Arms and the Woman

Gunners in dresses. (Courtesy Topham Picture Library, Kent, England)

Arms and the Woman

War, Gender, and

Literary Representation

Edited by Helen M. Cooper

Adrienne Auslander Munich

Susan Merrill Squier

The University
of North
Carolina Press

Chapel Hill
and London

© 1989 The University of North Carolina Press

Library of Congress Cataloging-in-Publication Data

Arms and the woman : war, gender, and literary representation / edited by
Helen M. Cooper, Adrienne Auslander Munich, and Susan Merrill Squier.
   p.   cm.
  Bibliography: p.
  Includes index.
   ISBN 8078-1860-7 (alk. paper). — ISBN 0-8078-4256-7 (pbk. : alk. paper)
   1. Women in literature. 2. War in literature. 3. Feminist literary
criticism. 4. Women and war. 5. Women in the military. I. Cooper,
Helen M. (Helen Margaret) II. Munich, Adrienne. III. Squier, Susan
Merrill.
PN98.W64A76   1989   89-5246
809'.93352042—dc19   CIP

The editors are grateful for permission to reproduce the following essays,
which have appeared in print in somewhat different form:

Gillian Brown, "Nuclear Domesticity: Sequence and Survival." *Yale
Journal of Criticism* 2, no. 1 (Fall 1988): 179–91.

Esther Fuchs, "Images of Love and War in Contemporary Israeli Fiction:
Toward Feminist Re-vision." *Modern Judaism* 6 (1986): 189–96.

Jane Marcus, "Corpus/Corps/Corpse: Writing the Body in/at War," which
appeared as the Afterword to a reprint of *Not So Quiet . . .* by Helen Zenna
Smith (Evadne Price) (New York: Feminist Press, 1988).

The following passages are reproduced from Mitsuye Yamada's *Camp
Notes*, copyright © 1976 Shameless Hussy Press: "The Night Before Good-
bye" (the entire poem); "Cincinnati" (selected lines); "Thirty Years
Under" (the entire poem). Used by permission of the publisher.

The paper in this book meets the guidelines for permanence and durability
of the Committee on Production Guidelines for Book Longevity of the
Council on Library Resources.

Manufactured in the United States of America
93 92 91 90 89   5 4 3 2 1

7-13-90

This volume is Edwin and Matthew
dedicated to our Caitlin and Toby
children: Clare and Sarah

Contents

Acknowledgments

We wish to thank our contributors for their tolerance of the complications entailed in working with three editors; the Stony Brook English Department for providing a research assistant for one semester; Barbara Scanlon for secretarial services; Walter Weil for a pleasant retreat in which to work; and our husbands, Gowen Roper, Jerome Tognoli, and Richard Munich, who have shared with us many personal and civic struggles about war and gender.

Helen Cooper
Adrienne Munich
Susan Squier

Introduction

[It] is much less significant that men's History is made of wars than that men's wars are made of stories.—Nancy Huston, "Tales of War and Tears of Women"

Neither *women* nor *war* is a self-evident category . . . war is an object of discourse central to historic understandings of politics in the West. Without war stories there would be many fewer stories to tell. —Jean Bethke Elshtain, *Women and War*

The paradigmatic narrative of "men's wars" builds on the Western literary tradition celebrating "arms and the man," to figure a culture in which men fight while women remain at home preserving the domestic front. To perpetuate this polarized gender system, female complicity in warmaking has been overlooked. Every girl loves a soldier, so the saying goes. Female adulation of male warriors has been labeled patriotism, obscuring women's aggressive involvement in the war system. The white feather used by female patriots in World War I to shame men into battle is but a late embodiment of the sexual bargaining dramatized by the seventh-century Arabian poet, Hind bint Utba:

Tambourine Song for Soldiers Going into Battle

Forward, sons of the tribe!
protect us
strike with spear thrust

Advance
and our embraces
and softest rugs
   await you

Retreat
and all our loving
we'll take
   and leave you[1]

Resistance to the war text appears in many forms when writers refuse to glorify the sexual bargain between woman and soldier articulated by Hind bint Utba. Sappho's poem, "To an Army Wife in Sardis," reinterprets the founding myth of the literary canon to decenter the ideology supporting war:

> To an Army Wife, in Sardis:
>
> Some say a cavalry corps,
> some infantry, some, again,
> will maintain that the swift oars
>
> of our fleet are the finest
> sight on dark earth; but I say
> that whatever one loves, is.
>
> This is easily proved: did
> not Helen—she who had scanned
> the flower of the world's manhood—
>
> choose as first among men one
> who laid Troy's honor in ruin?
> warped to his will, forgetting
>
> love due her own blood, her own
> child, she wandered far with him.
> So Anactoria, although you
>
> being far away forget us,
> the dear sound of your footstep
> and light glancing in your eyes
>
> would move me more than glitter
> of Lydian horse or armored
> tread of mainland infantry[2]

Sappho's redefinition of Helen of Troy's classic story imagines a Helen who disregards the heroic code in choosing a lover "who laid Troy's honor in ruins." This revision invokes family codes implicated in the institution of war in order to supplant them. Neither affirming nor denying the power of the famous couple, Sappho's poem rather dismisses that duo to commemorate another connection. Preferring the "light glancing" in Anactoria's eyes to the "Lydian horse or armored / tread of mainland infantry," Sappho subverts both the heterosexual love plot and the heroic sexuality of war to privilege her relationship with Anactoria over Anactoria's role as an army wife.

Although the themes of women's complicity in and resistance to war have been part of literature from early times, as these poems of Hint bint Utba and Sappho testify, they have not been fully integrated into conventional conceptions of the war narrative. This collection of essays aims to rectify this omission in two ways. First, it examines the relationship between war and gender as figured in literature. While feminist philosophers, historians, sociologists, and political scientists have considered the meaning of war in their disciplines, no one has yet considered the deeply gendered mutual influence war and literary representation have had upon each other. The essays examine that link in literature of the Trojan and Arthurian wars, the French Wars of Religion, the French Revolution, the Crimean War, the American and Nigerian civil wars, the two world wars, the Arab-Israeli conflict, and the nuclear age.

The second purpose of this volume is to identify and then interrogate the conventional war text, with its essentialist assumptions. While the essays consider texts that figure fighters as male, thereby maintaining the culturally endorsed split between warlike man and peaceful woman, they confirm that women's role in relation to war is much more complex and often complicitous than such essentializing suggests.

We consider gender as one crucial organizing principle in the war system. Not all of the essays focus on overt ties between the womanly and the warlike, but they all regard literature as implicated in both the war system and the gender system and as instrumental in perpetuating the ancient essentialist war myth. Our opening essay charts the terrain of the collection as a whole: it delineates the literary tradition of the war text, discusses variations that reveal the inconsistencies and pregnability of the tradition, and finally argues that in the twentieth century the basic polarity of man as fighter and woman as peacemaker miscarries. The remaining essays elaborate on this three-part configuration, a pattern that generally works chronologically, although we would not argue that the pattern is progressive or causal.

Five essays explore the paradigm of the war story. In Lorraine Helms's essay the literary figure of the Trojan War is a locus for examining the complex interconnections of eroticism and war in the Western literary tradition. Helms looks back at classical texts, the *Iliad*, the *Trojan Women*, and Chaucer's *Troilus and Cresseyde*, to illuminate Shakespeare's rewriting of military sexuality in *Troilus and Cressida*. Achilles, not Paris, is a feminized warrior; combat is eroticized, while the erotic is charged with the struggle for dominance. Cressida embodies one woman's effort to survive in this fatal coupling, but she inevitably suffers from the militarization of her sexuality. Choosing, like Helms, to focus on male writers, Esther Fuchs explores how submerged erotic tensions gradually dominate the manifest text of military conflict. Whereas Helms demonstrates that Shakespeare's text militarizes sexuality, Fuchs concludes that Israeli male writers portray male characters as victimized not by the Middle East wars, but by sexual battle. They perceive the real enemy to be not the Arabs across the border but the Israeli women at home.

Internecine conflicts cloak gender conflicts in the next three essays, which focus primarily on women writers. Patricia Cholakian examines *Les Desordres de l'amour*, an account of the sixteenth-century French Wars of Religion from a woman's perspective. Cholakian argues that its author, Mme de Villedieu, challenges the official version of those wars to reveal the private romantic subtext in which women manipulate male erotic desire not for their own female pleasure but to achieve the access to public power they are denied. The American Civil War also led to a rearrangement of the balance of public power, leaving Southern women in charge of a large domestic and agricultural domain. Jane Schultz argues that the Civil War exposed the dangers of a gender ideology that positions women as the protected and men as the protectors. Marshalling evidence from thirty-seven Civil War diaries and memoirs, only four of which were written for publication, this essay shows how the dominant gender ideology limited the ability of Southern women diarists to express what was happening to them and to their domain. As genteel women assaulted by the force of Sherman's army, they could note their assailants' vulgarity but not the sexual threat they posed. The destruction of social codes in the Civil War is mirrored in the gaps and silences of these diaries, signaling defeat. Margaret R. Higonnet challenges the androcentric bias of existing civil war analysis, showing how civil war becomes a metaphor for the battle of the sexes fought on both private and public terrain. Explicating fictions whose focus ranges from the French Revolution and the American Civil War to occupied Vichy France, the essay demonstrates that political and military conflict is deeply gendered while gender relations hold deeply political undertones. Higonnet distinguishes between two forms of internecine struggle, civil war and rebellion, and identifies as the major difference between men's and women's civil war novels the fact that men imagine the domestic realm as a retreat from politics, while women expose the profoundly political nature of domestic life.

Whereas domestic and political life necessarily begin to merge in civil war, with World War I the boundaries between battlefront and home front and public and private gendered spheres began to dissolve. Three essays about World War I consider the assault on gender divisions arising from the nascent women's movement and the death of the manly ideal of patriotic sacrifice in war. Arguing for the interconnections between the battle for women's suffrage, the battle for modern art, and the battle in the trenches, James Longenbach draws on "Epilogue," an unpublished manuscript by Ford Madox Ford, as well as fiction and nonfiction by major male and female modernists. He demonstrates that, rather than face the social reality of the women's movement as an independent force, modernist literature located the Great War as the point of origin for the rising tensions between men and women. Longenbach's essay contributes to the major critical reexamination of literary modernism in light of the contributions of feminist scholarship. Entering this debate about gender and World War I, the essays by Jane Marcus and Laura Stempel Mumford present opposed assessments of the relation of feminism to the war effort. Challenging the idea that women greeted World War I as a liberation from the domestic sphere, Jane Marcus's essay shifts the focus from men's war texts to women's to reveal the variety of their literary responses to war. Her parallel discussion of Helen Zenna Smith's *Not So Quiet . . .* with Erich Maria Remarque's *All Quiet on the Western Front* encourages us to read men's texts as ancillary to this provocative group of rediscovered war texts. Approaching the topic of feminist writers' response to World War I from a different perspective, Laura Stempel Mumford analyzes *The Tree of Heaven,* a war novel by the feminist novelist May Sinclair. Mumford traces the image of the vortex in Sinclair's novel to show how the "horrible harmony" born from the ecstasy of battle eclipses the "little vortex" of feminism and to demonstrate why some women abandoned the women's movement as trivial in the face of what they saw as the greater reality of war.

Whereas Sinclair's novel portrays women embracing the war effort for the exhilaration it offers, Sharon O'Brien's essay shows that Willa Cather's fascination with war originated in male identification as an escape from enforced female passivity. The essay demonstrates that the issues of gender, sexuality, and power portrayed in the text and subtext of Cather's *One of Ours* also structured her experiences of writing and publishing that battle novel. O'Brien finds beneath its overt plot of male warmaking a submerged drama of masculine anxiety over emasculation, infantilization, and female empowerment.

That there is no inherent link between one's gender and one's engagement with war is demonstrated in Sara Friedrichsmeyer's study of Käthe Kollwitz's developing pacifism. Kollwitz's unpublished diary documents the artist's progression from an initial endorsement of war to a total rejection not only of war but also of revolutionary violence as a program for social justice. Friedrichsmeyer rejects any simple essentialism to argue that Kollwitz's changed attitude toward war stemmed not from an automatically "womanly" pacifism but from a lengthy intellectual struggle to respond to the painful experience of her son's death during the early months of the war.

The pacifist position on war, represented by Kollwitz, will be more familiar to readers of this volume than the positions explored in the essays by Carol Adams and Susan Schweik. Beginning with the identification of a tradition of literary texts that expands the front and in so doing establishes the links between vegetarianism and pacifism, Adams's essay argues for a broader definition of female literary modernism. Interpreting a rich variety of nineteenth- and twentieth-century texts, from Gilman's *Herland* to Atwood's *The Edible Woman*, Adams reveals the writers' challenge to our repression of the links between warmaking and meat eating. The essay argues that feminist critics have silenced the vegetarian pacifist voice in their construction of modernism just as, earlier, feminism itself was silenced. Schweik's essay points out that a double silencing, caused by the author's race and sex, was responsible for the delay of several decades in the publication of the central section of Mitsuye Yamada's *Camp Notes*. Yamada was interned as a Japanese-American during World War II, and her volume of poetry challenges assumptions about both gender and warfare informing the prevailing canon of war poetry. Schweik argues that Yamada's work constructs a discourse of discontinuity, emphasizing her marginality from white America and its master discourse about war, while simultaneously celebrating the survival of both her personal and cultural identities during the war.

The rapprochement of battlefront and home front inaugurated by World War I culminated in the obliteration of such boundaries with the bombing of Hiroshima and Nagasaki in World War II. With the development of nuclear technology, the home front became the battlefront. The final essays in our book address the collapsing of polarities occurring in a nuclear age while pointing to the persistence of the ideology such polarities uphold. Barbara Freeman's essay argues that the dominant discourse on war as well as some feminist antiwar language describes men as implicated in nuclear warfare in a way that women are not. The essay considers ways in which women also contribute to the context that makes nuclear war imaginable. Bringing together nuclear war manuals, the Book of Revelation, and Marguerite Duras's *Hiroshima Mon Amour*, Freeman demonstrates that the familiar couples of man/woman, war/peace must be both acknowledged and challenged in order to understand how the nuclear holocaust has come to be imagined, even desired. Gillian Brown's essay draws on texts as diverse as nuclear protest literature and the FEMA (Federal Emergency Management Agency) civil defense survival manuals to show how the framers of the nuclear future have embedded a fantastic vision of domestic life in their nuclear "survival" plans. This vision has roots in the nineteenth-century American domestic ideology promoting a possessive individualism. In a chillingly circular and overdetermined process, the domestic ideology has set the stage for the contemporary fantasy of nuclear warfare, while the individualism it promotes also persists in the way we imagine postnuclear society. Brown's essay demonstrates that, in spite of drastic changes in war technology, dominant Western culture still subscribes to a war system that even in a nuclear era figures war as fought along the ancient, conventional lines of "arms and the man." While this collection exposes the heterosexual ideology of war narratives, race, religion, and class are equally fundamental categories in any consideration of power and conflict. "War and Memory," a poem by June Jordan that begins this collection, envisages a time when all such categories are rendered obsolete.

Notes

Since this collection went to press, two important books have appeared that further develop the links betweeen war and gender: Mary Lynn Broe and Angela Ingram, eds., *Women's Writing in Exile* (Chapel Hill: University of North Carolina Press, 1989) and Sara Ruddick, *Maternal Thinking: Toward a Politics of Peace* (Boston: Beacon Press, 1989).

1. Utba, *Women Poets of the World*, 95.
2. Sappho, no. 41.

Works Cited

Elshtain, Jean Bethke. *Women and War*. New York: Basic Books, 1987.

Huston, Nancy. "Tales of War and Tears of Women." *Women's Studies International Forum* 5, no. 3/4 (1982): 271–82.

Sappho. *Sappho: A New Translation*, by Mary Barnard. Berkeley: University of California Press, 1958.

Utba, Hind bint. *Women Poets of the World*. Edited by Joanna Bankier and Dierdre Lashgari and translated from the Arabic by Bridget Connelly and Dierdre Lashgari. New York: Macmillan Co., 1983.

Arms and the Woman

Dedicated to Jane Creighton

I

Daddy at the stove or sink. Large
knife nearby or artfully
suspended by his clean hand handsome
even in its menace
slamming the silverware drawer
open and shut the spoons
suddenly loud as the yelling
at my mother
no (she would say) no
Granville no
about: would he
be late/had she
hidden away the Chinese laundry shirts
again/did she think
it right that he (a man in his own house)
should serve himself a cup of tea a plate
of food/perhaps she thought that he
should cook the cabbage and the pot roast
for himself
as well?
It sure did seem she wanted him to lose
his job because she could not find
the keys
he could not find
and no (she would attempt to disagree)
no Granville no
but was he
trying to destroy her with his mouth?
"My mouth?!" my Daddy hunkered down
incredulous and burly now

with anger, "What you mean, 'My mouth?' You woman! Who
you talk to in that way?
I am master of this castle!" Here
he'd gesture with a kitchen fork
around the sagging clutter
laugh and choke the rage tears
watering his eyes: "You no to speak to me
like that: You hear?
You damn Black woman!"
And my mother backing up or hunching smaller
than frail bones should easily allow
began to munch on saltine
crackers
let the flat crumbs scatter on her full lips
and the oilcloth
"You answer me?" he'd scream, at last:
"I speak to you. You answer me!"
And she might struggle then
to swallow
or to mumble finally out loud:
"And who are you supposed to be? The Queen
of England? Or the King?"
And he
berserk with fury lifted
chair or frying pan
and I'd attack
in her defense: "No
Daddy! No!" rushing for his knees
and begging, "Please
don't, Daddy, please!"
He'd come down hard: My head
break into daylight pain
or rip me spinning crookedly across the floor.
I'd match him fast
for madness
lineage in wild display
age six
my pigtails long enough to hang me
from the ceiling
I would race about for weaponry

another chair a knife
a flowered glass
the radio
"You stop it, Daddy! Stop it!"
brandishing my arsenal
my mother silently
beside the point.
He'd seize me or he'd duck the glass
"You devil child!
You damn Black devil child!"
"And what are you supposed to be?"
My mother might inquire
from the doorway:
"White? Are you supposed to be a white man
Granville?"
"Not white, but right!" And I
would have to bite and kick
or race away
sometimes out the house and racing
still for blocks
my daddy chasing
after me

II

Daddy at the table reading
all about the Fiji Islanders or childhood
in Brazil
his favorite National Geographic research
into life beyond our
neighborhood
my mother looking into
the refrigerator
"Momma!" I cried, after staring at the front page
foto of The Daily News.
"What's this a picture of?"
It was Black and White.
But nothing else. No people
and no houses anywhere. My mother

came and took a look above my
shoulder. "It's about the Jews," she
said. "The Jews?"
"It's not! It's more about those Nazis!" Daddy
interjected. "No Granville, no!
It's about the Jews. In the war going on,"
my mother amplified, "the German soldiers
take away the Jewish families and they make
them march through snow until they die!"
"What kind of an ignorant
woman are you?" Daddy shouted out. "It's
not the snow. It's Nazi camps: the concentration
camps!"
"The camps?" I asked them, eagerly: "The Nazis?"
I was quite confused. "But in this picture,
Daddy, I can't see nobody."
"*Any*body," he corrected me: "You can't see
anybody!" "Yes, but what," I persevered, "what is this
a picture of?"
"That's the trail of blood left by the Jewish girls
and women on the snow because the Germans
make them march so long."
"Does snow make feet bleed, Momma?
Where does the bleeding come from?"
My mother told me I should put away
the papers and not continue to upset myself
about these things I could not understand
and I remember
wondering if my family was a war
going on
and if
there would soon be blood
someplace in the house
and where
the blood of my family would come from

III

The Spanish Civil War:
I think I read about that one.

IV

Joan DeFreitas/2 doors up
she latched onto a soldier
fat cat bulging at the belt
and he didn't look like Hollywood
said he should
so I couldn't picture him defending
me or anyone
but then I couldn't picture war or North
Korea
at that time

V

There was tv . . .
There were buses down to Washington, D.C.
You could go and meet your friends
from everywhere.
It was very exciting.
The tear gas burned like crazy.
The President kept lying to us.
Crowd counts at the rallies.
Body counts on the news.
Ketchup on the steps of universities.
Blood on the bandages around the head of the Vietnamese
woman shot between the eyes.
Big guys.
Aerial spray missions.
Little people
Shot at close range.
"Hell no! We won't go!"
"Hell no! We won't go!"
Make love.
Kill anything that moves.
Kent State.
American artillery unlimited at Jackson State.
Who raised these devil children?
Who invented these Americans with pony
tails and Afros and tee shirts and statistical

arguments against the mining of the harbors
of a country far away?

And I remember turning from the footage of the tat-tat-tat-
tat-tat-tat
helicopters
and I wondered how democracy would travel from the graves
at Kent State
to the hidden trenches
of Hanoi

VI

Plump during The War on Poverty
I remember making pretty good
money (5 bucks an hour)
as a city planner and my former
husband married my best
friend and I was never positive
about the next month's rent but
once I left my son sitting
on his lunchbox in the early rain
waiting for a day-care pickup and I went
to redesign low-income housing for The Lower
East Side of Manhattan and three hours after that
I got a phone call from my neighbors
that the pickup never came
that Christopher was waiting
on the sidewalk
in his yellow slicker
on his lunchbox
in the rain

VII

I used to sometimes call the government
to tell them how my parents
ate real butter or stole sugar

from The Victory Rations
we received

I sometimes called the Operator
asking for Police
to beat my father up for beating me
so bad
but no one listened to
a tattletale
like me:
I think I felt relieved
because the government didn't send a rescue
face or voice to my imagination
and I hated
the police
but what else could you do?

Peace never meant a thing to me.

I wanted everyone to mold
the plastic bag for margarine
save stamps
plant carrots
and
(imitating Joe "Brown Bomber" Louis)
fight hard
fight fair

*   *   *   *   *   *   *   *   *   *   *   *   *   *   *

And from the freedom days
that blazed outside my mind
I fell in love
I fell in love with Black men White
men Black
women White women
and I
dared myself to say The Palestinians
and I
worried about unilateral words like Lesbian or Nationalist
and I
tried to speak Spanish when I travelled to Managua

and I
dreamed about The Fourteenth Amendment
and I
defied the hatred of the hateful everywhere
as best I could
I mean
I took long nightly walks to emulate The Chinese Revolutionaries
and I
always wore one sweater less than absolutely necessary to keep
warm
and I
wrote everything I knew how to write against apartheid
and I
buried my father with all of the ceremony all of the music
    I could piece together
and I
lust for justice
and I
make that quest arthritic/pigeon-toed/however
and I
invent the mother of the courage I require
    not to quit

Helen Cooper
Adrienne Munich
Susan Squier

Arms and the Woman:
The Con[tra]ception of the War Text

"*A*rms and the Woman" echoes Virgil's heroic phrase not only to assert that women play a part in war but to affirm that in our culture "arms" when juxtaposed to "woman" evokes sexual and maternal love, eclipsing Virgil's masculine military reference. Since, as Mary Ellmann points out, "all human activities have been suspectible to the sexual analogy,"[1] it is not surprising that war has been linked with sex, as in "make love not war." That slogan brings into the twentieth century the cry of the Athenian women in *Lysistrata*; the opposition between love and war in both slogan and play joins a traditionally private affair with a conventionally political one. In what follows we develop the conjunction between the military and the amorous, according to some implications for the war narrative of the sexual trope, in which love figures as both sexual congress and sexual reproductivity. From the beginning of the Western tradition in the epic, the war narrative has been written in terms of that trope, making what is in fact a cultural event seem an essential one.

The epic tradition figures arms as being engendered through the mother by linking making babies and making arms. The pattern of associating a story of arms making with human birth begins in the *Iliad* with the story of Thetis approaching Hephaistos to make weapons for her son, Achilles. The epic presents her as Hephaistos's "good mother," the one who has nurtured him for nine years in a cave since his rejection as a cripple by Hera, his bad mother. In that womblike environment Hephaistos makes peaceable, domestic objects until Thetis's mortal son requires implements of war. The epic initially assigns passivity and pacifism, traits usually associated with women, to the male god of the forge. This compliant "son" takes orders from the militant mother. Thetis emphasizes to Achilles that the weapons are her maternal gifts: "Accept rather from me the glorious arms of Hephaistos, so splendid, and such as no man has ever worn on his shoulders."[2]

In the *Aeneid* Virgil expands upon Homer's suggestive birth imagery by conflating Thetis's approach to Hephaistos with the seduction of Zeus by Hera in Book 14 of the *Iliad*. Hera beguiles Zeus so that her side will win a battle; in his revision Virgil describes the lovemaking of Venus and Vulcan as a prerequisite to making weapons. Like Thetis, Venus pleads to the smith-god, and like Hera, she seduces her consort. The seduced Homeric father becomes Virgil's Vulcan, who fathers Aeneas's arms. In their pleas, both Thetis and Venus allude to the precedent of other militant mothers who had provided their sons' weapons. As Venus says to her consort:

> I do come now, begging your sacred power
> For arms, a mother begging for her son.
> The daughter of Nereus moved you, and Tithonus'
> Consort moved you by her tears to this.[3]

Virgil imagines the sexual scene of arms making, but he reverses the conventional gender configuration by making the woman the aggressor to a passive man. Expanding upon Homer, he constructs his scene of military buildup in the feminine embrace; without woman's sexual inducement, the neutral man might not make arms at all:

> The goddess spoke and wrapped her snowy arms
> This way and that about him as he lingered,
> Cherishing him in her swansdown embrace.
> And instantly he felt the flame of love
> Invading him as ever; into his marrow
> Ran the fire he knew.   [*Aeneid* 8.243]

In order to make arms, the deities first have to make love.

In presenting the dualities of man/woman, war/peace, classical epic both establishes the conception of the war narrative informing Western literary tradition and allows a questioning of those dualities. These originating figurations demonstrate that in a patriarchal world men may sign the war contract, but both sexes had a hand in drafting it. By examining the metaphors that link life making to warmaking and by decoding the invisible female signature on the military contract, we question the validity of any exclusively male construction of the war text.

The most explicit trope connecting love and war in classical literature occurs when the gods ensnare Mars and Venus in each other's arms. That the two polarized deities make such easy bedfellows illustrates how woman's complicity in the aggressivity and violence of war has been allegorized. Love, according to one possible interpretation, is the feminine counterpart to, not the opposite of, war. The role historically assigned to woman as peacemaker denies the possibilities of her warmaking wishes suggested by these literary representations. Chaucer reworks for English literature the sexual conjunction of Mars and Venus, in which making war is explicitly connected to making love. Yet, as in all revisions, Chaucer introduces a countertradition. In classical epic the war narrative is conceived of in all its metaphoric richness. In Chaucer, we find the possibility not only of a conception but also a contraception of the epic war narrative when Chaucer's heroine wishes for an alternative to the exclusive copula of love/war.

"The Knight's Tale" suggests a paradigm that allows Venus, the female deity, an aggressive part in battle while denying Emily, the woman, any active role. Two knights, men dedicated to the martial arts, love Emily; they vie for her hand in a ritualized battle, a duel. The same structural triangle that caused the Trojan War impels the knights to fight over the lady. On the dawn of the battle day the two knights pray to their particular deity, one to Venus, the other to Mars. Venus triumphs, and her knight Palamon wins Emily. Chaucer figures both the goddess of love and the god of war as sponsors of battle. In his story soldiers worship both deities. Venus triumphs, not because she is a mild unaggressive goddess but because she is more fierce, more warlike than the quintessential war-god. The point is not, as is commonly thought, that the mild, pacific idea of love is more powerful than the fierce, aggressive idea of war but that love is also aggressive and the better warrior.

In Chaucer's scheme, there seems to be no ground for the lady; she is merely the prize in an elemental battle. The story momentarily offers her an alternative but powerful position. Although that position is ultimately denied, it allows not a middle but an other ground, a glimpse of a way out of what seemed an inevitable polarity. When Palamon prays to Venus and Arcite prays to Mars, Emily prays to Diana, chaste goddess of the hunt. Her eloquent prayer asks the goddess for freedom from both knights, implicitly from both love and war. She prays for independence, to hunt and walk in the woods; notably, she also prays for freedom from childbearing. In her view, the knights of Venus and Mars are the same:

And fro me turne awey hir hertes so
That al hire hoote love and hir desir,

> And al hir bisy torment, and hir fir
> Be queynt, or turned in another place.[4]

By giving voice to a third term, Chaucer reveals that opposition is engagement; opposing love and war on the battlefield, he shows that the two terms share a common ground. To emphasize this point he makes the two knights indistinguishable.

Emily suggests a reason for her flight to chastity in her dislike of childbearing. If to avoid war one must also dispense with reproductivity, Emily's prayer for peace through chastity must go unanswered. To remain aloof from love and war in that configuration is to avoid having children, yet as long as childbearing is necessary for the continuation of the human race, history seems condemned to the cycle of love and war, endorsed in literary representation.

When the Victorians reimagine medieval myths of courtly love and chivalric heroism, they fragment and rearrange but nonetheless find in them signs of their precursors. When Tennyson recasts the Arthurian legends in *Idylls of the King* he also preserves some of the epic figuration that links birth and death by battle arms. Yet once again, the revision opens space for an alternative representation of love and war. Tennyson adapts his Arthurian story to accord with the figuration of classical epic, but he splits sexuality from engendering; mothering of arms appears as an involuted but fragmented presence.

Tennyson describes the first and last of his idylls as being about "the awfulness of Birth and Death." It is therefore fitting that these two books are the parts where the sword Excalibur figures most prominently. In "The Coming of Arthur," Arthur is born as a hero when he takes the sword from the Lake. Then sword and king are crowned together: "I beheld Excalibur / Before him at his crowning borne, the sword / That rose from out the bosom of the lake."[5] In "The Passing of Arthur," the sword is clearly coexistent with Arthur's heroic life. His life cannot end until Excalibur is returned to the Lady of the Lake; the Lady functions as mother of Excalibur: "Clothed in white samite, mystic, wonderful. / She gave the King his huge cross-hilted sword" ("The Coming of Arthur," ll. 284–85). Tennyson reduces the epic mother to an "arm," a significant pun in the context of the pattern we have been tracing. This Lady makes the weapon herself, with no male partner, but Tennyson retains temporal suggestions of birth: "nine years she wrought it, sitting in the deeps / Upon the hidden bases of the hills" ("Morte D'Arthur," ll. 105–6).

As it surfaces in Tennyson's transformation of Arthurian tradition to a predominantly Virgilian model, the inscription of the mother's voice determines the lifespan of Arthur's heroic age. Excalibur's two commandments, written on either side of the blade—"Take Me"; "Cast Me Away!"—signify Arthur's dependency on the Law-of-the-Mother, on her inscribed will. These are the commandments, not of the Lord but of the Lady. In the same way as engendering epic arms depends upon the Will-of-the-Mother, the authorizing of heroic prowess is tied to a mysterious but inexorable female realm, the awfulness, as Tennyson states, of Birth and Death. And because this mythologizing of female power represents a powerful figuration of (perhaps a defense against) the mother, it is inadequately resolved. Arthur "dies" when the sword returns to its maternal bosom and arm, but he dies only to return. This topos of death and rebirth is repeated in the figurations linking birth and death, creativity and destruction, that are legacy and curse in Western literary tradition.

Tennyson fragments without undermining the fantasy of the sword-bearing mother. The course of the sword's engendering—from the virtual origins of the tradition in Homer to its repression and consequently greater, though generally unacknowledged, presence in the spokesmen for their nations in Virgil and Tennyson—delineates what seems like a male tradition. In that dominant construction the sword symbolizes a "natural" phallic instrument. Yet those interpreters who accept the construction, "Man is for the sword," as a sign of the language and Law-of-the-Father need to acknowledge and interrogate the complex interdependency of war, gender, and engendering in war texts of the literary canon; the implication of the feminine in this canon; and the interrelatedness of creation and destruction. In epic tradition in which arms are given miraculous authority by linking them with miraculous birth, "arms and the man" springs as much from envy of woman's procreative function as from male military and sexual potency. In this tradition the voice and even written language of the mothers are therefore a great repressed source of power.

The tradition of arms and the man encounters the repressed tradition of arms and the mother when feminist consciousness achieves literary articulation. During the Victorian era, with its provocative private and public challenge to the rule of the father, as well as its collocation of technological and social changes, woman writers begin to revise the canonical representation of war. The work of Elizabeth Barrett Browning exemplifies one such moment of tension in the construction of the war narrative. Her poetry reveals the conflict between women's acceptance of the roles men have assigned to them in the war story and women's challenge both to those roles and to the privileging of that story, with its traditional focus on men at the front.

Shifting the focus of the epic from the military to the domestic, Elizabeth Barrett Browning's *Aurora Leigh* imagines the classical tradition as a masculine drama in order to create a place for herself as a writer. She revises the masculine epic with its militaristic conventions:

> The critics say that epics have died out
> With Agamemnon and the goat-nursed gods;
> I'll not believe it . . .
> [Poets'] sole work is to represent the age . . .
> [That] spends more passion, more heroic heat,
> Betwixt the mirrors of its drawing-rooms,
> Than Roland with his knights at Roncesvalles.[6]

Challenging the hierarchical relation between war and love, she acknowledges two culturally repressed activities for women's arms —war and writing—and mutes the militaristic bias of poetic tradition to share instead a novelistic vision of the "heroic heat / Betwixt the mirrors of [the] drawing-rooms." Yet in so doing, Barrett Browning reinscribes the opposition of love and war, claiming the terrain of love over war for her own literary purposes.

In letters written to friends during the Crimean War, Barrett Browning continues her strategic decentering of the war narrative to focus not on soldiers but on the plight of prostitutes: "War, war! It is terrible certainly. But there are worse plagues, deeper griefs, dreader wounds than the physical. What of the forty thousand wretched women in this city? The silent writhing of them is to me more appalling than the roar of the cannons."[7] Not simply reversing the dichotomies to privilege women over men, the sufferings of prostitutes over those of soldiers, Barrett Browning recalls the illicit connections and oppositions between love and war. Mars is still in bed with Venus.

Barrett Browning's Crimean War letters mock the convention that men fight to protect the women back home, revealing instead the war's links to both sexism and imperialism: "Oh, the Crimea! How dismal, how full of despair and horror! The results will, however, be good if we are induced to come down from the English pedestal in Europe of incessant self-glorification, and learn that our close, stifling, corrupt system gives no air nor scope for healthy and effective organisation anywhere. We are oligarchic in all things, from our parliament to our army" (L, 2:189–90). In shifting her focus to the corrupt system entwining imperialism with sexism, Barrett Browning only apparently displaces war as primary narrative; she tells Helen's story rather than Agamemnon's. At the same time, she resists some traditional stereotypes, objecting to the elevation of Florence Nightingale as saintly nurse. She repudiates this role for women, as merely a "revival of old virtues! Since the siege of Troy and earlier, we have had princesses binding wounds with their hands. . . . Every man is on his knees before ladies carrying lint, calling them 'angelic she's,' whereas, if they stir an inch as thinkers or artists from the beaten line . . . the very same men would curse the impudence of the very same women" (L, 2:189).

Confronted with war in the streets outside her Florentine home, Barrett Browning liberated herself from enforced female silence on the subject of war but accommodated to tradition by telling the canonical war story. In her poems of the Italian Risorgimento, *Casa Guidi Windows* and *Poems before Congress*, she functions as the poet-mother arming her warrior sons. When the Austrians march on Florence, she denounces those Florentine men who merely parade their military costumes but do not fight, encouraging "the struggle in the slippery fosse / Of dying men and horses, and the wave / Blood-bubbling." With the "faint heart of my womanhood," Barrett Browning urges men to a death she will not suffer herself, confirming the opposition between the protected woman and the protector "raking [his] . . . guns across / The world" (W, 3:301, 401–6).

In *Last Poems*, written just before her death, instead of internalizing the literary representation of herself as mother arming her sons, Barrett Browning redirects her inquiry to the "empty heart and home" left by war. In "Mother and Poet" the speaker is Laura Savio, an Italian poet and patriot whose two sons were killed fighting for the unification of Italy, a cause that both author and speaker shared. The speaker reconsiders the meaning of both motherhood and military heroism after the deaths of her sons, implicitly acknowledging woman's complicity in war when she connects the conception of her sons with their inception as warriors whom she armed with the lesson, "a country's a thing men should die for" (*W*, 6:72, 23). Barrett Browning's choice of a maternal narrator to explore the emotional costs of war reveals that the alternative she chooses is implicated in what she rejects.

The dualities of front and home front, militarist male and pacifist female that Barrett Browning maintained while privileging home and motherhood over war have traditionally structured—and so perpetuated—the war story. That dualistic structure is emphatically at variance with facts of war in the modern era that was inaugurated by woman's incursion with Florence Nightingale into battlefield nursing. The increasing toll of civilian casualties during the two world wars destroys the myth that in war men fight to protect their women, who remain secure at home caring for their children. Historically, women's new roles as war workers, ambulance drivers, soldiers, and terrorists, as well as victims of total war, put to rest the notion of inherently peaceable women, inherently warlike men. Betty Miller's World War II novel *On the Side of the Angels* dismantles the conventional dichotomies associated with this collective violence by interrogating the mythic attraction war holds for both sexes.

The novel, set far from the battlefield in a small English village, demonstrates that the symbols of war have a stronger hold on the imagination than the realities of the battlefield. Andrew, a young lawyer invalided out of the army not by a heroic wound, but by a heart condition, confronts his fiancée Claudia with the news of his demobilization. Seeing her dismay, he voices her conflicted feelings, "You're going to miss the purely military side aren't you?. . . [Y]ou enjoyed walking out with a soldier. . . . It's going to be rather a come-down, appearing on the arm of a civilian."[8]

The desire for arms in both of the senses we are discussing in this essay—"those 'beautiful bombs'" (77) or the status-enhancing arm of a soldier—Miller reveals as essentially gender-free. Both men and women in this community, with a military hospital at its center, are drawn to Colonel Herriot, who appears as a brave commando. Later, the police apprehend him as a fraud; a small-town bank manager, his yearning for glory has been satisfied by the pose of military

hero. As Andrew realizes: "We create a fiction out of our own desires. The fiction in this case happened to be the Commando hero:
the killer, tough, unscrupulous; outside the bounds of ordinary convention. A fiction so attractive to the law-abiding that we chose in
its favour to ignore the reality" (232). Andrew understands that the
allure of war lies in its collective function to express sublimated
desires: "It's the force of pent-up human emotion that wrecked
Amsterdam, Leningrad, Coventry, Cologne. Why? Because it's com-
pressed, tightly packed down into the shell-case of civilization.
Hence our joy in those 'beautiful bombs.' They say it all for us—
everything that we've been forbidden to say or think or do. . . .
We're not fighting something local and external, labelled Fascism—
we're wrestling with our own deepest inclinations and desires" (77–
78).

As Miller's novel reveals, modern military technology emphasizes war's function as the projection outward of repressed human
emotions. Similarly, reproductive technology has produced a parallel externalization of the previously private, emotional sphere of
human birth, manufacturing innovative means of conception, and
contraception. As birth has become subject to technological manip-
ulation, it has also become clear that even this biological function
is a cultural construct. Shulamith Firestone's vision of reproductive
technology imagined a world in which women were freed from
childbearing; Dorothy Dinnerstein's analysis revealed the lethal social implications of exclusively female mothering. Building on the
works of both writers we can recognize that both child-rearing and
war are culturally determined; hence their meaning in literary texts
is subject to renegotiation and revision.

A reconsideration of the culturally and historically dependent
meanings of war and conception is central to Chinua Achebe's
story "Girls at War," a tale set during the Nigerian civil war.[9]
Nwankwo, a government official, recalls a contingent of militia
girls from a local secondary school marching behind a banner: "WE
ARE IMPREGNABLE!" (100). Before the war, the joke's humor resided in the paradoxical double meaning of the female soldiers' slogan. While as members of the militia the girls may aim to be militarily invulnerable, in fact they are still impregnable, that is, capable of being impregnated. Hence they are sexually vulnerable. But
when the war begins, their comic slogan, with its paradoxical con-
flation of military invulnerability and sexual vulnerability, is re-

versed. Now, as "girls at war" who do not scruple at casual sex and who boldly demand the use of contraceptives, they are sexually impregnable, but they can die in battle.

The relationship of Nwankwo and Gladys, one of the militia girls, exemplifies the tangled meanings of war and sex. Nwankwo disapproves of her sexual looseness and her easy acceptance of consumer goods in return for sexual favors, akin in his mind to war profiteering. Gladys inverts the tradition; rather than using sex as a way of speaking of war, she uses war metaphors to speak of sex: " 'You want to shell?' she asked. And without waiting for an answer said, 'Go ahead but don't pour in troops!' " (113). She transgresses the sexual, economic, and military ideologies Nwankwo unconsciously valorizes. In that ideology, woman is an item in the patriarchal sexual exchange, whose reproductive potential belongs to men who defend it by making war.

Gladys inverts the war metaphor. Rather than conceiving arms, as does Venus with Vulcan, she wants to contracept them. Now that she herself is part of the militia, she controls the war-making machine that had been her uterus. She no longer needs to accept the man's "troops." In Nwankwo's moral condemnation of her, Achebe reinvokes but undercuts the illicit love/war coupling in Elizabeth Barrett Browning's Crimean letters. Barrett Browning excludes prostitutes from active participation in the political economy that makes war, seeing them rather as victims of an unjust system. Achebe understands that both soldier and "prostitute" are partners in the war system. Nwankwo's condemnation, "He might just as well have slept with a prostitute" (113), indicates that he categorizes women according to their position in the patriarchal sexual economy, particularly in terms of their emotional commitment to their sexual partners. Just as Gladys's willingness to sleep with, and accept gifts from, men whom she does not love defines her in Nwankwo's eyes as equivalent to a prostitute, so Gladys's power of contraception disturbingly frees her from the force of patriarchal authority.

Although the story condemns Nwankwo's exploitative wartime hypocrisy, it still holds open a place for military honor and valor through death. At the end of the story, Gladys, whose economic and sexual liberation had rendered her militarily suspect, dies trying to save a wounded soldier Nwankwo has abandoned. By the method of Gladys's death, Achebe definitively rejects any tendency to split the soldier and the girl; he forces us to see their connection. The story ends with Nwankwo's final vision of "the entangled remains of the girl and the soldier"; by selecting the word "entangled," Achebe emends the war narrative to incorporate its sexual valence (118). The woman joins the warrior, grimly mixing her flesh with his in a last embrace.

While Emily's chaste refusal of her reproductive powers enacts her antiwar position, Achebe's militia girl refuses reproductive economy while still endorsing war. Yet while Achebe's story decenters notions of heroism by making Gladys more conventionally heroic than Nwankwo, it does not present contraception as an alternative to the opposition of love and war. Instead, it reopens the question of war and gender to reveal the hidden links between the noncombatant woman and the combat soldier and to valorize in both an implicitly military heroism.

Both Chaucer's and Achebe's texts, however, pose the possibility of contraception—a closing off of the war text—to allow for other figures, alternative discourses. Achebe's story stresses the profoundly narrative component of war itself, reminding us that the meaning of war changes as the narrative is revised. The text reflects on the shifting meaning of war in its proliferation of war metaphors: war enters as a hairstyle ("air force base"), a pair of high-flying vultures ("a humorist in the crowd called them Fighter and Bomber and everyone laughed in relief"), a drink ("one fiery brand nicknamed 'tracer' which indeed sent a flame down your gullet"), and finally to the act of sexual intercourse ("You want to shell? . . . Go ahead but don't pour in troops") (99, 105, 110, 113).

As an object of discourse, war has no more self-evident a significance than does gender: its meaning also changes as culture codifies that meaning differently. "Girls at War" reveals not only the transformation of war metaphors, but also the changing construction of the war system. The cultural systematization of random conflict into war proceeds by defining what war is and is not, what a soldier is and is not, what a battle is and is not, where battles can and cannot take place, and what the roles are for combatants and noncombatants. In Achebe's story all such systematization is subject to debate, dependent on whether the reigning point of view is that of the man from the Ministry of Justice, the "wargirl," or the implied narrator.

The contraceptive moment is pivotal not only for Achebe's story but for the modern war text in general. Arguably, the modern woman's ability to prevent conception, resulting from wide-scale access to contraception and abortion, produces a different figuration of the gendered meaning of war in modern and postmodern writing. Nancy Huston reminds us of the Gnostic conundrum: "How long will men make war?—As long as women have children."[10] While war has customarily been linked by opposition to reproduction, twentieth-century advances in the technology of contraception and abortion as well as changes in social mores have decoupled the figuration of war and reproduction, with a resultant disruption of the entire sexual economy. When women decide to use contraception, they are no longer inevitably forced to "travaille pour l'armée." Contraception enables the woman to refuse to bear future warriors for the war hero without (like Chaucer's Emily) curtailing her sexual activity or relinquishing her right to sexual pleasure: with contraception, the modern woman can resist the role of circulating sexual object crucial to the war effort. Contemporary feminist theory reveals that the contraceptive choice can be understood as life-affirming rather than life-denying, as *within* society rather than above or beneath it, where women have traditionally been located. In canonical war literature women have been similarly marginal, represented as the woman at home, too physically weak or too morally pure to engage in battle, whom the soldier must defend. Manifestly not the act of a woman who denies her physicality, contraception challenges this stereotype. Contraceptive choice can symbolize the refusal of complicity with the war system.

Connecting war protest with contraception brings us back to a classical example and a modern revision of it. In a modernist retelling of *Lysistrata*, the ancient narrative of love and war, Virginia Woolf considers the relations between war and gender governing the antiwar or nonwar tale. "A Society"[11] invokes Aristophanes, challenging "a woman's duty to spend her youth in bearing children" in a society beset by social ills (119). In order to discover whether childbirth is worth continuing, members of "the society for asking questions" interrogate institutions of patriarchal power. They find a monumental contraceptive solution that will permit women to dispense with chastity, Aristophanes' ancient answer to social evil. Women can now experience sexual pleasure without becoming embroiled in the sex/gender system implicated in society's ills, the system organizing childbirth through the patriarchal family. A member describes "an invention of hers to be erected at Tube stations and other public resorts, which, upon payment of a small fee, would safeguard the nation's health, accommodate its sons, and relieve its daughters" (124).

Yet the initial optimism that a technologically based reorganization of the social meaning of sexuality can prevent social ills while still permitting women sexual love and motherhood is shortlived. The society's investigations are derailed by the question they have overlooked: " 'Why,' we cried, 'do men go to war?' " (128). Eradication of patriarchy will not cure all social ills: one must also eradicate the related war system. The story concludes by suggesting that if the society continues, its members may well advocate not only universal female literacy, but universal female chastity, at least until the invention of that convenient machine that will detach sexuality from the patriarchal family system.

Six centuries after Chaucer, Woolf is forced to resort to the persistent solution to the problem of war. Yet by connecting female literacy to a new understanding of the horrors of war, and particularly the horror of bearing "cannon fodder," Woolf begins to imagine an alternative: "If we hadn't learnt to read . . . we might still have been bearing children in ignorance and that I believe was the happiest life after all. I know what you're going to say about war . . . and the horror of bearing children to see them killed, but our mothers did it, and their mothers, and their mothers before them. And *they* didn't complain. They couldn't read. . . . [L]et us devise a method by which men may bear children! It is our only chance" (128–29). When coin slots in commuter stations channel the sexual economy, chastity will no longer be the only locus of war resistance. Woolf foresees the revolutionary impact of an alternative sex/gender system, in which biological and intellectual conception are no longer dichotomous, gender-linked terms. Such a radically reorganized society, in which women learn to read and men "learn" to bear children, would provide ample alternatives to the fruits of man's "unbridled activity," war.

In her World War II essay, "Thoughts on Peace in an Air Raid," Woolf appropriates war discourse for her own purposes, revising the metaphor of battle to urge "mental fight" against a system that relegates men to war and women to the position of weaponless spectators. Blake's "Milton," from which the phrase "mental fight" is drawn, participates, albeit subversively, in the patriarchal tradition of British literature that conceptualizes battle as the sanctioned male alternative to woman's childbearing. Thinking against the current, Woolf argues that if we are ever to undo the war system, we must dismantle the binary sex/gender system she labels "the instincts." Rather than the mother arming the hero, Woolf's essay offers the anticanonical proposition that mothers should disarm the hero by turning over to men the mothering role. She argues we must break the links between male glory and warfare, female glory and motherhood:

> The young airman up in the sky is driven [by] . . . instincts fostered and cherished by education and tradition. Is he to be blamed for those instincts? Could we switch off the maternal instinct at the command of a table full of politicians? . . . But if it were necessary, for the sake of humanity, for the peace of the world, that child-bearing should be restricted, the maternal instinct subdued, women would attempt it. Men would help them. . . . They would give them other openings for their creative power. . . . We must create more honorable activities for those who try to conquer in themselves their fighting instinct. . . . We must compensate the man for the loss of his gun.[12]

Woolf challenges the binary thinking that attributes to men responsibility for war, to women responsibility for peace. She argues that male warmaking joins female childbearing; the complex war system is grafted on to the ancient sex/gender system. She dismantles the dualistic figuration of war itself. In locating her concept of "mental fight" at the tea table rather than the officer table or the conference table, Woolf redefines the front, shifts the nature of battle from physical to mental, and repudiates such dualistic schemas as peaceful women and warlike men. Woolf not only accepts for women the challenge of restricting childbearing, she also accepts for men the challenge of restricting warfare. She thus questions both the culturally constructed meaning of childbirth and the binary opposition between war and masculinity, peace and femininity.

Where Barrett Browning counters the militaristic with the maternal preoccupation, Woolf counsels the repudiation of the maternal instinct as the only effective war resistance. For Woolf the only good war is a "mental battle," the figurative war waged by antiwar groups. Chaucer's Emily refuses the war economy but cannot escape the sexual economy, yet that option is more accessible in a world that undermines assured hierarchies and familiar dualities. We might imagine a modern Emily refusing both of those categories, challenging their status as necessary figurations. By accepting her own aggressive desires a modern Emily might help to defuse the charged metaphor linking sexuality to war.

Neither childbearing nor chastity, conception nor contraception, have meanings in themselves. No more does war, or the war text. All are elaborately socialized, constructed forms of human interaction that we must struggle to see together, like the entangled remains of Achebe's girl and soldier. To see how women and men have constructed war texts out of cultural data is not to recanonize those texts but rather to unload the can[n]on.

Notes

1. Ellmann, *Thinking about Women*, 7.
2. Homer, *Iliad*, 19.392.
3. Virgil, *Aeneid*, 9.243.
4. Chaucer, *Works*, p. 39, ll. 2318–21.
5. Tennyson, "The Coming of Arthur," *Idylls of the King*, in *Poems*, p. 1477, ll. 294–96. Hereafter references to *Poems* are given in text with poem title and line numbers in parentheses.
6. Barrett Browning, *Aurora Leigh*, bk. 5, ll. 139–207. Hereafter cited in the text as *W* followed by volume and line references.
7. Barrett Browning, *The Letters of Elizabeth Barrett Browning*, 2:213. Hereafter cited in the text as *L* followed by volume and page references.
8. Miller, *On the Side of the Angels*, 29.
9. Achebe, "Girls at War," 98–118.
10. Huston, "The Matrix of War," 119.
11. Woolf, "A Society," 118–30.
12. Woolf, "Thoughts on Peace," 246–47.

Works Cited

Achebe, Chinua. "The War Girls." In *Girls at War and Other Stories*. London: Heinemann, 1972.

Barrett Browning, Elizabeth. *The Complete Works of Elizabeth Barrett Browning*. Edited by Charlotte Porter and Helen A. Clarke. 6 vols. New York: Thomas Y. Crowell & Co., 1900. Reprint. New York: AMS Press, 1973.

———. *The Letters of Elizabeth Barrett Browning*. Edited by Frederic C. Kenyon. 2 vols. New York: Macmillan Co., 1897.

Chaucer, Geoffrey. *The Works of Geoffrey Chaucer*. Edited by F. N. Robinson. 2d ed. Boston: Houghton Mifflin, 1957.

Dinnerstein, Dorothy. *The Mermaid and the Minotaur: Sexual Arrangements and Human Malaise*. New York: Harper & Row, 1976.

Ellmann, Mary. *Thinking about Women*. New York: Harcourt, Brace & World, 1968.

Firestone, Shulamith. *The Dialectic of Sex*. New York: Bantam Books, 1971.

Homer. *The Iliad*. Translated by Richmond Lattimore. Chicago: University of Chicago Press, 1951.

Huston, Nancy. "The Matrix of War: Mothers and Heroes." In *The Female Body in Western Culture: Contemporary Perspectives*, edited by Susan Rubin Suleiman, 120–36. Cambridge, Mass.: Harvard University Press, 1986.

Miller, Betty. *On the Side of the Angels*. 1945. Reprint. London: Virago Press, 1985.

Tennyson, Alfred Lord. *The Poems of Tennyson*. Edited by Christopher Ricks. London: Longmans, 1969.

Virgil. *The Aeneid*. Translated by Robert Fitzgerald. New York: Random House, 1981.

Woolf, Virginia. "A Society." In *The Complete Shorter Fiction of Virginia Woolf*, edited by Susan Dick. New York: Harcourt Brace Jovanovich, 1985.

————. "Thoughts on Peace in an Air Raid." In *Death of the Moth and Other Essays*. New York: Harcourt Brace Jovanovich, 1970.

Lorraine   "Still Wars and Lechery":
Helms
          Shakespeare and

          the Last Trojan Woman

          Concidit virgo ac puer.
          Bellum peractum est.—Seneca, *Troades*

*T*hroughout Shakespeare's *Troilus and Cressida*, Thersites' bitter cry echoes and reechoes: "Lechery, lechery, still wars and lechery; nothing else holds fashion" (5.2.194–95). It is a cry from which Shakespeare scholars long turned in disgust, dismissing *Troilus and Cressida* as vicious and cynical, a cruel misrepresentation of both Homer's heroic warriors and Chaucer's courtly lovers. For commentators who have turned to *Troilus and Cressida* in the aftermath of twentieth-century wars, the play has become a "great dispute about the sense and cost of war, about the existence and cost of love"; its action seems "all part of the game of war" and its arguments "all ceremonies of rededication to the code that maintains the war." On the eroticized battlefields and in the militarized bedchambers of *Troilus and Cressida*, we have come to see the bleak and violent sexuality our world has bred from martial pomp and circumstance.[1]

Yet Shakespeare's "great dispute about the sense and cost of war, about the existence and cost of love" rises from the traditional discourse of the Trojan War. Even in its earliest literary formulations, the "matter of Troy" was distant and mythical, without fixed ideological content. When, in the later tradition, Rome and London fancifully traced their ancestry to the vanquished Trojans rather than the victorious Greeks, they could celebrate neither the rape of Helen nor the fall of Troy as a nationalistic exploit of martial prowess. Nor had the legends ever fully silenced the voices of the Trojan women. Even through the mediated texts of Homer, Euripides, Virgil, and Chaucer, the Trojan women speak of contradictions in the narrative and dramatic representation of war. This "matter of Troy" is the prehistory of *Troilus and Cressida*. It is not by devaluing but by assimilating it that Shakespeare arrives at his bitter appraisal of "wars and lechery."

The *Iliad* has served men as a monument to martial glory. It represents a masculinist world in which women are at best the mothers of heroes; at worst, slaves and war prizes.[2] The separate spheres of men and women are divided by the gates through which Troy's warriors go to confront the Greek invaders.[3] But the violence of war cannot be cordoned off; it threatens to spill from the field to the *polis* and from the *polis* to the *oikos* where the Trojan women wait. In Book 6, Hector returns from the battlefield to find Andromache mourning at the city wall. She offers advice to resolve "the pain of the warrior's role, of the man who, on behalf of his family must leave his family, so that his very defense of them becomes a betrayal":[4]

> Please take pity upon me then, stay here upon the rampart,
> that you may not leave your child an orphan, your wife
>   a widow,
> but draw your people up by the fig tree, there where the city
> is openest to attack, and where the wall may be
>   mounted.   [6.431–34]

Andromache's strategy would not keep Hector from battle, but from the forefront of battle where personal danger and hence personal glory are greatest.[5] She asks him to fight defensively, to shore up the weakness of the ramparts and protect the citadel. Hector rejects her plan: he must "fight always among the foremost ranks of the Trojans / winning for my own self great glory, and for my father" (6.445–46).

With the Greek army camped before Troy, Andromache does not challenge the war's necessity. Yet her intervention exposes the disjunction between the motive and the pretext for war. For Andromache, dominance and submission are not sources of glory and shame, but the terms of destruction or survival. Her advice to Hector initiates a challenge the Trojan women will repeatedly offer to the Homeric warriors. They do not counsel pacifism, but defense. Their fugitive and cloistered warfare does not sally forth to meet its adversaries. But neither does it respect chivalric rules of combat. Unlike the ritualized combat through which the Homeric warrior establishes hierarchy, its object is survival, not glory. Andromache fights a woman's war, a *guerre à outrance* to defend her home and children.[6]

In Homer's narrative, women's voices are audible only in occasional notes of warning and supplication. They are absent from the battlefield and silent in the councils of war. In Euripides' *The Trojan Women*, however, women's voices resound in the stillness that follows the noise of battle. Euripides transfers the focus from the epic siege of Troy to the tragedy of its sack. He transforms a narrative of the violence that accompanies war into a theatrical representation of the violence that follows it, acknowledging that the *oikos* has claims as great as the *polis* on a tragic dramatist's attention. A woman's wartime experience of rape, deracination, and concubinage can, like a man's death in battle, provide a locus of articulate suffering.

For the chorus of *The Trojan Women*, the aftermath of war is an interstice between marriage and concubinage. No longer the wives of Trojans, they are not yet the concubines of Greeks. As they cross the threshold of the *oikos*, they respond to the violence in this postwar exchange of women. For Cassandra, in whose own fate marriage, concubinage, rape, and death are interwoven, violence begins to obscure distinctions between male and female experience:[7]

> The Achaeans came beside Scamander's banks, and died
> day after day, though none sought to wrench their land
>   from them
> nor their own towering cities.
>
> · · · · · · · · · · · · · · · · · · ·
>
> The Trojans have that glory which is loveliest:
> They died for their own country. So the bodies of all
> who took the spears were carried home in loving hands,
> brought, in the land of their fathers, to the embrace of
>   earth
> and buried becomingly as the rite fell due.   [374–76, 386–90]

Through Euripides' metaphors of the embracing earth, the slaughtered Trojan warriors begin to merge with the women who survived them. They participate in the private world of the *oikos*, emerging from its protective walls only because they must, in self-defense. Their fates are intertwined with their city's; their bodies are bound to the earth that outlasts the battlefield the invaders have erected upon it. In defeat, the Trojans' military stance comes to resemble Andromache's strategy. It is the feminized stance of those for whom defeat means not only dishonor but destruction.

Euripides takes the Trojans' perspective to challenge the xenophobia and androcentrism he locates at the heart of war. When Virgil tells the story of Troy's fall, in Book 2 of the *Aeneid*, he too takes

the Trojans' perspective. The *Aeneid* is a national epic that serves
to create a patriotic prologue for Roman imperialism, and yet the
metaphors of Virgil's narrative resonate with Euripides' tragedy. In
The Trojan Women, the destruction of the city and its ruler's death
are the prelude to rape; in the *Aeneid*, they are indissolubly twined
in a language of sexual violation:

> And then, before the very porch, along
> the outer portal Pyrrhus leaps with pride;
> his armor glitters with a brazen brilliance
> he is like a snake that, fed on poisonous plants
> and swollen underground all winter, now
> his slough cast off, made new and bright with youth,
> uncoils his slippery body to the light;
> his breast erect, he towers toward the sun;
> he flickers from his mouth a three-forked tongue.
>
> . . . .
>   [Pyrrhus] takes up
> a two-edged ax and cracks the stubborn gates.
> He rips the bronze-bound portals off the hinges,
> cuts through a beam, digs out tough oak: the breach
> is vast, a gaping mouth. The inner house
> is naked now, the long halls, open; naked,
> the private rooms of Priam and the ancient
>   kings.   [2.627–35, 640–48]

As the serpentine Pyrrhus penetrates first Priam's chamber and
then his flesh, the king merges symbolically with the feminine
citadel. By placing war's cruelest violence in Troy's most private
chambers, the *Aeneid* identifies erotic and military domination,
representing the breached walls and the mutilated body as a unified
locus of violence.

The eroticized violence of Virgil's description reemerges in recurring analogies between the rape of women's bodies and the conquest of walled cities, analogies from which Renaissance literature
creates its "patriarchal territories."[8] For Shakespeare, the metaphor
of Troy's rape serves as an image and archetype of sexual violence.
In *The Rape of Lucrece*, Lucrece stands before a tapestry of Troy's
fall after Tarquin has raped her, finding in the images of Troy's ruin
the horror of her own. As Sinon came to Priam and betrayed him, so
Tarquin came to her: "As Priam him did cherish, / So did I Tarquin;
so my Troy did perish" (1541–47). Shakespeare, like Virgil, identi-

fies the citadel with its ruler; he associates the penetration of Troy's defenses with violent sexual penetration. Whatever is besieged, whatever is penetrated, becomes by analogy female. Defensive warfare becomes a feminine enterprise.[9]

Like *The Rape of Lucrece*, *Troilus and Cressida* draws on the legends of classical Troy, but the play also explores medieval traditions derived from Chaucer's *Troilus and Criseyde*. Chaucer's romance, like Euripides' tragedy, explores women's wartime struggle against rape and concubinage. In the romance, however, the protocols of courtly love and honor obscure, though they cannot obliterate, the force that drives the Trojan women from the citadel. The violence of war is represented as a symbolic violence for which the Trojan women, with Criseyde as their surrogate, can themselves be blamed.

Criseyde is a composite of two Homeric characters: Chryseis, whom Agamemnon returned to her father, the Trojan priest Chryses, and Briseis, whom Agamemnon took from Achilles after relinquishing Chryseis. For medieval chroniclers, there was "no essential difference between Homeric slave-girls . . . and a medieval lady who could be used as a slave-girl if it seemed militarily desirable";[10] thus Criseyde became a lady of the Trojan court infamous for betraying her lover. Yet the chroniclers do distinguish between slave-girl and lady when they claim that Criseyde freely chose Diomedes for her lover. In condemning Criseyde, they deny the violence of deracination and concubinage.

For Criseyde, unlike earlier Trojan women, it is not the destruction of the citadel that exposes her to the Greeks' rough pleasures. The Trojans themselves trade her to regain Antenor, a valuable prisoner of war. Only Hector challenges this ancient ceremony of war:

"Syres, she nys no prisonere," he seyde;
"I not on yow who that this charge leyde,
But, on my part, ye may eftsone hem telle,
We usen here no wommen for to selle."   [4.179–82]

Hector is shouted down, and the exchange goes forward:

"Ector," quod they, "what goost may yow enspyre,
This womman thus to shilde, and don us leese
Daun Antenor—a wrong wey now ye chese."   [4.187–89]

Although Troy still remains standing at the close of *Troilus and Criseyde*, violence nevertheless penetrates the citadel at this moment. Criseyde's exchange brings the war into the daily life of the besieged city. The demands of the battlefield determine the values of the marketplace: Criseyde can be bartered as a slave, since she has no other military value. Her expulsion confirms her marginal status. But in exchanging Criseyde for Antenor, the Trojans have forced Criseyde to exchange Trojans for Greeks. From Criseyde's perspective, the exchange exposes the interchangeable roles of her protectors and her assailants. As Criseyde rides to the Greek camp in Diomedes' custody, her Troy, like Lucrece's, perishes.

The exchange of Criseyde anticipates the fate of the other Trojan women, who will pass from the conquered city into the possession of the victorious Greeks. Like the other Trojan women, Criseyde is a victim of the war. But since the force that imposes her fate has been obscured, her strategy for survival can be equated with Helen's ambiguous complicity in violation. Helen can manipulate the patriarchal exchange of women at her pleasure. Criseyde is Helen tamed and conquered, Helen rendered vulnerable to men who may trade and barter her, Helen expelled from the citadel and punished at last for her lawless sexual choices. As a surrogate for the Trojan women, Criseyde obscures the violence of concubinage; as a surrogate for Helen, she invalidates women's power to take the offensive in their own survival. Her vulnerability transforms Helen's aggressive sexual posture into the defensive stance of the Trojan women.

Like Chaucer's romance, Shakespeare's play inserts a Euripidean focus on women's wartime experience into the framework of the Homeric siege. In a theatrical representation, however, Cressida's response first to Troilus's militarized courtship and then to the Greeks' violent eroticism is mediated through an actor's voice and body, not through a Chaucerian narrator who, taking her guilt for granted, explains that she "sory was for hire untrouthe" (5.1098) and excuses "hire yet for routhe" (5.1099). Shakespeare's "Arm'd Prologue" explicitly disavows responsibility for such mediation, noting that the interpretation of a play emerges from the dynamic relation between actors and audience: "Like or find fault, do as your pleasures are, / Now good or bad, 'tis but the chance of war" (Prologue, 22–31).[11]

The Prologue does not refer to the romance from which the play takes its title. The story of Troilus and Cressida is merely an episode of a war in which the *casus belli*, "the chance of war," dominates eros. For the chance of war gives time and circumstance their keenest weapons against humanity. Time and circumstance, em-

powered by violence, turn occasions for love and bravery into fur-
tive moments of pleasure and ignominious rites of domination.
Wars and lechery hold fashion, and make battlefields of public and
private life.

This world of wars and lechery transforms the traditional contrast between the aggressive masculinity of the Greek camp and the
feminized world within the citadel. Shakespeare's Troy takes the
political form of a chivalric fraternity that contrasts with the patriarchal hierarchy of the Greek army.[12] But the Trojans too are warmongers. *Troilus and Cressida* reexamines the tradition that feminizes the Trojans, making Troy participate actively in its own victimization. The Trojans keep Helen, for the Greeks keep Priam's
sister Hesione (2.2.80). Greek retaliations follow Trojan raids; Trojan retaliations follow Greek raids. The Trojans' defensive stance
merely logs their current military position in a long conflict during
which the exchange of women has repeatedly served as a pretext for
the circulation of violence.

Violence underwrites the power of every cultural rite and representation in both the Trojan citadel and the Greek camp. The
Greeks speak of ending the stalemate; the Trojans speak of ending
the siege. Neither can end the interminable *agon* from which the
stalemate and the siege result. Their councils are merely the war's
epiphenomena. They display the forms of power that Michel Foucault describes when he inverts Clausewitz's aphorism: "Politics is
a continuation of war by other means. . . . The role of political
power . . . is perpetually to inscribe [the disequilibrium of war] in
social institutions, in economic inequalities, in language, in the
bodies themselves of each and every one of us."[13]

In *Troilus and Cressida*, the political continuation of war assimi-
lates a Machiavellianism that anticipates Foucault's remarks. In
the Proheme to *The Arte of Warre*, translated into English in 1560,
Machiavelli argues that war is the foundation of public life and
military structure society's best model. Whatever diligence has
been employed in civil life "to maintain men faithful, peaceable,
and full of the fear of God, in the service of war, it was doubled." In
the interests of civic order, military life should be "with all study
followed and imitated."[14] Machiavelli's statecraft enables rulers to
direct violence with a technician's skill. Yet they can only create
order sufficient to continue war by the "other means" of political
discourse.

In *Troilus and Cressida*, the creation of this Machiavellian order is Ulysses' task. His degree speech, sometimes celebrated as Shakespeare's most eloquent statement of "the Elizabethan world picture" of a divinely instituted hierarchy,[15] seems, in its dramatic context, rather to expose the fragility of an arbitrary social structure of power and privilege:[16]

> O, when degree is shak'd,
> Which is the ladder of all high designs,
> The enterprise is sick. How could communities,
> Degrees in schools, and brotherhoods in cities,
> Peaceful commerce from dividable shores,
> The primogenity and due of birth,
> Prerogative of age, crowns, sceptres, laurels,
> But by degree stand in authentic place?
> Take but degree away, untune that string,
> And hark what discord follows.   [1.3.101–10]

For Ulysses, "it is not the differences, but the loss of them that gives rise to violence and chaos."[17] He pits the forms of power against the chaos of violence; he creates authority by molding force into shapes that will serve the state. Social structure depends, not on cosmic harmony, but on political power, and political power, as Tudor statesmen recognized, consists of monopolizing violence.[18] Like Machiavelli, Ulysses predicates his statecraft on the art of war. His hierarchical society, with its "specialty of rule," its "primogenity and due of birth," and its "prerogative of age," is a well-organized army.

In the degree speech, Ulysses addresses the leaders of a military expedition. While his subject ostensibly encompasses all arts and sciences, all products and processes of peace, Ulysses' vision, like Machiavelli's, makes military subordination the foundation for social relations. He describes academic communities, civic associations, commercial trade, and, as his instance of familial order, the obedience a son owes his father. These homosocial relationships are all analogues to the military hierarchy that is his real concern. But he ignores entirely one cornerstone of "the Elizabethan world view," the subordination of wife to husband. He silently suppresses the military significance of the hierarchy of gender. A subsequent speech, however, reveals the patriarchal foundation for his militarization of peacetime institutions:

[Achilles and Patroclus] tax our policy, and call
    it cowardice,
Count wisdom as no member of the war,
Forestall prescience, and esteem no act
But that of hand. The still and mental parts,
That do contrive how many hands shall strike
When fitness calls them on, and know by measure
Of their observant toil the enemies' weight—
Why, this hath not a finger's dignity.
They call this bed-work, mapp'ry, closet-war;
So that the ram that batters down the wall,
For the great swinge and rudeness of his poise,
They place before his hand that made the engine,
Or those that with the fineness of their souls
By reason guide his execution.   [1.3.197–210]

With the petulance of neglected age, Ulysses advocates a gerontocracy. Young men become instruments of violence in the hands of
the old, the means by which the power of the elders is maintained.
By giving old men the political power to send the young to war,
gerontocracy controls violence; by giving them the domestic power
to silence and sequester women, it controls eros. Ulysses' hierarchy
requires the isolation of the field from the *polis* and the *polis* from
the *oikos*. To maintain it, he must keep Achilles in combat; and he
must keep Cressida silent, for in her eye, cheek, and lip there is a
speech "so glib" (4.5.58) that it seems to challenge his power.
    Achilles is Greece's greatest warrior. He is also bisexual, and,
when *Troilus and Cressida* opens, has withdrawn to his tent with
his lover Patroclus, mingling military comraderie with sexual companionship. In rejecting the agonistic activity that defines masculinity, Achilles has become as vulnerable to men's judgments as
the Trojan women. Unlike the women, Achilles withdraws from
the public world voluntarily and temporarily, but in his privacy he
too becomes subject to incursions from the public discourse of
violence:

Ulysses: But 'gainst your privacy
The reasons are more potent and heroical.
'Tis known, Achilles, that you are in love
With one of Priam's daughters.
Achilles: Ha? known?

Ulysses: Is that a wonder?

. . . .

There is a mystery (with whom relation
Durst never meddle) in the soul of state,
Which hath an operation more divine
Than breath or pen can give expressure to.
All the commerce that you have had with Troy
As perfectly is ours as yours, my lord,
And better would it fit Achilles much
To throw down Hector than Polyxena.   [3.3.191–95, 201–8]

The rationally apprehensible cosmos of the degree speech gives way
to a fideistic resolution that further mystifies the power of the
state. In capitulating to it, Achilles does "throw down" Hector
rather than Polyxena, in a combat more eroticized than his courtship had been. In his desire for battle, Achilles suffers

        a woman's longing,
An appetite that I am sick withal,
To see great Hector in his weeds of peace,
To talk with him, and to behold his visage,
Even to my full of view.   [3.3.237–41]

When, during a truce, Hector comes to the Greek camp, Achilles
watches him with a still keener passion:

Now Hector, I have fed mine eyes on thee;
I have with exact view perus'd thee, Hector,
And quoted joint by joint.   [4.5.231–33]

Achilles' ambiguous sexuality becomes an element in his military
power, since his "woman's longing" arms him with intimate knowledge of his adversary's body. Combat *is* a form of intimacy, for it
demands empathy to foresee and forestall the enemies' maneuvers.
But the erotic valence of combat becomes particularly lethal in
Achilles because he is an androgynous warrior who exploits both
masculine strategies for dominance and feminine tactics for survival. Achilles wages a *guerre à outrance*, killing Hector in an am-
bush, not in the face-to-face combat to which Hector's chivalric
credo restricts him.

    Thus concludes the representation of war's eroticized violence. In
the parallel representation of lechery's militarized sexuality, the art
of war is adapted for the battle of the sexes. There is a Machiavel-

lianism for the citadel as well as the camp. For Machiavelli, only sexual violence can control the feminine power that would otherwise disrupt the state. "Fortune," Machiavelli warns the ruler, "is a woman, and it is necessary, if one wishes to hold her down, to beat her and fight with her" (*The Prince*, 25). The goddess Fortuna, thus tamed by the man of *virtù*, grants him power and prestige. Machiavelli's imagery eroticizes political power and military conquest, while sexuality becomes a campaign of conquest, with advances, retreats, feints, strategic and tactical failures and successes.[19] To control Fortuna, the Machiavellian must control the sexuality of those he would govern, weaving and reweaving patterns of eros and domination. When a woman triumphs in the battle of the sexes, Fortuna conquers *virtù*, to universal disaster. When Helen transforms abduction into conquest, she destroys the Machiavellian structures of erotic domination on which patriarchal hierarchy depends: "This love will undo us all. O Cupid, Cupid, Cupid!" (3.1.110).

Shakespeare's Trojan women retain the defensive roles the literary tradition has given them. Andromache exposes the "bloody . . . intent" (5.3.8) of Hector's martial credo; Cassandra mourns the common ruin of "virgins and boys, mid-age and wrinkled [eld]" (2.2.104); Cressida, the last Trojan woman, defends herself against the violence of deracination and concubinage. Like the warriors and politicians, she too pits *virtù* against *fortuna*. But fortune and virtue operate rather differently for women than they do for men. In women's lives, the acts of Machiavelli's capricious goddess are mediated by her equally capricious worshippers among the warriors and politicians. *Virtù*, an offensive weapon for Machiavelli's statesmen, devolves into the defensive virtue of female chastity.

Troilus and Cressida's two plots open with this distinction between masculine and feminine *virtù*. Initiating the war plot, Agamemnon insists that the army must, despite the apparent futility of their seven years' siege, continue actively to pit valor against fortune (1.3.1–30). In his first scene, Troilus also describes a long and wearing siege: "Why should I war without the walls of Troy / That find such cruel battle here within?" (1.1.2–3). Troilus has laid siege to Cressida, as the Greek army has laid siege to Troy, and he too complains of the time involved: "Still have I tarried" (1.1.22). Where wars and lechery hold fashion, cities and women are on the defensive:

Pandarus: You are such a woman, a man knows not at what ward you lie.
Cressida: Upon my back, to defend my belly, upon my wit, to defend my wiles, upon my secrecy, to defend mine honesty, my mask, to defend my beauty, and you, to defend all these; and at all these wards I lie, at a thousand watches.   [1.2.258–64]

Besieged by Troilus, Cressida tries to defend herself by taking the position of abject surrender. She cannot take the offensive in this martial courtship:

> I wish'd myself a man,
> Or that we women had men's privilege
> Of speaking first.   [3.2.127–29]

Cressida's defensive tactics do not permit a frontal attack. Yet she practices a martial art of love to escape erotic domination, to transform her sexual surrender into a strategic triumph:

> Perchance, my lord, I show more craft than love,
> And fell so roundly to a large confession,
> To angle for your thoughts.   [3.2.153–55]

At best, these tactics can camouflage her weakness for a little while, during which the besieged Cressida is, if not "hard to win," at least "hard to seem won" (3.2.116–17). In playing the role of the coquette, Cressida is imitating Helen, the femme fatale who is so "hard to seem won" that she alone, of all the women in Troy, is not vulnerable to the inconsistency of male desire.[20]

In practicing the martial art of love, Cressida encounters the dangers with which the Machiavellian strategist must contend. If, Machiavelli advises, the statesman remains flexible, he can perfect his control over destiny: "If one could change one's nature with time and circumstance, fortune would never change" (*The Prince*, 25). But time and circumstance are even more problematic in the wars of love than in the wars of state:

> Women are angels, wooing:
> Things won are done, joy's soul lies in the doing.
> That she belov'd knows nought that knows not this:
> Men prize the thing ungain'd more than it is.
> That she was never yet, that ever knew
> Love got so sweet as when desire did sue.
> Therefore this maxim out of love I teach:

Achievement is command; ungain'd, beseech;
Then, though my heart's content firm love doth bear,
Nothing of that shall from mine eyes appear.   [1.2.286–95]

There is a biological and psychological disparity between men and women that makes Cressida's love for Troilus a source of despair. Cressida, like the warriors and politicians, must move through a wartime world, a universe in continual flux. But men and women experience that flux at different rates. Troilus's desire will be satisfied only too quickly. Cressida can anticipate but cannot alter the course of war or lechery:

> Prithee tarry,
> You men will never tarry.
> O foolish Cressid! I might have still held off,
> And then you would have tarried.   [4.2.15–18]

Cressida's complaint illuminates the course of courtly love: if she wishes Troilus to believe that "Her bed is India" and "there she lies a pearl" (1.1.100), she must lie in it alone.

The chance of war forbids such refinements of thwarted sexuality. Cressida will be sent to the Greek camp, bearing the memory of Troilus's eager return ·to the homosocial world of war. Ulysses will construct a ceremonial welcome in which the Greek generals, begging kisses from their prisoner, give a courtly color to their sexual demands: "Despite the elaborate courtesy of begging kisses, the Greek generals are taking what Cressida, essentially a captive, has no real power to refuse."[21] Yet Cressida uses her wit, as she had told Pandarus, to defend her wiles; she eludes the full humiliation Ulysses requires:

> Fie, fie upon her!
> There's language in her eye, her cheek, her lip,
> Nay, her foot speaks; her wanton spirits look out
> At every joint and motive of her body.
> O, these encounters, so glib of tongue,
> That give a coasting welcome ere it comes,
> And wide unclasp the tables of their thoughts
> To every ticklish reader! set them down
> For sluttish spoils of opportunity,
> And daughters of the game.   [4.5.54–63]

Ulysses' ceremony has not silenced the language of Cressida's sexuality. But her initiation into concubinage continues, and she surrenders to Diomedes' sexual blackmail. As surrender becomes her last line of defense, the rest of her banter is realized: she will lie on her back to defend her belly. She will accept concubinage to avoid rape.

Yet concubinage is no defense against the symbolic violence of war. For the victims of power, resistance and collusion may often merge "in the very condition of their survival."²² So, for Cressida, survival demands surrender, and surrender entails collusion. The terms of surrender are to internalize the patriarchal vision of female sexuality:

> Troilus, farewell! one eye yet looks on thee,
> But with my heart the other eye doth see.
> Ah, poor our sex! this fault in us I find,
> The error of our eyes directs our mind.
> What error leads must err; O, then conclude,
> Minds sway'd by eyes are full of turpitude.   [5.2.107–12]

Cressida's capitulation is one of the rare Shakespearean soliloquies for a female character. Her earlier speech, "Women are angels, wooing," fulfills the conventional expectation that a soliloquy represents the character's own interpretation of events. But in this speech, the eye, tongue, and cheek that Ulysses found so "glib" seem silent. Cressida seems instead to speak "the language of the victim," the language in which women join men in blaming women.²³ The eavesdropper Thersites underscores her alienation, ending the scene with a contemptuous commentary: "A proof of strength she could not publish more / Unless she said, 'My mind is now turn'd whore'" (5.2.113–14).

Yet even in speaking the language of submission, Cressida still articulates a subtext of defense.²⁴ She still imitates Helen and tries to "show more craft than love." When Cressida claims Diomedes, as Helen claimed Paris, for her own erotic choice, she is trying to disguise the stance of the victim in the posture of a whore. In this militarized world, where the *oikos* has become a besieged citadel and the *polis* an armed camp, where combat is eroticized and eros a struggle for dominance, Cressida pits the art of love against the chance of war. She does not, like Homer's Andromache, offer defensive military strategies nor, like Euripides' Cassandra, distinguish invasion from protection. But, like other Trojan women, Cressida wages a defensive *guerre à outrance*. From deracination and concubinage, she constructs a strategy for survival, negotiating her way between the patriarchal categories of victim and whore. Yet while the war continues, Cressida will not elude the militarization of her sexuality. It is time to declare a truce for the last Trojan woman.

Notes

1. I single out these quotations from Kott (*Shakespeare Our Contemporary*, 77) and Yoder (" 'Sons and Daughters,' " 19), who explicitly identify their responses to *Troilus and Cressida* with their reactions to twentieth-century wars, but one can trace the rise of the play's critical fortunes in the history of twentieth-century warfare. Burns, "The Worst of Both Worlds," and Dollimore, *Radical Tragedy*, could also be cited. Feminist critics, including Greene, "Shakespeare's Cressida"; Adelman, "This Is and Is Not Cressid"; and Okerlund, "In Defense of Cressida," have contributed substantially to this reappraisal, though without treating the war theme in detail.

2. Redfield, *Nature and Culture*, 119–27; Hartsock, *Money, Sex, and Power*, 186–90.

3. Arthur, "The Divided World," 20.

4. Redfield, *Nature and Culture*, 123.

5. Arthur, "The Divided World," 32.

6. Judith Stiehm notes that "Margaret Mead has said there is no society that places women in offensive warfare. She argues that women may be too vicious and too violent for combat because they have traditionally wielded weapons only in immediate defense of the home" (*Bring Me Men and Women*, 293). See also Huston, "The Matrix of War," and, on Renaissance views of women and war, Woodbridge, *Women and the English Renaissance*.

7. I am here and throughout this essay indebted to Joplin's analysis of violence in mythical and literary representations of the exchange of women in "The Voice of the Shuttle."

8. Stallybrass, "Patriarchal Territories," 123–47.

9. For important discussions of *The Rape of Lucrece*, see Kahn, "The Rape in Shakespeare's *Lucrece*," and Vickers, "This Heraldry" and " 'The Blazon.' "

10. Donaldson, "The Progress of a Heroine," 10–11.

11. While theatrical representation, unlike narrative, provides each character with an advocate, directors have, no less than literary scholars, imposed patriarchal evaluations of Cressida for which Shakespeare's text provides no warrant. For a comparison of Shakespeare's textual cues and twentieth-century directorial choices, see LaBranche, "The Theatrical Dimension."

12. Knight, *The Wheel of Fire*, 47; Roy, "War and Manliness," 108–10.

13. Foucault, *Power/Knowledge*, 90.

14. Machiavelli, *The Arte of Warre*. I have modernized the spelling and punctuation of this 1560 translation by Peter Whitehorne.

15. Tillyard, *The Elizabethan World Picture*, 7–15.

16. Elton, "Shakespeare's Ulysses," 98–100; Dollimore, *Radical Tragedy*, 42–43.

17. Girard, *Violence and the Sacred*, 51.

18. Stone, *The Crisis of the Aristocracy*, 96–113.

19. Pitkin, *Fortune Is a Woman*, 25; Elshtain, *Public Man, Private Woman*, 94.

20. In "The Politics of Desire," Girard suggests that Pandarus exploits Helen's "erotic prestige" to promote the affair between Troilus and a "bovaryesque" Cressida whom Pandarus manipulates into desiring what she believes Helen desires. In focusing on the "mimetic rivalry" of the male characters, Girard neglects the possibility I wish to bring out here: that Helen is Cressida's model for a role in which she would be less vulnerable to the inconsistency of male desire.

21. Yoder, " 'Sons and Daughters,' " 20.

22. Eagleton, *The Rape of Clarissa*, 82.

23. Joplin, "The Voice of the Shuttle," 40.

24. The recovery of the subtext is problematic, and this speech has often been interpreted as capitulation *tout court*. Still, the speech is hardly comprehensible, much less performable, without uncovering some sort of subtext, the most plausible of which, I believe, denies the patriarchal text its traditional hegemony.

Works Cited

Adelman, Janet. "This Is and Is Not Cressid." In *The (M)other Tongue: Essays in Feminist Psychoanalytic Interpretation*, edited by Shirley Nelson Garner, Claire Kahane, and Madelon Spregnether, 119–41. Ithaca, N.Y.: Cornell University Press, 1985.

Arthur, Marilyn B. "The Divided World of *Iliad* VI." In *Reflections of Women in Antiquity*, edited by Helene P. Foley, 19–44. New York: Gordon & Breach, 1981.

Burns, M. M. "*Troilus and Cressida*: The Worst of Both Worlds." *Shakespeare Studies* 13 (1980): 105–30.

Chaucer, Geoffrey. *The Works of Geoffrey Chaucer*. Edited by F. N. Robinson. 2d ed. Boston: Houghton Mifflin, 1957.

Dollimore, Jonathan. *Radical Tragedy*. Chicago: University of Chicago Press, 1984.

Donaldson, E. Talbot. "Briseis, Briseida, Criseyde, Cresseid, Cressid: Progress of a Heroine." In *Chaucerian Problems and Perspectives*, edited by Edward Vasta and Zacharias P. Thundy, 3–12. Notre Dame: University of Notre Dame Press, 1979.

Eagleton, Terry. *The Rape of Clarissa*. Minneapolis: University of Minnesota Press, 1982.

Elshtain, Jean Bethke. *Public Man, Private Woman: Women in Social and Political Thought*. Princeton, N.J.: Princeton University Press, 1981.

Elton, W. R. "Shakespeare's Ulysses and the Problem of Value." *Shakespeare Studies* 2 (1966): 95–111.

Euripides. *The Trojan Women*. Translated by Richmond Lattimore. New York: Random House, 1958. In Vol. 6 of *The Complete Greek Tragedies*, edited by David Grene and Richmond Lattimore. 8 vols. 1956–58.

Foucault, Michel. *Power/Knowledge: Selected Interviews and Other Writings, 1972–77*. Edited by Colin Gordon. New York: Pantheon, 1980.

Girard, René. "The Politics of Desire in *Troilus and Cressida*." In *Shakespeare and the Question of Theory*, edited by Patricia Parker and Geoffrey Hartman, 188–209. New York: Methuen, 1985.

———. *Violence and the Sacred*. Translated by Patrick Gregory. Baltimore: Johns Hopkins University Press, 1977.

Greene, Gayle. "Shakespeare's Cressida: 'A kind of self.'" In *The Woman's Part: Feminist Criticism of Shakespeare*, edited by Carolyn Ruth Swift Lenz, Gayle Greene, and Carol Thomas Neely, 133–49. Urbana: University of Illinois Press, 1980.

Hartsock, Nancy C. *Money, Sex, and Power: Toward a Feminist Historical Materialism*. Boston: Northeastern University Press, 1985.

Homer. *The Iliad*. Translated by Richmond Lattimore. Chicago: University of Chicago Press, 1951.

Huston, Nancy. "The Matrix of War: Mothers and Heroes." In *The Female Body in Western Culture: Contemporary Perspectives*, edited by Susan Rubin Suleiman, 120–36. Cambridge, Mass.: Harvard University Press, 1986.

Joplin, Patricia Klindienst. "The Voice of the Shuttle Is Ours." *Stanford Literature Review* 1 (1984): 25–53.

Kahn, Coppélia. "The Rape in Shakespeare's Lucrece." *Shakespeare Studies* 9 (1976): 45–72.

Knight, G. Wilson. *The Wheel of Fire*. Oxford: Oxford University Press, 1930.

Kott, Jan. *Shakespeare Our Contemporary*. Translated by Boleslaw Taborski. New York: Doubleday, 1966.

LaBranche, Linda Berning. "The Theatrical Dimension of *Troilus and Cressida*." Ph.D. dissertation, Northwestern University, 1984.

Machiavelli, Niccolò. *The Arte of Warre*. Translated by Peter Whitehorne.

1560. Reprint. New York: Da Capo, 1969.

————.*The Prince.* Translated by Mark Musa. New York: St. Martin's Press, 1964.

Okerlund, Arlene N. "In Defense of Cressida: Character as Metaphor." *Women's Studies* 7 (1980): 1–17.

Pitkin, Hannah. *Fortune Is a Woman: Gender and Politics in the Thought of Niccolo Machiavelli.* Berkeley: University of California Press, 1984.

Redfield, James. *Nature and Culture in the Iliad: The Tragedy of Hector.* Chicago: University of Chicago Press, 1975.

Roy, Emil. "War and Manliness in Shakespeare's *Troilus and Cressida.*" *Comparative Drama* 7 (1973): 107–20.

Shakespeare, William. *The Riverside Shakespeare.* Boston: Houghton Mifflin, 1974.

Stallybrass, Peter. "Patriarchal Territories: The Body Enclosed." In *Rewriting the Renaissance: The Discourses of Sexual Difference in Early Modern Europe*, edited by Margaret W. Ferguson, Maureen Quilligan, and Nancy J. Vickers, 123–42. Chicago: University of Chicago Press, 1986.

Stiehm, Judith Hicks. *Bring Me Men and Women: Mandated Change at the U.S. Air Force Academy.* Berkeley: University of California Press, 1981.

Stone, Lawrence. *The Crisis of the Aristocracy: 1558–1660.* Oxford: Oxford University Press, 1967.

Tillyard, E. M. W. *The Elizabethan World Picture.* 1943. Reprint. New York: Random House, n.d.

Vickers, Nancy. " 'The Blazon of Sweet Beauty's Best': Shakespeare's *Lucrece.*" In *Shakespeare and the Question of Theory*, edited by Patricia Parker and Geoffrey Hartman, 95–115. New York: Methuen, 1985.

————. "This Heraldry in Lucrece's Face." In *The Female Body in Western Culture*, edited by Susan Rubin Suleiman, 209–22. Cambridge, Mass.: Harvard University Press, 1986.

Virgil. *The Aeneid.* Translated by Allan Mandelbaum. New York: Bantam Books, 1971.

Woodbridge, Linda. *Women and the English Renaissance: Literature and the Nature of Womankind, 1540–1620.* Urbana: University of Illinois Press, 1984.

Yoder, R. A. " 'Sons and Daughters of the Game': An Essay on Shakespeare's *Troilus and Cressida.*" *Shakespeare Survey* 25 (1972): 11–25.

Patricia
Francis
Cholakian Rewriting History:

Madame de Villedieu and

the Wars of Religion

*I*t has been a commonplace of literature since Homer to blame women for causing wars. Such fictional histories appropriate women as pretexts, jealously guarding the text itself for the exploits of the hero. However, they contain the subversive idea that women's power shapes events. We may regard historical fiction, therefore, as the genre through which women take their place in history.

Les Désordres de l'amour, published in 1675 by the French novelist Madame de Villedieu, inscribes women into one of the most turbulent periods of history, the Wars of Religion, which devastated France in the second half of the sixteenth century.[1] It consists of three novellas, all of which deal with amorous intrigues in the court of Henri III.[2] Madame de Villedieu,[3] believed to be the first French woman to support herself by writing fiction, composed more than thirty works, of which *Les Désordres de l'amour* was the last. One of the most popular and widely read writers of her time, Villedieu addressed herself primarily to a female audience. As Micheline Cuénin writes in her critical edition, "[t]he novel's public is first of all women, whose natural curiosity, sentimental ups and downs, or lack of occupation led them naturally towards works of imagination and amusement."[4]

By recounting the romantic adventures of the beautiful and famous during her great-grandmothers' day, Villedieu offered to her women readers, often unhappily married and perpetually pregnant, a type of fictional distraction that was just beginning to be popular in France. To women living under Louis XIV, the Wars of Religion must have appeared much as the American Civil War appears to American women today. The divisions and bitterness it had engendered, although largely laid to rest, would have been vaguely understood, and its causes, events, and leaders would have been at once legendary and familiar. In the earlier part of the century the need for fictional escape had been satisfied by pastoral romances set in mythical countries. The multiple tomes of Urfé's *L'Astrée* and Scudéry's *Clélie* had diverted their readers with the refined gallantries of improbable shepherds and shepherdesses. By contrast, the places and people of *Les Désordres de l'amour* had really existed. Readers were able to identify with their heroines in a new and different way. Stories about the private lives of dead kings and queens satisfied a desire for realistic fiction that the pastoral romances had not.

Les *Désordres de l'amour* was more than a "woman's novel" meant to while away the time, however. Seriously documented and carefully composed, it purported to demonstrate the role that love had played in history. As René Démoris suggests, the vogue for historical fiction that inspired Villedieu to compose *Les Désordres de l'amour* had political causes, representing a form of protest against an absolute monarch who had imposed an official version of history on his subjects.[5] In fiction it was possible to tell the "truth" about the past by depicting the wickedness, vanity, and folly of the great "in an epoch neither too near or too distant." Those who resorted to historical fiction in order to comment indirectly on the deficiencies of the monarchy were those who did not have direct access to power: "Those who adapted themselves to this deconstruction were both those who were excluded from the political sphere by birth (grosso modo, the Bourgeoisie) and those who had been excluded by accident (the [feudal] Aristocracy). The result was at one and the same time a politicization of Eros and an eroticization of politics."[6]

Not surprisingly, Démoris's analysis of the reasons behind the rise of historical fiction in the second half of the seventeenth century suppresses mention of a group that did not have direct access to political power under Louis XIV, or indeed under any other monarch. I refer, of course, to women. That is why the last sentence of the above citation appears to be a non sequitur. The "eroticization of politics" in the historical novel results not from exclusion based on class, but from exclusion based on gender.

To take up where Démoris's analysis leaves off, when a female novelist like Villedieu rewrote history her text questioned not only the assumptions of Louis XIV's regime but the more general assumption that men were more fit than women to exercise power. Historical fiction written by and for women fantasizes a context in which the rules governing power no longer apply. *Les Désordres de l'amour* is usually interpreted as a warning against the dangers of love: "The honest women who read novels took pleasure in the defeat of the 'femme fatale' [Madame de Sauve], who comes between husbands and wives. . . . Everything comes together to praise sincerity and to denounce the falseness of love."[7] But in her review of Cuénin's doctoral thesis on Villedieu, Elizabeth Berg sees beneath the surface "message" to the feminist implications of these stories:

> Villedieu's work constitutes a rewriting of history that takes into account the *galanteries* responsible for major historical events; it is a history designed to correct the bias of historians who discount the role played by women in influencing the course of politics. While this revision of historical writing may seem—and be—a distortion of facts in favor of a romantic delusion of women's power "behind the scenes," it must also be read as a first attempt by a woman to reread history from a woman's point of view, to substitute a woman's history—"herstory"—for the history of male domination that Madame de Villedieu knew so well.[8]

Berg's remarks are particularly applicable to the first novella in the collection. Situated in the years 1574–77, it begins with the French nation's fervent hopes for peace at the moment of Henri III's accession to the throne and ends with the formation of the ultra-Catholic *Ligue* by the Duc de Guise, which put an end to these hopes. On the historical level, therefore, it narrates Henri III's failure to bring peace and prosperity to his kingdom. These historical events are merely the frame, however, for an "inside story," the amorous intrigues surrounding the bewitching Madame de Sauve. The novella's plot may be likened to two concentric circles. In the outer circle, the leaders of the two religiopolitical factions play out the events that culminate in civil war; in the inner circle, they are manipulated by the women they love. Villedieu bases this feminized version of events on the most highly respected history of her time, François Eudes de Mézeray's *Histoire de France contenant le règne du Roi Henri III et celui du Roi Henri IV*. Composed in the years before Louis XIV came to power, Mézeray's account of the Wars of Religion was considered a model until the middle of the eighteenth century.[9] Villedieu also took certain episodes from the *Mémoires* of Marguerite de Valois, Queen of Navarre, who as sister of Henri III and wife of the future Henri IV, had witnessed the events at first hand.[10]

Writing in a dry and dispassionate style, Villedieu constructs her narrative by extracting from her sources the passages that speak of romantic affairs at Henri III's court and eliminating almost everything else. For instance, Mézeray offers a complex series of explanations for the wars that troubled the reign of Henri III: the grievances of the Huguenots; the ambitions of the House of Guise; the resentment of the Princes of the Blood; the seditious temper of the people; the debauchery of the clergy; the corruptive influence of Machiavelli's writings; and, only incidentally, the degeneracy of the court, "infected" by "deceit, treachery, assassinations, and shameless manners."[11] Villedieu ignores or minimizes all but the last of these, concentrating on a portrayal of the "shameless manners" in a court seething with amorous intrigue.

Both Mézeray and Marguerite de Valois explain that Henri III's brother (known as Monsieur) and the king of Navarre (who became Henri IV) deserted the court and joined the seditious forces because they resented being treated as virtual prisoners by the king. Completely ignoring this explanation, Villedieu embroiders on Mézeray's statement that Madame de Sauve "used her charms no less on the queen-mother's behalf than for her own satisfaction."[12] She invents a scenario in which Monsieur and Navarre join the Protestant enemies of the Guises because they learn of Madame de Sauve's secret amours with their rival the Duc de Guise. Since strictly speaking Villedieu invents almost nothing, the stories she tells are verifiably "true." They therefore become incontrovertible evidence in support of her text's thesis: *History is shaped behind the scenes by erotic desire.*

The inside story of the real causes behind the war begins when the queen-mother, the notorious Catherine de Médicis, becomes fearful of losing control over her son and promises to back the woman who can become his mistress. Madame de Sauve succeeds in this enterprise, but her jealous rivals and disappointed suitors form a "ligue" that vows to bring about her downfall.[13] Terrified that she will be banished from court as a troublemaker, Madame de Sauve manages to persuade each of the male conspirators that he is her favorite. When her suitors learn the truth, their enmity spills over into the political arena and war becomes inevitable.

Villedieu's stated purpose, to prove that passion was the true cause of the Wars of Religion, is set forth in the form of a theorem which serves as epigraph to Part I: "*That love is the mainspring of all the soul's other passions*" (3). The story of the femme fatale, Madame de Sauve, is thus announced as an exemplum, and the final page of the novella reminds the reader of this fact: "It is all too amply proven by the diverse intrigues which make up this example that love is the mainspring of all the soul's passions and that if one examined carefully the secret motives of the revolutions which occur in monarchies, one would find it [love] without fail either guilty or implicated in all of them" (65–66). As Nancy K. Miller comments, "What one might say is at stake in this collection of stories is the proper relation between the spheres of love and state. If by virtue of the logic of the maxim that underwrites the whole work—'*Que l'amour est le ressort de toutes les autres passions*'—love rules all human relations, what in their representations can distinguish, for example, the state of love from affairs of state, private life from public life, women from men?"[14]

The old idea that women are responsible for causing wars thus becomes the basis for an examination of women's access to the mechanisms of power. The novella asks the question: What is the relationship between the private (woman's) domain of passion and the public (man's) domain of politics? The book's title, as well as a series of authorial incursions into the plot, would seem to indicate clearly that the author intends to prove that it is love, the private relationship between two individuals, which is responsible for public disorder.

As has often been pointed out, such disorders were all too prevalent in Villedieu's own day at the court of Louis XIV. The so-called Sun King carried on his adulterous relationships with Louise de La Vallière and Madame de Montespan (to name only two of his mistresses) in full view of the nation, and love, which in literature had heretofore been treated as a beneficent force in human affairs, was now held responsible for the greatest misfortunes. This revised attitude toward love was most compellingly enunciated in Racine's tragedies. In Jean-Michel Pelous's opinion, Madame de Villedieu, always sensitive to the demands of her readers, was "converted" to this "new" attitude toward love, which became popular in the very decade which saw the publication of *Les Désordres de l'amour*. "The work of this successful novelist," he writes, "gives an accurate indication of the average beliefs of her time."[15] At the end of Part 2, the author acknowledges that her attitude toward love has changed: "I do not doubt that at this point more than one reader is saying ironically that I have not always talked like this [about love]" (118). Upon close examination, however, disastrous passion in this novella is very different from the universally debilitating malady that afflicts Racine's characters—for the very good reason that women do not seem to suffer from it at all.[16]

Three verse maxims inserted into the narrative enunciate the destructive power of love. The first appears at the end of the second paragraph and tells how Henri III's determination to bring peace and prosperity to his realm failed because Love interfered: "But Love, that tyrant over the most illustrious souls, that secret enemy of our prosperities, who disguises its flames under false pleasures to make our ills pass as felicities, causes its chimeras to shine in the new king's eyes. He let himself be charmed by their vain sweetness and their lying delights, and seducing his senses, they soften his heart" (5). The second maxim is inserted at the moment when Guise believes that he at last possesses the elusive Madame de Sauve. It speaks of the transitory nature of such happiness and how love blinds those whom it seduces, concluding, "All that we know of grandeur on earth, all that makes up its most beautiful adornments, law, honor, peace, war, all are subject to its enchantments" (43). The third maxim appears just as war seems about to break out despite Catherine de Médicis' efforts to arrange a truce: "How many misfortunes, present and future, always accompany love and its madness! How many evils does this jealousy cause us, and how much time is necessary to see to their reparation! Fatal passion, souls' enchantment, Ah! how Heaven was angered with us when it was written there that your deadly flames would offer something so sweet to our desires" (61).

Because of the gender-neutral language of these passages, they would seem to apply to both sexes, but in fact these maxims point to the connection between *masculine* vulnerability and political disaster. The "Love" of which the first maxim speaks is the woman who distracts Henri III from carrying out his high resolves; similarly the second maxim mocks the Duc de Guise's blind trust in Madame de Sauve's love; while the third refers to his fit of jealousy, which eventually destroys the truce.

According to Cuénin the insertion of verse passages into prose was also widespread at this time.[17] La Fontaine followed the same practice in *Le Songe de Vaux* (1665–1671) and *Les Amours de Psyché et de Cupidon* (1669). Thus these verse maxims inveighing against love may have been introduced primarily as a concession to literary vogues.[18] Whereas Arthur Flannigan believes that "it is through the maxims that the narrative voice reveals parenthetically the moral 'causes' which permit the reader to understand fully the particular political and social 'effects' under consideration and, at the same time, to transcend the particularities of the events in question," in actual fact, these discursive generalizations obscure what is really happening in the story.[19] When we analyze the story alone, we find that it does not demonstrate the moral causes set forth in the maxims. Rather it deconstructs the *stereotypes* of men and women in love.

It may even be argued that these verse maxims serve as a diversionary tactic, drawing attention away from the antimasculinist message hidden in the plot. Elaine Showalter has demonstrated how nineteenth-century Englishwomen camouflaged their feminism with superficial conformity to patriarchal conventions.[20] And Gilbert and Gubar have revealed the "madwoman in the attic" concealed behind Brontë's docile Jane Eyre. If such subterfuges were necessary in Victorian England, they were certainly no less so under a paternalistic monarch who considered himself God's representative on earth. These sententious authorial pronouncements introduce into the story's plot attitudes prevalent in Villedieu's time, but it is not at all certain that, as Cuénin believes, they were aimed at "honest women" who took pleasure in the defeat of a femme fatale.[21] For one thing, the femme fatale Madame de Sauve is *not* defeated, as becomes clear later.

If one excludes the discursive interruptions, one finds a critique not of female passion but of the men who wield power. The male figures are consistently portrayed as weaklings, incapable of carrying out a single good deed. The king is quickly distracted from implementing his plans for peace and devotes all his energies to his love life. As for the king's brother Monsieur and his brother-in-law Henri de Navarre, their honorable inclinations are never strong enough to prevent them from performing acts they *know* to be reprehensible. Navarre's code of honor is superseded by his mistress's demand that he publicly humiliate Madame de Sauve; nor does he hesitate later to go back on his promise when he himself falls under the coquette's spell. Likewise Monsieur, who has steadfastly refused to join the Protestants, changes his mind when he finds out that he has been deceived by Madame de Sauve. Wilier and more perceptive than the others, the Duc de Guise nevertheless allows himself to be ruled by his passion for the coquette. His desire to punish her drives him to ally himself with her female enemies. When Madame de Sauve begins to sigh and make eyes at him, however, his cohorts guess rightly that he will betray their cause; and it is not long before he has proved them right. Rendered euphoric by her favors, he forgets all his political concerns and realizes too late that he has been the dupe of his emotions: "How he reproached himself for having waited so long to discover the truth! He accused himself of weakness and blindness; he regretted a thousand times the day when he had put his faith in this coquette" (59). But things have already gone too far. Although Catherine de Médicis succeeds in averting war temporarily, Guise eventually decides to ally himself with the Catholic *Ligue*, and thus he "laid the foundations for that internecine war which for many years tore the kingdom apart" (65).

The leaders who appear so strong in public are in fact powerless in private. What Villedieu's story demonstrates is that the two domains cannot be kept separate. The men's private weakness is responsible for the disaster of their public performance. The queen-mother, who understands this perfectly, is able to manipulate them into doing what she wants by arousing their erotic desires. Catherine brings along the prettiest women at court to make sure that she gets her way at the conference table—"she had herself attended by women who were so beautiful and knew so well how to please that they softened the hearts of these warriors, and brought them to agree to a part of what was desired of them" (64).[22]

None of the female characters has direct access to political power, however. Although they are the prime movers in the romantic plot, they are confined to the private domain. Even the queen-mother, the character most adept at shaping events to her own ends, must act indirectly through her son the king. As a woman she can only wield power at second hand. That is why all her undertakings are aimed at preserving her "credit" with her son. Despite her central position in both the historical and the fictional plots, Catherine de Médicis' power is in reality indirect and temporary. It is her awareness of this fact that causes her to place self-interest above the common good. By furthering what she perceives to be her son's desire for peace, she tries to prove to him that she is indispensable to his government. To this end she even incites the rival factions to go to war in order to display her talent as a peacemaker: "During that time, the queen-mother's skills had not been idle. She had secretly sowed division between the Chiefs. She [then] caused proposals of peace to be made which could not reasonably be rejected" (22).

The figure of the queen-mother stands at the intersection between the men's world of senseless military conflict and the women's world of petty quarrels. The three female conspirators, Mademoiselle de Châteauneuf, Mademoiselle d'Elbeuf, and the Queen of Navarre, are completely enclosed within the confines of the court. While the princes make and break alliances on the frontiers, the women conspire behind palace walls. This court is a world apart, an oasis of lavish entertainments in which illusion and pretense not only conceal the harsh realities of the times but mask the true feelings of the participants. Its principal attractions are its lavish festivities, which emblemize by their artificiality the court's separation from the "real world" and the deceptive relationships it harbors: "The wide paths were lit with torches and lanterns *hidden* among the branches; the point to which they all led had been prepared to *represent an Italian comedy,* another part of the woods *served as* a ball room, and in the transversal alleys which had purposely been left *obscure* . . . there were *false figures,* lighted from the inside and *painted the color of fire,* which by *agreeably deceiving the eye* enabled it to make out objects" (36–38; emphasis added). The creation of illusion represents the highest achievement of this court. Formed by its false values, the women's most effective weapon is their ability to deceive and dissimulate. They convince the King of Navarre to pretend to fall in love with Madame de Sauve. To achieve this Mademoiselle de Châteauneuf makes a false promise to become his mistress. Likewise, when the Queen of Navarre complains to her brother Monsieur of her husband's infidelity, she is not sincerely jealous. Her pretended sadness is merely a ruse to incite him to take action against the hated Madame de Sauve.

It is the women's second-class status which makes it necessary for them to resort constantly to lies and subterfuge, the devious behavior traditionally attributed to the female character. There is none of the mystification or murky unpredictability so often set forth in male constructions of female figures, however. Villedieu's women are not dark goddesses mindlessly subjecting their male victims to cruel whims. The women of the little *ligue* act as they do because of their confinement to the private sector. The obsessive erotic desire from which the men suffer is entirely foreign to them. Like the queen-mother, they too desire not to be loved but to be powerful. Villedieu's text corroborates Nancy Miller's thesis that the true female fantasy is the fantasy of power: "The repressed content [of female fantasy], I think, would be, not erotic impulses, but an impulse to power: a fantasy of power that would revise the social grammar in which women are never defined as subjects; a fantasy of power that disdains a sexual exchange in which women can participate only as objects of circulation."[23] But at this court the only way women can hold power is by winning the king's affections—thus their chagrin when Madame de Sauve succeeds where they have failed, and their desire to punish her. Like all oppressed people, their lack of insight into the true causes of their oppression makes them direct their hostility toward the member of their own group who has gained admittance to the power structure from which they have been excluded. Their sexual uninvolvement enables them to pursue this goal with a single-mindedness far surpassing the men's. They never question or revise their project. Despite their lucidity and their high powers of concentration, however, they cannot bring about Madame de Sauve's disgrace and exile. Even here they must find male allies who will act for them— Guise, Navarre, Monsieur. The female conspirators are powerless to accomplish anything at first hand. They must manipulate men into fighting their battles.

The figure of their enemy Madame de Sauve stands apart. Her power lies in her refusal to reveal her true feelings; she remains a mystery even to the other women. "What charms and spells does this coquette use?" exclaims Mademoiselle d'Elbeuf (25). In this she is like Célimène in the *Misanthrope* by Villedieu's contemporary Molière. Both Célimène and Madame de Sauve know that to name a favorite is to let their admirers slip out of their grasp.[24] Her "taste for making new conquests" (11) drives Madame de Sauve to place herself at the head of a miniempire composed of subjugated suitors. Women cannot participate in the game of war, but love is also a game that can be won or lost by conquest. In love, Madame de Sauve is the greatest general, for it is she who possesses the most power over her lovers. She does not conceive of power in masculine terms, however. The mystique of her femininity leads her to define her power in terms of male admiration. That is what valorizes her existence: "Her beauty came so much into vogue that a man would have passed for an outcast if he had not displayed some small mark of passion for Madame de Sauve" (10–11).

Although she acts as the queen-mother's agent, there is no real indication within the story that Madame de Sauve values the political influence afforded by her status as the king's favorite. Rather, what she seems to appreciate most is the opportunity to be the erotic center of the court whose values and pleasures define the limits of her existence. Only the king's threat of banishment can arouse in her a sincere emotion: "This was one of the most cruel adventures which could happen to a woman of her character. She loved the Court, she had a mortal hatred of solitude, and she spared neither presents nor flattery to have such a terrible order revoked" (35). In her determination not to be separated from the artificial pleasures of the court, Madame de Sauve incarnates its isolation from the cataclysm taking place in the world outside. She clings to its illusions in the same way that she refuses to participate in the kill climaxing the King of Navarre's hunting party: "The hunt was successful, and the ladies were guided so skilfully that after having seen the stag five or six times, they were able to be present at its death. But this was not an amusement which suited Madame de Sauve. She said that it aroused her pity to see this animal at bay, and she withdrew to sit under some trees" (16). As Madame de Sauve cuts herself off from the real purpose of the hunting party, so the text carefully separates the passages that speak of her from those that describe the political events taking place in the world outside the court. It depicts her as completely unaware that her behavior has led to disastrous consequences. What happens in the political domain is no concern of hers. So long as she is allowed to display her charms at court, she remains untouched by external events. She knows her place and she occupies it without either hindsight or foresight.

In the final pages summarizing the political consequences of her gallantries, the name of Madame de Sauve disappears completely. In the last passage that mentions her, she remains unrepentant and unafraid, despite Guise's threats to unmask her: "These threats didn't overly frighten Madame de Sauve. She had already put her power to the test and it promised her a thousand new miracles" (60). For the coquette, power consists of successfully walking the tightrope of romance. Although the historical plot eventually leads to violent deaths for Guise, Navarre, and the king, the story of which Madame de Sauve is the heroine never ends. The private domain of amorous fantasy may hold many other adventures for her.

Villedieu's novella hardly presents a flattering view of women. The politically ambitious Catherine de Médicis adroitly advances her own interests by manipulating male desire. The women of the little "ligue" seek compensation for their disenfranchisement in petty intrigues against a successful female rival; and the narcissistic Madame de Sauve, oblivious to the world of war, gratifies her need for male adulation by systematically deceiving her admirers.

Henri Coulet has remarked in his study of the French novel before the Revolution that Madame de Villedieu portrays "beings who are without heroism."[25] But is not the concept of the hero itself a masculine invention? The age of Louis XIV venerated the king's grandfather, Henri IV de Navarre, as the founder of the Bourbon dynasty and the savior of the nation. In *Les Désordres*, Navarre is a fickle, vacillating traitor to the crown. This corroborates Démoris's analysis of the way in which historical fiction undermined the official history of Louis' reign. Villedieu subverts not only political mythology but gender mythology as well, claiming that both women and men interact with history, albeit in different ways. Although women's power may be indirect, it nevertheless exists and influences the shape of public events. The outside world of war and the inside world of love are shown to be inextricably linked, a truth that is incorporated into the structure of the story itself as it moves from public events—Henri III's projects for peace—to private adventures—the "heroes'" involvement with Madame de Sauve—and returns to the realm of history in the final paragraphs that sum up the consequences.

Since women are excluded from direct participation in history, however, they are not subject to its closure. The story ends by revealing the destiny of the men caught up in a war fought over the length and breadth of France. The reader never learns what finally happens to its female characters. As the narrative moves from the inner circle of the court to the outer circle of history, the women are left behind. When last heard of both Madame de Sauve and her sponsor Catherine de Médicis have achieved their goals. The former is still firmly entrenched at the court and is looking forward to performing "new miracles" with her charms. The queen-mother's machinations have appreciably increased her influence over the king. Each is abandoned by the narrative at a moment when she is in full control of the power she desired.

The "honest women" whom Cuénin imagines taking satisfaction in reading this text would not find there the lesson she extrapolates—the defeat of the femme fatale. Instead they would find one of the few cases in all literature where female erotic desire does not lead to the heroines' downfall and where "wicked" women are not punished by disgrace or death. Madame de Villedieu does more than rewrite the past to include women. She creates through fiction a historical space in which their fantasies of power can come true.

Notes

1. It is difficult to fix a date for the beginning of this long civil conflict. The "Affaire des Placards" in 1534 caused François I to take a hard line with the reformers, and a series of crises followed under the reign of his son Henri II. Many historians date the actual wars from 1575 to 1596, after which the Edict of Nantes guaranteed civil and military rights to Protestants. All are in agreement, however, that the situation became critical following the St. Bartholomew's Day Massacre (August 25, 1572), when many Protestant leaders were assassinated.

2. The book is divided into four parts, but the third and fourth are in reality two halves of the same story.

3. Née Marie-Catherine Desjardins (1638?–1683).

4. Cuénin, Introduction to *Les Désordres de l'amour*, xiii. All translations from the French in this article are my own. Page numbers within parentheses in the text refer to the Cuénin edition of *Les Désordres*. A more recent edition by Arthur Flannigan is perhaps easier to read, but is not so rich in background material.

5. The king engaged a series of court historiographers, including Jean Racine. The writing of history thus became a form of political propaganda. See Ranum, *Artisans of Glory*.

6. Démoris, "Aux Origines de l'homme historique," 30, 31.

7. Cuénin, Introduction, lii.

8. Berg, Review, 117–18.

9. See Evans, *L'Historien Mézeray*.

10. Micheline Cuénin's edition provides references to all the passages on which Villedieu based her narrative. See also her Introduction (xxviii–xliii).

11. Mézeray, *Histoire de France*, 2.

12. Ibid., 44.

13. The use of the word "ligue" to designate the alliance against Madame de Sauve may be a conscious parody of the name by which history designates the ultra-Catholic Guise faction. See *Les Désordres*, 13: "[T]he duke entered into this 'ligue,' joining to the ladies' resentments a fearless courage and a perfect knowledge of all the characters involved."

14. Miller, "Tender Economies," 82.

15. Pelous, *Amour précieux*, 464. Micheline Cuénin notes in this regard, "In fact, it is really beginning with Madame de Villedieu that the French novel would take on for centuries the psychological determinism which Racine, quite precisely at the same date, implanted in the theatre" (*Roman*

et Société, 724). Lassalle, "Enonciation de la fatalité," and Lever, *Le Roman français*, also see in *Les Désordres de l'amour* the enunciation of passion as fatality.

16. Although in Part 1, women seem to be immune to love, in the other parts of *Les Désordres de l'amour*, they too are subject to passion. Marguerite de Saluces is in love with her husband's nephew at the beginning of Part 2, a passion that turns to hate after their marriage. Madame de Martigues remains desperately attached to Givry despite his callous infidelity in Parts 3 and 4. A careful comparison of their loves and those of the book's male characters would reveal, however, that Villedieu portrays the manifestations of love very differently in men and in women. Since the other two novellas in the series are not directly concerned with the causes of war, however, I have limited this essay as much as possible to a discussion of Part 1. For a good analysis of the third novella, see Miller's "Tender Economies." Miller describes *Les Désordres* as "(bleak) stories of love not returned in kind, of agitation and *despair* . . . structured by an essentially dysphoric model: the woman in love—or the man in love *like a woman* (in love)" (83). (Emphasis in original.)

17. Cuénin, Introduction, xlviii.

18. The number of maxims dwindles progressively. There are only two in Part 2, none in Part 3, and only a short quatrain at the end of Part 4.

19. Flannigan, "The Feminization of History," 97. For Flannigan's view of the way "discours" functions in relationship to "récit" see ibid. and his *Mme de Villedieu's Les Désordres de l'amour*. Flannigan also argues in "The Feminization of History" that while history's form is linear (masculine), Villedieu's fictionalized version is discontinuous: "a feminine discourse similar to what has been postulated as 'female subjectivity' " (104). He explicitly stops short, however, of suggesting "that it is gender alone that has determined Mme de Villedieu's conceptualization and writing of history. The fact that Mézeray is male and Villedieu female is perhaps coincidental; for even if one can identify their works as man-text and woman-text respectively, I maintain (with Hélène Cixous) that there is no 'attributable difference' between the writing of *a* man and that of *a* woman" (106). Flannigan's analysis is therefore essentially formalistic and not really concerned with the role of gender in determining textual signs. I believe, on the other hand, that Villedieu's rewriting of history grew out of her membership in a disenfranchised collectivity—women—and was thus the result of her gender.

20. See Showalter, *A Literature of Their Own*.

21. Cuénin, Introduction, lii.

22. This passage is based directly on Mézeray's account of the negotiations at Chastenay-le-Château, *Histoire de France*, 97.

23. Miller, "Emphasis Added," 41.

24. This play was first produced in 1666 and the character of Madame de

Sauve as conceived by Madame de Villedieu may have owed something to Molière's portrait of the coquette. The exchange between Guise and Madame de Sauve on pages 12 and 13 is very similar to that between Célimène and Alceste in act 2, scene 1. For an analysis of Célimène's coquetry, see my article, "The 'Woman Question' in Molière's *Misanthrope*."

25. Coulet, *Le Roman jusqu'à la Révolution*, 267.

Works Cited

Berg, Elizabeth. Review of Micheline Cuénin, *Roman et Société*. In *L'Esprit Créateur* 23, no. 2 (Summer 1983): 117–18.

Cholakian, Patricia Francis. "The 'Woman Question' in Molière's *Misanthrope*." *French Review* 58, no. 4 (March 1985): 524–32.

Coulet, Henri. *Le Roman jusqu'à la Révolution*. Paris: Armand Colin, 1967.

Cuénin, Micheline. *Madame de Villedieu, Les Désordres de l'amour. Edition critique*. Genève: Droz, 1970.

———. *Roman et Société sous Louis XIV: Madame de Villedieu*. Vol. 1. Paris: Champion, 1979.

Démoris, René. "Aux Origines de l'homme historique: le croisement, au XVIIe siècle, du roman et de l'histoire." In *Le Roman historique (XVIIe–XXe siècles)*. Actes de Marseilles réunis par Pierre Ronzeaud. Biblio 17. *Papers on French Seventeenth Century Literature* 15 (1983): 23–41.

Evans, Wilfrid Hugo. *L'Historien Mézeray et la conception de l'histoire de France au XVIIe siècle*. Paris: Presses Modernes, 1931.

Flannigan, Arthur. *Les Désordres de l'amour, a critical edition*. Washington, D.C.: University Press of America, 1982.

———. *Mme de Villedieu's Les Désordres de l'amour: History, Literature, and the Nouvelle Historique*. Washington, D.C.: University Press of America, 1982.

———. "Mme de Villedieu's *Les Désordres de l'amour*: The Feminization of History." *L'Esprit Créateur* 23, no. 2 (Summer 1983): 94–106.

Gilbert, Sandra, and Gubar, Susan. *The Madwoman in the Attic*. New Haven: Yale University Press, 1979.

Lassalle, Thérèse. "Enonciation de la fatalité et structure du récit: Quelques remarques sur *Les Désordres de l'amour* et *La Princesse de Clèves*." *Cahiers de littérature du dix-septième siècle* 6(84): 292–300.

Lever, Maurice. *Le Roman français au XVIIe siècle*. Paris: PUF, 1981.

Mézeray, François Eudes de. *Histoire de France contenant le règne du Roi Henri III et celui du Roi Henri IV*, vol. 3, Paris, 1651.

Miller, Nancy K. "Emphasis Added: Plots and Plausibilities in Women's Fiction." *PMLA* 96, no. 1 (January 1981): 36–48.

———. "Tender Economies: Mme de Villedieu and the Costs of Indifference." *L'Esprit Créateur* 23, no. 2 (Summer 1983): 80–93.

Pelous, Jean-Michel. *Amour précieux, amour galant (1654–1675)*. Paris: Klincksieck, 1980.

Ranum, Orest. *Artisans of Glory: Writers and Historical Thought in Seventeenth-Century France*. Chapel Hill: University of North Carolina Press, 1980.

Showalter, Elaine. *A Literature of Their Own: British Women Novelists from Brontë to Lessing*. Princeton, N.J.: Princeton University Press, 1977.

Valois, Marguerite de. *Mémoires et autres écrits de Marguerite de Valois, La Reine Margot*. Edited by Yves Cazaux. Paris: Mercure de France, 1971.

Jane E. Mute Fury:
Schultz

Southern Women's Diaries

of Sherman's March to the Sea,

1864–1865

William Tecumseh Sherman was a pragmatist at heart.
When reflecting on the great marches from Atlanta to
Savannah and Savannah to Goldsboro, North Carolina, he wrote that Southerners had been unduly
afraid of his men: "[T]hey had invented such ghost-like stories of
our prowess in Georgia, that they were scared by their own inventions. Still, this was a power, and I intended to utilize it."[1]

Sherman was well aware of the relationship between power and
fear, and he did not really expect any serious challenge to his
troops' preeminence in a country populated by women, children,
and old men. His object was to wage "total war," by which he
meant destruction not only of military targets but of domestic
property and land.[2] In effect Sherman became the first general in
American history to declare war on a civilian population.

As ex officio heads of households, women had coped for months
at a time with agricultural and mercantile responsibilities. While
managing their homes, businesses, and farms had made them self-
reliant and self-confident, they nonetheless dreaded the prospect of
meeting face to face with Yankee marauders. In the absence of their
own men, they looked to other men for protection—particularly
those who wore gray uniforms and camped in the yard. Or they
implored their husbands to return home, in spite of the trials they
knew would follow such a course of action.[3]

A social code that taught women deference to male power in return for protection was upended as Sherman's sixty thousand troops
razed a landscape through three states over an eight-month period.
Women's experience with the enemy was to teach them that they
could not depend on male protection during wartime. With the
policy of domestic vandalism in effect, Southern women, who con-

sidered themselves the quintessentially Protected, knew that the Federal soldiers sweeping the countryside were more often a danger to them than a source of protection.[4] Though some of these soldiers might be ordered to guard civilian property, the great majority of them foraged liberally off the civilian population. Their presence constituted not only a threat to familiar patterns of social conduct but a physical threat to the women charged with upholding the standard of conduct. Women lived in continual dread of physical violation, and their frequent mention of their reluctance to undress indicates that they feared the possibility of rape. Rape became for them an unspeakable crime—never named but referred to in oblique language as something that happened to other women.

Yet women along Sherman's route found themselves in something of a double bind: even though they were aware that the Yankees had been known to harm civilians, they believed that the Yankees, as men, must also respond to feminine pleas for protection. Indeed Sherman and other generals under his command dispatched guards to the homes of women who had had the presence of mind to petition them directly for such aid. Some women found their guards to be trustworthy, and thus permitted them to play the role of protector. But other women found their alleged protectors wanting in honesty: they stole family possessions or abandoned the household before their term of duty had expired. These less dependable guards made women mistrust their own instincts about male protection: they wanted to trust men as the natural protectors of women, but how could they distinguish the good from the evil man? Without their own protectors at home, women sought protection from the only individuals empowered to deliver it—the men whom militarily they had least reason to trust. But after their homes had been raided, they recognized that they could no longer depend on men—even their own men—to protect them.

Knowing little about when or where raids would commence, women regarded themselves as victims of psychological torture. They were shocked by the cruelty and vulgarity of these Northern men who had been commanded to plunder their genteel homes. Writing about Sherman's assault on Fayetteville, North Carolina, Sarah Tillinghast was still perplexed years later at the brazen dishonesty of those who ought to have known better: "Even after the experience of those days, it is a mystery to me yet, that officers of high standing, men, who one would think might be gentlemen, could bow their pride enough to walk into a private house and carry off articles belonging to the occupants."[5] Tillinghast's response to the raids as well as the more immediate responses of many other Southern women imply that nothing in previous experience had prepared them for this utter abandonment of chivalrous conduct. Without an intimate understanding of military prerogative and the uses of force, women responded angrily to what they perceived foremost as a masculine abuse of power.

That is, they saw their foes not so much as soldiers as errant men. And as such, they believed they might appeal to them on personal grounds. Kate Whitehead Rowland's anger at a Michigan soldier also named Whitehead illustrates this point. When the soldier appropriated an engraved dipper, claiming that it was his because it said "Whitehead," Kate's response was not to see the theft as part of the larger cycle of authorized pillage but as a malicious act committed by an ill-bred boy. When the soldier asked as an afterthought if they were related, she recorded in her journal, "I felt like taking off his head."[6] Women like Rowland regarded violation in personal terms; violation was a gendered offense, not merely the inevitable result of a military command to lay waste.

Cues in the language of this circumstantially bound group of Southern women suggest that their experience of Federal raids was rather different from men's. Most male Southerners writing about the war were likely to extrapolate political truths from their observations of military might. They regarded the raids as an emblem of disintegration; as inheritors of a precious aristocratic past they feared the spectral image of a shiftless future, where the very fabric of cultural continuity would be threadbare.[7] While women too lamented the passing of an old and familiar way of life, they perceived the military threat much more literally. Instead of viewing singular acts, like destruction of personal property, from an abstract political perspective, they were more likely to dwell on the social meaning of an incident.

Women's diaries provided a natural forum for the consideration of social questions. Writers used them as largely private receptacles to comment and pass judgment on personal relationships and on daily occurrences. Judy Nolte Lensink has argued that although the diary's virtual exclusion from critical praxis has been viewed as a function of its idiomatic fluctuations in form and content, in fact it reflects critics' lack of tools to systematize the reading of diaries. More importantly, Lensink points out that the diary's generic liminality makes it the representative female autobiographical text. To the extent that the diarist creates a form for her "story," which is shaped by content, each diary looks different from every other. The writer chooses what kind of details to include—whether routine reports of domestic events or intimate appraisals of acquaintances or a few lines of poetry about the weather—all without generic constraints. Out of this freedom to create a formless form emerges a quilt-text of unique meanings and metaphors. As Lensink phrases it, diary writing "ma[kes] coherent [women's] experiential lives."[8] That is, the act of writing carries with it the power to shape a generic standard, whereas the tangible product itself may argue against generic standardization.

Women's accounts of Sherman's raids reflect both their view of themselves as social commentators and their predisposition to autobiography. Perceiving themselves to be objects of the enemy's wrath, they write as victims—with defensiveness and a Southern brand of civil disobedience. They are not only "the other" in terms of gender but in regional and social class distinctions (or so it seems to them) as well. As a manifestation of "the other" mentality, the diarists often define themselves by saying what they are *not*, or will not tolerate. Despite their oft-expressed desire to preserve the record of outrageous incidents for posterity, if the diarists have a mission, it is a profoundly transhistorical one. Nevertheless, they neither devalue their personal perspective nor regard their writing as less serious or influential than historical writing. The diarists' reluctance to privilege the historical over the personal offers a key to understanding their autobiographical bent.

Thirty-seven diaries and memoirs constitute the body of texts considered here. Only four writers actively published their accounts; several others intended them to be preserved in family archives. The remainder are for the most part self-contained works, several of which have been extracted without editing from diaries that cover entire adult lifetimes or the entire Civil War period. Mrs. Campbell Bryce of Columbia, South Carolina, dedicates her memoir to her children, "remembering well how eagerly I sought for and cherished every tradition and scrap of history handed down to me by my parents of their parents." Sarah Tillinghast gives voice to that part of human experience not yet included under the rubric of history; she writes a young female relative that although she may read about the war, its causes, and military strategies, "history does not tell all those items, that belong to family affairs, and I would like you all to know what I know from experience of that part of the war." For women like Grace Beard, more was at stake than to preserve what was not destined to make the history books; it was no less than the writer's duty to protect modern readers from "erroneous ideas" about the raids.[9]

Whether considered as entities or as parts of larger texts, these accounts illustrate a cycle of changes in women's language as violence escalates. Women initially used precise and detailed language to depict Federal depredations. Diarists tell us down to the last crumb how much food was stolen, how much livestock killed, and how many orchards, gardens, and fields annihilated. Mary Beth Norton has illumined an eighteenth-century precedent for this careful accounting of losses in testimony of loyalist women pursuing property claims with the British government in the wake of the Revolutionary War.[10] Although women may have had little knowledge of their husbands' or fathers' financial dealings, they knew just how many barrels of sorghum their farms had produced, and for how many days their supply of sugar would last. This clerical zeal, contrasted with men's relative obliviousness to material specifics, notwithstanding their mastery of larger financial affairs, is one of many denotative characteristics setting women's observations of the raids apart from men's.

Although memoir writers are not as precise in their quantification, they vividly recall the extent of the damage and the debilitating fear of starvation that stayed with them for months afterwards. At the same time, they are insistent that they have underplayed events in the past rather than exaggerated them, defending the value of their less immediate but more contemplative narratives. All accounts—whether unretouched diaries or memoirs written years later—are filled with observations about Yankee conduct, an affirmation of the writers' keen interest in social nuance. For example, they assess how polite, clean, and sober the soldiers are, and whether or not the officers are more well behaved than the men.

A detail that surfaces over and over again concerns what the writer was wearing at the time of the first intrusion, an indication of the anxiety she felt in preparing for the unknown. Many tell us that they were not dressed when nighttime invaders appeared, revealing a feeling of physical vulnerability. Others who feared being caught in deshabille would not undress for several days at a time when they knew the Yankees were in the vicinity. Sue Richardson wrote in her diary, "afraid to undress; dreadful to live in such suspense, not knowing what hour the ruffians will break in." Months later she was still wary: "We sleep in our clothes, terrible fore-bodings."[11] Grace Beard, Emily Geiger Goodlett, and Maria Hayns-worth tell us precisely what kind and how many articles of clothing they wore in the face of invasion.[12] Implicitly, the writers were donning clothing as armor. To look physically bigger was to do psy-chological battle with an even bigger enemy: the more clothing they wore, the more explicit was their message to the enemy that they would not tolerate sexual violation.

To give some idea of what these accounts are like in style and substance, I include brief excerpts from three. Dolly Lunt Burge, forty-seven-year-old mistress of a large plantation near Covington, Georgia, related that her first thought upon hearing of the Yankees' arrival on August 2, 1864, was that she was not dressed.[13] As it happened, however, her estate was not raided until August 19. Note the care with which Dolly itemized her losses. Note also her use of present tense narration, unusual even in diaries that are kept on a day-to-day basis:

> [L]ike Demons they rush in! My yards are full. To my smoke-house, my Dairy, Pantry, Kitchen & Cellar, like famished wolves they come, breaking locks and whatever is in their way. The thousand pounds of meat in my smoke-house is gone in a twinkling, my flour, my meat, my lard, butter, eggs, pickles of various kinds, both in vinegar & brine, wine, jars, & jugs, are all gone. My eighteen fat turkeys, my hens, chickens & fowls, my young pigs, are all shot down in my yard and hunted as if they were rebels themselves.[14]

Emma LeConte was only seventeen when she recorded the burning of Columbia. Her diary, full of observations about the intimidating soldiery, is exceptional for her sophisticated description of the in-ferno and her attention to visual and auditory detail. On February 17, 1865, she wrote,

> My God! What a scene! It was about 4 o'clock and the State House was one grand conflagration. Imagine night turned into noonday, only with a blazing, scorching glare that was horri-ble—a copper colored sky across which swept columns of black rolling smoke glittering with sparks and flying embers, while all around us were falling thickly showers of burning flakes. Everywhere the palpitating blaze walling the streets with solid masses of flames as far as the eye could reach, filling the air

with its horrible roar. On every side the crackling and devouring fire, while every instant came the crashing of timbers and the thunder of falling buildings. . . . Such a scene as this with the drunken fiendish soldiery in their dark uniforms, infuriated, cursing, screaming, exulting in their work, came nearer realizing the material ideal of hell than anything I ever expect to see again.[15]

In Lenoir, North Carolina, Cornelia Spencer recounted the trials of Mrs. Boone Clark and her young daughter at the hands of a particularly unruly band of Federals.

[The daughter's] hat and garments were placed on the floor and loathesomely polluted. . . . They compelled her and her little daughter to remain and witness the destruction; and, finally, when there was nothing more to break and steal, one of them approached [Mrs. Clark] and thrust his fist in her face. As she raised her head to avoid it, he struck her forehead, seized her by the throat, cursing her furiously . . . seizing the neck of her dress, tore it open, snatched the gold watch, which hung by a ribbon, tore it off and left her.[16]

Spencer's excerpt is exceptionally graphic, perhaps because she describes another's trials. Women were uneasy about assessing violence done to themselves in such graphic terms, but they spoke more frankly about violence done to others.

As the foregoing examples demonstrate, women's accounts of Federal depredations were filled with pathos, fear, and rage. The cyclical nature of their responses corresponded to the different stages of women's awareness of the enemy. The woman who had only heard about the raids would think of the Yankees less indignantly than the woman who had met them face to face in her own home. Tales of Sherman's brutality exacted a fearful response from those who knew that it was only a matter of time before their homes would be ravaged. Atlanta teenager Mary Rawson wrote on August 31, 1864, before the evacuation of that city, "Time after time had we been told of the severity of Gen. Sherman until we came to dread his approach as we would that of a mighty hurricane which sweeps all before it caring naught for justice or humanity."[17] Once women heard rumors of Yankees in the vicinity, their concern for their property set them to work "preparing" for the invasion, although there could be little psychological preparation for the unknown, as Sarah Tillinghast attested in her reminiscence: "Although I had read of raids and of people losing much by them, I never realized for a moment what was before us."[18] Indeed, without a concrete idea of what was before them, women could not overemphasize the issue of their own physical security.

Rumors of raids did not inspire awe in every case, however. Malvina Black Gist was a twenty-two-year-old widowed Confederate treasury department worker living with her parents in Columbia and disenchanted with what she viewed as their overprotectiveness. Once the Yankees left Savannah and moved on toward Columbia, Malvina learned that her department would be transferred to Richmond ("[M]y father does not consider the track of a great army the safest place for young women," she complained), and her exasperation played itself out in the form of bravado:

> There are other reasons why I should like to remain here to receive Sherman: it is high time I was having some experiences out of the ordinary, and if anything remarkable is going to happen, I want to know something about it. It might be worth relating to my grandchildren! Anyhow, it is frightfully monotonous, just because you are a woman, to be always tucked away in the safe places. I want to stay. I want to have a taste of danger.[19]

Malvina was like other diarists in her frank assessment of her situation, but her sentiments were unique: it was one thing to court danger by ignoring rumors of the invasion, but quite another to welcome danger before danger arrived. Malvina's romantic notion of the historical role she might play was common enough among young Southern women early in the war, but unusual as late as February 1865.

It was standard practice for rural households to bury trunks of china, jewelry, and silver, but Federal forces caught on quickly. Cornelia E. Screven of Liberty County, Georgia, hid silver in the sofa. When two Federal guards sat down to an audible jingle, she coolly responded that the springs were loose. When they got up to sit elsewhere, the sofa once again jingled. The officers exchanged a knowing glance, more amused than covetous.[20] Both Sally Hawthorne's and Robena Tillinghast's reminiscences of raids in Fayetteville mention soldiers piercing the ground with bayonets in search of buried treasure.[21] Other raiders found it easier to probe with their wits, extorting information about valuables from family servants, sometimes at gunpoint.

City dwellers devised more ingenious ways to protect property. They prepared by sewing compartments and elaborate bustles into their dresses to conceal silver and jewelry, and in at least one case, a gun. Women in Covington, Georgia, sat quietly knitting while their homes were plundered, their gold watches and rings at the center of large balls of yarn.[22] When it became known that invaders were after more than heirlooms—that they might tear up silk dresses to dispose of quids of tobacco[23]—women began to wear as many dresses and sets of underwear as possible. Federal diarists relate humorous tales of misshapen young women attempting to look unobtrusive in all their sartorial heft. But this was no laughing matter to women living in a blockaded region who had watched a season's cotton crop go up in smoke. And as I have already suggested, this tendency to preserve wardrobe went hand in hand with the more salient psychological impact of dress: to look more physically imposing made women feel more secure about bodily safety.

In Columbia women brought furniture and rugs to holding pens, where they received assurances that the Provost Marshal's office would protect their goods. These stockpiles were gold mines to stragglers when the provost guard was obliged to move on with the troops. Occasionally women did not even have the chance to attempt to safeguard their valuables. Several cases in South Carolina bear witness to women who had wrestled extremely heavy trunks out of attics only to be stopped by invaders outside their homes, whereupon the trunks were hacked open and the contents stolen.[24] Even women who had had the foresight to secure guards for their residences were often foiled: the soldier would ingratiate himself with the family and then disappear in several days' time with some valued possession.

Many women, believing that there was safety in numbers, went to relatives' homes hauling furniture and household goods, particularly if they lived in rural areas, which were thought less well fortified than towns. Or they might send their children to relatives and remain at home on the logic that an occupied dwelling was not as likely to be burned down as an abandoned one. Mrs. Campbell Bryce and a neighbor, convinced of the invaders' malevolent intentions, persuaded their husbands to leave town while they remained with the children to guard the property. Surely, Mrs. Bryce calmed herself, the Yankees would not do the women any physical harm, but news of able-bodied men who had been hung by the enemy had not escaped her notice. After the burning of Columbia on February 17, 1865, many women and children, including the Bryces (some already refugeed from the hinterlands), sought protection at the local insane asylum and convent. Other recently destitute families fled to Federal camps seeking protection and instead were robbed of what possessions they had managed to salvage.[25]

After a tortured period of waiting, the first reaction to the onslaught among those who remained at home was characterized by immobility or paralysis. Mary Jones Mallard ended the day of the assault on her Liberty County, Georgia, plantation by entering in her diary, "It was vain to utter a word, for we were completely paralyzed by the fury of these ruffians." A seventeen-year-old widow of Sandersville, Georgia, wrote just after her parents' house was sacked, "Like statues mother and I stood looking on, and saw them take all the provisions we had . . . [We] stood silent and sad." Another Georgia woman, who attempted to meet the invaders who had forced their way into her sister-in-law's home, wrote, "I tried to move across the hall . . . but for the moment I seemed rooted to the spot." Judith Brockenbrough McGuire wrote of the Federal storming of Richmond on April 3, 1865, in similar terms: "I turned to come home, but what was my horror, to see a regiment of Yankee cavalry come dashing up, yelling, shouting. . . . I stood riveted to the spot; I could not move nor speak." Still others described the initial shock of invasion as an uncontrollable plummet. At first sight of the blue coats, Mrs. Alfred P. Aldrich of Barnwell, South Carolina, wrote, "I felt like falling, for I remembered the horrible accounts we had for months been listening to of the brutal treatment of the army to the women of Georgia."[26]

As food and durable goods were carried off or wantonly destroyed, writers tried to reason with assailants, often reminding them that they, too, had wives and children. However, such attempts usually culminated in pleas for mercy. When yet another group of raiders descended on Grace Beard's South Carolina plantation demanding money, she explained that an earlier raiding party had already cleaned her out. When the men threatened to burn the house down, Beard's supplication earned her a temporary stay: they fired every building on her property except the house.[27]

With the failure of such appeals, writers expressed various combinations of anger, grief, and defiance. Cornelia McDonald exploded with anger when on Christmas Eve soldiers interrupted her meager holiday preparations by walking off with a pan of rolls: "A man had opened the stove and taken out the pan of nice light brown rusks, and was running out with them. A fit of heroism seized me and I darted after him, and just as he reached the porch steps, I caught him by the collar of his great coat, and held him tight till the hot pan burnt his hands." Minerva McClatchey displayed a similar brand of defiance when she was told to flee during the fall of Atlanta. "I told them I should not leave my home while there was a roof over my head unless General Sherman ordered me personally. . . . This is my home, I have a right to stay at it." Similarly, Louise Caroline Reese Cornwell of Hillsborough, Georgia, reported that under orders to vacate her home, she told her captors that they'd have to burn her house down with her and her children in it.[28] On a more somber note, Grace Elmore wrote of the Federal army's departure from Columbia on February 21: "How my whole soul rose against that army as it passed, that band of highway robbers, the insulters of women and children. My whole nature is changed. I feel so hard, so pitiless."[29] For Elmore, that anger had transforming power; she recognized, with some chagrin, that her encounter with the enemy had ruined forever her implicit trust in men as protectors.

Pitiless was also Henrietta Lee's frame of mind in writing a lengthy and vituperous letter to Gen. David Hunter, whose troops had recently burned down her house. A distant relative of Robert E. Lee, she appealed to Hunter's sense of shame in this excerpt: "The house was built by my father, a Revolutionary soldier, who served the whole seven years for your independence. There was I born; there the sacred dead repose. It was my house and my home, and there has your niece . . . met with all kindness and hospitality at my hands. Was it for this that you turned me, my young daughter and little son out upon the world without a shelter?"[30] Mrs. Lee's impassioned letter is that of an enraged soul lashing out at a crime perceived in personal terms only; the political justification for mass depredations in wartime held no interest for her, much like Kate Whitehead Rowland's response to the dipper incident mentioned earlier.

Mrs. Campbell Bryce's appeal to General Sherman produced somewhat better results. An initial interview with Sherman won her two guards. But on her second visit to the general (her guards having moved on with their units), the nettled Sherman instructed his aide to secure an entire regiment to guard "the poor woman's" estate. Feeling humiliated by this brush-off, Mrs. Bryce supplicated, "If you have mother, wife, or sister, pray God they may never be called upon to suffer the anguish and terror the women of Columbia have been called upon to endure."[31] Luckier than most who gave themselves to passionate displays, Mrs. Bryce got her guard but not much in the way of self-respect. Insofar as statements and acts of defiance might be regarded as attempts to assert the self, these were usually fruitless attempts. And the satisfaction of revenge, in light of so much want, was evanescent at best.

In the aftermath of the raids, writers often felt humiliated and demoralized, and the quality and quantity of their writing changed noticeably. Many, like Grace Beard and Sue Richardson, whose homes were repeatedly ransacked, seemed unable to extricate themselves from the verbal lull that usually followed descriptive passages written at a fevered pitch. Perhaps because the diary is among the most private of genres, the diary writer's use of language fluctuates in direct proportion to her equanimity: if she is anxious and agitated, her writing is likely to exhibit a lively syntactical pace; if she is despondent, her verbal acuity may desert her.

Katherine Couse should be cited as an example here, even though she was not directly in Sherman's path. From May 4 to 20, 1864, during the battles of the Wilderness and Spottsylvania Courthouse, her home was repeatedly raided. Each time she believed the intrusion over, she sought consolation in her diary, and with each unexpected return of the army, she relived the anxiety, anger, and finally despair of her previous entries. On May 4, 7, 12, and 15, Katherine winced at the roar of artillery. On the 12th, she noted, "Oh God there is now the most murderous battle raging, the continuous roar of cannons, the still more terrible musketry sounds awful indeed. My feelings are intensely awful, beyond description." On May 14 and 19, Katherine described the makeshift hospital set up on her family's property. The entry of May 19 was significantly brief ("house full of surgeons and others most of the time") after a detailed account on May 17 of the by now standard depredations. Katherine's final entry on May 20 represents a long pent-up outpouring of feelings that culminates in despair:

> The confederacy is heir to so many ills—we take no pleasure in life,—and could not be worse punished if we were expiating some horrid crime, Delapidation and decay mark the course of

everything at old Laurel Hill, both people and places are gradually falling into ruins ... an air of suffocating loneliness remains ... but my very soul rebels against the many other harrassing annoyances we are subject to, there is no peace in living in this God forsaken country. it [*sic*] is fearful to see with what impunity—all kinds of robbery and roguishness are carried on—Might makes right here, we wake up in the morning and find the thing we prize most highly gone. We are suffering from such lawless times as existed in the dark ages, but no knights-errant rise up with the times to protect the helpless and redress grievances.[32]

With decay as her metaphor, Couse conveyed a spiritual emptiness materially evident in the desecration of a familiar landscape. Further, she projected her sense of personal loss on a morally bankrupt society, where no knights-errant could be found to salvage the old aristocratic conventions.

A similar pattern emerges in Elizabeth Allston's journal. With her family at one of their several estates in Florence, South Carolina, she described on March 1, 2, and 4 their elaborate preparations in anticipation of Sherman. The next entry, on March 6, briefly mentioned the household raid of the previous day and ended with a demoralized Allston recounting an interview with a Yankee officer who claimed he'd fight ten years more to see the South and her pretensions to independence crushed.[33] Allston responded to this affront by leaving her journal alone for the next six days.

There is much debate about the incidence of violent crime in invaded territory. It was not uncommon for a woman to be assaulted by soldiers looking for valuables hidden about her person. In Washington County, Georgia, and Cheraw, South Carolina, women were made to undress before packs of onlookers.[34] Mae Jett, alone on her modest farm near Atlanta, wrote to her husband Richard that a soldier threatened "to shoot [her] brains out" if she could not provide food for him from her already depleted stores. Emma Rankin was also threatened with physical violence when she refused to surrender an inexpensive but sentimentally valued brooch to an inebriated soldier.[35]

Although women would not have spoken plainly about their fear of molestation, it was an ever-present concern among them. Cornelia Spencer argued in 1866 that many cases of assault and battery went unreported. According to soldiers' diaries, women both white and black were raped as the army passed through Milledgeville, Georgia, on the way to Savannah, and on the night of the conflagration in Columbia. Black women were particularly at risk. As one writer reported from Columbia, "the next morning their unclothed bodies, bearing the marks of detestable sex crimes, were found about the city," and at least one slave's body was found raped and murdered.[36] Emma Manley of Spauling County, Georgia, noted that when General Blair's troops appeared in the vicinity on November 17, 1864, the slave women hid in the plantation house. Likewise, Dolly Burge's servants spent the night of the assault on her plantation in their mistress's bedroom; every time they attempted to set foot out of the house, their Yankee "guards" grossly insulted them.[37] In cases such as these, sexual innuendo was nearly as powerful a tool for social control as any more visible weapon.

Upon hearing that Sherman's men were in the area, twenty-five-year-old Grace Elmore considered with a girlfriend "the justification of suicide under certain tyrannies. Would to God I could feel sure of his forgiveness, did I have to choose between death and dishonor."[38] Elmore reasoned that death would be preferable to living the life of a raped woman; once others learned of such an incident, the victim might be branded indefinitely, sexual assault being tantamount to social expulsion.

Curiously, not one of the writers sampled used the word "rape." Rape—both potential and real—became the unspeakable crime. Women made a tacit agreement not to call rape by its name, referring to it obliquely instead. Cornelia Spencer's cataloguing of crimes against property extended to women: "[N]or were darker and nameless tragedies wanting in lonely situations. No; [we] hardly dare trust [our]selves to think of these things."[39] Spencer alludes to sexual violence by calling it nameless; she suggests that even the thought of this thing-without-a-name has the power to taint—not unlike Grace Elmore's hypothetical choice between "death and dishonor." Somewhat more explicit is Anna Maria Green's diary entry of November 23, 1864, at Milledgeville: "The worst of [the Yankees'] acts was committed to [*sic*] poor Mrs. N.—violence done, an atrocity committed that ought to make her husband an enemy unto death."[40] "Violence" and "atrocity" are as close as Anna and other writers confined by linguistic convention can come to speaking about sexual assault.

With the possibility of rape ever before them, incidents in which women confronted physical violence brought out their anger rather than fear. But venting their anger did nothing to win back the protection to which they believed themselves entitled. In each of these accounts, the power of depiction diminished as the writer moved beyond anger into a feeling of powerlessness to control her own fate. Mary Rawson bespoke her powerlessness by comparing Sherman's invading forces to "a mighty hurricane which sweeps all before it." An Atlanta refugee near Milledgeville compared Sherman to "a huge octopus, stretch[ing] out his long arms and gather[ing] everything in, leaving only ruin and desolation behind him." Still another refugee likened Sherman to an "avalanche of terror sweep[ing] down on us."[41]

Sarah Jane Graham Sams's journal graphically exemplifies her sense of powerlessness. A refugee from Beaufort County, South Carolina, Sams was temporarily housed at Barnwell during the ten days and nights it took Sherman's infantry and Kilpatrick's cavalry to pass through. On February 8, she wrote a lengthy entry about the burning of Barnwell. On February 9, she said very little about the incendiary spectacle of the previous day: "They behaved more like enraged tigers, than human beings running all over the town, kicking down fences, breaking in doors and smashing glasses, also stealing and tearing up clothing. I've no plans for the future."[42] The sudden shift from narrative to Sarah's pronouncement about the future takes us by surprise. After months of running from the enemy, living from moment to moment was the best one could do. Now the destruction of her temporary homestead suspended Sams in time and language: as far as she could tell, there was no future— only moments in the present to be endured. The passage of time, once a familiar constant, had been arrested. Without the power to imagine what came next, she could not write, and indeed wrote nothing for two days following.

Ultimately, many writers acknowledged their futile search for words to describe what they saw and how it affected them. Three Columbians, Mary Rowe, Emma LeConte, and refugee Emily Ellis remarked at their inability to describe the indescribable: Mary Rowe, sick with exhaustion from four nights' vigil, was roused from her first moments of sleep upon learning that her house was on fire. She later wrote, "What we experienced that night is indescribable. . . . I have not yet found words to express half of the suffering we witnessed and my feeling during the reign of Satan Sherman and his imps." After taking a tour of the smouldering city on February 18, Emma LeConte wrote, "It would be impossible to describe or even to conceive the pandemonium and horror." After her family was compelled to flee to Camden, Emily Ellis got more bad news: her husband had been taken prisoner. "I have not words to describe my feeling," she wrote.[43] Charlotte St. John Ravenel of Pooshee plantation in Berkeley County, South Carolina, wrote on the night of March 1, 1865, that her property had been raided by a group of black Federals (the most dreaded variety of Yankee to Southerners): "I have attempted to describe that dreadful night, but nothing can come up to the reality."[44]

Despairing of finding language that could adequately convey the trauma of invasion, each of the previous writers abruptly terminated her written record. There were often periods of days or weeks at a time when nothing was written in an otherwise daily journal. Of course, women whose homes had been destroyed spent much of their energy looking for new shelter; if their homes had been spared, they were preoccupied with taking stock of their losses and securing food. Many previously wealthy households were reduced to dependence on charity, a humiliating experience for women whose sense of self-sufficiency had been forged by hard work. But aside from pragmatic reasons, it is likely that some writers made a conscious decision to stop writing when the language they were accustomed to using no longer seemed adequate.

Although the exigencies of war weighed heavily upon the entire civilian population of the South, women who found themselves in the path of Sherman's army were particularly moved to vent their rage by expressing in conventional terms the failure of the protection they felt had been due them. But in this brave new world of "total war," women were neither revered as objects worthy of protection nor immune to the enemy's destructive will. An inability or unwillingness to continue writing, marked by the gaps in their diaries, now betokened a transition in their feeling about the war. If the enemy's object was not in fact to bully defenseless civilians like themselves, then perhaps the war they had fought with Sherman's invaders existed only in their imagination. If those who had denied them protection did so not out of social animus but because their object was to cripple the Confederacy economically, then Southern women's visceral response to Sherman was nothing more than the mute fury of players without an audience.

Having enjoyed a privileged status before the war, women sensed that it was precisely the inescapable fact of their womanhood, their gender difference, that made them such an easy target during it.

Without protection, privilege was a thing of the past. Thus language as the agent of social convention (i.e., the customs and behavioral patterns that empowered privilege) lost its combative force. And one wonders if, for at least a portion of these women, the end of the war was prefigured in their verbal acquiescence. When Confederate military officials despaired of making any strategic headway in the last year of the war, it had been the women who spurred them on. With language as ammunition, women might wage war indefinitely. But their emotional exhaustion, their utter dejection in the wake of Sherman's army silenced them. If language no longer carried the power to console them, then the invaders had robbed them not only of worldly goods but of their will to defend themselves.

In thus acknowledging their defenselessness, women in the path of Sherman's great march to the sea recognized the failure of social convention, as they knew it, to provide form and structure in daily life. On the Monday after Federal forces pulled out of Columbia, one diarist wrote, "A dead and solemn silence seemed to have fallen upon the town. No sound of wheels or horse-hoofs. There was nothing left to disturb the mournful silence."[45] Without the social structure that assured them protection and without the forms in language that had sustained them early on in their struggles with the enemy, Southern women for the first time during the war acknowledged defeat in silence.

Notes

1. Sherman, *Memoirs*, 2:254.

2. Although General Order No. 100, Instruction for the Government of Armies of the United States in the Field, specified that no civilian should be harmed, Sherman interpreted this order in his own way. See Walters, *Merchant of Terror*, xi–xiii.

3. Although war historians have depicted Southern women as goading their men to remain at the front, women's testimony, beginning with the siege of Atlanta in the summer of 1864, provides evidence to the contrary. See Julia Davidson's letters to John Mitchell Davidson, July and August, 1864; and Kate Whitehead Rowland Journal, entries of July 1864.

4. For a discussion of the gendered relationship between the protector and the protected, see Stiehm, "The Protected, the Protector, the Defender."

5. Sarah Tillinghast Reminiscence, 31–32.

6. Kate Whitehead Rowland Journal, Nov. 29, 1864.

7. Taylor, *Cavalier and Yankee*, 261–341.

8. Lensink, "Expanding the Boundaries of Criticism," 1–6.

9. Bryce, "Personal Experiences," preface; Sarah Tillinghast Reminiscence, 1; Beard, "A Series of True Incidents," 15.

10. Norton, "Eighteenth-Century Women in Peace and War."

11. Sue Richardson Diary, Jan. 2, 1864; Sept. 21, 1864.

12. Beard, "A Series of True Incidents," 6; Goodlett, "The Burning of Columbia"; Maria L. Haynsworth Letters, Apr. 28–May 6, 1865.

13. Robertson, *The Diary of Dolly Lunt Burge*, 94.

14. Ibid., 101.

15. Miers, *When the World Ended*, 45–46.

16. Spencer, *The Last Ninety Days*, 221.

17. Jones, *Heroines of Dixie*, 336.

18. Sarah Tillinghast Reminiscence, 17.

19. Jones, *Heroines of Dixie*, 359.

20. Jones, *When Sherman Came*, 72.

21. Hawthorne, "Memories," 63; Tillinghast, "Aunt Bena's Account of Sherman's Raid," 3.

22. Wheeler, *Sherman's March*, 69.

23. Spencer, *The Last Ninety Days*, 220.

24. Barrett, *Sherman's March through the Carolinas*, 84.

25. Bryce, "Personal Experiences," 13–14; Barrett, *Sherman's March through the Carolinas*, 84.

26. Jones, *When Sherman Came*, 66; Wheeler, *Sherman's March*, 93, 179; Jones, *Heroines of Dixie*, 398; Wheeler, *Sherman's March*, 168.

27. Beard, "A Series of True Incidents," 7.

28. McDonald, *A Diary*, Dec. 24, 1862; Bryan, "Journal of Minerva Leah Rowles McClatchey," Sept. 19, 1864; Jones, *When Sherman Came*, 22.

29. Grace Elmore Diary, Feb. 21, 1865.

30. Underwood, *The Women of the Confederacy*, 159.

31. Bryce, "Personal Experiences," 48.

32. Katherine Couse Letter, May 4–20, 1864.

33. Jones, *When Sherman Came*, 251–55.

34. Walters, *Merchant of Terror*, 169; Barrett, *Sherman's March through the Carolinas*, 111.

35. Mae Jett to Richard B. Jett, Sept. 2, 1864; Rankin, "Stoneman's Raid."

36. Spencer, *The Last Ninety Days*, 222; Walters, *Merchant of Terror*, 200; Barrett, *Sherman's March through the Carolinas*, 85.

37. Jones, *When Sherman Came*, 17; Robertson, *The Diary of Dolly Lunt Burge*, 104.

38. Grace Elmore Diary, Nov. 26, 1864.

39. Spencer, *The Last Ninety Days*, 51.

40. Jones, *When Sherman Came*, 30.

41. Jones, *Heroines of Dixie*, 336; Jones, *When Sherman Came*, 26, 132.

42. Sarah Jane Graham Sams Journal, Feb. 3–Mar. 25, 1865.
43. Jones, *When Sherman Came*, 166; Miers, *When the World Ended*, 58–59; Ellis, "The Flight of the Clan," Feb. 25, 1865.
44. Jones, *Heroines of Dixie*, 371.
45. Bryce, "Personal Experiences," 51.

Geographical Distribution of Sources

Lucy Johnston Ambler, Morven, Virginia
Grace Pierson James Beard, Columbia, South Carolina
Mrs. Campbell Bryce, Columbia, South Carolina
Katherine Couse, Spottsylvania County, Virginia
Julia Davidson, Atlanta, Georgia
Emily Caroline Ellis, Columbia and Camden, South Carolina
Grace Elmore, Columbia, South Carolina
Emily Geiger Goodlett, Columbia, South Carolina
Sally Hawthorne, Fayetteville, North Carolina
Maria L. Haynsworth, Camden, South Carolina
L. F. J., Sandersville, Georgia
Mae Jett, Atlanta, Georgia
Floride Cantey Johnson, Camden, South Carolina
Cornelia Peake McDonald, Winchester, Virginia
Emma Lydia Rankin, McDowell County, North Carolina
Sue Richardson, Front Royal, Virginia
Kate Whitehead Rowland, Macon, Georgia
Sarah Jane Graham Sams, Barnwell, South Carolina
Harriet Hyrne Simons, Columbia, South Carolina
Sophie Sosnowski, Columbia, South Carolina
Sarah and Robena Tillinghast, Fayetteville, North Carolina

Works Cited

Ambler, Lucy Johnston. Diary. Manuscripts, Acc. #5191. Alderman Library, University of Virginia, Charlottesville, Virginia.
Barrett, John G. *Sherman's March through the Carolinas*. Chapel Hill: University of North Carolina Press, 1956.
Beard, Grace Pierson James. "A Series of True Incidents Connected with Sherman's March to the Sea." Southern Historical Collection, University of North Carolina, Chapel Hill, North Carolina.
Bryan, T. Conn. "A Georgia Woman's Civil War Diary: The Journal of Minerva Leah Rowles McClatchey, 1864–65." *Georgia Historical Quarterly* 15, no. 2 (1967): 197–216.

Bryce, Mrs. Campbell. "The Personal Experiences of Mrs. Campbell Bryce during the Burning of Columbia, South Carolina by General W. T. Sherman's Army, Feb. 17, 1865." Philadelphia: N.p., 1899.

Couse, Katherine. Letter, May 4–20, 1864. Manuscripts, Acc. #10441. Alderman Library, University of Virginia, Charlottesville, Virginia.

Davidson, Julia. Letters to John Mitchell Davidson. John Mitchell Davidson Papers. Special Collections, Woodruff Library, Emory University, Atlanta, Georgia.

Ellis, Emily Caroline. "The Flight of the Clan," Feb. 25, 1865. Manuscript Division, South Caroliniana Library, University of South Carolina, Columbia, South Carolina.

Elmore, Grace. Diary. Manuscript Division, South Caroliniana Library, University of South Carolina, Columbia, South Carolina.

Goodlett, Emily Geiger. "The Burning of Columbia by Sherman, February 17, 1865." Manuscript Division, South Caroliniana Library, University of South Carolina, Columbia, South Carolina.

Hawthorne, Sally. "Memories." North Carolina Department of Archives and History, Raleigh, North Carolina.

Haynsworth, Maria L. Letters. Southern Historical Collection, University of North Carolina, Chapel Hill, North Carolina.

Jett, Mae. Mae Jett to Richard B. Jett, Sept. 2, 1864. Richard B. Jett Papers. Special Collections, Woodruff Library, Emory University, Atlanta, Georgia.

Johnson, Floride Cantey. Reminiscence. Thomas J. Myers Papers. North Carolina Department of Archives and History, Raleigh, North Carolina.

Jones, Katharine M. *Heroines of Dixie: Confederate Women Tell Their Story of the War.* Indianapolis and New York: Bobbs-Merrill Co., 1955.
———. *When Sherman Came: Southern Women and the "Great March."* Indianapolis: Bobbs-Merrill Co., 1964.

Lensink, Judy Nolte. "Expanding the Boundaries of Criticism: The Diary as Autobiography." Paper presented at the Tenth Biennial Convention of the American Studies Association, San Diego, 1985.

McDonald, Cornelia Peake. *A Diary with Reminiscences of the War and Refugee Life in the Shenandoah Valley, 1860–1865.* Nashville: Cullom & Ghertner, 1934.

Miers, Earl Schenck, ed. *When the World Ended: The Diary of Emma LeConte.* New York: Oxford University Press, 1957.

Norton, Mary Beth. "Eighteenth-Century Women in Peace and War: The Case of the Loyalists." *William and Mary Quarterly* 33 (July 1976): 386–409.

Rankin, Emma Lydia. "Stoneman's Raid." Southern Historical Collection, University of North Carolina, Chapel Hill, North Carolina.

Richardson, Sue. Diary. Special Collections, Woodruff Library, Emory University, Atlanta, Georgia.

Robertson, James I., ed. *The Diary of Dolly Lunt Burge*. Athens: University of Georgia Press, 1962.

Rowland, Kate Whitehead. Journal. Special Collections, Woodruff Library, Emory University, Atlanta, Georgia.

Sams, Sarah Jane Graham. Journal. Manuscript Division, South Caroliniana Library, University of South Carolina, Columbia, South Carolina.

Sherman, William Tecumseh. *Memoirs of William Tecumseh Sherman by Himself*. Bloomington: Indiana University Press, 1957.

Simons, Harriet Hyrne. "The Burning of Columbia." Manuscript Division, South Caroliniana Library, University of South Carolina, Columbia, South Carolina.

Sosnowski, Sophie. "Burning of Columbia." *Georgia Historical Quarterly* 8, no. 3 (1924): 195–214.

Spencer, Cornelia Phillips. *The Last Ninety Days of the War in North-Carolina*. New York: Watchman Publishing Co., 1866.

Stiehm, Judith Hicks. "The Protected, the Protector, the Defender." *Women's Studies International Forum* 5, nos. 3–4 (1982): 367–76.

Taylor, William R. *Cavalier and Yankee: The Old South and American National Character*. New York: Harper & Row, 1969.

Tillinghast, Robena. "Aunt Bena's Account of Sherman's Raid." Tillinghast Family Papers. Manuscript Division, Perkins Library, Duke University, Durham, North Carolina.

Tillinghast, Sarah. Reminiscence. Tillinghast Family Papers. Manuscript Division, Perkins Library, Duke University, Durham, North Carolina.

Underwood, John L. *The Women of the Confederacy*. New York and Washington: Neale Publishing Co., 1906.

Walters, John Bennett. *Merchant of Terror: General Sherman and Total War*. Indianapolis: Bobbs-Merrill Co., 1973.

Wheeler, Richard. *Sherman's March*. New York: Thomas Y. Crowell & Co., 1978.

Margaret R.
Higonnet Civil Wars

and Sexual Territories

*I*n the past, analyses of civil war, considered as a "family"
matter, have focused on men: on *Bruderkrieg* or fratricide.
This essay pursues civil war as a metaphor for the "battle of
the sexes." Since the French Revolution, a number of major
writers have used their fiction to explore the links between political struggles to restructure the national "family" and social struggles to realign the relationships between men and women. The resulting literature of civil war is strikingly overdetermined: by metaphoric transfer, political actions are shown to be personal and the
private public. Men and women both perceive these transfers of
meaning between the political and the personal realms, but as this
study of prose fiction will show, the structures they use to represent
changes in gender relations differ fundamentally.

Wars may awaken our awareness of the ways sexual territory is
mapped because they disrupt the normal division of labor by gender. In modern times, for example, we have seen women entering
heavy industry and engaged in guerrilla warfare alongside men.
Peace in turn reverses many wartime changes in gender assignments. These ephemeral but radical shifts in women's situation reveal how arbitrary our definitions of masculine and feminine roles
truly are.[1]

It is my thesis that civil wars, which take place on "home" territory, have more potential than other wars to transform women's
expectations. In all wars roles traditionally assigned to women are
political in the sense that to maintain the hearth takes on ideological coloration. Yet *nationalist* wars against an external enemy repress internal political divisions and with them feminist movements. *Civil* wars by contrast may occasion explicit political choices
for women. Once a change in government can be conceived, sexual
politics can also become an overt political issue; thus in the legend
of Lucretia, her rape and suicide precipitate the revolt of Brutus
against the Tarquins. The sexual struggle lays bare political tyr-

anny. Inversely, civil war serves as emblem and catalyst of change in the social prescription of sexual roles.

Depending on the position of the viewer, internecine struggle may appear to take one of two forms. Where the opposed groups are thought to be moral or military equals, an internal war is most likely to be termed a "civil" war. Where one group is thought to be distinctly inferior in justification or strength, the struggle is termed a "revolution," with the stress on reversal of a political order. Because such moral distinctions are largely a matter of perspective, I have included in this discussion works that represent the French Revolution and occupied Vichy France.[2] These two patterns, the struggle between equals and the rebellion of inferiors, bear on sexual as well as national politics. Not surprisingly, even where the struggle is represented as a civil war, a change in gender roles is most often represented as a reversal of order, in short, as revolutionary. For women, the struggle to shift from subordination to equality is necessarily an act of insubordination and must therefore be assimilated to regicide, the murder of the *pater populi*, rather than fratricide. The process works both ways. Political relations acquire the color of gender. Not only are women's claims aligned with insurrection, but dissidents are aligned with unnatural women.[3] In order to describe a revolution, many historians and novelists draw on familial metaphors, above all that of the topsy-turvy marriage or the exchange of authority between husband and wife.

Certainly one of the topics we need to pursue in the literature of civil war is the thematic pairing of challenges to the political order with challenges to the traditional territorial assignments of gender. Outside feminist criticism, the field of thematics has largely been neglected in recent years because it has seemed to foster a mechanistic version of literary history and a mode of criticism so sociological or philosophical as to seem nonliterary. A feminist thematics must face these challenges. The most obvious point to make is that gender is not an extractable feature of literary texts but an aspect of the relationships among characters and in turn therefore of plot. The fictional network of characterization marks out systematically what one may call "sexual territory." In turn, just as the events of war may shape narrative sequence, so do changes in gender relations.

To study gender is to see how patterns of characterization and of narration merge. In the literature of civil war, it is virtually a rule that the external conflict, which serves as catalyst of social change and narrative sequence, also becomes a metaphor for inner conflicts and the experience of inner emigration. The axis of narrative, to borrow a phrase from Jakobson, is displaced onto the axis of character.[4] In addition, the theme of civil war becomes a metaphor for reversals in emotional and sexual relationships; with striking frequency, gender roles under the pressure of social change become inverted. And finally, we may see how authors explore the gendering of political discourse; not only voices but political attitudes are encoded as masculine and feminine, and it is not unusual to find that female figures serve to criticize established political ideology. By comparing the works of women such as Madame de Staël, Louisa May Alcott, or Simone de Beauvoir, to those by men such as Henry James, Ernest Hemingway, or Boris Pilniak, we can examine whether these issues are handled differently by female and male intellectuals whose careers took shape at moments of political upheaval.

Madame de Staël's *Delphine* (1802) offers a particularly rich text for the study of civil war as a metaphor for social conflict over the appropriate roles of women and men and for the resulting psychological conflicts. Usually read as a sentimental novel, *Delphine* is actually a very political novel in which the French Revolution is insistently present. Set between 1790 and 1792, the novel witnesses the first enthusiastic attempts to legislate an enlightened society, the royal family's flight to Varennes and the emigration of loyalist noblemen, and then the September massacres and the uprising in the Vendée. The struggle between republicans and royalists aligns Delphine and her friend Monsieur de Lebensei against an aristocratic Parisian milieu, and above all against her lover Léonce de Mondoville and her suitor Monsieur de Valorbe, both of them noblemen of the old school. Her political values lead her to actions that make her seem personally suspect to Léonce, who therefore marries her cousin. Likewise, her personal loyalties force her to violate abstractly defined political duties. The revolutionary conflict occasions wrenching choices for Delphine.

The narrative unfolds against the backdrop of France's ongoing war with the other monarchies of Europe, whose armies the émigrés are joining. From this perspective, the émigré turns a nationalist war into a civil war and initiates the political narrative. Léonce foresees that he will go over to the enemy of the new republic:

"Amid the present events, I could find myself engaged though with regret in a civil war."[5] Because his sense of identity is inseparable from his paternal name and sense of class, he cannot embrace revolutionary ideals, however much he respects them. For him, the Constituent Assembly (which had drawn up a new constitution grounded in the rights of man) necessarily does violence to the feudalistic institutions of the past. He clings to the legitimacy of the past against the Revolution.

By contrast, Delphine's identification is not with class but with the new nation, and she perceives the counterrevolutionaries as illegitimate. One crisis in her relationship to Léonce is precipitated by her realization that the reactionaries are preparing a "civil," that is moral, war. "When you pronounce the horrible words 'civil war,' how can I not be afflicted by how little importance you give to personal convictions in addressing political questions?" (1:470). A humanist, she fuses the personal with the political: civil war is uncivil.

The political division between the protagonists mirrors the separation caused by Léonce's social prejudices, which blind him to her love, her fidelity, and even his own desires. He cannot conceive that her offer to shelter a political victim might have a motive other than sexual; he misreads every act that violates the narrow rules governing women's conduct. Léonce goes so far as to argue that women should distance themselves from political power in order to preserve their feminine otherness: "It seems to me proper that you should always belong to the party of victims" (1:469). Clearly politics has a gender.

The conflict over women's proper social role divides not only the lovers but the community of women. Women who stand to profit from political conservatism naturally define the domain of women as moral and apolitical. Madame de Mondoville mère, for example, speaks for the inherited values of religion and nobility, attacking the "new ideas" that might permit a "superior" mind like Delphine's "to rule" her son. The new individualism that defies the proprieties in the name of reason seems to her supremely absurd in a woman: "Our conduct is delineated for us, our birth marks our place, our status imposes our opinions on us" (2:204). "Notre état nous impose nos opinions." The state imposes our status. The pun on "état" in this text, which is by one of the most important commentators on the Revolution and on the formation of public opinion, indicates that there is another estate as rigidly determined by politics as the "Fourth Estate" of the poor. "Birth" into a socially defined sexual class determines not only our "place" and condition but our right to have ideas.

Friends and enemies alike urge Delphine to silence as well as inactivity, and she herself erroneously believes that "[i]t does not befit a woman to participate in political debates; her destiny shelters her from all the dangers they involve, and her actions can never lend importance or dignity to her words" (1:118). Because women are "sheltered" from the political fray, their words lack the meaning that acts could lend them. (Later, Delphine will find that women are not sheltered from political dangers, nor are their actions devoid of political resonance.) Indeed, the silencing of one's opinions and desires is a social law for women, who are "the victims of all social institutions" (1:333). As Delphine's friend Madame de Vernon recalls, in her childhood, "they silenced my spirit, as if it were improper for a woman to have one" (1:330).

If Léonce symbolically begins civil war through his political choices and emigration, Delphine by her refusal to remain within the confines of feminine *"convenances"* initiates a social and sexual conflict. She intrudes into men's conversations at polite receptions. She emigrates socially from the oppressive atmosphere of Parisian salons to alternative spaces of her own, first to her garden estate Bellerive and then to a convent—spaces that turn out to be ironically confining.

Parallel to political and social conflicts run the inner conflicts of Delphine and Léonce, figured also as civil wars. An "army" of duties combats a person of feeling, as Delphine "struggles" against her own desires (1:497, 506; 2:218). Léonce, in turn, is torn in an "atrocious combat" between his principles and his love (2:388, 391). His obstacle lies within: "Can I have an enemy more cruel than myself?" he asks (2:392).

In the end, if the lovers are divided by internal and external civil wars, they are also joined by them. Paradoxically, suicide promises to heal inner splits, perhaps especially so because of its metaphoric erotic content. In the first version of the novel, Madame de Staël risked a conclusion that was in fact a double suicide. Delphine takes a swift but gentle Italian poison a few hours before Léonce's execution; when she succumbs to its effects, the soldiers are so softened by the sight of Léonce's despair that he must insult them before they will shoot.[6]

Military metaphors pervade and heighten erotic discourse. But this traditional figure is extended by the political insights of the novel. When Léonce enters civil war as his only means of gaining control over his life—even if it means the loss of that very life—he has summed up Staël's identification of personal with political struggle.[7]

The metaphoric transfer of conflict from a military to a psychological plane, linking violent death to erotic "death" and defeated love, so clear in Staël's novel, permeates most fictions about civil war. In Simone de Beauvoir's novel about the French Resistance, *The Blood of Others*, the political and military strands of her narrative double the inner conflict of her male protagonist, Jean Blomart. The novel depicts France both before and during the war, but the central political and moral dilemma is the violence begotten by violence. On the political plane, in the prewar period capitalist exploitation leads to a Communist strike whose cost is the death of a boy. Then the German Occupation leads to the French Resistance, whose terrorist attacks on Germans in turn lead to reprisals against randomly selected French citizens. Arguably, this very indirect version of the costs of the Resistance was the only political vision acceptable at the time. Still, Beauvoir's critique of the instrumental sacrifice of lives on behalf of "transcendent" political goals foreshadows much more recent debates over Resistance tactics and transforms what is usually considered a nationalist struggle into something that looks much more like a civil war.

On the personal plane, Beauvoir's existentialism leads her to depict Jean as divided by the question of responsibility for violence, whether bloodshed on the streets or the botched and bloody abortion of Hélène. Though horrified by the Anschluss, he rejects war; only the German invasion forces Jean to recognize the impracticality of pacifism. As leader of a Resistance unit, Jean faces the existentialist dilemma of asserting autonomy while also recognizing the consequences of one's actions.[8] He is anguished, "torn," brought up short by the knowledge that for all his attempt to respect the liberty of others, his acts lead to their sufferings and ultimate deaths, including the death of Hélène that frames the story. The shattering problems of preserving humanity in the face of disease, class warfare, and violence are filtered through the language of existentialism. To participate in the Resistance is to "choose," to face death is to "choose" liberty, to sacrifice one life for another is to "decide." And inversely, Beauvoir applies the language of personal self-division to politics. Austrian acquiescence in the Anschluss (like the truce that established Vichy) is for one character "a suicide story" (142).

For Beauvoir as for Staël the dilemma is gendered; Jean's masculine commitment to an abstract political ideal conflicts with a horror at its costs that is figured as feminine. He must choose between his father, capitalist and nationalist subsidizer of the Resistance effort, and his humanitarian mother, from whom he has inherited "the sense of guilt" for the poverty and suffering of others (6). Already, when Jean sets up a terrorist organization after the French defeat, he "makes it up" with his father, from whom he has been alienated by his pacifism and his involvement with the Communist party (262). The father endorses Jean's actions, even when the Germans retaliate by shooting hostages. In a bizarrely Oedipal fantasy, Jean imagines he and his father are one, as males: "He is very proud. He threw the bomb and he does not regret his act: he's a strong man" (271). By contrast, his mother condemns this terrorism as an "outrage" (though she does not know her son was involved). For her, Jean has "murdered Frenchmen." She sums up Jean's insistent preoccupation with the conflict between autonomy and the possibility of political action by saying "[L]et them shed their own blood" (271). The familial conflict between mother and father, important for its own gender symbolism, also makes clear the analogy between Resistance work, which sets the French against the French, and civil war. And of course it is a psychological conflict that Jean internalizes with sexual attributes.

Although the narrative perspective is that of a man, who finally decides to continue his work for the Resistance, the occasion of the narrative and emblem of his decision is a woman, Jean's dying friend Hélène, who has been fatally wounded on a rescue mission. Her dying moments catalyze Jean's brooding memories and anguish about his responsibility for "the blood of others." Ironically, at the same time, this slight figure, stubbornly self-centered and hedonistic for most of the novel, teaches Jean in her last moments an existential lesson. Hélène has found herself slowly forced by her love for Jean into political commitment and action; she rather than he is able to say, "It is for me to decide." She represents choice without regret, and therefore "liberty" (288).

Like Delphine, Jean wrestles with silence. Horrified by the masculine moral instrumentalism that symbolically leads to death, he resists making choices. He questions the social teleologies that people use to justify their actions; he is an outsider in relation to public discourse. "My life must be silent." But such withdrawal is futile. The impossibility of purely individual choice reveals the impurity of narrative, which enfolds its objects within the embrace of the "voice" and of the perceiver. In a symbolic attempt to resist that embrace, Beauvoir fractures the narrative line; Jean's associative memories interrupt each other, minimizing the control of a narrator who is occupied by his conflicting memories.

While both Madame de Staël and Simone de Beauvoir, politically engaged women, explicitly link civil war to internal conflicts and conflicts between their male and female protagonists, other writers such as Henry James do so indirectly. James, who wished to write the "unwritten," found in civil war an occasion to write experimental fiction about women. In his first published tale, "The Story of a Year" (1865), one of three similar pieces about the American Civil War and the French Revolution, James describes his project: "My own taste has always been for unwritten history, and my present business is with the reverse of the picture" (35). On his "reversed" canvas he traces not battle strategy but his heroines' choices between suitors on the home front. The most political of these choices is that made by Gabrielle de Bergerac in the tale bearing her name; she casts off her aristocratic name and a wealthy aristocratic suitor in order to marry a penniless veteran of the American wars, a tutor named Pierre de Coquelin. She calls upon him to speak not only "for the great mass of *petits gens*" but "for poor portionless girls" too (225–26). Somewhat more ironically, in James's story "Poor Richard," the heroine hopes that to choose the right husband, to renounce the privilege of wealth, will enable her to cast off the "chains" of slavery (480). Such metaphors join these women's inner struggle to redefine themselves with vast social struggles to redress oppression.

The most obvious feature of all these narratives is the metaphoric transfer of civil war from an external, political realm to inner conflict over sexual choice and the proper gender roles. In an extension of this theme, social upheaval both causes and is represented by an inversion of gender roles. Louisa May Alcott's *Work, A Story of Experience* (1861–73) unites these two features, moving from a metaphorical "battle" for female equality to the social rearrangements that flow from the actual Civil War.

The novel opens strategically with a debate between two women.

The comic metaphors of baking through which they exchange ideas conceal Alcott's profound insistence on the way women's development is shaped (and impeded) by differences within the female community (an insight already developed in *Delphine*). In the first sentence, the heroine Christie stakes out a claim to new sexual territory: "Aunt Betsey, there's going to be a new Declaration of Independence" (1). Her ideals of "self-knowledge, self-control, self-help" lead her to seek the same autonomy that would have been forced upon an orphaned boy in her economic situation. Thus Christie consciously applies her political metaphor to her rejection of the feminine stereotype held out by her aunt, whose marriage is governed by "a most old-fashioned and dutiful awe of her lord and master" (10).

In her first job as a servant, Christie encounters the former slave Hepsey Johnson, who teaches her that willing work for pay is not degrading: "I's a free woman" (22). It is a lesson she does not forget. When the condescending, spoiled Philip Fletcher proposes to her later on, Christie responds, "It is what we *are*, not what we *have*, that makes one human being superior to another" (87). Later, she will "invest" her earnings in Hepsey's efforts to free other slaves: "[S]hares in the Underground Railroad pay splendid dividends that never fail" (128). The alliance between an educated white girl and the illiterate former slave prepares us for the major political event of the novel, the outbreak of the Civil War, at the same time that it records the perception of suffragists and abolitionists of the period that the political goals of women and blacks were parallel, if not identical. Alcott, like Madame de Staël, realized that genuine autonomy for women would require not just individual effort but political and economic change.

The course of nineteenth-century social and industrial transformations gave Alcott a consciousness of class conflicts that her French predecessor lacked. For the poor, the space for individual development and self-sufficiency is tragically limited. Christie is rapidly drawn into wage serfdom; indeed, it is so difficult to find even piecework that she almost commits suicide. If in her courage and practical gifts she earlier seemed a typical New England girl, here she is Everywoman face to face with capitalist misogyny and exploitation: "If one steps out from the ranks of needle-women it is very hard to press in again, so crowded are they, and so desperate the need of money" (155). For these social ills, of course, there is no simple answer; but Alcott rejects the status and gender divisions of labor. Christie becomes an emblem of a nonhierarchical view of labor because she can slip from one social class to another through her different types of performance, and she finally unites her friends from all social strata in one circle.

The relationship between the sexes is the true testing ground for Christie's "Declaration of Independence." It is not enough that she should gain the experience and self-confidence that flow from work; she must find a way to defend her redefined self against the pressures to surrender independence that are brought to bear on all of us in every relationship. The complex development of this protagonist clarified Alcott's "domestic feminism." In her youth Christie refuses to "wait for any man to give me independence, if I can earn it for myself" (8). She knows a bad marriage forced Matty Stone "to crush and curb her needs and aspirations" and finally to drown herself. Yet when, exhausted and despairing, she finds refuge in work with the florist David Sterling, Christie begins to feel "home was woman's sphere after all" (288) and wishes "he'd be masterful, and order me about" (236). Such a patriarchal idyll, however, is glimpsed only to prove an illusion. Slowly, through the trials of self-doubt and a renewed offer of marriage from Philip Fletcher, Christie comes to realize that "she would never make a good slave" (324). In love then, as well as at work, Alcott embraces the view that "[w]omen who stand alone in the world, and have their own way to make, have a better chance to know men truly than those who sit safe at home and only see one side of mankind" (268).

Marriage, however, is a powerful institution that does not readily accommodate equality. The novel uses the Civil War to remove David and achieve the inversion of roles that is the sine qua non of a civil war novel. (Indeed, the war makes the covert role reversal in the Watkins family overt, when Cindy becomes the general commanding her husband to enlist.) David's death in battle forces Christie to become head of the Sterling household and business. More important, she creates a community of women, or Herland, that cuts across class lines.

The economic and social density of Alcott's analysis gives unusual depth to her realignment of gender roles, but role reversal seems to be a key metaphor in most of these fictions. Delphine's inner strength, for example, contrasts with Léonce's weakness. While she is "independent" in thought and conduct, Léonce sacrifices desire to marital duty. To play the woman's role, however, may be a sign of his growth as when he speaks through the words of Milton's Eve: "God is thy law, thou mine" (1:422). In countless letters he confesses, "My will is submitted to yours" (1:449), yet his tragedy lies in the incompleteness of Delphine's "fatal rule" over him. A similar growth through traversal of old dichotomies marks the end of Beauvoir's novel. It is Hélène who undertakes the dangerous mission leading to her death while Jean, as the mind of the operation, must not expose himself to danger. By inverting the roles they played at the opening of their affair, when Jean undertook the mission of stealing a bicycle for her, this final mission demonstrates Hélène's new autonomy.

In fictions by men, by contrast, role reversal more commonly has sexual connotations and figures political upheaval. An excellent example of such inversion can be found in Hemingway's *For Whom the Bell Tolls*. One of the basic problems in civil war is that of delineating the new moral unity within an older, fallen order; because the enemy is within, we must be able to tell "ours"—our planes, for example—from "theirs." Simple failure of the will may turn a friend into an enemy, and new strengths become necessary. When Hemingway's protagonist, Robert Jordan, joins a Spanish Republican guerrilla group to blow up a bridge and slow the Fascist advance, he finds the group is no longer led by Pablo, but by his wife Pilar. The line between man and wife is redrawn, reassigning power —as the men see it, "barbarously."

Such popular attitudes also color Margaret Mitchell's treatment of the theme in *Gone with the Wind*, which describes how topsy-turvy conditions make Scarlett the head of an extended family, while the men she supports (her father, Ashley, even Will Benteen and Frank Kennedy) are broken in body and spirit. Frank thinks she has "unsexed" herself (625), and Grandma Fontaine observes that she is smart "in a man's way of being smart" (704). The true woman in this novel is of course Rhett Butler, the male whore with a heart of gold.

These pervasive inversions of gender roles prepare the realization that sexual politics are indeed political. Only at critical moments, however, can gender definitions become an overt political issue. If politics at the outset of *Delphine* are an issue that divides the sexes, an arena into which only men may enter, by the end of the novel Madame de Staël has shown that sexual definition and constraints are a political matter. Two episodes underline this radical perception. In the first, Monsieur de Lebensei, the democratic friend of Delphine, suggests that Léonce should obtain a divorce as soon as the Constituent Assembly ratifies this measure. In a world of arranged marriages, both men and women suffer from living "under civil slavery as well as political slavery" (2:73). For Delphine, politics should be able to reshape family structures: she accepts divorce in principle, even if her situation in fact precludes it.

In the second and more vivid episode, the oppressive social determination of sexual relations again betrays its political nature. Delphine departs from the convent in which she had taken refuge and plans to marry Léonce. The Revolution has released her from her vows—vows that in any case were illegitimate, since they were forced upon her by blackmail and before the prescribed waiting period had elapsed. But from the counterrevolutionary perspective of provincial villagers the wedding license of this former nun seems to echo the September massacres. Violation of the sexual order is equated with violence.

A materialist view of revolutionary sexual politics emerges from a reading of the works of Hemingway, James, and Pilniak. In *For Whom the Bell Tolls*, the quintessential example of a "territory" that must be redefined is Maria, emblem of the Spanish nation. Gang raped by the Franquistas, she must be retaken by Jordan. "If we do everything together, the other maybe never will have been" (72). The barbaric treatment of female civilians by the Fascists, like the rape of Lucretia by Tarquin, is emblematic of political tyranny; it is also a narrative motive for resistance that humanizes the republican struggle. Here sexual politics not only define moral values but enter directly into the broader political struggle. At the same time, Jordan's symbolic cure for political tyranny patently lies outside history and indeed any pragmatic hope for social transformation.

The Naked Year (1922), Boris Pilniak's remarkable novel about the Russian Revolution, likewise figures political change as the liberation of sexual acts. Like Henry James, Pilniak focuses on the daily lives of individuals rather than the violence of civil war. As it happens, the ordinary people conceive of the impact of the Revolution through images of women and the transformation of women's roles. "Mister comrade, will women be freed from the eight hour day during their monthly?" (67). For them, Russia is their "mother," and like "woman" she is also "a fiction, an illusion" composed of many Russias (117). Pilniak's women, ranging from the new celibate surgeon to the syphilitic whore of the past, evoke in their very diversity the stereotypes Beauvoir catalogs in *The Second Sex*. The anarchist Irina, for example, rejects humanism and ethics to take up with a horse thief; he knows enough, she says, to "thrash a woman." "I am beautiful and free, and . . . am cramped by my freedom. . . . I look at myself in the mirror—and a woman with eyes as black as the confusion of rebellion . . . looks out at me" (178–79). As one might expect, the revolutionary Pilniak depicts female sexuality as antirevolutionary, and "rebellion" as feminine. Near the end, two men try to enact an apocalypse by arranging a love feast with the flirtatious clerk Ollie Kuntz in a nunnery, then setting the building on fire. Such erotic scenes point to the ideological blending of violence with sexuality formulated in Pilniak's most famous line: "I feel that the whole revolution smells of sexual organs" (26). Pilniak draws energy from this fusion of themes, but he himself slips into the same ideological confusion.

Because the stakes are moral in civil wars, the protagonists are often inner émigrés whose social alienation and psychological distance permit them to comment incisively on the struggle. This is true of both men and women—of Beauvoir's Jean Blomart and Hemingway's Robert Jordan, as well as Staël's Delphine. But with striking frequency the social outsider who becomes a critic of patriotic, militarist ideology is a woman. This may be so precisely because of the traditional definition of woman's territory as moral rather than political, a perch that gives the woman's voice particular authority in the context of the moral civil war.

A particularly poignant instance of the social outsider who retreats inward is Iduzza, the heroine of Elsa Morante's *History: A Novel*, whose rape by a German soldier multiplies her sense of alienation as epileptic and Jew. By contrast, the male author shows the dangers of moral vision for the man engaged in political struggle. Hemingway's old republican fighter Anselmo knows that "to shoot a man gives a feeling as though one had struck one's own brother," but he also knows that to keep from becoming effeminate, he must repress this knowledge: "Nay, do not think of that. That gave thee too much emotion and thee ran blubbering down the bridge like a woman" (442). Moral vision, then, feminizes men and hyperfeminizes women, endangering their political purity and personal security.

Realist writers like James, who use women for their critique of militarism, do so ironically, playing the heroine's narcissism and desire for materialist pleasures against the hero's infatuation with abstractions and noble rhetoric. In "Story of a Year," just as Lizzie Crowe refuses to attend improving lectures—"All the battles and things described, you know" (54)—James himself refuses to record the military exploits of Lizzie's fiancé Jack (35). If he depicts Lizzie as a "childish" and trivial actress who soon becomes a "veteran" bored with love, he likewise reveals that the noble Jack is deceived by hope that a sublime battle will quickly lead to the end of the war (25). "War is an infamy," as James writes in "Poor Richard" (476). Scarlett O'Hara is another example of the silly, even selfish woman who indirectly points up the shabbiness and baseness of war itself: "War didn't seem to be a holy affair, but a nuisance that killed men senselessly and cost money and made luxuries hard to get" (170).

From the male author's perspective, the family seems insulated from conflict; from that of the female author, political discourse and familial order lie in a continuum. Significantly, men rather than women construe the family as a depoliticized idyllic terrain. Staël explicitly politicizes family relations; Hemingway, by contrast, imagines sexual union as taking place on a transcendent plane. Women writers interpret the moral claims of civil wars in terms of an individual emotional and relational context. Carol Gilligan's theory that women learn skills of moral negotiation and balance through identification with the mother (as opposed to the male model of development through separation from the mother) may explain the tendency to individualize and contextualize judgment in these women's novels. Beauvoir's protagonist ponders the meaning of his broadly aimed social struggle in terms of the individuals he has known who have died, while Hemingway's protagonist at several points treats war as a matter of mathematical calculations and military timing. For Beauvoir, instrumentalism destroys existential values; for Hemingway, it is just one outcome of large-scale strategic analysis. To Robert Jordan, lives are "instruments" "on which the future of the human race can turn" (43). And in turn, Jordan's own life becomes an instrument, as Hemingway subverts sacrificial tragedy to the service of ideology.

In some of these fictions of civil war, the identification of women's voice with privileged political insight leads to narrative experimentation with point of view, for the theme of civil war seems to demand a narrative violation of expectations. A number of these texts splice masculine and feminine voices, marking significant political moments by shifts in perspective. Set into Hemingway's third-person, relatively staccato narrative focused on Jordan, we find the gypsy woman Pilar's story of a village massacre. Her narrative pause (Chapter 10) delays Jordan's encounter with El Sordo, the deaf guerrilla, and speaks the unspeakable, ironically, what a woman should not hear (134). Jordan grudgingly admits, "I've always known about the other. . . . What we did to them at the start. . . . But that damned woman made me see it as though I had been there" (135). Elsa Morante also splits her narrative into two: one voice lists telegraphically the political and military events of the year, while the other narrates Iduzza's story. Louisa May Alcott, in her first publication, *Hospital Sketches* (1863), weaves across the strands of men's "tragic" experience the warp of a woman's ironic perspective. The polyphonic juxtaposition of voices becomes an anarchic metaphor in Pilniak's modernist novel. In Pilniak's mosaic of female portraits suggesting a new "mother Russia," the most amusing is that of Ollie Kuntz, a comic projection of the narrator's own experiment. This nubile notary public "was remodelling her grammar—she thought it wasn't decent, impersonal enough, to use any form of the verb but the infinitive, and so instead of 'do you love me?' she would say 'you to love me?'" (152). Like Ollie, Pilniak attacks the formal structures that hierarchically define subject and object.

The internal splits that define civil war reproduce themselves in the representation of gender relations and in the process of representation itself. To reconceive social and political structures requires that one reconceive oneself: civil war is paired with inner struggle. That self-division or inner struggle in turn may lead to productive change, but far more often in these fictions it leads to inner exile, silence, and suicide. The tenuous possibility of change that is raised by civil war finds its poetic figure in the reversal of gender roles. Typically, these narratives trace inverted trajectories for their male and female protagonists; if they start with a gender gap, they also end on one.

For all the similarities among these novels in their narrative structures and recurrent metaphors, significant differences also emerge. Among the male authors, the realm of the feminine remains emblematic of withdrawal from politics, whether into anarchy or into a protected idyll. By contrast, the women authors expose sexual politics as a truly political issue. They raise the problem of women's access to political discourse—can words without acts have any authority? And, finally, they show that the difficulties of literary representation are also difficulties of political representation.

Notes

I wish to thank those who at various points have read and whose ideas have fed this essay: Guy and Marge Cardwell, Patrice Higonnet, Regina Barreca, Cornelia Nixon, Barbara Rosen, and the editors of this volume.

1. That arbitrariness cannot be acknowledged. In order to mask the swift transformations of men's and women's roles, an organicist discourse naturalizes the politics of gender. Similarly, the gendering of politics gives an illusion of naturalness. See Higonnet and Higonnet, "The Double Helix," 37–41.

2. External wars indeed are often initiated in order to derail internal dissension and to justify the repression of dissidence. Similarly, the occupation of a country both creates and masks internal political divisions. It is important to avoid the complacent faith that the French Resistance under the Vichy regime was a struggle against a foreign nation rather than a civil war.

3. Marat, for example, links aristocrats to women, and more generally the clerical and peasant resistance to the French Revolution was thought to be supported by women.

4. Jakobson, "Closing Statement: Linguistics and Poetics," 358.

5. Staël, *Delphine*, 1:467. All translations from Madame de Staël are my own; hereafter volume and page numbers are given in text in parentheses.

6. While Delphine is active, Léonce is passive in his suicide. Delphine's act is deliberate; Léonce depends on others to complete his act. It is perhaps not an accident that Delphine, like Dido, suffers from calumny and that her lover abandons her for battle.

7. The political and personal conflicts also intersect in the conclusion of the second version, published posthumously. Léonce announces his marriage to Delphine the very day that the news of the September massacres arrives in the province where they have taken refuge (near the Vendée). As a defrocked nun about to marry, Delphine represents the anticlerical revolutionary tendencies that had just climaxed in the slaughter on the streets of Paris. In a chain reaction, the popular condemnation of the marriage causes Léonce to faint, and his inability to embrace her in the face of social prejudice deals a mortal blow to Delphine. She is a victim of the counterrevolution.

8. See Marks, *Simone de Beauvoir*, 38–40, 66–68.

Works Cited

Alcott, Louisa May. *Hospital Sketches*. New York: Sagmore Press, 1957.
———. *Work: A Story of Experience*. New York: Schocken Books, 1977.
Beauvoir, Simone de. *The Blood of Others*. Translated by Roger Senhouse, 1948. Reprint. New York: Pantheon, 1983.
———. *The Second Sex*. Translated by H. M. Parshley. New York: Vintage, 1974.
Hemingway, Ernest. *For Whom the Bell Tolls*. New York: Charles Scribner's Sons, 1940, 1968.
Higonnet, Margaret R., and Patrice L.-R. Higonnet. "The Double Helix." In *Behind the Lines: Gender and the Two World Wars*, edited by Margaret Randolph Higonnet, Jane Jenson, Sonya Michel, and Margaret Collins Weitz, 31–47. New Haven: Yale University Press, 1987.
Jakobson, Roman. "Closing Statement: Linguistics and Poetics." In *Style in Language*, edited by Thomas A. Sebeok, 350–77. Cambridge, Mass.: MIT Press, 1958.
James, Henry. "Poor Richard." In *The Novels and Stories of Henry James*, 25:417–96. London: Macmillan & Co., 1923.
———. "The Story of a Year" and "Gabrielle de Bergerac." In *Eight Uncollected Tales of Henry James*, edited by Edna Kenton. New Brunswick, N.J.: Rutgers University Press, 1950.
Marks, Elaine. *Simone de Beauvoir: Encounter with Death*. New Brunswick, N.J.: Rutgers University Press, 1973.
Mitchell, Margaret. *Gone with the Wind*. 2 vols. London: Macmillan & Co., 1957.
Morante, Elsa. *History: A Novel*. Translated by William Weaver. New York: Alfred A. Knopf, 1977.
Pilniak, Boris [Boris Vogau]. *The Naked Year*. Translated by Alec Brown. New York: Payson & Clarke, 1928.
Staël, Germaine de. *Delphine*. 2 vols. Paris: Des Femmes, 1981.

*I*n an essay on Wyndham Lewis published on June 15, 1914, Ezra Pound named his fellow Vorticist "a man at war."[1] The remark was prescient, for exactly one week after Lewis's public declaration of war on Edwardian taste appeared in the June 20 issue of *Blast*, the Archduke Franz Ferdinand was shot at Sarajevo. Soon Lewis donned a helmet, and along with Ford Madox Ford, he became one of the few self-proclaimed "men of 1914" who participated in both the battle of modernism and the battle of the Somme.

There were other wars taking place in Edwardian society before the Great War began on August 4, 1914, when the time limit on Britain's ultimatum to Germany ran out. During the first half of 1914, Emmeline Pankhurst (organizer of the Women's Social and Political Union) was imprisoned four times, responding each time with a hunger strike and raising her total number of strikes to twelve. At the same time, her army of suffragettes had set an arsonist's record, burning 107 buildings, including two ancient churches at Wargrave and Breadsall. The windows at 10 Downing Street had already been broken. Velázquez's Venus was slashed and a mummy case in the British Museum was damaged.[2] In the first issue of *Blast* Lewis offered these words of advice addressed "TO SUFFRAGETTES":

IN DESTRUCTION, AS IN OTHER THINGS,
  stick to what you understand.
WE MAKE YOU A PRESENT OF OUR VOTES.
ONLY LEAVE WORKS OF ART ALONE.
   YOU MIGHT SOME DAY DESTROY A
   GOOD PICTURE BY ACCIDENT.
THEN!—
  MAIS SOYEZ BONNES FILLES!
  NOUS VOUS AIMONS!
WE ADMIRE YOUR ENERGY. YOU AND ARTISTS
  ARE THE ONLY THINGS (YOU DON'T MIND
  BEING CALLED THINGS?) LEFT IN ENGLAND
  WITH A LITTLE LIFE IN THEM.

IF YOU DESTROY A GREAT WORK OF ART you
are destroying a greater soul than if you
annihilated a whole district of London.
LEAVE ART ALONE, BRAVE COMRADES![3]

For Lewis, the suffragettes' war was productive so long as it did not
interfere with his exclusively male war against Edwardian taste; in
the rhetoric of his Vorticist manifesto, "artists" and "suffragettes"
are mutually exclusive groups. What Lewis did not see, however,
was that the battle for women's suffrage, the battle for modern art,
and the battle in the trenches could not be separated. All three wars
conspired, each fueled by the energy of the others, to change the
face of modern culture. May Sinclair, who as novelist, suffragette,
and ambulance driver had participated in all three wars, was more
insightful than Pound or Lewis. In her novel *The Tree of Heaven*
(1917) she borrowed the male modernists' Vorticist rhetoric to describe not only the "vortex of revolutionary Art" but also the "vortex of the fighting Suffrage women." And although one of the male
characters in the novel mistakenly considers the revolution in the
arts to be "*the* Vortex," both his vortex and the "Feminist Vortex"
are "swept without a sound into the immense vortex of the War."[4]

To see the Great War as the instigator of the downfall of Edwardian society would be to ignore the tensions that twisted that society out of shape in the years prior to the war. It was "on or about
December, 1910"—not 1914—that Virginia Woolf said that "human
character changed."[5] When the war finally came, its rhetoric was
already in place, honed by the soldiers of modernism and suffrage.
Military rhetoric appeared in *Blast* before the war, and it appeared
even more strenuously in the *Suffragette*, the weekly newspaper of
the WSPU, edited by Emmeline Pankhurst's daughter Christabel. In
the June 19, 1914 issue (published the day before the first *Blast*),
Christabel Pankhurst addressed antifeminists who maintained that
"ordinary warfare as waged by men is more civilised than the meth-
ods of the Suffragettes."

> The fact is that warfare as developed by men has become a
> horror unspeakable—a horror upon which the mind's eye dare
> hardly look.
> . . . War is now a mechanical and soulless massacre of multi-
> tudes of soldiers, mere boys some of them, others husbands
> and fathers. . . .
> Well may women strive for the Vote! For war as it is and as it

is going to be is the tragic result of the unnatural system of government by men only.[6]

These sentences were written before Britain declared war, before Germany invaded Belgium, even before the assassination of the archduke. Suffragettes justified their military tactics by proving that government is based on physical force while merely pretending to be an agent of moral force: "The proof of that fact is that as soon as women rebel against being voteless, even if they only try to petition the Prime Minister or the King, force is used against them and they are arrested and sent to prison, and if they resent this are tortured into the bargain."[7]

Despite the obvious disparity in their goals, the male modernists' war and the suffragettes' war were sometimes forced to join forces if only because they shared a common rhetoric and a common enemy—Edwardian culture. Ironically, Rebecca West's short story "Indissoluble Matrimony," a depiction of the war between women and men, was published just pages away from Lewis's proclamation to the suffragettes in *Blast*. As if in response to Lewis's shortsighted dismissal of female power, West presents the story of George Silverton, a proper Edwardian businessman, and his wife Evadne, a woman who "had black blood in her"—and worse, had "passed through [her husband's] own orthodox Radicalism to a passionate Socialism, . . . [and] had begun to write for the Socialist press and to speak successfully at meetings." After an unusually violent row over one of her speaking engagements ("You shan't speak!" repeats George until the phrase gains a universality that denies Evadne any claim to subjectivity), Evadne runs from the house. George follows her, expecting to apprehend her in the tryst that will enable him to divorce her. ("All those Browning lectures for nothing," he laments.) Instead, George discovers Evadne in a long black bathing dress, standing in the moonlight, preparing to dive into Whimsey Pond. When the two protagonists face each other, the rhetoric of military confrontation—which has been subliminal throughout the story—now becomes explicit:

They perceived that God is war and his creatures are meant to fight. When dogs walk through the world cats must climb trees. The virgin must snare the wanton, the fine lover must put the prude to the sword. The gross man of action walks, spurred on the bloodless bodies of the men of thought, who lie quiet and cunningly do not tell him where his grossness leads him. The flesh must smother the spirit, the spirit must set the flesh on fire and watch it burn. And those who were gentle by nature and shrank from the ordained brutality were betrayers of their kind, surrendering the earth to the seed of their enemies. In this war there is no discharge. If they succumbed to peace now, the rest of their lives would be dishonourable, like the exile of a rebel who has begged his life as the reward of cowardice.

"With an uplifting sense of responsibility," continues West, "they realised they must kill each other." Neither is successful, however, and the story ends, all passion spent, with George climbing into bed "as he had done every night for ten years, and as he would do every night until he died. Still sleeping, Evadne caressed him with warm arms."[8] Their war would have neither a Waterloo nor an armistice.

Ezra Pound would have been even more prescient if he had named Rebecca West a woman at war; her cause was represented between the shocking pink covers of *Blast* at the same time that it was rendered subservient to Lewis's Vorticist war. But just two weeks after Pound gave that name to Lewis, he published in the *Egoist* (originally the feminist *New Freewoman* before Pound persuaded Dora Marsden to change its title) an essay titled "Suffragettes."

Miss Christabel Pankhurst has about as much intellect as a guinea-pig but she has a sense of values, of subjective emotional values, which is sound beyond question. And Sylvia, her sister, is also getting a lot out of life. It is glorious and stimulating to ride on a stretcher at the head of a loyal mob. I do not pity these young ladies. I regard them with envy, at least they "will have lived," they will always have that to look back upon if they survive it.

The women of 1914 were receiving more publicity than the men who grouped themselves under a similar epithet. Pound suggests that instead of attempting to "make hell less hell-like for the lower classes," the "duty of all literate men and of all women is to keep alight some spark of civilization at the summit of things." The modernist war should subsume the energy of the suffragettes, says Pound. And although he calls all literate men and all women (whether literate or illiterate) to the battle, it is clear that his secret society of modernism is finally the Edwardian gentlemen's club writ large: "The enlightened men should foregather with other enlightened men and plot for the preservation of enlightenment. That is to say, he should form his syndicat."[9]

During the summer of 1914, the modernist war and the suffrage war were engaged in battle with each other, yet on August 4 another war arose to subsume them both. In one sense, all three wars merged as the Great War quickly became the apparent stimulus for social and artistic revolution; in October 1915, the WSPU changed the name of its periodical from the *Suffragette* to *Britannia*, a name better suited to the common cause. Yet as Sandra Gilbert has pointed out, it is important to see how the women and men of 1914 reacted to the war differently: "[A]s young men became increasingly alienated from their prewar selves, increasingly immured in the muck and blood of No Man's Land, women seemed to become, as if by some uncanny swing of history's pendulum, ever more powerful. As nurses, as mistresses, as munitions workers, bus drivers, or soldiers in the 'land army,' even as wives and mothers, these formerly subservient creatures began to loom malevolently larger."[10]

Gilbert has oversimplified the effect of the war somewhat by saying that women were subservient prior to its inception. Although women took over men's jobs, for instance, they were rarely paid men's wages. Even more importantly, the Great War was not the first military conflict in which British women played a prominent part, and the women of 1914 had several role models. The chapter on "Women and War" in Olive Schreiner's *Women and Labour* (adopted by many suffragettes as their "bible" when it was first published in 1911 and given an even wider circulation when the chapter was reissued as a pamphlet in 1914) advised that women had always had a "far more intimate" relation to war than men because they *"pay the first cost on all human life."* Schreiner felt that women should take an active role on the battlefield: "On that day, when the woman takes her place beside the man in the governance and arrangement of external affairs of her race will also be that day that heralds the death of war as a means of arranging human differences."[11] As Schreiner wrote, other women were undertaking this challenge. St. Clair Stobart was frustrated by the liberal establishment's reaction to the suffragettes, and she saw the beginning of the Balkan Wars (October 1912) as the opportunity "to give a practical demonstration of the fact that women are capable of taking an independent and servicable share in National Defense":

> Concerning the right of women to the parliamentary franchise,
> how, I argued, could women *prove* that they were capable of
> taking a share in the work of national and imperial parlia-
> ments, unless and until they had shown their capacity for tak-
> ing an *interest* in national and imperial affairs?
>
> So long as women's interests were purely personal and paro-
> chial, so long must their influence remain personal and paro-
> chial.[12]

With the ultimate purpose of enlarging women's roles in domestic
politics, Stobart organized the Women's Convey Corps, a medical
unit stationed between the front and the base hospitals: the commandant, doctors, nurses, cooks, and dressers were all women. Both
the effort and the book Stobart wrote about it, *War and Women*
(1913), were an acclaimed success.

Just as Hardy's poems about the Boer War offered an important
model for the poets of the Great War, these Edwardian women's
involvement in warfare prepared for the greater advances achieved
by the women of 1914. As Stobart predicted, the international conflict had important repercussions at home. The April 16, 1915 issue
of the *Suffragette* reported that "two women conductors are being
employed, as an experiment" because nearly two thousand men
employed by the Glasgow Corporation Tramways Department had
left to join the armed forces. "The women, who have both had considerable experience on the clerical staff of the Tramways Department, have been supplied with neat blue uniforms—a coat and
skirt with yellow facings, and a distinctive cap. In spite of the
amount of attention they attracted on their first appearance, the
women went about their work in a practical and business-like
manner, and the result of their first two days' work is regarded as
perfectly satisfactory."[13] D. H. Lawrence's short story "Tickets,
Please" (1919) presents the male response to this development. As
women take over the duties on a midland tram line, the one remaining male conductor futilely continues to assert his dominance
until his female coworkers descend upon him in a baccanalian fury
that leaves him emasculated. "Who wants him?" cries Laura to the
rest of the women. "Nobody" is their unison response—except for
Annie, who seems to have had some genuine feeling for John
Thomas.[14] She stands as the victim who represents Lawrence's anger even more fully than John Thomas: the woman who wished to
love a man, but found herself undone by the new-found power of

wartime women. Before the war, in West's "Indissoluble Matrimony," the battle between women and men was fought but had no effect. Now, West's new woman does not shrink from battle. At the climax of "Indissoluble Matrimony," when George and Evadne are poised for fisticuffs, Evadne becomes possessed by "the primitive woman who is the curse of all women: a creature of the most utter femaleness, useless, save for childbirth, with no strong brain to make her physical weakness a light accident, abjectly and corruptingly afraid of men. A squaw, she dared not strike her lord."[15] Before the war, the rhetoric of social revolution was in place, but the bonds of social codes seemed indissoluble.

Lawrence expressed his resentment at women's increasing power (especially their threat to the exclusively male revolution in the arts) even more violently in a pair of poems that were written during wartime but remained unpublished until 1940. In "Reach Over" the spirit of a dead soldier calls to his living brothers to

> reach over, reach over,
> and give me a hand.
> I come back to you
> men dumb in the dusk
> but men,
> and dearer to me
> than anything else
> than woman, or triumph, money or success
> men in the dusk
> dumb
> but masculine as the sun,
> waiting for the sun to rise on you.

Yet the spirit of the dead man cannot make the passage, as the companion poem "Softly, then, Softly" reveals, because women stand in his way:

> Do they block the way?
> Do they obstruct?
> Tripping about with their ladylike hams
> And their groomed and mushroom-like faces?

"But softly, softly and ruthlessly / Down with them!" the poem concludes.[16] If before the Great War Pound could call women to lay down their arms at the male "syndicate" of modernism, women had now become an insurmountable threat to male comradery.

The suffragettes, in contrast, saw male comradery as the very thing that had caused the war. The first issue of the *Suffragette* to appear after Britain's declaration of war confronted its readers with a graphic cartoon of men at battle, subtitled "Worse than *Women's* Militancy." In a bold-print editorial titled "THE WAR," Christabel Pankhurst declared that the Great War

> is Nature's vengeance—is God's vengeance upon the people who held women in subjection, and by doing that have de-stroyed the perfect human balance. Just as when the laws gov-erning the human body are defied we have disease, so when the law of right government is defied—the law that men and women shall co-operate in managing their affairs—we have a civilisation imperfect, unjust, savage at its best and fore-doomed to destruction.
>
> Had women been equal partners with men from the begin-ning, human civilisation would have been wholly different from what it is. The whole march of humanity would have been to a point other than we have reached at this moment of horrible calamity.[17]

The readers of the *Suffragette* knew that the war was not the point of origin for tensions between women and men. They even began to see the Great War as an extension of their own. Christabel Pank-hurst wrote in "We will not be Prussianised" that the "women's cause is one and the same as that of the Belgians."[18] The suffrag-ettes were proud that their patriotism was seen as a sign "that this war and the women's fight for the vote are part of the old old con-flict between freedom and tyranny. The very same hopes, the very same aspirations that inspire British women to fight for political liberty are inspiring the peoples of Europe to fight for national liberty."[19]

If women saw the Great War as the natural outcome of years of sexual and political repression, men such as Lawrence perceived it as the calamity that initiated the war between women and men. This distortion of the war's effect on sexual politics is itself histori-cally important: while it is clear that the Great War was not the point of origin for the rising tensions between men and women (any more than it was the origin of the modernist revolution in the arts), it quickly became *perceived* as such because people who lived through these troubled years (as well as the historians and literary critics who have documented them) were soothed by the idea that social tensions had a point of origin that was fixed and thrust upon them by powers divorced from personal experience. The real terror of the war made it possible to fabricate a prelapsarian era in which the war between men and women had not yet been declared. But as the *Freewoman* pointed out in "Speculations on Sex War" (1911)— three years before the Great War began—"the war started long before Votes for Women was first whispered."[20]

The transformation of World War I into a decisive historical turning point that created the illusion of a sexual golden age may be seen vividly in another work that first saw publication in Lewis's *Blast*: Ford Madox Ford's *The Good Soldier*. When the first three and a half chapters appeared in *Blast* in 1914, the novel was still titled *The Saddest Story* and Ford was still named Hueffer (he would change his surname after the war). Yet the opening of the novel appeared in much the same form as would be published in 1915 after the war began. *The Good Soldier* is a paradigmatic story of the disintegration of Edwardian society, a time when the king stood as an icon of moral respectability at the same time that his gambling and his many mistresses were common knowledge. Ford's novel is likewise a book in which contradictory social codes exist side by side, cemented together with a thin coating of convenient ignorance. The novel's narrator, John Dowell, and his wife Florence meet Edward and Leonora Ashburnham annually at a German spa. But unknown to John, Florence and Edward have conducted an annual affair—with Leonora's knowledge. Florence kills herself when Edward falls in love with his ward Nancy Rufford. Being a gentleman (a good soldier) Edward then kills himself in turn, unable to commit the unthinkable act of seducing Nancy. All these events emerge from *The Good Soldier* only slowly, however, as the inept Dowell attempts to reconstruct the events of this "saddest story I have ever heard."[21]

Ford intended *The Good Soldier* to be a book about endings. "I fully intended it to be my last book," he recalled in his 1927 dedication of the novel.[22] And even in the pages of *Blast* we can see how this novel of intricate sexual politics was designed to express an eschatological vision of international politics:

> You may well ask why I write. Yet my reasons are quite many. For it is not unusual in human beings who have witnessed the sack of a city or the falling to pieces of a people to

desire to set down what they have witnessed for the benefit of unknown heirs or of generations infinitely remote; or, if you please just to get the sight out of their heads.

Someone has said that the death of a mouse from cancer is the whole sack of Rome by the Goths, and I swear to you that the breaking up of our little four-square coterie was such another unthinkable event.[23]

These sentences were published in *Blast* before the war began; the artistic and moral battles that predated the actual fighting had already persuaded Ford that civilization as he knew it was drawing to a close. Yet as he revised and renamed the novel after the war began on August 4, he wove an allegory of the Great War into *The Good Soldier*. Throughout the novel the war is never mentioned; the book remains a portrayal of sexual intrigue and a mind's unraveling. Yet every major event in the novel takes place on August 4—the day the war began:

The death of Mrs. Maiden [another of Edward's lovers] occurred on the 4th of August 1904. And then nothing happened until the 4th of August 1913. There is the curious coincidence of dates, but I do not know whether that is one of those sinister, as if half-jocular and altogether merciless proceedings on the part of a cruel Providence that we call a coincidence. Because it may just as well have been the superstitious mind of Florence that forced her to certain acts, as if she had been hypnotized. It is, however, certain that the 4th of August always proved a significant date for her. To begin with, she was born on the 4th of August. Then, on that date in the year 1899, she set out with her uncle for the tour round the world [. . . .] Then, on the 4th of August 1900, she yielded to an action that certainly coloured her whole life—as well as mine [. . . .] On the 4th of August 1901, she married me, and set sail for Europe in a great gale of wind—the gale that affected her heart.[24]

And on August 4, 1913, Dowell neglects to mention, Florence discovered Edward's love for Nancy and committed suicide, the action that brought down the Edwardian house of cards with which the novel's sexual codes are constructed. Dowell, who reconstructs the events of the novel after many years, also neglects to mention the most striking coincidence: that the war also began on August 4. It is not, as he suspects, "the superstitious mind of Florence" that caused the coincidences, but rather his own reordering of the events after the war. It was, indeed, Ford's superstitious mind that created the coincidences: as he completed *The Good Soldier* after the declaration of war, he wanted its eschatological plot and tone to appear to be the outcome of the war even though the action of the novel takes place before the war. By having all the major events of *The Good Soldier* occur on August 4, he suggests both that these events "caused" the war and that the war was the "source" of all the sexual confusion in the novel. The war had already begun to be seen as a point of origin for disrupted social codes rather than a force that exacerbated the disintegration of an ailing society. Ford went on to make this interpretation of the war's relationship to sexual politics explicit in *Parade's End*, his postwar tetralogy of novels. Standing in the trenches, Christopher Tietjens says, "[M]y problem will remain the same whether I'm here or not. For it's insoluble. It's the whole problem of the relations of the sexes."[25]

The work of Ford Madox Ford and that of his lover Violet Hunt (a novelist and sometimes suffragette) presents a complicated portrait of the intertwining of the women's movement and the Great War in the early years of our century. Ford's character is puzzling to the point of irritation. On the one hand, he was the only male modernist to hold open sympathies with the women of 1914; indeed, he was the only "man of 1914" to have been engaged directly in the battles of art, sexism, and the Somme. In 1913 he wrote a pamphlet for the Women's Freedom League titled *This Monstrous Regiment of Women*, and in one of his memoirs, *Return to Yesterday*, he recalled that "at the time of the Suffragette agitations I wrote a great deal that Miss Pankhurst published, where and how she liked," implying that other contributions appeared anonymously.[26] In his own magazine, the *English Review*, Ford adopted the rhetoric of war to champion the suffragettes, justifying their "militant tactics" and the necessary violence of their "revolution," calling for the "surrender" of the government, and concluding that once it had capitulated, the government was to expect "very little gratitude from its conquerors."[27] In a series of essays published in the Women's Freedom League's journal *The Vote* (later collected in *The Critical Attitude* [1911]), Ford amalgamated the aesthetic and sexual wars in which he was involved by criticizing modern novelists for their perpetuation of the "convenient labour-saving contrivance" of the idealized female character. "But you have the matter a great deal in your own hands," he advised his female readership, for to such an extent is the writer of imaginative literature dependent on your suffrages, that if woman only refused to read the works of any writer who unreasonably idealises their sex, such writers must starve to death. For it should be a self-evident proposition that it would be much better for you to be, as a sex, reviled in books. Then men coming to you in real life would find how delightful you actually are, how logical, how sensible, how unemotional, how capable of conducting the affairs of the world.[28]

Ford took pleasure in feeling more qualified to diagnose the problem with women than women themselves; his own books present "reviled" women with intentions more vindictive than revolutionary. Ford was sensitive to the novelist's surreptitious reinforcement of sexual repression, but at the same time he was incapable of disentangling himself from the already outmoded sexual codes of his day. A subtle instance of his resentment is contained in the title of the pamphlet he wrote for the Women's Freedom League; he borrowed it from John Knox's *The First Blast of the Trumpet against the Monstrous Regiment of Women* (1558), a condemnation of the role Mary I and other women played in opposing the Reformation. In the pamphlet Ford points out that England had always enjoyed its greatest moments of prosperity under female rulers: "And it seems to me that if it is profitable that a woman should occupy the highest place, it is only reasonable to carry the argument one or two stages further." But Ford's portraits of female power would hardly have been condoned by the Olive Schreiner who believed that women's militancy would eventually destroy war's power as an enforcer of sexual difference:

And so Elizabeth paid nobody, cheated everybody, and was mean in a manner in which no man could have been mean. Had she been a fine lady living to-day she would have been the sort of person who would have underpaid her cabman, docked half the wages of her footman, ridden first-class with a third-class ticket—and at the cabman, at the footman, at the ticket collectors she would have made such eyes that not one of them but would have protested that she was the most charming lady in the world. No man, nowadays, could do such a thing, just as no King in her time could have done it.[29]

In print, Ford did his best to appear as the "new man," but in person his ambivalences ran deep, and the "new woman" was far more than he could handle. In 1894 (when he was still named Hueffer) Ford married Elsie Martindale, but the marriage quickly soured; the first and (as it would turn out) only woman to be named Mrs. Hueffer legally became the first of a long sequence of companions. In 1907 Ford met Violet Hunt, and in 1909 they became lovers. Hunt described herself in her memoirs as "not the Newest Woman of all, but I happen to be the New Woman that people wrote about in the nineties."[30] As the editors of her diaries have observed, she "seems to have had conflicting impulses, to be drawn both to the socially and artistically adventurous and to the wholly conventional, respectable upper-middle class: she wanted to be shocking and to be respected."[31] Hunt and Ford (Hueffer) tried to persuade his wife to grant him a divorce, but Mrs. Hueffer's devoutly Catholic family would not hear of it. Neither would some of Hunt's closest friends. When she confided in Henry James, the novelist replied that her "lamentable position" compelled him "to regard all agreeable or unembarrassed communications between us as impossible."[32] The author of *What Mazie Knew* could not be counted on for sympathy in such matters when they occurred outside the house of fiction.

In 1910, Ford moved into South Lodge, Hunt's family home, but kept up appearances by paying £3 a week rent. Later that year he decided that he and Hunt should move to Germany, where he would attempt to regain his father's German citizenship and then obtain a German divorce. The couple resided in Giessen, and Ford passed the time by beginning a book called *Women and Men*, his most extended analysis of Edwardian sexual politics. If Ford had been able to live by the precepts outlined in *Women and Men*, he would have saved both Hunt and himself a good deal of pain. "Let me postulate for the sake of clearness of thought," Ford begins, "that there is no difference between men and women." After a survey of examples from literature and his own experience, Ford concludes that what differences there might be are culturally determined:

> The theory is that instead of this Western world being made up of two opposing bands, distinguished from each other in morals, ethics, points of view, habits of mind and ideas of honour and dishonour—that we are all just people, distinguished from each other by functions that we perform in society. [. . .] Roughly speaking, what I mean to say is, that what

we have always been taught to regard as the difference between sexes is very little more actually than the difference between employments.[33]

Compared with Rebecca West's analysis of sexual difference in "Indissoluble Matrimony," Ford's analysis may be seen as typically male because of his desire to expose a social infrastructure that eradicates difference; for the women of 1914, it was often more important to assert and define the difference in terms of power. For West, the Western world was "made up of two opposing bands," and their war was real even if their differences were merely apparent.[34]

Attractive as the eradication of sexual difference might have seemed to Ford, however, he remained unable to act on such a presupposition in his relations with Hunt. His discussion of sexual politics in *Women and Men* is finally not socially prescriptive but akin to the idealistic ramblings of his poem "On Heaven"—dedicated to Hunt—in which he dreams of a world in which "poor lovers, married or never yet married" are all part of "His estate."[35] At the same time that Ford wrote *Women and Men* he was unable to see the arbitrariness of his socially codified marital status and devote himself unequivocally to Hunt. Evidence has recently arisen to suggest that Ford and Hunt were actually married in Germany, Ford having convinced his partner that his German citizenship and divorce had been granted.[36] Over the following few years, their relationship deteriorated rapidly, and when the war broke out, Ford exchanged his stakes in the war between women and men for a commission in the British Army.

Ford's poem "On Heaven" was published in a book of poems "written in active duty," and although Ford did not intend the ambiguity, it is difficult to tell which "war" he meant. One senses that Ford sought the commission not only because of a latent streak of patriotism but because it was the only way to extricate himself from an impossibly complicated personal life. Hunt felt that a more drastic alternative was required: "I told him when he left me that he was no longer free like other men[,] that if he found he couldn't bear to live with me, his only remedy before having let me into such an impasse was to cut his throat."[37] Yet when Ford left for France Hunt published "Merciful Aphasia," a poem expressing her irrepressible desire for him to return to her:

When you are with me it is Life.
Réveillés, alarms

The thrust, the parry, the séance in the trenches . . .
Feints of passion
Too starved, too ill-equipped to succeed. . . .
But still we are washed and laid out, and our eyelids closed.
At peace. . . .
It is a merciful dispensation.
Yet you'll come back?[38]

As Ford went to the Great War, Hunt stayed behind, a casualty in a war of genders. Her overt use of military rhetoric to describe her relationship with Ford in "Merciful Aphasia" once again reveals how each war nurtured the others. Yet unlike Ford, Hunt was trapped in a losing battle, unable to exchange her uniform or name. She dramatized her dilemma in "Love's Last Leave," a novella about two sisters (Aggie and Gussy Tremlett) who marry two brothers (Willy and George Leclerc). Both men are "swallowed in the war machine," but Hunt maintains that they "had the best of it; it was either kill or cure with them over there."

> But women, who had no vote, fought too, for they worked too and endured the beastliness of living in what were practically beleaguered cities. Food queues and tramping for lack of transit wore them out by day, while nights, punctuated by Zeppelins, put the finishing touch to the instability of their nerve centres and horrified their children so that they threatened to grow up idiots.
>
> The men foregathered behind the line in comparative safety; even in the trenches, when the Boches were quiet, they enjoyed the concert parties that were sent out to them. But women . . . were now forced to live the lives of hermits.

At Willy's request, Aggie finds employment in a government office. There her boss (like Ford) tells her that the war had rendered marriage obsolete and made polygamy a national necessity: "Every woman in England belonged individually and collectively to the men who had endured hell for her."[39] When Willy hears of this talk he forces his wife to quit the job; Aggie loses the one thing that had lightened the tedium of wartime England. Later, when Willy fails to fulfill his promise to come home for Christmas, Aggie insists that he visited her in spirit (though her sister Gussy suspects that the mysterious visit may have been facilitated by the all too physical presence of Willy's brother George, who did get leave). Willy is reported missing, presumed dead, and after a few months of uncertain despair, Aggie's body is found, along with her son's, at the bottom of the lake.

Ford finally had to admit in *Women and Men* that he had no answers for Hunt's difficult questions concerning the war's effect on women. When he first began the book at Giessen, he was excited about its prospects, writing to his literary agent that "whilst it is deeply serious it is also wildly amusing and it will be bought in large quantities by my large following of suffragettes."[40] Yet for reasons that have never been clear, Ford did not finish the book. Parts of it were published in the *Little Review* in 1918 (Pound called the essays "specimens of [Ford's] Impressionist mode at its best"[41]), and these parts were then collected and published as a slim volume in 1923. A manuscript that Ford probably wrote while he was stationed in the Ypres Salient shows why he was unable to complete the book. This manuscript, titled "Epilogue" (a sign, corroborated by the subject matter, that he may have intended the manuscript to be a coda to the truncated *Women and Men*), ends with these sentences:

> Just as every human face differs, if just by the hairs breadth turn of an instant, from every other human face, so every human life differs from every other human life if only by a little dimple on the stream of it. And the hairs breadth turn of the instant & the hairs breadth dimple in the stream of life when they come in contact with the lives of others just make all the difference—all the huge difference in the fates of men & women. Perhaps as one's eyes close in death one might be qualified to write a book entitled "Women & Men." But one won't be able to.[42]

Before the war, Ford tried to obliterate sexual difference; after visiting the trenches, he was overwhelmed by difference to such an extent that generalization was no longer possible. The direct experience of the war made the already complicated issue of sexual difference intractable. Ford always exaggerated his duties as an officer in the Transportation Corps; he saw only a little action, though what little he did see caused him two nervous breakdowns and a memory loss. Yet his emotional reactions to the fighting are emblematic of the loss he felt Western civilization had incurred. In his "Epilogue" he states explicitly the idea of cultural memory loss that would recur throughout the war memoirs of Blunden, Graves, and Sassoon.

> If, before the war, one had any function it was that of historian. Basing, as it were, one's mortality on the Europe of Charlemagne as modified by the Europe of Napoleon, I once had something to go upon. One could approach with composure the Lex Allemannica, the Feudal System, problems of Aerial Flight, the price of wheat or the relations of the Sexes. But now, it seems to me, we have no method of approach to any of these problems.[43]

To Ford, the war seemed to create irresolvable sexual differences when in actuality it revealed to him more clearly the tensions that had existed all along. Immersed in the reality of the Great War, Ford had already forgotten just how problematic the relations of the sexes had been in both his personal life and in England at large even when the Europe of Charlemagne and Napoleon lay intact. Like most of his male comrades, Ford was rendered myopically nostalgic by the war, and the prewar bombings by the suffragettes turned into retrospective echoes of the shells across the channel. In Ford's mind, the trouble began on August 4.

While Ford idealized an unruffled Edwardian era, the suffragettes, as Virginia Woolf would recall in *Three Guineas*, unconsciously "desired our splendid war" precisely because it ripped apart Edwardian society as their own bombs could not.[44] Woolf's comment, coming nearly twenty years after the armistice, is a retrospective simplification of female response to the war. Some suffragettes reacted as Woolf suggests, but even the Pankhurst women diverged dramatically. Emmeline and her daughter Christabel considered their fight for women's rights to be coequal with the fight against "Prussianism." In a speech titled "What Is Our Duty?" (reprinted in the April 23, 1915 issue of the *Suffragette*) Emmeline Pankhurst maintained that women should "ask men to fight for bigger reasons than are advanced ordinarily. We say to men, 'In this war there are issues at stake bigger even than the safety of your homes and your own country. Your honour as a nation is at stake.'"[45] Some members of the WSPU resented this shift from feminist to nationalist politics—despite Emmeline Pankhurst's rebuttal that a German victory would set the women's movement back by fifty years. Mrs. Pankhurst's daughter Sylvia had objections to the war that ran deeper. She separated from the WSPU and began publishing her own *Women's Dreadnought* (later the *Worker's Dreadnought* as socialism absorbed her feminism) to counteract the *Suffragette*. "No intelligent person," she wrote in "Why Governments Refuse to Tell," ". . . can believe either the one-sided story that the Allies are entirely blameless, and that the Central Powers alone caused the War, or can still be under the delusion that any of the great Powers are fighting a war of freedom and liberation."[46] While on an American lecture tour in 1916, Emmeline Pankhurst was informed of Sylvia's antiwar demonstrations, and she sent a telegram to WSPU headquarters that was then published in *Britannia* (formerly the *Suffragette*) as "A Message from Mrs. Pankhurst": "Strongly repudiate Sylvia's foolish and unpatriotic conduct. Regret I cannot prevent use of [Pankhurst] name. Make this public."[47]

Despite this mixed response to the war, however, Woolf was in one sense right to remember that suffragettes welcomed the fighting: whether they supported the allied cause or not, the war allowed them to penetrate more fully the male world of international politics. If Ford did believe that sexual differences arose from differences in "occupation," as he wrote in *Women and Men*, then the war simultaneously closed the gap and made the difference insurmountable. On the one hand, men were stationed in the trenches, engaged in the male world of combat; resentment for what they imagined as the "easy lives" of women in drawing rooms ran deep. On the other hand, women quickly usurped the positions vacated by soldiers, taking over what previously had been the male dominion of politics, public service, business—and the literary wars. For Violet Hunt, these domestic battles seemed more strenuous than those across the channel.

The Great War created not so much a turning point as an intensification of the war between women and men. Perhaps the greatest effect it had on Ford's conception of sexual politics was that it made the retrospectively easy speculations of *Women and Men* impossible. The book could not be finished and never would be. After Ford returned to England, he and Violet Hunt published poems side by side in *Poetry* magazine. "I must plod along the road / That leads to Germany," wrote Ford in "The Silver Music"; "Dear, were you ever here? / It has all grown so faint," replied Hunt in "Is It Worth While?"[48] After they had put on such knowledge, this man and woman were placed at odds permanently. Hunt recorded this wartime conversation with Ford in her diary on March 27, 1917: "You know dear [said Ford], I am not the sort of animal that makes love to women. . . . I am cold and I have one passion now, the Army & that England should win."[49] After the armistice, Ford left Hunt for good and moved into a cottage in Sussex with a new companion, Stella Bowen. He played the healing war hero to a captive audience. "Beneath the sagging roof," Pound would write of him in *Hugh Selwyn Mauberley* (1920), the "stylist has taken shelter . . . with a placid and uneducated mistress."[50] It was "heaven" at last.

After the armistice the time for manifestos had passed. For both feminists and Vorticists, the *Suffragette* and *Blast* were no more. And in some ways, the wars these manifestos had initiated seemed to be won: not only was the peace signed in 1918, but the vote was granted to women over thirty and the first chapters of *Ulysses* were published in the *Little Review*. Yet the tensions continued.[51] Lytton Strachey's *Eminent Victorians* (1918) extended the modernist battle against nineteenth-century taste with rhetoric borrowed from the Great War: a biographer must "attack his subject in unexpected places; he will fall upon the flank, or the rear; he will shoot a sudden, revealing searchlight into obscure recesses, hitherto undivined." The male modernist war also continued to resist an alliance with the feminist war. "Surrender to a woman," wrote Lewis in *Tarr* (first published in book form in 1918) "was a sort of suicide for an artist." And at the same time the feminists took stock of the Great War's effect on their own. In *The Return of the Soldier* (1918) Rebecca West's narrator pictures her soldier brother "somewhere behind the front," walking past a ruined French village: "I am no more dear [to him] than the bare-armed slut at the neighbouring door."[52]

May Sinclair was right to see that the vortex of the Great War had subsumed the energy of the vortices of art and feminism. Each movement, as she wrote in *The Tree of Heaven*, was part of "the immense Vortex of the young century. If you had youth and life in you, you were in revolt."[53] Not only *The Tree of Heaven* gives evidence of this precept. In the early years of our century, these three wars were inextricably intertwined in the work of both male and female artists who tried to come to terms with the construction of gender in a postwar world. Although the pressure of the war is most keenly felt in *Mrs. Dalloway* (1925), it is no exaggeration to say that every postwar novel by Virginia Woolf examines the linked battles of modernism, sexism, and the Somme. In January 1916 Woolf wrote that the war was a "preposterous masculine fiction."[54]

At the same time, she was writing fictions that self-consciously avoided the public world of the war; in *To the Lighthouse* (1927) the duration of the war and the death of Andrew Ramsey would be reduced to two brief sentences: "A shell exploded. Twenty or thirty young men were blown up in France, among them Andrew Ramsey, whose death, mercifully, was instantaneous."[55] When Woolf wrote in "Modern Fiction" (1919) that writers should not "take it for granted that life exists more fully in what is commonly thought big than in what is commonly thought small,"[56] she was not only defending her "modern" writing but exploring what would commonly be thought of as a feminine perspective on war. In *Jacob's Room* (1922), Woolf's first novel to embody fully the dicta of "Modern Fiction," the life of the ominously named Jacob Flanders (who would die in the war) is told not so much in terms of the masculine world of public history as in the feminine world of domestic detail. Jacob's biography implicitly provides a negative answer to the question asked in an essay he wrote at Cambridge: "Does History Consist of the Biographies of Great Men?"[57]

Yet even as Woolf establishes these parallel dualisms (male and female, public and private, heroic and domestic), she immediately undermines them. It is not that the war exists only in the public world of masculine heroism; the war also takes place in the private space of feminine detail. Woolf expresses this deconstruction of culturally enforced dualisms most dramatically at the end of *Jacob's Room* when Betty Flanders hears the roar of the sea and transforms the sound into both artillery fire across the channel and an army of women engaged in domestic battle:

> "The guns?" said Betty Flanders, half asleep, getting out of bed and going to the window, which was decorated with a fringe of dark leaves.
>
> "Not at this distance," she thought. "It is the sea."
>
> Again, far away, she heard the dull sound, as if nocturnal women were beating great carpets. There was Morty lost, and Seabrook dead; her sons fighting for their country. But were the chickens safe? Was that some one moving downstairs? Rebecca with the toothache? No. The nocturnal women were beating great carpets. Her hens shifted slightly on their perches.[58]

As Woolf declared war on the "preposterous masculine fictions" of Wells, Bennett, and Galsworthy, she had no choice but to address the other wars of her time. Even *The Waste Land*, perhaps the most utterly canonical text of Anglo-American literary modernism, was necessarily an examination of the war and its relationship to sexual politics at the same time that it was (in Pound's words) "the justification of the 'movement,' of our modern experiment, since 1900."[59]

> When Lil's husband was coming back out of the Transport
>   Corps
> I didn't mince my words, I said to her myself,
> HURRY UP PLEASE IT'S TIME.
> "Now Albert's coming back, make yourself a bit smart.
> . . . .
> "He's been in the army four years, he wants a good time,
> "And if you don't give it him, there's many another will".
> "Other women", she said, "Something of that", I said.
> "Then I'll know who to thank", she said, and gave me a
>   straight look.
> HURRY UP PLEASE IT'S TIME.
> "No, ma'am, you needn't look old-fashioned at me", I said,
> "Others can pick and choose if you can't.[60]

In this draft for lines in "A Game of Chess" (the references to the "Transport Corps," the "army," and the "old-fashioned" look were eventually deleted) we can see more clearly that the poem addressed not only an "old-fashioned" conception of poetry but an "old-fashioned" sexual morality that the war seemed to have destroyed. But a quick gambol through Eliot's prewar poetry shows that the tensions were there all along; from a historical point of view, the only difference between Prufrock's and Tiresias's sexual conundrums is that the latter persona is given a soothing halo of cultural resonance that offers an epochal explanation for a personal crisis.

Quickly hailed as the apocalypse, the Great War made it easy for some soldiers in the war between men and women to believe that their troubles subsided as the dust settled in Flanders—that society had been transformed utterly. Despite the fact that votes for women came at the same time as the armistice, the effect of the war on British society, as we have seen, was not so unambiguous. Both Ford Madox Ford's *Parade's End* and Rebecca West's *The Return of the Soldier* revolve around a male character who fights in the trenches and loses his memory. While Ford's Christopher Tietjens forgets the entire history of civilization and reads the encyclopedia to regain it, West's Christopher Baldry forgets his wife and remembers only an earlier lost love. Both characters are cured of their delusions. Before and during the war, Teitjens is plagued by his estranged wife Sylvia; though he loves Valentine, he is unable (being another good soldier) to consummate their relationship because of his strongly bred Edwardian morality. After the war, however, he overcomes this obstacle, and he and Valentine plan to consummate their love on armistice day. It is a perfect ending—too perfect, in fact, for it implies that peace between women and men came naturally with peace between England and Germany. Rebecca West presents a similar scenario more sternly. When Baldry is cured of his memory lapse, he must return to a woman he does not love, a life he does not value—and a war that has not yet ended. Ford's protagonist is reborn into a new life; West's is reborn into the life he has always known, and there is no sense that one age has ended and a new age begun. Neither the Great War nor the war between women and men comes to an easy conclusion in *The Return of the Soldier*. Even before the war began some suffragettes recognized that their "sex war" was initiated "long before Votes for Women was first whispered." And if the men of 1914 wanted to believe that the battle of the sexes had been won with the Great War, the women of 1914 suspected that more battles would be fought.

Notes

In writing this essay I have benefited from the advice and criticism of Carol Barash, Samuel Hynes, A. Walton Litz, Bette London, Joanna Scott, and Keith Waldrop.

1. Pound, "Wyndham Lewis," 233.

2. For a discussion of prewar suffragette militancy see Vicinus, *Independent Women*. The most sophisticated discussion of the movement's battles (in both public and private spheres) is Kent, *Sex and Suffrage*. Useful information may also be found in Liddington and Norris, *One Hand Tied Behind Us*; Mitchell, *Monstrous Regiment*; and Rosen, *Rise Up, Women*. For a discussion of changing constructions of gender during the prewar period see Smith-Rosenberg, *Disorderly Conduct*; for a discussion of the war's effect on gender construction in psychotherapy see Showalter, *The Female Malady*, 167–94.

3. Lewis, "TO SUFFRAGETTES," 151–52.

4. Sinclair, *The Tree of Heaven*, 233, 162, 233, 299.

5. Woolf, *The Captain's Death Bed*, 96. Woolf made this comment in "Mr. Bennett and Mrs. Brown," first delivered as a lecture at Cambridge on May 18, 1924.

6. Christabel Pankhurst, "How Men Fight," 163.

7. "Moral versus Physical Force," 161.

8. West, "Indissoluble Matrimony," 98, 102, 104, 110, 117.

9. Pound, "Suffragettes," 254–55. Before it was named the *Egoist* or the *New Freewoman*, the magazine was called the *Freewoman*. See Barash, "Dora Marsden's Feminism," for an analysis of the magazine's nominal and ideological transformations.

10. Gilbert, "Soldier's Heart," 425. Gilbert and Gubar have more recently expanded some aspects of this essay's argument in the first volume of *No Man's Land*; they promise a more detailed treatment of the Great War in the forthcoming volumes of their trilogy.

11. Schreiner, *An Olive Schreiner Reader*, 206, 207. For the suffragettes' response to *Women and Labour* see Barash's introduction to this volume, 17, and Kent, *Sex and Suffrage*, 147.

12. Stobart, *War and Women*, xi, 8.

13. "Women Tram Conductors," 12.

14. Lawrence, *Complete Short Stories*, 2:345.

15. West, "Indissoluble Matrimony," 111.

16. Lawrence, *Complete Poems*, 763–66.

17. Christabel Pankhurst, "THE WAR," 301.

18. Christabel Pankhurst, "We Will Not Be Prussianized," 6.

19. " 'The Suffragette' Welcomed," 19.

20. "Speculations on Sex War," 65.

21. Ford, *The Good Soldier*, 3. This first sentence was added to the novel after Ford's publisher persuaded him to change the title from *The Saddest Story* (under which the first three and a half chapters appeared in *Blast* in 1914).

22. Ibid., xviii.

23. Ibid., 5. This passage may also be found in the portion of the novel published as "The Saddest Story," 87–88.

24. Ibid., 77–78. Ford employs an unusually large number of ellipses in his writing; to distinguish mine from his, I place mine in brackets.

25. Ford, *Parade's End*, 491.

26. Ford, *Return to Yesterday*, 349.

27. Hueffer [Ford], "Militants Here on Earth," 137, 141, 142.

28. Hueffer [Ford], *The Critical Attitude*, 168.

29. Hueffer [Ford], *This Monstrous Regiment of Women*, 26–27, 18–19.

30. Hunt, *I Have This to Say*, 73.

31. Secor and Secor, *Return of the Good Soldier*, 8. See also Mizener, *The Saddest Story*, 171–284, for a detailed account of Ford and Hunt's relationship.

32. Henry James to Violet Hunt, November 2, 1909; in Mizener, *The Saddest Story*, 196.

33. Ford, *Women and Men*, 14, 46.

34. Compare Woolf in *Three Guineas*, 4: There is "a gulf so deeply cut between [women and men] . . . that for three years and more I have been sitting on my side of it wondering if it is any use to try to speak across it."

35. Hueffer [Ford], *On Heaven*, 110.

36. See Secor and Secor, *Return of the Good Soldier*, 19.

37. Ibid., 23.

38. Hunt, "Merciful Aphasia," 271.

39. Hunt, *More Tales of the Uneasy*, 88, 83, 90.

40. Hueffer [Ford] to J. B. Pinker, March 9, 1911; in Mizener, *The Saddest Story*, 210.

41. Pound, *Pound/Ford*, 70.

42. Ford, "Epilogue," 152. Portions of this manuscript were worked into Ford's autobiographical novel, *No Enemy* (1929).

43. Ibid., 161–62.

44. Woolf, *Three Guineas*, 39.

45. Emmeline Pankhurst, "What Is Our Duty?," 25.

46. E. Sylvia Pankhurst, "Why Governments Refuse to Tell," 640.

47. Emmeline Pankhurst, "A Message from Mrs. Pankhurst," 174. For Sylvia Pankhurst's account of this quarrel see her *Suffragette Movement*, 594–95.

48. Hueffer [Ford], "The Silver Music," 19; Hunt, "Is It Worth While?," 21.

49. Secor and Secor, *Return of the Good Soldier*, 152.

50. Pound, *Personae*, 195.

51. See Kent, *Sex and Suffrage*, 220–31, for an analysis of the postwar decline of the feminist movement in Britain. Not only was there intense pressure on women to leave their wartime jobs and return to prewar domesticity; Kent also points out that gaining the vote was only part of the battle: "Because feminists accepted the terms of liberal political discourse —that power lay in the vote—they directed the brunt of their attack on the centralized power of the state. Feminists gained access to state institutions, but they failed to gain control of the sexual discourse—particularly that sexual discourse articulated by the psychoanalytic profession—and thereby reconstruct the models of 'masculinity' and 'femininity'" (227).

52. Strachey, *Eminent Victorians*, v; Lewis, *Tarr*, 215; West, *The Return of the Soldier*, 135, 136.

53. Sinclair, *The Tree of Heaven*, 163.

54. Woolf, *Letters*, 2:76.

55. Woolf, *To the Lighthouse*, 201.

56. Woolf, *The Common Reader*, 155.

57. Woolf, *Jacob's Room*, 39.

58. Ibid., 175. Woolf's intermingling of public and private discourse enacts what Susan Kent sees as the suffragettes' goal—"The elimination of separate sphere ideology that justified the sexual classification of women":

"Nineteenth-century feminists argued . . . that the public and the private were not distinct spheres but were inseparable from one another; the public was private, the personal was political" (*Sex and Suffrage*, 205, 5).

59. Pound, *Selected Letters*, 180.

60. Eliot, *The Waste Land: A Facsimile*, 13.

Works Cited

Barash, Carol L. "Dora Marsden's Feminism, the *Freewoman*, and the Gender Politics of Early Modernism." *Princeton University Library Chronicle* 49 (Autumn 1987): 31–56.

Eliot, T. S. *The Waste Land: A Facsimile and Transcript of the Original Drafts*. Edited by Valerie Eliot. New York: Harcourt, Brace & World, 1971.

Ford, Ford Madox. "Epilogue." Manuscript in the Princeton University Library. Quoted in James Longenbach, "Ford Madox Ford: The Novelist as Historian." *Princeton University Library Chronicle* 45 (Winter 1984): 150–66.

———. *The Good Soldier*. New York: Vintage Books, 1951.

———. *Parade's End*. New York: Vintage Books, 1979.

———. *Return to Yesterday*. New York: Horace Liveright, 1932.

———. *Women and Men*. Paris: Three Mountains Press, 1923.

Gilbert, Sandra M. "Soldier's Heart: Literary Men, Literary Women, and the Great War." *Signs* 8, no. 3 (Spring 1983): 422–50.

Gilbert, Sandra M., and Susan Gubar. *No Man's Land: The Place of the Woman Writer in the Twentieth Century*. Vol. 1, *The War of the Words*. New Haven: Yale University Press, 1988.

Hueffer [Ford], Ford Madox. *The Critical Attitude*. Freeport, N.Y.: Books for Library Press, 1967.

———. "Militants Here on Earth." *English Review* 3 (August 1909): 137–42.

———. *On Heaven and Other Poems Written in Active Service*. London: John Lane, 1918.

———. "The Saddest Story." *Blast* 1 (June 20, 1914): 87–97.

———. "The Silver Music." *Poetry* 12 (April 1918): 19–20.

———. *This Monstrous Regiment of Women*. London: Women's Freedom League, n.d. [1913].

Hunt, Violet. *I Have This to Say*. New York: Boni & Liveright, 1926.

———. "Is It Worth While?" *Poetry* 12 (April 1918): 21.

———. "Merciful Aphasia." *Outlook* 36 (August 28, 1915): 271.

———. *More Tales of the Uneasy*. London: Heinemann, 1925.

Kent, Susan. *Sex and Suffrage in Britain, 1860–1914*. Princeton, N.J.: Princeton University Press, 1987.

Lawrence, D. H. *The Complete Poems*. Edited by Vivian de Sola Pinto. New York: Penguin Books, 1980.

———. *The Complete Short Stories*, vol. 2. New York: Penguin Books, 1976.

Lewis, Wyndham. *Tarr*. New York: Penguin Books, 1982.

———. "TO SUFFRAGETTES." *Blast* 1 (June 20, 1914): 151–52.

Liddington, Jill, and Jill Norris. *One Hand Tied Behind Us: The Rise of the Women's Suffrage Movement*. London: Virago Press, 1978.

Mitchell, David. *Monstrous Regiment: The Story of the Women of the First World War*. New York: Macmillan Co., 1965.

Mizener, Arthur. *The Saddest Story: A Biography of Ford Madox Ford*. New York: World Publishing Co., 1971.

"Moral versus Physical Force." *Suffragette* 3 (June 19, 1914): 161.

Pankhurst, Christabel. "How Men Fight." *Suffragette* 3 (June 19, 1914): 163.

———. "THE WAR." *Suffragette* 3 (August 7, 1914): 301.

———. "We Will Not Be Prussianized." *Suffragette* 4 (April 16, 1915): 6.

Pankhurst, E. Sylvia. *The Suffragette Movement: An Intimate Account of Persons and Ideals*. New York: Longmans, Green, 1931.

———. "Why Governments Refuse to Tell." *Women's Dreadnought* 3 (January 6, 1917): 640.

Pankhurst, Emmeline. "A Message from Mrs. Pankhurst." *Britannia* 5 (April 23, 1916): 174.

———. "What Is Our Duty?" *Suffragette* 4 (April 23, 1915): 25–26.

Pound, Ezra. *Personae: The Collected Shorter Poems*. New York: New Directions, 1971.

———. *Pound/Ford: The Story of a Literary Friendship*. Edited by Brita Lindberg-Seyersted. New York: New Directions, 1982.

———. *Selected Letters, 1907–1941*. Edited by D. D. Paige. New York: New Directions, 1971.

———. "Suffragettes." *Egoist* 1 (July 1, 1914): 254–56.

———. "Wyndham Lewis." *Egoist* 1 (July 15, 1914): 233–34.

Rosen, Andrew. *Rise Up, Women! The Militant Campaign of the Women's Social and Political Union, 1903–1914*. London: Routledge & Kegan Paul, 1974.

Schreiner, Olive. *An Olive Schreiner Reader: Writings on Women and South Africa*. Edited by Carol Barash. London: Pandora, 1987.

Secor, Robert, and Marie Secor. *The Return of the Good Soldier: Ford Madox Ford and Violet Hunt's 1917 Diary*. Victoria, British Columbia: English Literary Studies, 1983.

Showalter, Elaine. *The Female Malady: Women, Madness, and English Culture, 1830–1980*. New York: Pantheon, 1985.

Sinclair, May. *The Tree of Heaven*. New York: Macmillan Co., 1917.

Smith-Rosenberg, Carroll. *Disorderly Conduct: Visions of Gender in Victorian America.* New York: Alfred A. Knopf, 1985.

"Speculations on Sex War." *Freewoman* 1 (December 14, 1911): 65.

Stobart, St. Clair. *War and Women: From Experience in the Balkans and Elsewhere.* London: G. Bell & Sons, 1913.

Strachey, Lytton. *Eminent Victorians.* New York: Capricorn Books, 1963.

" 'The Suffragette' Welcomed." *Suffragette* 4 (April 23, 1915): 19.

Vicinus, Martha. *Independent Women: Work and Community for Single Women, 1850–1920.* Chicago: University of Chicago Press, 1985.

West, Rebecca. "Indissoluble Matrimony." *Blast* 1 (June 20, 1914): 98–117.

————. *The Return of the Soldier.* New York: Dial Press, 1980.

"Women Tram Conductors." *Suffragette* 4 (April 16, 1915): 12.

Woolf, Virginia. *The Captain's Death Bed and Other Essays.* New York: Harcourt, Brace & World, 1950.

————. *The Common Reader, First Series.* New York: Harcourt, Brace & World, 1953.

————. *Jacob's Room.* New York: Harcourt, Brace & World, 1960.

————. *The Letters of Virginia Woolf,* vol. 2. Edited by Nigel Nicolson. New York: Harcourt, Brace & World, 1976.

————. *Three Guineas.* New York: Harcourt, Brace & World, 1966.

————. *To the Lighthouse.* New York: Harcourt, Brace & World, 1955.

Jane Marcus

Corpus/Corps/Corpse:
Writing the Body in/at War

> [A] declaration of war should be a kind of popular festival with entrance-tickets and bands, like a bull fight. Then in the arena the ministers and generals of the two countries, dressed in bathing-drawers and armed with clubs, can have it out among themselves. Whoever survives, his country wins. That would be much simpler and more just than this arrangement, where the wrong people do the fighting.—Erich Maria Remarque, *All Quiet on the Western Front*

> Any day and in every way this can be seen, eating and vomiting and war.—Gertrude Stein, *Wars I Have Seen*

La Zone Interdite

Helen Zenna Smith's *Not So Quiet . . .* (1930) is a book about the body. Specifically, it chronicles the experience of a corps of six English gentlewomen, whose average age is twenty-one, as they drive field ambulances of wounded men picked up by trains at the front to hospitals set up just behind the fighting lines, in what Mary Borden has also memorialized as "the forbidden zone" in France in 1918.[1] Their war is not a popular festival, like Erich Maria Remarque's in *All Quiet on the Western Front*. It is a grotesque of the "brotherhood" felt by the German men, an inversion of "sisterhood." Helen and her companions are volunteer ambulance drivers. They, like VAD (Volunteer Aid Detachment) nurses, have actually paid for the privilege of serving at the front, their patriotic upper-class families proud to sacrifice daughters as well as sons for the war effort, providing their passage money and their uniforms, sending packages of cocoa and carbolic body belts to keep off the lice.

These body belts, personal disinfectants, always fighting a losing battle against the invasion of delicately bred female bodies by lice and fleas, worn between skin and rough clothing, suggest a "forbidden zone" on the body, dividing upper and lower, the spiritual and the physical. They remind us of the chastity belts with which men of an earlier age "protected" the bodies of their womenfolk from invasion by other men while they were at war, an age when women's bodies were clearly defined as the property of men. Like the forbidden zone itself, marked neutral by signs and barbed wire, an unholy territory of dead and dying men, the wounded and their hospitals, the ambulance drivers and VAD nurses were marked out for the most polluted of war work. Like gravediggers in peacetime they were shunned by the society whose dirty work they did. They were neither the "ladies" they had been brought up to be, nor were they paid professionals, like the working-class nurses in the Women's Army Auxiliary Corps (WAAC) or Women's Royal Naval Service (WREN), who were respected and rewarded for their labor. They were both terrorized and scorned by women in the regular armed services, precisely because they were volunteers but also because they were ladies exposed to the most acute physical horrors, suffering themselves under severe hardships for which a comfortable life at home with servants had hardly prepared them. They made everyone except their patriotic parents at home feel ashamed.

Like a company of Wagnerian Valkyries (though of course they would not have made such a Germanic comparison themselves), the ambulance drivers resembled Amazon goddesses, carrying slain soldiers from the battlefield to glory in Valhalla or to hospitals where they could recover to fight again. The ambulances were the mythical horses of the modern Valkyries, and the women drivers cared for their engines as if they were horses. European intellectuals welcomed the war as a mystical purification of decadence, a revolution against greed and materialism. Women would, as usual, clean up the mess. Transporting the dead or dying is a dangerous job, but it has also always been invested with mythological significance. The ferryman who guards the borders of life and death is a ghostly figure in our cultural myths. This corps of ferrywomen seems unreal as well, ghosts whose bodies had disappeared from history until revived by the reprinting of *Not So Quiet . . . .*[2] All motor vehicles were rare and glamorous creatures at this time, and driving itself a male and upper-class activity. In stiff-upper-lipped long-suffering bravery, the women had to be superhuman, driving for weeks on three hours of sleep a night, eating spoiled food, and very little of that (no decent army rations for volunteers). They became experts at the geography of hell, driving at night with their lights off in the freezing cold and snow (the cabs were open to the elements, the backs of the lorries covered with canvas) with their loads of screaming and moaning wounded.

One assumes that the War Office counted on class codes of honor to keep the women from telling or writing what they had seen or heard. *Not So Quiet . . .* brilliantly broke the sound barrier about what "Our Splendid Women" had really seen and heard and done in the war, offending all of those who had blocked their ears. When *Not So Quiet . . .* was published, one English reviewer suggested that it be burned (but the French gave it the Prix Sevigne as "the novel most calculated to promote international peace"). Young, healthy, well-educated women became the charwomen of the battlefield, the cleaners of the worst human waste we produce, the symbolic bearers of all its pollution and disease. Like the mythological ferryman, their bodies became *la zone interdite*, for themselves as well as for those who sent them to the battlefields, forbidden, dangerous, polluted carriers of a terrible knowledge. This knowledge effectively separated them from the complacent, jingoist home front and the mobile battlefronts, which left these polluted zones behind as they moved on.

Because women's role in World War I and women's writing about that war is just beginning to receive attention, I want to begin with a discussion of the issues surrounding historical and literary revaluation. In particular, because *Not So Quiet . . .* is not in any sense an example of *écriture feminine* but a textual deconstruction of gender stereotypes in writing, it is important to place it in relation to other women's war writing.

In 1929, the American VAD nurse, Mary Borden, published her poems and sketches, written during 1914–18 when she was with the French Army, along with five stories written after the war: "I have called the collection of fragments 'The Forbidden Zone' because the strip of land immediately behind the zone of fire where I was stationed went by that name in the French Army. We were moved up and down inside it; our hospital unit was shifted from Flanders to the Somme, then to Champagne, and then back again to Belgium, but we never left 'La Zone Interdite.' "[3] The horrors of the forbidden territories also extended to an unspoken ban on writing about it—Enid Bagnold was dismissed from her VAD post after publishing *A Diary without Dates* in 1918.[4] Both of these collections of fragments document women's wartime experience in essentially "feminine" voices. Serious literary achievements, the books are marked by the fragmentation and dislocation of poignant love/war battles and the romantic and chivalric, almost religious, ethos of self-sacrifice. Enid Bagnold is proud of her nursing ability, which brings order and tranquillity to a hospital full of wounded men. Like a nun, she domesticates devastation. She writes:

> I lay my spoons and forks. Sixty-five trays. It takes an hour to do. Thirteen pieces on each tray. Thirteen times sixty-five . . . eight hundred and forty-five things to collect, lay, square up symmetrically. I make little absurd reflections and arrangements—taking a dislike to the knives because they will not lie still on the polished metal of the tray, but pivot on their shafts, and swing out at angles after my fingers have left them.[5]

Her pride in gleaming trays and scrubbed corridors is obviously a little human success after the failure to bring such healing graces to the suffering soldiers. (Though the knives will truly never lie still.) The women drivers in her later *The Happy Foreigner* are as attentive to the material objects in their charge—the cars they drive for the French Army—and the heroine puts a whole village to work making a dress for her to wear to a dance with a French officer.

Mary Borden's book is equally interesting on an aesthetic level. While Bagnold's voice is lyrically nostalgic and romantic, despite the chronicle of hardship for volunteer nurses, Borden is a modernist, obviously influenced by Gertrude Stein. She carried Stein and Flaubert to the front with her, and *The Forbidden Zone* speaks in her flat Chicago accent. It is hallucinatory and yet detached. The voice seems submerged in the unconscious like a nightmare that numbs with repetition. She, too, turns to material objects for solace at the sight of maimed men:

> I had received by post that same morning a dozen beautiful new platinum needles. I was very pleased with them. I said to one of the dressers as I fixed a needle on my syringe and held it up, squirting the liquid through it: "Look, I've got some lovely new needles." He said: "Come and help me a moment. Just cut this bandage, please." I went over to his dressing table. He darted off to a voice that was shrieking somewhere. There was a man stretched on the table. His brain came off in my hands when I lifted the bandage from his head. When the dresser came back I said: "His brain came off on the bandage." "Where have you put it?" "I put it in the pail under the table." "It's

only one half of his brain," he said, looking into the man's skull. "The rest is here." I left him to finish the dressing and went about my own business. I had much to do. It was my business to sort out the wounded as they were brought in from the ambulances and to keep them from dying before they got to the operating rooms: It was my business to sort out the nearly dying from the dying. I was there to sort them and tell how fast life was ebbing in them. Life was leaking away from all of them; but with some there was no hurry, with others it was a case of minutes. It was my business to create a counter-wave of life, to create the flow against the ebb. It was like a tug of war with the tide.[6]

The repetition of the word "business" in such circumstances, and the brief emotionless descriptive sentences, mark a detachment that has a calculated effect on the reader. We understand her pleasure in her new needles. Borden simply cannot bear the burden of womanhood and continue to work with wounded men.

It is impossible to be a woman here. One must be dead. . . . There are no men here, so why should I be a woman? There are heads and knees and mangled testicles. There are chests with holes as big as your fist, and pulpy thighs, shapeless; and stumps where legs once were fastened. There are eyes—eyes of sick dogs, sick cats, blind eyes, eyes of delirium; and mouths that cannot articulate; and parts of faces—the nose gone, or the jaw. There are these things, but no men . . . [7]

The fragmented bodies of men are reproduced in the fragmented parts of women's war texts, the texts themselves a "forbidden zone" long ignored by historians and literary critics. Writers of war produce pieces of texts, like parts of a body that will never be whole. The texts are specific to World War I and the kinds of warfare specific to that particularly horrible war and its mutilation of millions of bodies. They wrote the body of war, the wounded soldier's body and their own newly sexualized (only to be numbed) bodies as well as the effect of war on the body politic. The textual fragmentation marks the pages of their books as the forbidden zone of writing what hasn't been written before, and their books actually look like battlefields where the body of Mother Earth has been torn apart by shells and bombs. The works of Mary Borden and Enid Bagnold, cited above, are not exceptional. There are many important women war writers. A materialist analysis of the fragmented texts would look immediately to the passage in Irene Rathbone's *We That Were Young* (1932) that excruciatingly details the step-by-step process by which a nurse removes fragments of shrapnel from a soldier's wound. One might then observe that the fragmentation described as typical of modernist texts has an origin in the writing practice of women nurses and ambulance drivers. The recent discovery and reprinting of many "lost" examples of women's war writing by Virago Press and the Feminist Press may be linked to the work of feminist scholars in many disciplines over the last fifteen years. This work ranges from psychological studies of gender and aggression, to new historical studies of pacifism, to philosophical treatises, such as Nancy Huston's provocative essay on the relation between war and motherhood, which explores the hypothesis that men make war *because* women make babies.[8]

The study of World War I and its effect on women in England begins with the acknowledgment that all wars destroy women's culture, returning women to the restricted roles of childbearing and nursing and only the work that helps the war effort. The struggle for women's own political equality becomes almost treasonous in wartime. World War I practically destroyed the women's movement in England, an extraordinary mass movement of women who struggled for nearly fifty years to obtain political justice and equality with regard to education, the vote, and legislation concerning marriage, divorce, child custody, and labor practices. Any account of women's energetic and responsible performance of social labor during wartime must recognize that their performance in the public sphere came from the previous struggle against an immensely hostile state to win the elements of education, knowledge, and skills which any democracy customarily grants its citizens today, but which, in Edwardian England, were systematically denied to half the population. The self-education in political organization, public speaking, social work, and other areas that thousands of English women *provided for themselves* as they worked tirelessly in the suffrage movement against the ruthless repression of the Liberal government is the source of such strengths commonly attributed by historians to a mythical "natural" female ethic of heroic self-sacrifice.[9]

In *The Daily Chronicle* in 1916, Rebecca West reminded her readers that it was "the rough and tumble" of the suffrage movement that hardened women for their wartime tasks:

The story of the Scottish Suffrage Societies' Hospital in Serbia and Rumania is immortal. The biggest factory in France which supplies an article most necessary to our armies is under the sole charge of a woman under thirty, who was formerly a suffrage organiser. One could cite many such cases. And one doubts that women would have gone into the dangerous high explosive factories, the engineering shops and the fields, and worked with quite such fidelity and enthusiasm if it had not been so vigorously affirmed by the suffragists in the last few years that women ought to be independent and courageous and capable.[10]

We cannot assume that it was easy for women experiencing this newly transformed collective feminist consciousness to give up the struggle for freedom, despite the alacrity with which Emmeline Pankhurst and her daughter, Christabel, the militant suffrage leaders, began to harass conscientious objectors, or the fact that many women did identify with the ethic of self-sacrifice and produced books urging nursing and ambulance driving as opportunities for the full expression of the female need to suffer. But Rebecca West and other (especially left-wing) feminist theorists had already before the war punched holes in the idea of self-sacrifice as natural to women, and there is no reason to suppose that these brilliant deflations of the reigning ideology were so easily forgotten. And yet, even feminists "forgot." One agrees with Rebecca West's assessment of May Sinclair's *Journal of Impressions in Belgium* as "one of the few books of permanent value produced by the war." It should be read as a companion volume to *Not So Quiet* . . . . But her novel, *The Romantic*, mocks the unmanly man as viciously as scandalized old ladies wrote to the papers about "She-men" in uniforms.

Certainly F. Tennyson Jesse's *The Sword of Deborah* (1919) is sheer propaganda for recruiting VADs and WAACs: "How could we bear to do nothing when the men are doing the most wonderful thing in the world?" And when Charlotte Redhead in May Sinclair's *The Romantic* (1920) rejects John Conway, her lover, because of his cowardice (and her own fearlessness) as they drive field ambulances in Belgium, she seems to support Sandra Gilbert's thesis that women rose at the expense of man's fall. It seems just as logical to suppose that women who had fought in the streets to protect and demand votes for women should be ready for action at the front.

Obviously, war values dispensed horrifying shame to men who were deemed cowards. Early in the war Rose Macaulay wrote, "Oh, it's you that have the luck, out there in the blood and muck / . . . In a trench you are sitting, while I am knitting / A hopeless sock that never gets done."[11]

But May Sinclair in *The Romantic* created a realistically revengeful portrait of the weak male from the point of view of the strong female. Why did gender distinctions keep her from action? Charlotte's psychoanalyst condemns Conway. A more human analysis would allow more room for men lacking in the brutal, aggressive qualities required for war:

Conway was an out and out degenerate. He couldn't help *that*. He suffered from some physical disability. It went through everything. It made him so that he couldn't live a man's life. He was afraid to enter a profession. He was afraid of women . . . the balance had to be righted somehow. His whole life must have been a struggle to right it. Unconscious, of course. Instinctive. His platonics were just a glorifying of his disability. All that romancing was a gorgeous transformation of his funk . . . so that his very lying was a sort of truth. I mean it was part of the whole desperate effort after completion. He jumped at everything that helped him to get compensation, to get power. He jumped at your feeling for him because it gave him power. He sucked manhood out of you. He sucked it out of everything—out of blood and wound.[12]

There it is. In wartime, the impotent male is a vampire. The language of popular psychology joins the discourse of martial valor—degenerate, disability, funk, jumped, sucked—to condemn those who don't fit the most polarized gender categories. Men must be potent. Women must be maternal. Sinclair's voicing of the popular fear of male weakness in war also reveals the unspoken truth that men were just as terrified of war as women. Virginia Woolf valorizes the impotent suicidal Septimus Smith in *Mrs. Dalloway*. And Sylvia Townsend Warner brilliantly mocks the enforced rigidity of wartime sex roles in her splendid poem, "Cottage Mantleshelf," which celebrates the "uncomely" portrait of "young Osbert who died at the war," a "nancy boy" with enormous ears, whose "beseeching swagger" endears him to the reader. The poem is an English "red and black" tribute to a victim of the ideology, "Keep the home fires burning."[13]

Joan Scott's introductory essay in *Behind the Lines* is the most sophisticated guide to date to a methodology for feminist historiography in the service of a cultural critique. She warns against facile reversals of established theories, the projection of present concerns onto the past, and the simple search for heroines. Women's literature of World War I runs the gamut from patriotic propaganda to pacifist protest. For all those who jeered at conscientious objectors and handed them white feathers, there were also the founders of the Women's International League for Peace and Freedom. Artistic standards will have to acknowledge the greatness of "Cottage Mantleshelf" as well as much other writing by women about the war, now that patriotism no longer dictates that the combatant's writing is superior to that of the noncombatant. We need to examine the war ministries' posters and propaganda images of men and women for all the countries involved in the war, to contextualize German and French writing with British fiction and the autobiographies of American volunteer nurses.

The effort to expand the literary canon is greatly aided by publishers such as the Feminist Press and Virago Press in reprinting lost texts. For example, the reprinting of Katharine Burdekin's *Swastika Night*, a feminist dystopia from the thirties, allows for fresh and interesting ways to read George Orwell's classic *1984* and to view Nazi ideology from the perspective of its misogyny, a neglected area since historians have concentrated particularly on anti-Semitism. While I intend here to examine Helen Zenna Smith's *Not So Quiet . . .* in conjunction with Erich Maria Remarque's classic *All Quiet on the Western Front*, on which it was based, a more thorough examination of the issues raised would have to take into account the French and Belgian women's experiences of invasion and bombardment. Dorothy Canfield's *Home Fires in France* (1919), a collection of short stories, might be analyzed, as well as Colette's wartime newspaper articles.

Women's history asks that we look not only at war texts but at those particular fictions in which suffrage and war overlap and intermix. There are some excellent examples: Cecily Hamilton's *William, An Englishman*, May Sinclair's *The Tree of Heaven*, and Ford Madox Ford's *Some Do Not* and *No More Parades*, two of the Tietjens novels, which tell the same events from different characters' viewpoints, wonderfully deconstructing the meanings of feminism, patriotism, marriage, war, religion, and all the social issues of the period. Ford's two novels are perhaps the best literary representations of all the issues under discussion here. Ford himself seems to have been anything but an admirable character, but his brilliant modernist fictional techniques—in particular, the undermining of narrative authority, schooling his readers in the unreliability of all narratives—evoke the instability of an age of conflicting values more powerfully than the more valorized work of T. S. Eliot or Ezra Pound. In addition, these novels, like Irene Rathbone's *We That Were Young*, allow the reader to escape from the standard historical confines of wartime and peacetime. Rathbone's later *They Call It Peace* (1936) in fact deconstructs this convenient historical fiction, showing that the government continued to wage war against women and the working class between the wars.

William, An Englishman is another story. Cecily Hamilton had certainly earned her credentials as an active suffragette and had written plays and polemics for the cause. Yet its "feminism" is disturbing, despite the fact that it won the Femina Prize in 1919. "Neither William nor Griselda had ever entertained the idea of a European War; it was not entertained by any of their friends or their pamphlets." William and Griselda are socialists and activists in the suffrage campaign. He, a clerk, inherits a small amount of money from his mother and throws himself into political action and public speaking, "a ferment of protestation and grievance." Griselda, a suburban suffragette, is attracted to him because of the pleasure they share in denouncing the enemies of their cause. Hamilton's ruthless satire of political activists is amusing, for we all know the type—"cocksure, contemptuous, intolerant, self-sacrificing after the manner of their kind." However, their punishment for not knowing the war has begun when they go off to honeymoon in Belgium is a little excessive. Moved to leave their woodland retreat because Griselda "missed the weekly temper into which she worked herself in sympathy with her weekly *Suffragette*," they are devastated by seeing the Germans shoot innocent villagers. She is raped and he is put in a work camp. Escaping to find her again, William is horrified by her silence; then, melodramatically, "she die[s] very quietly in the straw at the bottom of the cart."[14]

Hamilton rather overdoes the death of Griselda as "real" suffering compared to her previous choice to go on a hunger strike and be forcibly fed in Holloway Gaol for the cause of suffrage. The newly patriotic William is rejected by the British Army and dies unheroically in a bombing raid. This novel is a shameless example of the ideological repression of both socialism and feminism that was one of the major social achievements of World War I. Certainly in England, the war was a stunning setback to the struggle for liberty at home. Arthur Marwick's *The Deluge: British Society and the First World War* is the honorable exception to histories of the war that ignore "the forbidden zone" of the class struggle and the repression of women. His *Women at War*, along with Gail Braybon's *Women Workers in the First World War* and Anne Wiltsher's *Most Dangerous Women: Feminist Peace Campaigners of the Great War*, have trespassed quite firmly on the forbidden zone of World War I history. For other examples of how quickly the European intellectuals rallied around their respective flags, see Roland N. Stromberg's *Redemption by War: The Intellectuals and 1914*, though he doesn't include women among the "intellectuals."

Like Hamilton's *William, An Englishman*, the insularity of the ordinary English folk is also the point of H. G. Wells's *Mr. Britling Sees It Through*, but suffrage again becomes the scapegoat in May Sinclair's *The Tree of Heaven* (1917). Frances and Anthony refuse to face up to the Boer War, but they and their children eventually reject suffrage and pacifism and movements for political justice at home for an almost evangelical devotion to "the Great War of Redemption." All the authors cited here (male and female) were active in the suffrage campaign. Their fiction is the field on which we may see a great ideological battle fought, where the struggle for sexual freedom becomes "silly" and the leaders, like the Pankhursts, are called protofascists as the war mentality condones militarism, nationalism, and patriotism. On the pages of these obscure novels we see how quickly the intellectuals come to the aid of their country, embracing violence and war as a mystical cleansing, rejecting the feminist, pacifist, and socialist reforms needed at home to agree to internationalist slaughter of a whole generation in the name of democracy. Stromberg documents the ideology of destruction as spiritual and idealistic renewal. The authoritarian nature of the ideological powers to which this generation submitted is then displaced onto a critique of authoritarianism within the suffrage movement (perhaps out of guilt for their joy in war [?] and abandonment of the struggle for real social change at home).

This is not to argue that there was not some justice in the earlier claim by Mrs. Charlotte Despard and the Women's Freedom League that the Women's Social and Political Union (WSPU) was an autocratic paramilitary organization. In many ways it was. But those young women—who had pledged total commitment to the suffrage cause and obedience to its leaders, who had learned to speak in public and defy their families and the law to march in the streets, who had been attacked by hecklers and ruffians, gone on hunger strikes in prison, and been forcibly fed—were the perfect recruits for war work. They were disciplined and self-controlled. It has always seemed to me very curious that historians do not mention the suffrage campaign as the training ground for ambulance drivers and VAD nurses in World War I. Bravery, physical courage, chivalry, group solidarity, strategic planning, honor—these things women had learned in the streets and jails of London, the *first* "forbidden zone" they had entered. The spiritual and sacramental aspects of the suffrage movement as a "holy war" were exploited by idealist figurations of the war as a purge of bourgeois materialism.

Then again, historians also neglect to mention that the work of these women, glamorous heroines to younger generations, was for a long time refused by the British government. "My good lady, go home and sit still" was what the War Office told the distinguished Dr. Elsie Inglis when she offered them a fully staffed medical unit with women doctors and nurses![15] The French government hired her to take this staff to Serbia. Cecily Hamilton remarked in her autobiography that the British were so opposed to hospitals *run* by women that all the British women's hospital units were employed by the Allies, France and Russia, and operated in France, the Balkans, and in Russia. These fully trained groups of women doctors and nurses were far less popular than the volunteer upper-class girls who could be shown in uniform in the picture papers, glamorous, pretty, and clearly unprofessional. The "Balkanization" of British women doctors and nurses in Serbia and Russia may be seen as part of the larger historical repression of the Eastern Front in favor of the story of Western Europe in histories of the war. The Eastern Front is the female "other" of World War I history. Where all is *really* quiet is on the Eastern Front, perhaps because attention to the other front would mean attention to the other back—that is, the background of capitalism and imperialism and colonialism that were behind the curtain of the European theater of war. This is echoed in *Mrs. Dalloway* when Lady Bruton espouses the cause of the Armenians and, fearing that she will not be taken seriously as a woman, convinces Richard Dalloway and other important men to help her frame her letter to the London *Times*.

As we recover the history of women in this period, these oppositions—Western Front/Eastern Front, manly/womanly, professional/

volunteer, patriot/feminist—in addition to the others that reinforce them—male/female, killer/coward, martyr/traitor—need to be undone, along with the class and gender biases that intersect with them. Looking back, we can see the message in May Sinclair's 1917 satire on Christabel Pankhurst—the hysterical man-hating Miss Dorothy Blackadder in *The Tree of Heaven*—as sheer propaganda for the authority of the nation, party, and government that had oppressed women. Dorothy "was afraid of the Feminist Vortex. . . . She was afraid of the herded women. She disliked the excited faces, and the high voices skirling their battle-cries, and the silly business of committees, and the platform slang. She was sick and shy before the tremor and surge of collective feeling; she loathed the gestures and the movements of the collective soul, the swaying and heaving forward of the many as one."[16] There is nothing like an appeal to individualism and personal freedom to sway the reader. Examine the skillful rhetoric of this passage, as a "feminist" discredits her own movement. The class bias against the masses, human beings in the collective, is unabashed. What else was service in the war but joining a similar "herd," swirling in a far more destructive "vortex?" It was "women in the collective," struggling for their own freedom, who were now marked as Public Enemy No. 1. This propaganda was so effective that another exsuffragette, Amber Blanco White, was able to argue later in the thirties that the suffragettes had actually brought dangerous fascist (read "foreign") political techniques to "democratic" England. (Blame the victim. Name the freedom-fighter as a fascist. Reinscribe the mass hysteria of war as individual heroism.)[17]

From a literary perspective, the reprinting of women's wartime writing will also allow us to contextualize the classics, reading *A Farewell to Arms* along with the experience of an American nurse, Ellen La Motte, whose powerful *The Backwash of War: The Human Wreckage of the Battlefield as Witnessed by an American Nurse* (1916) was banned during the war and not reprinted until 1934.[18] La Motte's prose style stands up to Ernest Hemingway's, drained of emotion and restrained in the face of the bodies of wounded men: "From the operating room they are brought into the wards, these bandaged heaps from the operating tables, these heaps that once were men. The clean beds of the ward are turned back to receive them, to receive the motionless, bandaged heaps that are lifted, shoved or rolled from the stretchers to the beds."[19]

We could also read Richard Aldington's *Death of a Hero* with

H.D.'s *Bid Me to Live* or Irene Rathbone's *We That Were Young* (which Aldington supposedly got published); H. G. Wells's *Mr. Britling Sees It Through* with Amber Reeves's *Give and Take* or E. M. Delafield's *The War Workers*; Robert Graves's *Goodbye to All That* with Laura Riding's *A Trojan Ending*; Siegfried Sassoon's *Memoirs of a Fox-Hunting Man* with Sylvia Thompson's *The Hounds of Spring*. Virginia Woolf's *Mrs. Dalloway* and *Jacob's Room* and Rebecca West's *The Return of the Soldier* are already being read as classic feminist antiwar novels. Their distinguishing feature is the insertion of class into the narrative of war and gender. It is the class critique that also distinguishes Helen Zenna Smith's *Not So Quiet . . .* from much other women's war fiction, as a relentlessly realistic document in brutally masculinized prose of what war does to women at the front. Not only does this brilliant novel overturn the stereotypes of "male" writing and "female" writing by writing from the subject position of the masculinized woman, as Erich Remarque writes from the subject position of the feminized soldier in *All Quiet on the Western Front*, it unforgettably inscribes better than any other fiction I know the female body in/at war. The hero of *A Farewell to Arms* (1925) is embarrassed by the words "sacred," "glorious," and "sacrifice." The heroine of *Not So Quiet . . .* is also driven mad by patriotic words. The corruption of language is war's first casualty. Hemingway writes, *"There were many words that you could not stand to hear* [emphasis added] and finally only the names of the places had dignity."[20]

Ears Only

Governments stamp their secret documents "Eyes Only." I call this section "Ears Only" to mark the experience of war in *Not So Quiet . . .* as a violation of the eardrums, and Helen Zenna Smith's writing as a bombardment of the reader's ears in a text pockmarked with ellipses of silence and rushes of noisy belligerent words. Despite Mary Cadogan and Patricia Craig's dismissal of this novel and its sequels as "crude" socialist realism and "emotional melodrama,"[21] the genius of *Not So Quiet . . .* lies in its unswervingly truthful reportage of a war that was both crude and emotionally melodramatic, its prose style revealing the death of the feminine sentence, or at least exposing the myth that writing comes from gender rather than experience. I mean these remarks about the assault on the ears as a compliment, of course. In *Paris France* (1940) Gertrude Stein characterized the experience of World War I as "Music in the Air": "War naturally does make music but certainly this war with everybody really everybody listening to the radio, there is nothing but music."[22] My subtitle, "Ears Only," is not only meant to convey the urgency and secrecy of messages sent in wartime. It also suggests that if Freud interprets blinding or the assault on the eyes in dreams as representing the fear of castration, we might consider the ear as an image of female sexuality, with its outer folds and inner labyrinthine passages where balance and equilibrium are lodged. If we experience noise as rape, what does it mean if the woman writer writes a noisy text? To use Julia Kristeva's terms, it is a "semiotic" rather than a symbolic text. But by her criteria, the semiotic text is in touch with the child's experience of learning sounds from the mother before it is initiated into masculine or symbolic language.[23] Yet the whole force of this novel on the level of content is rage against the mother, refusal to deal with the father as a war-maker. The heroine of this novel is truly "up to her ears" in war; it disorients and unbalances her. As an ambulance driver at the front, she is not only overwhelmed by the noise of battle, she is a noise maker herself. By taking over a man's job, she both experiences the rape of the ear and "ears" herself, in the Old English use of the word as a verb for ploughing, an apt term for driving an ambulance across no-man's-land.

Helen Zenna Smith was the pseudonym of Evadne Price. The National Union Catalogue lists her birthdate as 1896, but Kenneth Attiwill, her second husband (of fifty-four years), claims she was born in 1901. (The narrator of *Not So Quiet* . . . would have been born in 1896 or 1897.)[24] When Angela Ingram and I began to work on these novels (*Not So Quiet* . . . and its sequels, *Women of the Aftermath* [1931], *Shadow Women* [1932], *Luxury Ladies* [1933], and *They Lived with Me* [1934]), information on the author was hard to come by. Zenna was spelled Zennor in some places, but Evadne Price was revived by Cadogan and Craig in *You're a Brick, Angela!*, a popular account of the history of English girls' books, and *Women and Children First: The Fiction of the Two World Wars*. Evadne Price was a very successful free-lance journalist, and her career included everything from children's books to romances, serious stage parts to acting and writing for several films, as well as playwriting. Her Helen Zenna Smith books were serialized in *The People*, and she was their war correspondent from 1943, covering the Allied invasion and all the major war stories through the Nuremberg Trials. Her husband was a POW in Japan, and for two years she believed he was dead. She wrote a great deal of popular fiction with titles like *Society Girl, Glamour Girl, Escape to Marriage,* and *Air Hostess in Love.* Her play *Big Ben,* written for the Malvern Festival in 1939, was successful (the *Times* called it "a large, comfortable play with a soul to call its own"). *The Phantom Light* (1937) was a stage version of her novel, *The Haunted Light,* and it was also made into a film starring Gordon Harker. *Once a Crook,* on which Kenneth Attiwill collaborated (1939), was also both a play and a film.

The author of several hundred paperback romances first serialized in *Novel Magazine,* Evadne Price had another career when television began, as a broadcast storyteller. An afternoon horoscope show called "Fun with the Stars" led to a long-running evening horoscope program. Price was "our new astrologer extraordinaire" for twenty-five years for *SHE* magazine and published a successful collection of these columns as *SHE Stargazers.* When she and her husband retired to Australia in 1976, Evadne Price wrote the monthly horoscope column for Australian *Vogue.* Before she died in April 1985, she had begun work on an autobiography to be called *Mother Painted Nudes.*

As I write, the press is having a field day over the revelation that Nancy and Ronald Reagan consult astrologers. What is the feminist scholar to make of a talent that spanned social realism and pulp fiction, a talent that composed sensational reports of World War II battlefronts and also concocted horoscopes for fashion magazines? Can we include in our feminist project the magnetic, feminine "little" personality with "raven black hair," a "cultivated" accent, and "English rose complexion," the born performer who longed to be in the public eye and said, "I was a real little show-off. . . . I loved reciting, singing, dancing, telling make-believe stories, making people laugh or cry, anything to be the center of attention. And when they took me to my first ever theatre—it was a pantomime—I *knew* that I wanted to be an actress and have my name up in electric lights. . . . I wanted to be a star and shine."[25]

Evadne Price's authorship is a challenge for feminist criticism. Would unacknowledged snobbery about "high" and "low" culture dismiss Evadne Price as a commercial opportunist? Is our reading of the Helen Zenna Smith books contaminated by the astrological charts? Is *Not So Quiet . . .* diminished by the fact that its author adored housekeeping and gardening in Sussex and prided herself on being a very good cook? We claim that aesthetic judgments are no longer based on such considerations. Critical theory insists that the "author" is dead. But what if the dead author is not Shakespeare or Virginia Woolf, but Evadne Price?

Evadne Price's career is a twentieth-century woman's success story. She had enormous mimetic gifts; she was extraordinarily *adaptive*, a trait that feminist psychologists document in many women's lives. Evadne Price was a genuinely popular writer. She knew what the public wanted and she gave it to them. Readers of thirties novels of socialist realism will have no trouble recognizing the genre of *Not So Quiet* . . . and its sequels, the lost heroines of the later books, bored and weary mistresses and kept women, enacting the general social malaise of the depression in a female "depression" at being culturally deprived of *work*. Like Jean Rhys's miserable heroines, "Nello," as she is called in the later novels, is downwardly mobile and ends up sleeping on the Embankment when what prostitutes now call "sex work" is no longer available. Helen Zenna Smith does not write as lyrically as Jean Rhys. There are almost no figures of speech in her brutal, tense, angry narrative. But the technique of dramatic monologue, of inner and outer soliloquy and mental scene making are superb examples of what Bakhtin calls "dialogism" in fiction.[26]

Evadne Price here shapes a new form of cinematic, dialogic, and dramatic interior monologue for modernism, a very tightly controlled but daring form very different from James Joyce, Dorothy Richardson, or Virginia Woolf. One consciousness, Helen's, is a kind of mistress of ceremonies of the "carnival" of voices in her imagination. She jerks the puppet strings and they all "act out." Furious with her mother and Mrs. Evans-Mawnington (her mother's rival in war work and village recruiting) for their pious, smug inability to conceive of the terrors of trench life for soldiers or the unspeakable conditions in which the women drive ambulances, she hallucinates that they are on the scene, wanting to imagine their response: "Shut your ears, Mother and Mrs. Evans-Mawnington, lest their groans and heart-rending cries linger in your memory as in the memory of the daughter you sent out to help win the War."

Erich Maria Remarque's *All Quiet on the Western Front* appeared in 1929 to instant international acclaim. It remains a classic antiwar novel, a touching, comic, life-affirming first-person narrative of a young German soldier's experience. Albert Marriot, the publisher, approached Evadne Price with a free-lance project to write a spoof from a woman's point of view (*All Quaint on the Western Front*). She read Remarque and found "quaint" an unsuitable response to its power. She herself had never been at the front, so she convinced Winifred Young, who had kept diaries of her experience as an ambulance driver, to let her write a novel faithful to Young's experience of actual life at the front. We do not have those diaries to compare to *Not So Quiet . . . .* We know that Evadne Price locked herself up with them for six weeks and wrote a novel fit to put on the shelf next to Erich Maria Remarque. The question of its origins as a work of art, its originality or creativity in the face of Evadne Price's deliberate mimesis of *All Quiet on the Western Front* and her use of Winifred Young's diaries is fascinating.

Not So Quiet . . . is a multiauthored text, like the *King James Bible*, which was written by a committee, and it seems to demonstrate Virginia Woolf's thesis in *A Room of One's Own* that "masterpieces are not single and solitary births. They are the product of thinking by the body of the people." The many voices of *Not So Quiet . . .*, its "heteroglossia" in Bakhtin's terms, come from Evadne Price's extraordinary ability to hear and read the popular experience of the horror of this particular war, the popular revulsion at the destruction of a whole generation of European youth, male and female alike.[27] Socialist feminists in particular should be interested in a fiction that makes no pretense at "individual genius" and enacts as well a female literary class demobilization in the narrative of Helen's move from volunteer ambulance driving, a breakdown, and home leave to the deliberate rejection of class privilege and her return to the front as a cook's assistant with working-class WAACs.

Virginia Woolf, in "Professions for Women" (1931), imagined that women would be able to tell the truth about the body in fifty years' time.[28] She meant, of course, female sexual experience. But if she read popular fiction, she would have seen that Evadne Price (and other women war novelists) could tell the truth about the body in/at war—though some subjects remained taboo. Helen never tells us, except in veiled allusion, what happens to the menstruating body at the front. Did the harsh conditions stop the menstrual flow? Did women connect menstrual blood with the blood of wounded soldiers? Some anthropologists have argued that men's wars are a form of menstruation envy. Did death-blood, flowing so ceaselessly from men's bodies, affect women's perceptions of their own life-blood? Menstruation may still have been in *la zone inter-*

dite for women's fiction in 1929, but the body covered with lice was an arresting and shocking substitute. May I warn the gentle reader to cut her fingernails before reading *Not So Quiet . . . ?* Even on the second and third readings this novel will send you into a fit of itching and scratching, so graphic is its description of the horrors of lice in the hair and sleeping bags (which are called "flea bags").

The disorder and disorientation of the body at war are evoked immediately by the narrative voice in the modernist "continuous present" of Gertrude Stein (though more familiar to readers in the work of Hemingway and Remarque). The first-person speaker seems to be unreeling a black and white cinematic series of graphic images in the flat (but ominous) monotone of an old newsreel. The personal, reportorial "I" deliberately suppresses emotion, but extends the I-narrative with more private forms—the diary, the letter, the waking dream—so that she creates the illusion of multiple voices trying to speak over the static of a field radio, the continual rumble and whine of guns and bombs, and the screaming and moaning of the wounded. This "background noise," the deafening roar of the engines of death, is the source of the title, as well as a reversal of Remarque.

The word "quiet" in both titles indicates war's insistence on gender reversal. Man, the noise-making animal, is forced to lie still in the trenches, while the silent woman, used to domestic peace, must participate in the incessant noise of warfare. She must take and give orders, run machines, think and act quickly during the infernal din of shelling attacks, rev up her engines. Remarque's Paul Baumer and his comrades must leave the male world of active speaking and noisy work for the eerie *longuers* and passive, silent waiting for attack, which fills them with fear and makes them into "women." The ambulance drivers are equally made into "men" by the requirements of their jobs. They must overcome their fear of open spaces and the dark and drive long distances in the night with their cargo of maimed men. Self-reliance, courage, nerve, and bravery must be summoned.

Both experience war through the body of the other. Paul is feminized by war; Helen is masculinized. Both novels write the body in distress, as much for gender reversal as for fatigue, sleep deprivation, hunger, rotten food, the invasion of fleas and rats, cold. Remarque writes the claustrophobia of the falsely domestic trench/hearth and Price writes the agoraphobia of the mine-trapped open space, with its blinding snow and wind, its bombs falling from the sky. Unhoused, she must learn to operate Outside. Housed in holes of trenches, the German soldiers must learn containment, self-control, and all the female virtues of the aware and alert Inside. Woman makes noise; man maintains silence. The trench warfare and the writer of trench warfare experience profound gender traumas. The speaker becomes the listener; the listener becomes the speaker. The war/peace, front/back gender oppositions must be negotiated for survival.

Yet gender identity must be maintained despite the experience of living in the body of the other sex (Helen strenuously imagines the preparations for her coming-out party while driving a particularly stressful ambulance run, and Paul and his friends risk court-martial to make love to some French girls). The first opposition in the dialogic experience of reading the two novels together is in the meaning of the word "quiet." For the woman, the new meaning in war of her speech or silence is all the more disconcerting because of the accumulated cultural associations of female virtue with silence in a cultural script that asserts (against reality) that women talk too much. In addition, the new subject position of the woman at war undoes her ordinary sexual role. Heightened sexuality is part of her active role. In contrast, the men in *All Quiet on the Western Front* mostly masturbate. Helen casually sleeps with the first man she meets as she gets off the boat for leave in England, an action unthinkable for a girl of her class before the war. Sandra Gilbert's argument about gender warfare seems inappropriate to those for whom gender identity remains a serious test of endurance and of new respect for the *Other*. Paul, on home leave, feels a tender respect for his mother, a respect born of his own feminization in the trenches. He can now empathize with her body, which is dying of cancer, when all of civilian life enrages and disgusts him. Helen falls in love with Roy Evans-Mawnington because she knows in her body's stress what he has experienced as a soldier. The notion that woman's "potency" derived from men's "impotence" is a far too simple interpretation of gender roles in World War I. The most silent soldier in Remarque's novel, the one who hears and smells, can find food, and "read" the world around him (like a woman), is the most revered. And Tosh is the heroine of *Not So Quiet . . .*, with her foul mouth, continual banter, singing, joking, cursing, and clowning. Helen and her comrades cannot tell their families what they suffer. They write lying, cheerful letters and fantasize about telling the truth as they would have "before the world turned khaki and blood-coloured": "Tell them that all the ideals and beliefs you ever had have crashed about your gun-deafened ears—that you don't believe in God or them or the infallibility of England or anything but bloody war and wounds and foul smells and smutty stories and smoke and bombs and lice and filth and noise, noise, noise—that you live in a world of cold sick fear, a dirty world of darkness and despair."[29]

Psychically speaking, what both sexes experience in these novels is a Freudian version of "the uncanny." Though Freud associates the fear of castration with deprivation of sight, in the war experience it is hearing, noise or silence, that indicates the desexualization of the characters. Remarque's narrator, Paul Baumer, associates silence with the mass murder of a battle, the final impotence of passive endurance of enemy assault; he refers to "the soundless apparitions that speak to me,"[30] and a similar procession of silent maimed men appears in *Not So Quiet* . . . (163). Yet Helen fixates on one particular noise as the cause of her suffering,[31] the "loathly arrogant summons" of the Commandant's police whistle. Rousing her to roll call at 7:30 A.M. when she went to bed at 5, the whistle focuses her hatred:

> [It] ruin[ed] my pre-War disposition entirely. It rouses everything vile within me. Not long ago I was a gentle pliable creature of no particular virtues or vices, my temper was even, my nature amiable and my emotions practically non-existent. Now I am a sullen, smouldering thing, liable to burst Vesuvius fashion into a flaming fire of rage without the slightest warning. Commandant's police whistle. . . .
>
> If I am bathing or attending to my body with carbolic ointment or soothing lotion . . . it orders me to stop. If I am writing a hasty letter, or glancing at a newspaper . . . it shrieks its mocking summons. Whatever I am doing it gives me no peace. But worst of all, whenever I am asleep . . . it wakens me, and gloats and glories in the action. If only I could ram it down the Commandant's throat, I could die happy in the knowledge that I had not lived in vain.   [47]

Later Helen's sadistic fantasies again enact the invasion of the deep throat of the Commandant: "I wonder what she would do if I suddenly sprang at her and dug my fingers into her throat, her strong, red, thick throat that is never sore, that laughs scornfully at germs, that needs no wrapping up even when the snow is whirling, blinding and smothering" (57).

Note, first of all, that these passages are marked heavily by ellipses. In the first-person narrative dramatic monologue or soliloquy, the ellipses indicate self-interruption and the repression of even more rage than is on the page. *Not So Quiet . . .* is punctuated by these elliptical absences throughout. The text looks like letters received and sent during wartime, stamped and opened by the censor with marked-out passages (read by other eyes). The reader is reading as much silence as text, constantly filling in the blanks, supplying the left-out words, decoding the coded wartime message. The ellipses, like the censor's black lines crossing out sentences, sometimes paragraphs, indicate Helen's self-censorship, but also the utter lack of truthful communication possible in war. Partial messages, missent and misread; propaganda; rumor; lies; the reports of spies; secret codes—these are the messages of war. *Not So Quiet . . .* , already because of its multiple authorship in its imitation of Remarque and its pseudonymous rendering of Winifred Young's diaries in fictional form, is a particularly rich document in which to examine gender and war issues in World War I England. The punctuation asks the reader to read between the lines, to guess at the unsaid and the unsayable. The reading experience is a reproduction of the ambulance driver's route, swerving to avoid obstacles and holes, zigzagging with Helen Z. Smith. Passages from letters, bits of remembered newspaper articles, and phrases like "Our Splendid Women" are rendered in italics, further marking the text as an intertext with all the other cultural productions of war, as well as Remarque's novel. We seem to read secretly, behind the editorial blackout curtain of censorship in conspiracy with Helen Zenna Smith. Her textual practice is a version of the Kristevan "semiotic," those human noises excluded from "symbolic" discourse, marking a repression that marks another repression. This opens the novel to deconstructive feminism and other modes of contemporary critical discourse.

But it is interesting to note that Evadne Price's writing practice here is not the feminine "writing the body" of Hélène Cixous and some French feminist theory. It is not in the least erotic. The words on the page—so full of stops and starts and diacritical messages in italic and so many sentences framed as questions and requiring an answer from the reader—are a textual version of *la zone interdite,* fragmented like the bodies that litter this forbidden territory with arms and legs and headless trunks. The body of the text is "not whole"; it is a war casualty. This is a remarkable literary achievement and clearly related to Evadne Price's brilliance as a reporter. She reproduces the minefield of the forbidden zone as a dotted landscape on the body of the text, setting up disquieting relations between text and white space on the book's pages, the sight of which invades our ears as well as our eyes. Our eye contact with the fragmented text makes us feel the disorientation of the body at war, and it activates the reading "ear" as if a silent newsreel suddenly connected with its sound track, but faded in and out, as such reports continue to do, keeping the viewer on edge about the physical safety of the reporter.[32]

The content of the quoted passages is also significant. The Commandant is the phallic mother, the whistle her phallus, the very voice of violence and war. In the male masquerade that is required of the young women who shoulder these abhorrent wartime duties, Helen's hatred is directed exactly onto the object the Propaganda Office has chosen for its posters, the fearful huge matriarch who points the way to the front, the enormous maternal nurse who cradles the wounded. She is the Home Front, the Mother Country, the one who gives birth and also kills. It would never do to blame the old men who make war, the kings and kaisers and their counselors. The Commandant's whistle is, of course, a convenient disguise for the male voice of nationalist authority, the patriarchs in whose interest the war is fought. When Helen figures war as an invasion of her ears, the phallic mother is the rapist. She is the one who is "not so quiet," the literal *disturber of the peace*. She is War.

The repression of the male authority figures and displacement of their roles as killers onto the militant and militaristic mother figure is a precise reading of the cultural needs of the warmongers, and Helen Zenna Smith constructs a plot in which the bad mother is the villain. Edwards recognizes the real enemy, "the politicians": "[T]he men are failures." Women should "refuse to bring children into the world to be maimed and murdered." "Let the people who make the wars fight them" (55). As Angela Ingram so carefully and wittily demonstrates in "Un/Reproductions," the ideology of war insists on a primitive call to women to construct themselves socially as mothers first and then argues that the war is being fought to protect those mothers and, by extension, that it is their fault that men are dying.

But Helen's war is fought with the Commandant, known as "Mrs. Bitch," who "would have made a good wife for Napoleon." She can't understand how Mrs. Bitch could be a mother: "No woman who has suffered the pangs of childbirth could have so little understanding of pain in other women's daughters." She is a "hungry vulture" who loves "bossing the show." "Why is it that women in authority almost invariably fall victims to megalomania?" she asks (49). This cultural and social displacement of the drive for power onto the mother rather than the father, and women's internalization of it as enacted in this fiction, may be a clue to the problem of why humanity is unable to stop war. The portrait of the Commandant recalls, of course, Mrs. Breakspeare, "the very maternal general" of *The Well of Loneliness*.[33]

Not So Quiet . . . is subtitled *Stepdaughters of War*. In this drama, which problematizes the relation of the family to martial values, war is not the father but the mother, and not a real mother, but a wicked stepmother. The stepdaughter is a Cinderella of the battlefront, sweeping up the ashes and cinders, the blood and vomit of her wounded prince. But no fairy godmother comes to rescue her. Bello changes into Bella, ferocious goddess of war. We might call the "stepdaughter" of war Bellona, as Evadne Price chronicles the transformation of her heroine from "Helen" to "Nell" to "Nello." Virginia Woolf obviously recalls the figure of the stepdaughter of war in a footnote in *Three Guineas*, written in 1938:

> Englishwomen were much criticized for using force in the battle for the franchise. . . . The vote indeed was given to women largely because of the help they gave to Englishmen in using force in that war. . . . This raises the difficult question whether those who did not aid in the prosecution of the war, but did what they could to hinder the prosecution of the war, ought to use the vote to which they are entitled chiefly because others "aided in the prosecution of the war"? That they are stepdaughters, not full daughters, of England, is shown by the fact that they change nationality on marriage. A woman, whether or not she helped to beat the Germans, becomes a German if she marries a German. Her political views must then be entirely reversed, and her filial piety transferred.[34]

Woolf's logic exposes the ideological reversals by which patriarchy and militarism manipulate women in wartime, as ruthlessly as does Evadne Price's antilogical narrative.

There are only two figurative passages in this novel. One is the description of "an ancient tree that never buds into leaf nor yet rots," which is called the "Witch's Hand" for its gnarled trunk that looks like a gigantic palm and "five malformed branches that stretch like fingers into the valley below" (114), where Helen and her companions drive the dead in their ambulances to the military cemetery. The Witch's Hand is evil, sinister, greedy, demanding, never denied. Helen and the men struggle with the coffins in the mud. The snow, a "white glove that has so graciously hidden" the "claw-like and avaricious" hand, has disappeared, leaving the tree to grab ghoulishly at the dead. "It reaches down evilly, the claws snatching at us as we stand defenseless, as though to squeeze the youth from us until we are dry and lifeless" (119). The Witch's Hand is part of the enormous ideological effort of the novel to mask the paternity of war and its complicity with patriarchy and to blame the mothers. In a massive reversal of reality, Helen Zenna Smith makes the life-giving body of the mother the source of death and war in the same way that Claire Culleton documents the insidious propaganda campaign that enacted a popular transformation of the bombs of the munitions factories into breasts and wombs.[35] (Evadne Price is supposed to have worked for the War Ministry during the war, where doubtless such brilliant propagandistic tricks were hatched. There might be a connection with her astrology columns after all. *Not So Quiet . . .* could be read as the propagandist's star turn, if it did not so forcefully turn the reader against war.)

It is a common characteristic of the literature of this war to figure the home front as a phallic mother, especially in the homoerotic poetry of the lost brother. But Helen Zenna Smith doubles the "terrible mother" with a classic pair of belligerents who outdo even Woolf's Lady Bruton and Lady Bradshaw in matriarchal militarism. The two matrons, her mother and Mrs. Evans-Mawnington, compete with one another over who can recruit more young men and how many of their own they can sacrifice for the war. With capitalism, imperialism, and jingoism shoring up their flag-waving patriotism, they make a grotesque twin-headed statue of Bella-Bello. War will always exist "as long as we breed women like my mother and Mrs. Evans-Mawnington" (90). The dialogic structure of the novel is most apparent in the use of the letters from the mother and her aunt in fragments separated by ellipses. Helen dramatizes the letters in her head as reading them enrages her. She creates their voices, then mocks and mimics them (Mother "has seventeen more recruits than Mrs. Evans-Mawnington up to date" [17]). The front becomes a *theatre of war* where Helen acts out all the roles. The letters are dialogized into short plays with stage directions, including "Curtain," as the war itself is imagined as scenes in a drama whose most important aspect is that it will end. Helen hallucinates that her mother and Mrs. Evans-Mawnington join her on her nightly ambulance run:

> Oh, come with me, Mother and Mrs. Evans-Mawnington. Let me show you the exhibits straight from the battlefield. This will be something original to tell your committees, while they knit their endless miles of khaki scarves. . . . Something to spout from the platform at your recruiting meetings. Come with me. Stand just there.   [90]
>
> See the stretcher-bearers lifting the trays one by one, slotting them deftly into my ambulance. Out of the way quickly, Mother and Mrs. Evans-Mawnington—lift your silken skirts aside . . . a man is spewing blood, the moving has upset him, finished him. . . . He will die on the way to hospital if he doesn't die before the ambulance is loaded.   [91]
>
> See the man they are fitting into the bottom slot. He is coughing badly. No, not pneumonia. Not tuberculosis. Nothing so picturesque. Gently, gently, stretcher-bearers . . . he is about done. He is coughing up clots of pinky-green filth. Only his lungs, Mother and Mrs. Evans-Mawnington. He is coughing well tonight. That is gas. You've heard of gas, haven't you? It burns and shrivels the lungs to . . . to the mess you see on the ambulance floor there. He's about the age of Bertie, Mother. . . . The son you are so eager to send out to the trenches, in case Mrs. Evans-Mawnington scores over you at the next recruiting meeting. . . . "I have given my only son."
>
> Cough, cough, little fair-haired boy. Perhaps somewhere your mother is thinking of you . . . boasting of the life she has so nobly given . . . the life you thought was your own, but which is hers to squander as she thinks fit.   [92–93]

Such brutal writing might be understandable in the description of the enemy, but it is clear that for these young women the real enemy is Mother. When we compare this murderous prose with the gentle, pacifist tone of *All Quiet on the Western Front*, we can make the argument that, because of the gender reversals demanded by war, Erich Maria Remarque has produced a *woman's novel* and

Helen Zenna Smith a *man's novel*. The *subject positions* of the experience of the writers, not their *gender*, produces different forms of *écriture féminine* and *écriture masculine*. Remarque and Price are important as war novelists because, more than other writers, they have marked their prose and their narratives with the profound experience of gender reversal and the battle to recover the lost gendered subject position that was the real experience of male and female bodies in World War I.

The "Witch's Hand," the gloved and ungloved (mailed fist?) hand formed by the bent tree, seems a deliberate answer to the exquisite flowering cherry tree in *All Quiet on the Western Front*, which so overpowers Detering, a man in Paul's company, that he deserts out of a desperate desire for home. Home is a death-dealing monster to the British girl, an orchard full of promise to the German peasant. When Paul kills a Frenchman in hand-to-hand combat, he is overcome with remorse, reads his identity card, sees the photo of the man's wife and child, and vows to replace him: the dead man, Gerard Duval, was a compositor and printer, and Paul becomes a writer.

Helen's experience of the enemy, when for her the real enemy is the wicked stepmother (her own mother, the Commandant, England as her Mother Country), is a puzzled woman's experience of the male gaze when the German POWs assess her body parts. (She is puzzled because part of her masculine role as a driver is to be the gazer, not the object of men's gaze.) Paul's knowledge of the patriarchal authority that makes war fills him with sorrow and pity. He is feminized and civilized by the humiliations and submissions required by the army, whereas Helen is brutalized and numbed. Paul and his friends play schoolboy pranks on their officer and keep their difference and distance from authoritarian values. Much as Helen, Tosh, and their companions hate Mrs. Bitch, they *become* her, or junior versions of her matriarchal militarism, when they scapegoat, torture, and expel the lesbian in their midst.

One of the most moving scenes in *All Quiet on the Western Front* is a tender and comic story of Lewandowski's Polish wife's visit to the hospital. He hasn't seen her for two years and is almost recovered from a severe abdominal wound. The men on the ward insist that the little woman with the black mantilla get into bed with her husband. They stand guard, hold the baby, and play cards so the couple can make love, "like one big family," and then eat sausage with the "sweating and beaming" Lewandowski. Having been feminized by the trenches, the men experience an almost communal desire to be reinvested in the social roles of husband and father, rather than killer or shivering victim.[36] This is a story of what we now think of as "female" behavior. It is interesting to compare the men's struggle to return to male life-giving rather than death-dealing roles in a man's novel with Rebecca West's portrait in *The Return of the Soldier* of Chris Baldry regressing because of shell shock to a youthful self before he became a husband and father. His name, Bal/dry, clues the reader to a kind of pacifism of the body, the refusal to engender. This is also why the psychiatrists are so enraged with Septimus Smith in Virginia Woolf's *Mrs. Dalloway*. His body has become a pacifist and he refuses to sleep with Rezia and give her the child she wants.

In *Not So Quiet* . . . Helen's one-night stand with Robin when she returns to England seems to spring from her acquired "masculinity"; it is an act motivated by the fear of a loss of sexual identity. But it is clear that the fear of a lesbian in the women's barracks comes from a deeper fear of the pacifist body. It is not so much deviance that frightens them as the body, which enacts its pacifism by refusing to bear children. The "carnivalesque" in this scene is a dreadful ritualized eating and speech-making ceremony that ends, like some tribal ritual, by expelling the scapegoat. The carnivalesque in Remarque's novel enacts bonding by erasing shame. The battlefield has no privileged toilet of one's own. Both novels are mired in the body, as their narrators' own bodies are mired in muddy battlefields. The communal latrines in *All Quiet on the Western Front* relax the boundaries between the men and they become as close as women. Their bodies, humiliated in *evacuation* and emission, are weak and humanized. The woman ambulance drivers are also deep in others' excrement, but suffer more from *invasion* by fleas. They become brutalized and individualized, acting out their own hatred of authority by sacrificing one of their members rather than sticking together.[37]

There is an extraordinary scene at the opening of *Not So Quiet* . . . when the gallant heroine Tosh cuts her gorgeous red hair and burns the fleas and lice. This sordid ritual scene with its descriptions of filth and food that resembles shit does not unite the women but separates the sadistic Tosh, burning one louse at a time, as the "heroine," different from the other girls who don't dare to cut their hair for fear it would "put the helmet on the womanliness" they desperately need to maintain. It is only because she is an aris-

tocrat that Tosh doesn't fear being "unsexed" by short hair. "Unsexed? Me? With the breasts of a nursing mother?" (17). Tosh winks
to Bertina Farmer (called The B.F. for Bloody Fool).

The scene emphasizes the class distinctions among the girls:
Tosh, The B.F., The Bug, Skinny, Etta Potato (Etta Potter), and
Smithy, the narrator. The class distinctions are erased for the German soldiers, but since the women are in a volunteer outfit, they
range in class from being, like Tosh, the niece of an earl to being
upper-middle-class debutantes like The B.F.; daughters of government administrators, like Skinny, whose father is important in the
War Office; or girls like Nell, whose father made jam and then settled in Wimbledon Common—"we sheltered young women who
smilingly stumbled from the chintz-covered drawing-rooms of the
suburbs straight into hell" (165). Tosh calls them *mes petits har-
lots*; she's their leader and spokesperson. She even compiles a war
alphabet for them: "B for Bastard—obsolete term meaning war
baby. . . . I for Illegitimate—(see B). . . . V for Virgin—a term of re-
proach" (160). Tosh's alphabet inscribes the complicity of motherhood and war. She is, in reality, a budding "Mrs. Bitch," a candidate
for the role of Helen's mother or Mrs. Evans-Mawnington, the British matriarch in the making. She both writes and embodies the
gender reversal of women at war. Helen thinks that the War Office
sends only upper-class girls to the front because they will obey a
code of honor and remain silent and stiff-upper-lipped about the
horror. But their "voice" is Tosh's noisy swaggering fearlessness, a
voice in training to blow the Commandant's whistle:

> She is wandering around in the flickering candlelight dressed in
> a soiled woollen undervest and a voluminous pair of navy blue
> bloomers, chain-smoking yellow perils at a furious rate. There
> is something vaguely comforting in the Amazonian height and
> breadth of Tosh. She has the hips of a matron—intensified by
> the four pairs of thick combinations she always wears for
> warmth, a mind like a sewer (her own definition), the courage
> of a giant, the vocabulary of a Smithfield butcher, and the
> round, wind-reddened face of a dairymaid.   [11]

Georgina Toshington, who posthumously becomes a classic
schoolgirl storybook heroine in England after she has been killed
by a bomb while driving the Commandant's ambulance (Smithy
wishes the bomb would kill Mrs. Bitch, but it kills Tosh instead),
is the Edwardian version of England as Victoria, a large, imperial-

ist, terrifying maternal figure. When Smithy is driving under the bombs, she is terrified by the "flattening sound, as though the sky were jealous of the earth and determined to wipe it out of existence. Each time a bomb drops I see myself under it, flat, like the skin of a dead tiger that has been made into a rug with a little nicked half-inch of cloth all round the edges . . . flat, all the flesh and blood and bones knocked flat . . ." (156). This is the second figurative passage in *Not So Quiet . . .* , and it is repeated during the scene in which the bomb fragment kills Tosh. Its meaning is more deeply repressed than the figure of the dead tree as the Witch's Hand. Nellie Smith's *own* fear of annihilation (rather than her disgust at the maimed men whose bodies she ferries to hospital or the grave) is at issue here. While she talks about being a sacrificial victim to home front patriotism, her fear connects her own body, flattened like the tiger skin, to those earlier trophies of imperialistic adventures in India and Africa that grace English hearths. She, too, might become a hearth rug for safe, warm (not gangrenous or frozen) feet, to lay before the home fires that have been kept burning by the sacrifice of so many colonial lives. (This vivid image of home front trophies should be compared to Sylvia Townsend Warner's description of the photo of young Osbert in "Cottage Mantleshelf," in which the picture is isolated and "un-paired" when everything else on the shelf is locked into a couple or "married." The image of the female body at war as a flattened rug made out of her hide recalls Barbara Comyns's splendid novel *The Skin Chairs*.) Actually, Helen does not die like the hero-narrator of *All Quiet on the Western Front*. It is the intrepid Tosh who dies—though not before she has performed her role as keeper of the heterosexual flame.

Margaret Higonnet has argued that the fiction of nationalist wars equates heterosexuality with political correctness, that the linear narrative enforces gender stability.[38] Civil war novels break from linear narrative, often invoking Kristeva's "women's time," allowing more complicated temporal inversions, memories, and incestuous plots. The perfect example, for me, of this argument is Marguerite Yourcenar's *Coup de Grâce*, set in the Baltic states just after the First World War. By inserting an authoritarian preface in the reprint, cautioning the reader against reading for the woman's text and arguing that Eric, her protofascist narrator, is not as "unreliable" as we had supposed, Yourcenar has provided one of the most disturbing versions of the interconnections between gender and war. She is also the most stunning example of the woman writing from the male subject position, not in struggle with literary masculinizing as Helen Zenna Smith is in *Not So Quiet . . .* , but valorizing that very "valor" that Evadne Price and Erich Maria Remarque call into question.

Not So Quiet . . . runs on a present-tense time frame that we might call "fast forward," while *All Quiet on the Western Front* moves in a slow, nostalgic present toward the silence at the end of the war. The fact that *Not So Quiet . . .* does not end, but continues in sequels, with the life of the war-damaged narrator getting worse and worse, indicates Price's realization that, for women, the effects of war last a lifetime and can never be forgotten. Vera Brittain's memoirs indicate that she never got over the loss of lover and brother. The war is not over when it's over in historical time. Irene Rathbone's *We That Were Young* and *They Call It Peace* also demonstrate that patriarchal, capitalist, and imperialist "peacetimes" are still wartimes for the exploited.

The politics of *Not So Quiet . . .* are another matter. The portrait of Tosh, though it's meant to be complimentary, reminds me of the concentration camp commandant in Lina Wertmüller's film *Seven Beauties*. If *Not So Quiet . . .* was intended as a "politically correct" version of English ambulance drivers' experiences, specifically to counter the effects of Radclyffe Hall's *The Well of Loneliness*, which appeared in 1928 and was banned in a sensational censorship trial (and I believe it was), Helen Zenna Smith is writing to clear the volunteers of the charge of lesbianism. Hall's version of the war is very different—romantic, heroic, celebrating the hotbed of lesbian lovers in the Ambulance Corps.[39] Tosh is the "Niece of an Earl." One of the most well-known heroines among the ambulance drivers was Radclyffe Hall's friend, "Toupie" Lowther. She was actually the *daughter* of an earl and, as Barbara, Lady Lowther, ran a unit operating in Compeigne from 1917 on and also headed the London Branch of Relief for Belgian Prisoners in Germany. "Toupie" is described as "a bulky tall woman of extremely masculine appearance who had a considerable reputation as a fencer and tennis player." She and four of the women in her unit won the Croix de Guerre.[40] The scandal of *The Well of Loneliness* and its revelations that there were "inverts" among "Our Splendid Women" also made a specific link between the upper classes and lesbianism. Hence, Evadne Price has Tosh leading the sadistic purge of the lesbian figure, Skinny, in *Not So Quiet . . . .* Skinny is described as "yellow" and thin (and she is the only member of the company to have dysentery—a "male" form of pollution?). Virginia Woolf's description of Radclyffe Hall when she attended the censorship trial for *The Well of Loneliness* calls her "stringy" and "yellow." The word yellow, of course, indicates both cowardice and jaundice. Her skinniness is a deliberate opposition to Tosh's maternal Amazon's body. Evadne Price effectively rewrites the lesbian body at war to rob it of the healthy romantic glow with which Radclyffe Hall had surrounded it in *The Well of Loneliness*.

Tosh sees that Skinny is separated from her "particular friend," Frost (another naming of the nonmaternal), as soon as they arrive. At the party (which is a strange counterpart to the grand eating scenes in *All Quiet on the Western Front*, when the German soldiers steal pigs and geese, and roast and eat them with Paul making potato pancakes as the bombs fall around them, a wonderful Bakhtinian carnivalization of war), Tosh ignores, insults, and taunts Skinny, who has a hysterical fit. Skinny and Frost get sent home for "refusing to obey orders," in an unspoken agreement between Tosh and the Commandant that allows Tosh to retain her "honor" and makes clear to the reader that perversion has been routed and heterosexuality holds sway. The scene is a perfect example of Mary Douglas's arguments in *Purity and Danger* about scapegoating the "polluted" victim. The drivers are polluted in their role as the charwomen of the battlefield, and they sacrifice Skinny to purify themselves. This "purity" is not virginity but the flaunting of credentials of heterosexual experience. The female body at war must announce that it is made for motherhood. In his biography of Radclyffe Hall, Lovat Dickson implies that lesbianism caused an English defeat in the war, deftly reversing Una Troubridge's claim that her husband, the admiral, who refused to pursue the German fleet in an Eastern engagement, had syphilis, and blaming the admiral's "cowardice" on his wife's relationship with Radclyffe Hall.[41]

Helen's mother tolerates a pregnant servant when she had fired one in a similar situation before the war. Yet Nell's sister Trix, who washes dishes in a VAD nursing unit, gets pregnant and has an abortion with money Helen has obtained from another patriotic matriarch, her Aunt Helen. Class values are stronger than the need to reproduce cannon fodder. Helen, who has refused to return to the front, enlists in the WAACs as an assistant cook, infuriating and shaming her family by rejecting the class glamor of the ambulance unit for the drudgery of peeling vegetables with working-class girls, for whom the war salary is a great boost in status. Deliberately suppressing her experience, which would have given her an officer's commission, Helen *chooses* to be declassed, to do women's traditional dirty work, preparing food rather than cleaning the remains of killing. This textual swerve in the rejection of her own class and its complicity in the war is what makes *Not So Quiet . . .* so interesting and problematic a text. While it has followed the narrative of gender normality in its lesbian bashing (as May Sinclair's *The Romantic* creates the cowardly soldier—read "homosexual"—as a vampire), *Not So Quiet . . .* figures a kind of freedom for Helen in the break from her family and class. She trades the "khaki and red" world of ambulance driving at the front for the (relatively) "green" world of preparing food for the WAACs.

A feminist reader recognizes that this is a refusal of the glorification of death-work and a connection made to the eternal round of woman's work in the kitchen, life-work. The new class alliance is a move to another *zone interdite*, the repressed but always present class divisions of English society, which remain in force in wartime segregation. This suggests to me that Evadne Price had read Virginia Woolf's essay, "The Niece of an Earl," published in *Life and Letters* in 1928, in which Woolf set out to prove that she was wrong in asserting that there is no communication between classes—"We are enclosed, and separate, and cut off." This is the great "disability" of the English novelist—"a gulf yawns before us; on the other side are the working classes," who become "objects of pity, examples of curiosity."[42] Did Evadne Price, the journalist, have any ambitions that might have caused her to meet the challenge of Woolf's statement? I think so. Her pseudonym, Helen Zenna Smith, is a case in point. "Helen" is the figure man has created to name the cause of war as female. Male war novelists are always finding "another Troy for her to burn," and women are always revising, contending with, repudiating, or exonerating their own versions of the classical Helen. Smith is the most common English name, Everywoman. She writes, "How jealously I preserve the secret of that Z., that ludicrous Z. bestowed on me by my mother. Z. was the heroine of a book mother read the month before I arrived on earth. She wanted me to grow up like Z. Z. was the paragon of beauty, virtue, and womanliness" (15–16).

The textual Z is, of course, a semiotic signal for sleep, which is the ambulance drivers' lost luxury. It is also the sign for noise, a textual buzz addressed to the reader's ear. As the letter at the end of the alphabet, it signifies the end of writing, perhaps the end of a certain kind of writing. As Zenna, on the title page, the mysterious name looks like a diminutive for Zenobia. There were two Zenobias in history, one who died a Christian martyr, the other the great queen of Palmyra, who refused to be subjugated to Roman rule and was famous for her love and support of literature (Longinus wrote at her court) and her achievements as a military strategist. The letter Z, like King Lear's "thou whoreson Zed, thou unnecessary Letter," marks the "third sex," the masculinized woman or the "war baby," as Z in mathematics is the third symbol for the unknown, after X and Y. Evadne Price is the third person in the writing triangle of Remarque/Winifred Young/Helen Z. Smith. She is the "Z-woman," as a "Z-man" was an army reservist and a "Z-gun" an anti-aircraft rocket, a secret weapon. The "Zenna" also suggests the word for an Indian and Persian harem, *zenana*, a code for the position of all women during war. The person who invented the name "Helen Zenna Smith" wanted to write the great feminist war book.

The most brutally realistic scenes in *Not So Quiet* . . . are not so much the night horrors of driving the wounded but the daytime, stomach-churning job of cleaning out the ambulances of the material wastes of the men—blood, shit, and vomit—hosing and scrubbing with chilblained hands, disinfecting the vans in below-freezing weather. The drivers actually *become* their ambulances. Helen says "all the time they unload *me* the bombs are getting nearer." Mary Borden uses images of ambulances as wombs/tombs, pregnant, polluted bodies—"the motor lorries crouch in the square ashamed, deformed, very weary; their unspeakable burdens bulge under canvas coverings"; the men lie "on their backs in the dark canvas bellies of the ambulances staring at death."[43] The drivers feel as if they are undergoing abortions, birth has gone horribly wrong. Accepting this role, they act out the pollution of a distorted ideology that implicates motherhood with war, the female body with dirt and death. They are war's charwomen, and Smith returns again and again to this theme—bearing both men's and women's roles, the drivers must do all their own dirty work with their machines, but in addition they have to clean their own latrines and quarters and are served rotten and spoiled food by a filthy and lazy cook. Both *Not So Quiet* . . . and *All Quiet on the Western Front* fetishize food because, of course, getting enough to eat is everyone's primary concern in wartime. This is why the breasts of the phallic mother (Tosh, the Commandant, the matriarchal figures on the posters) become such important propagandistic signifiers in the literature of war. Everyone is hungry. Bare-breasted pinups in soldiers' bunks probably had more meaning in relation to hunger than to sex. Smithy's Aunt Helen is an incompetent waitress in the War Workers' Canteen in London, and she observes that it would be more productive if she stayed home and did the housework and let one of her competent maids serve the workers.

When Helen enlists in the WAACs as a domestic worker, it is for revenge on her class: "Put that on your needles and knit it, my patriotic aunt" (212). But she soon becomes attached to the other young women, Misery, Cheery, and Blimey, who, along with Smithy, make up "the Four Whys" who peel potatoes and onions together. Army uniforms are their first experience of good clothes. They have never brushed their teeth nor bathed very often, so the war does improve their circumstances. Helen alone survives the bombing raid that kills these spirited young women, under an "aggressively radiant" she-moon (another matriarchal figure), and she returns home to marry her impotent wounded fiance—"I have kids, anyway" (232). "The trench is like a slaughterhouse"; Blimey's new Burberry trench coat is covered with blood. It is this image one takes away from the novel, the dirty, blood-spattered trench coat, the sign of women's transvestism as soldiers in World War I, still worn and called "trench coats" after their original role. The Burberry recalls the scene where Tosh dies in Helen's arms, the blood soaking the coat. The dirty trench coat worn by Miss Kilman enrages Woolf's Mrs. Dalloway, and it marks the class of the hero's first beloved in Rebecca West's *Return of the Soldier*. The trench coat is a class and gender mark covering the body of women at/in this war. Jenny Gould's essay in *Behind the Lines* examines the profound discomfort aroused by the sight of women in khaki uniforms recorded in *Retrospect* (1938) by the Marchioness of Londonderry, founder of the Women's Legion. Amazons who aped men frightened people, who, of course, wrote letters to the papers demanding that women not be allowed to wear khaki; and the militarism was connected to lesbianism. In an anonymous letter of outrage to *The Morning Post* in 1915, a woman complained of the cropped hair of the "She-men": "I noticed that these women assumed mannish attitudes, stood with legs apart while they smote their riding whips, and looked like self-conscious and not very attractive boys."

Near these ridiculous "poseuses" stood the real thing—a British Officer in mufti. He had lost his left arm and right leg. . . . [I]f these women had a spark of shame left they should have blushed to be seen wearing a parody of the uniform which this officer and thousands like him have made a symbol of honour and glory by their deeds. I do not know the corps to which these ladies belong, but if they cannot become nurses or ward maids in hospital, let them put on sunbonnets and print frocks and go and make hay or pick fruit or make jam.[44]

Some of these blood-soaked (and gender-marked) coats are exhibited in the museum of World War I at Le Linge in Alsace, where trenches dating from the war are still in place, the German concrete bunkers a vivid contrast to the flimsy French earthworks. Signs tell visitors not to stray from the path, as mines may still be active. The pathetic and moving personal belongings of soldiers are on view, along with strategic maps of every battle in the war. The propaganda posters and literature of both sides are equally bloody-minded. I am writing this essay in Strasbourg, where Gutenberg invented the printing press and where Rouget de Lisle sang the Marseillaise for the first time in 1792; where Drivier's unique sculpture (1936) in the Place de la Republique shows a mother with two sons, one dead for Germany and the other dead for France. The other night there was a small demonstration by Alsatian socialists in the Cathedral Square to commemorate the anniversary of the Paris Commune. A group of young women sang in high, sweet voices, surrounded by votive candles, as others carried signs supporting the current struggles in New Caledonia and South Africa. It rains here all the time. I am never out of my trench coat.

Notes

This essay appears as the Afterword to the 1988 reprint of *Not So Quiet . . .* and is reprinted with some changes by the kind permission of Florence Howe and the Feminist Press, New York. I am grateful to the staff at the Feminist Press, particularly my editor, Joanne O'Hare, and Eliza Galaher, who typed the manuscript, for a judicious combination of critique and support.

1. Borden, *The Forbidden Zone.*
2. For photographs of women engaged in various kinds of war work, see Condell and Liddiard, *Working for Victory!*

3. Borden, *The Forbidden Zone*, preface.

4. Bagnold, *A Diary without Dates* (1918; reprinted by Virago, 1978). Virago has also reprinted *The Happy Foreigner* (1920), Bagnold's novel about driving for the French Army just after the war ended. Both books are brilliant and beautifully written. But Enid Bagnold's most disturbing novel is *The Squire* (1938), which makes clear how devastating war values are in domestic society. *The Squire* is about the militarization of motherhood as an institution between the wars.

5. Bagnold, *A Diary without Dates*, 5.

6. Borden, *The Forbidden Zone*, 142. See also Williams's "Mary Borden's Experimental Fiction," which argues that Borden portrays war as a seductive rapist and airplanes and motor lorries as rakish, teasing "creatures of pleasure" even as they are the bearers of death.

7. Borden, *The Forbidden Zone*, 60.

8. Huston, "The Matrix of War," 120–36. For a recent study of the history and literature, see Higonnet et al., *Behind the Lines*. Note also the work of a group of scholars working on the World War I archives at the University of Tulsa. The Tulsa group, which includes Jan Calloway, Claire Culleton, George Otte, Linda Palumbo, Susan Millar Williams, and Angela Ingram, presented their work at the 1987 MLA meeting. Culleton's "Gender-Charged Munitions," a study of the popular representations of women munitions workers in England in World War I, was presented at the International Feminist meeting in Dublin in 1987. See also Ingram's essay on the banning of women's writing, " 'Unutterable Putrefaction' and 'Foul Stuff,' " and her "Un/Reproductions." Tylee's essay, "Maleness Run Riot," takes issue with a provocative article by Gilbert, "Soldier's Heart," which presents the basic thesis of her new three-volume study (with Susan Gubar), *No Man's Land*. Tylee's rebuttal of Gilbert's thesis (that British women were empowered, psychologically, economically, and erotically, by World War I) is an important corrective to misleading arguments and quotations taken out of context. Gilbert's argument is also interrogated by the Tulsa group, by Mayhall's "The Indescribable Barrier," and by my "The Asylums of Antaeus." A different version of "Asylums" appears in Veeser's *The New Historicism*. See Joanne Glasgow's review of Gilbert and Gubar's first volume in *New Directions for Women*, Jan./Feb., 1988, p. 16; and Susan Stanford Friedman's review in the *Women's Review of Books*, July 1988. Gilbert's "sex war" construct is a limited paradigm, which only succeeds in reinforcing the male canon because women writers of the period are only quoted to support the claim that they hated men. This technique appears to be a "feminist" version of the New Historicism, searching texts for evidence to support the argument rather than letting the history emerge with as much force as the literature. "The battle of the sexes" paradigm was outlined many years ago in Samuel Hynes's *The Edwardian Turn of Mind*, based on an argument made by historian George Dangerfield in *The*

Strange Death of Liberal England, which, in turn, was taken directly from Sylvia Pankhurst's *The Suffragette Movement*. For an analysis of the rhetoric and ideology provided by Sylvia Pankhurst to future historians, see my essay in *Suffrage and the Pankhursts*.

9. See West, *The Young Rebecca West: 1911–1917*. The most useful feminist history of English women's struggle is Vicinus's *Independent Women*. Other contemporary socialist feminist theory is to be found in Hamilton's *Marriage as a Trade*. Hamilton regarded birth control as the most important woman's issue, arguing in *Life Errant* that there would be no advances for women "except under a system of voluntary motherhood" (65). Her rebellion was directed against "the dependence implied in the idea of 'destined' marriage, 'destined' motherhood—the identification of success with marriage, of failure with spinsterhood, the artificial concentration of the hopes of girlhood on sexual attraction and maternity." Beauman in *A Very Great Profession* regards Hamilton's *William, An Englishman* (1919) as the best of the women's novels about World War I, "a masterpiece," "incomparable," though her praise enforces an ideological design in the text that prefers a privatized "feminism" to the collective political action of the suffragettes. See also the chapter on the impact of the war on the suffrage movement in Holton's *Feminism and Democracy*. Holton argues that this "was not a time of dormancy, defeatism or depression among suffragists" (116). They "remained intact" by organizing relief work.

10. West, *The Young Rebecca West*, 392.

11. Rose Macaulay's "Many Sisters to Many Brothers" is reprinted in *Scars upon My Heart*, quoted on p. xxv. On Macauley see Passty, *Eros and Androgyny*. Jesse's *The Sword of Deborah* was published by Heinemann in 1919. Sinclair's *The Romantic* is as much a novel about psychoanalysis as it is about the war. Katherine Mansfield despised its "cheap psychoanalysis," "turning life into a *case*" (Beauman, *A Very Great Profession*). Rebecca West's review of Sinclair's report on Belgium describes the effectiveness of the writing as being due to its narrative as a record of "humiliations," and praises her "gallant humiliated book" (*The Young Rebecca West*, 307). Does that experience of humiliation relate to her later humiliation of the "unmanly" man in the novel?

12. Sinclair, *The Romantic*, 245.

13. Warner, "Cottage Mantleshelf," 21–22.

14. Hamilton, *William, An Englishman*, quoted in Beauman.

15. Balfour, *Dr. Elsie Inglis*, 144. See also Cannan, *Grey Ghosts and Voices*, and Hamilton, *Life Errant*, 98. Claire Tylee in "Madness Run Riot" also cites Mrs. St. Clair Stobart, whose memoir, *The Flaming Sword*, was a release from the anger, "cursing in my heart," she felt as a pacifist, easily transferring her feminism to "votes for life, justice for humankind" after the horrors she had seen in the Women's Convoy Corps, which she headed in the Balkan War, and in hospital units in Antwerp, Cherbourg, and Serbia.

16. Sinclair, *The Tree of Heaven*, 104.

17. See Marcus, "Asylums of Antaeus," for a discussion of these ideas.

18. For the banning of books during the war, see Ingram's "Un/Reproductions."

19. La Motte, *The Backwash of War*, 10.

20. Quoted in Stromberg, *Redemption by War*, 235.

21. Cadogan and Craig, *Women and Children First*, 42.

22. Stein, *Paris France*, 38.

23. Kristeva, *Revolution in Poetic Language*.

24. Evadne Price died in Australia in 1985. These autobiographical materials were supplied to Virago Press by Kenneth Attiwill. She married him in 1929 but told him little of her past except that she had been born of English parents off the coast of New South Wales in 1901. When her father died she went on stage to support herself. She was understudy to Dorothy Dix in *The Bird of Paradise* and played Princess Angelica in *The Rose and the Ring*. In 1918 she began work as a journalist with a column called "As a Woman Sees It" in *The Sunday Chronicle*, which also published Rebecca West and George Bernard Shaw. From there she went to *The Sunday Chronicle* and *The Daily Sketch*, and in the late 1920s began to write for serialization in *Novel Magazine* the Jane Turpin children's books, which became very popular.

25. Quoted in Kenneth Attiwill's notes for Virago Press, London.

26. Bakhtin, *The Dialogic Imagination*. Bakhtin's idea of the "carnival-esque" has proved useful for discussing black literature and relates directly to the macabre humor of war novels as well as the latrine scenes of male bonding in Remarque's *All Quiet on the Western Front*.

27. The concepts of "dialogism," "carnival," and "heteroglossia" that I use here were developed by Mikhail Bakhtin in his *Rabelais* and *The Dialogic Imagination*. Gender was not a serious category for Bakhtin, but a feminist revision of his theories is useful, particularly for the intertextual reading of *All Quiet on the Western Front* and *Not So Quiet . . .*, which is my project here, as well as for the carnivalistic aspects of eating, bleeding, defecating, and vomiting in the bodily experience of war, which characterize the two texts.

28. Woolf, "Professions for Women," 163–67.

29. Smith, *Not So Quiet . . . .* Hereafter page numbers in the text refer to the Albert E. Marriott edition of *Not So Quiet . . .*, London, 1930.

30. Remarque, *All Quiet on the Western Front*, 120–21.

31. Feminist critics like Luce Irigaray have written about specularity and touch in female experience and writing as very different from the male. We might think of analyzing whether the woman's experience of hearing and her relation to her own ears is different. See Irigaray, *Speculum of the Other Woman*.

32. In *Women and Children First*, Cadogan and Craig write, "[T]he

method is blunt, brutal and ferociously expository. Subjective indignation has a corrosive effect, however, and the pile-up of disasters tends toward farce" (42). They find the series of novels "strangely crude and offensive in tone," "a violent, unconsidered reaction to an extreme social condition." Helen's husband Roy commits suicide in the sequel, and she is blamed for it. *Women of the Aftermath* deals with the problem of joblessness after the war and the anger of the excluded women. However, Arnold Bennett reviewed *Not So Quiet . . .* in *The Evening Standard*: "Documentary detail about the war is still thousands of miles from being completed. One might have assumed that everything had been said about the Front—until Miss Helen Zenna Smith published her affrighting book . . . which portrays minutely the daily existence of women-chauffeurs and other women workers just behind the Front. This work may well become a prime source for historians. I am glad I read it. But no war book has appalled me more" (see *Arnold Bennett: The Evening Standard Years*). My thanks to Angela Ingram for this reference as well as her invaluable help on all aspects of this essay.

33. Hall, *Well of Loneliness.*

34. Woolf, *Three Guineas*, 148.

35. Colleton, "Gender-Charged Munitions."

36. Remarque, *All Quiet on the Western Front*, 264–68.

37. In *All Quiet on the Western Front*, the bowels are the most important part of the body, as in Bakhtinian carnivalesque. There are lavatory jokes in *Not So Quiet . . .* , but they are not so blatant. The macabre humor of war novels in relation to gender is also worth study. It is clear that Remarque's novel changed the subject of war fictions roughly from epic invocations of individual heroism to initiation into brotherhood, and this influence can be felt in *Catch-22* and *M*A*S*H*.

38. Higonnet, "Civil Wars and Sexual Territories." A version of this paper is included in this volume.

39. For further discussion of *The Well of Loneliness*, see Ingram's " 'Unutterable Putrefaction' and 'Foul Stuff' " and "Narration as Lesbian Seduction in *A Room of One's Own*," in my *Languages of Patriarchy*. See also the scene in *The Well of Loneliness* in which the "general" cautions Stephen about her "emotional friendship" with Mary Llewellyn (330–31).

40. My thanks to Angela Ingram for pointing out the references to Toupie Lowther. The quotations are from Baker, *Our Three Selves*, 125. The Hackett-Lowther papers are in the Imperial War Museum and deserve further study.

41. Dickson, *Radclyffe Hall.*

42. Virginia Woolf, "The Niece of an Earl," 193–97.

43. Quoted in Williams, "Mary Borden's Experimental Fiction."

44. Higonnet et al., *Behind the Lines*, 119.

Works Cited

Aldington, Richard. *Death of a Hero*. London: Chatto & Windus, 1929.

Bagnold, Enid. *A Diary without Dates*. London: Heinemann, 1918. Reprint. London: Virago Press, 1978.

_____. *The Happy Foreigner*. 1920. Reprint. London: Virago Press, 1987.

_____. *The Squire*. 1938. Reprint. London: Virago Press, 1987.

Baker, Michael. *Our Three Selves*. London: Hamish Hamilton, 1985.

Bakhtin, Mikhail. *The Dialogic Imagination*. Edited and translated by Michael Holquist and Caryl Emerson. Austin: University of Texas Press, 1981.

_____. *Rabelais and His Works*. Translated by Hélène Iswalsky. Bloomington: Indiana University Press, 1984.

Balfour, Frances (Lady). *Dr. Elsie Inglis*. London: Hodder & Stoughton, 1918.

Beauman, Nicola. *A Very Great Profession: The Women's Novel, 1914–1939*. London: Virago Press, 1983.

Bennett, Arnold. *Arnold Bennett: The Evening Standard Years*. Edited by Andrew Mylett. London: Chatto & Windus/Archon, 1974.

Blanco White, Amber. *The New Propaganda*. London: Left Bookclub, 1939.

Borden, Mary. *The Forbidden Zone*. London: Heinemann, 1929.

Braybon, Gail. *Women Workers and the First World War*. London: Croom Helm, 1981.

_____, and Penny Summerfield. *Our of the Cage: Women's Experiences in Two World Wars*. London and New York: Pandora, 1987.

Burdekin, Katharine. *Swastika Night*. London: Victor Gollancz, 1937. Reprinted with introduction by Daphne Patai. New York: Feminist Press, 1985.

Cadogan, Mary, and Patricia Craig. *Women and Children First: The Fiction of the Two World Wars*. London: Victor Gollancz, 1978.

_____. *You're a Brick, Angela!: A New Look at Girls' Fiction from 1839 to 1975*. London: Victor Gollancz, 1976.

Cannan, May Wedderburn. *Grey Ghosts and Voices*. London: Roundwood Press, 1976.

Colleton, Claire. "Gender-Charged Munitions: The Language of World War I Munitions Reports." *Women's Studies International Forum* 11, no. 2 (1988): 109–16.

Comyns, Barbara. *The Skin Chairs*. 1962. Reprint. London: Penguin Books, 1987.

Condell, Diana, and Jean Liddiard. *Working for Victory?: Images of Women in the First World War*. London: Routledge & Kegan Paul, 1987.

Dangerfield, George. *The Strange Death of Liberal England*. 1935. Reprint. New York: Capricorn Books, 1961.

Dickson, Lovat. *Radclyffe Hall at the Well of Loneliness: A Sapphic*

Chronicle. New York: Charles Scribner's Sons, 1975.

Ford, Ford Madox, *No More Parades*. 1925. Reprint. New York: New American Library, 1964.

Gilbert, Sandra M. "Soldier's Heart: Literary Men, Literary Women, and the Great War." *Signs* 8, no. 3 (Spring 1983): 422–50.

————, and Susan Gubar. *No Man's Land*. New Haven: Yale University Press, 1988.

Gould, Jenny. "Women's Military Service in First World War Britain." In *Behind the Lines: Gender and the Two World Wars*, edited by Margaret Higonnet, Jane Jensen, Sonya Michel, and Margaret Weitz, 114–25. New Haven: Yale University Press, 1987.

Graves, Robert. *Good-bye to All That*. Hammondsmith, Eng.: Penguin Books, 1957.

Hall, Radclyffe. *The Well of Loneliness*. Garden City, New York: Blue Ribbon Books, 1928.

Hamilton, Cecily. *Life Errant*. London: J. M. Dent, 1935.

————. *Marriage as a Trade*. London: Chapman & Hall, 1909. Reprinted with introduction by Jane Lewis. London: Women's Press, 1981.

————. *William, An Englishman*. London: Skeffington & Son, 1919.

Hemingway, Ernest. *A Farewell to Arms*. New York: Charles Scribner's Sons, 1925.

Higonnet, Margaret R. "Civil Wars and Sexual Territories." Paper delivered at the Second International Conference on Feminist Theory, Dubrovnik, May 1988, also in this volume.

————, Jane Jensen, Sonya Michel, and Margaret Collins Weitz. *Behind the Lines: Gender and the Two World Wars*. New Haven: Yale University Press, 1987.

Holton, Sandra. *Feminism and Democracy*. New York: Cambridge University Press, 1986.

Huston, Nancy. "The Matrix of War: Mothers and Heroes." In *The Female Body in Western Culture: Contemporary Perspectives*, edited by Susan Rubin Suleiman, 120–36. Cambridge, Mass.: Harvard University Press, 1986.

Hynes, Samuel. *The Edwardian Turn of Mind*. Princeton, N.J.: Princeton University Press, 1968.

Ingram, Angela. "Un/Reproductions: States of Banishment in Some English Novels after the Great War." In *Women's Writing in Exile*, edited by Mary Lynn Broe and Angela Ingram. Chapel Hill: University of North Carolina Press, 1989.

————. " 'Unutterable Putrefaction' and 'Foul Stuff': Two Obscene Novels of the 1920s." *Women's Studies International Forum* 9, no. 4 (1986): 341–54.

Irigaray, Luce. *Speculum of the Other Woman*. Ithaca, N.Y.: Cornell University Press, 1980.

Jesse, F. Tennyson. *The Sword of Deborah*. London: Heinemann, 1919.

Kristeva, Julia. *Revolution in Poetic Language*. New York: Columbia University Press, 1985.

———. "Women's Time." *Signs* 7 (Autumn 1981): 5–12.

La Motte, Ellen. *The Backwash of War: The Human Wreckage of the Battlefield as Witnessed by an American Nurse*. New York: Putnam's, 1916. Banned and reprinted 1934.

Macaulay, Rose. "Many Sisters to Many Brothers." In *Scars upon My Heart: Women's Poetry and Verse of the First World War*, edited by Judith Kazantis and Catherine Reilly. London: Virago Press, 1981.

Marcus, Jane. "The Asylums of Antaeus: Women, War, and Madness: Is There a Feminist Fetishism?" In *The Difference Within: Feminism and Critical Theory*, edited by Elizabeth Meese and Alice Parker, 49–83. Amsterdam: John Benjamins, 1989.

———. *Virginia Woolf and the Languages of Patriarchy*. Bloomington: Indiana University Press, 1987.

———, ed. *Suffrage and the Pankhursts*. London and New York: Routledge & Kegan Paul, 1988.

Marwick, Arthur. *The Deluge: British Society and the First World War*. New York: Norton, 1970.

———. *Women at War*. London: Fontana, 1977.

Mayhall, Laura. "The Indescribable Barrier: English Women and the Effect of the First World War." Unpublished paper, Stanford University.

Pankhurst, Sylvia. *The Suffragette Movement*. London: Lovat Dickson & Thompson, 1931.

Passty, Jeanette. *Eros and Androgyny: The Legacy of Rose Macaulay*. Cranbury, N. J.: Fairleigh Dickinson University Press, 1988.

Price, Evadne. See Helen Zenna Smith.

Rathbone, Irene. *They Call It Peace*. London: J. M. Dent, 1936.

———. *We That Were Young*. London: Chatto & Windus, 1932. Reprint. New York: Feminist Press, 1988.

Remarque, Erich Maria. *All Quiet on the Western Front*. Translated by A. W. Wheen. New York: Fawcett/Crest, 1929.

Scott, Joan. "Rewriting History." In *Behind the Lines: Gender and the Two World Wars*, edited by Margaret R. Higonnet, Jane Jensen, Sonya Michel, and Margaret Weitz, 21–30. New Haven: Yale University Press, 1987.

Sinclair, May. *Journal of Impressions in Belgium*. London: 1916.

———. *The Romantic*. London: Collin, 1920.

———. *The Tree of Heaven*. New York: Macmillan Co., 1918.

Smith, Helen Zenna. *Luxury Ladies*. London: John Long, 1933.

———. *Not So Quiet . . .: Stepdaughters of War*. London: Albert E. Marriott, 1930. Reprint. New York: Feminist Press, 1988.

———. *Shadow Women*. London: John Long, 1932.

———. *They Lived with Me*. London: John Long, 1934.

————. *Women of the Aftermath.* London: John Long, 1931.

Stein, Gertrude. *Paris France.* 1940. Reprint. New York: Liveright, 1970.

————. *Wars I Have Seen.* 1945. Reprint. London: Brilliance Books, 1984.

Stobart, Mrs. St. Clair. *The Flaming Sword in Serbia and Elsewhere.* London: Hodder & Stoughton, 1916.

Stromberg, Roland N. *Redemption by War: Intellectuals and 1914.* Lawrence, Kans.: Regents Press of Kansas, 1982.

Tylee, Claire. "Maleness Run Riot: The Great War and Women's Resistance to Militarism." *Women's Studies International Forum* 11, no. 3 (1988), 199–210.

Veeser, Harold. *The New Historicism.* New York: Methuen, 1988.

Vicinus, Martha. *Independent Women.* Chicago: University of Chicago Press, 1985.

Warner, Sylvia Townsend. "Cottage Mantleshelf." In *Collected Poems,* edited by Claire Harman, 21–22. New York: Viking, 1982.

Wells, H. G. *Mr. Britling Sees It Through.* London: Cassell, 1916.

West, Rebecca. *The Return of the Soldier.* London: Nisbet & Co., 1918.

[West, Rebecca.] *War Nurse.* New York: Cosmopolitan, 1930.

West, Rebecca. *The Young Rebecca West: 1911–1917.* Edited by Jane Marcus. New York: Viking, 1978.

Williams, Susan Millar. "Mary Borden's Experimental Fiction: Female Sexuality and the Language of War." Paper delivered at 1987 MLA session on Women's Writing in World War I.

Wiltsher, Ann. *Most Dangerous Women: Feminist Peace Campaigners of the Great War.* London: Pandora, 1986.

Woolf, Virginia. *Mrs. Dalloway.* New York: Harcourt, Brace & World, 1925.

————. *Jacob's Room.* New York: Harcourt, Brace & World, 1922.

————. "The Niece of an Earl." In *The Second Common Reader,* 193–97. New York: Harcourt, Brace & World, 1932.

————. "Professions for Women." 1931. Reprint of the long version in *The Partigers,* edited by Mitchell Leaska. New York: New York Public Library and Reader Books, 1977.

Yourcenar, Marguerite. *Coup de Grâce.* New York: Farrar, Straus & Giroux, 1957.

Laura
Stempel
Mumford May Sinclair's

The Tree of Heaven:

The Vortex of Feminism,

the Community of War

One of the common beliefs of British suffrage-era feminists was that women's equal participation in politics and government would contribute to the abolition of war. Whether because women were viewed as innately pacific, or as having a special investment in the preservation of human life because of their roles as childbearers,[1] it was widely expected that the enfranchisement of women would herald a major change in the means by which international disputes were decided. Until World War I, the issue of women's relation to war was an important touchstone in debates over the position of women, and arguments against women's enfranchisement often rested on the contention that men's role in warfare justified superior civil and political rights.[2] In general, feminists countered this argument with the fact of women's crucial contributions to culture and civilization, even going so far as to say, as did Olive Schreiner, that the risks women ran in giving birth, providing "the primal munition of war," greatly outweighed the risks men took on the battlefield.[3] This was not, however, a universal feminist assumption, and more conservative members of the suffrage movement even conceded the idea of men's greater contribution. Nor were all feminists united in opposing war as a means of settling international conflicts, although such a prowar stance was much more common among antifeminists like Mrs. Humphry Ward.

All of this altered with World War I, however, for it was, ironically, the war that heralded a change in feminist activity, with suffragists converted into war workers, and even the most militant activists released from prison on condition that they pledge to refrain from violence for the duration. While the majority of feminist organizations disbanded, including the militant Women's Social and Political Union, a new split developed regarding women's relation to war. Committed pacifist feminists like Crystal Eastman and Olive Schreiner continued to work against warfare and even counseled conscientious objectors, refusing altogether to participate in the feminist organizations that had become, in their view, part of the machinery of war.[4] But these women were in the minority. Among those who supported the feminist war effort was novelist May Sinclair, best known today for her 1918 psychological novel *Mary Olivier* and her coinage of the phrase "stream of consciousness" to describe the work of Dorothy Richardson. Although Sinclair, an active participant in the suffrage movement, wrote twenty-four novels, only one—*The Tree of Heaven*, published in 1917—focuses on the feminist movement, and it is interesting both because of its direct attack on militant feminism and because of its view of war as the site of genuine community. Throughout the novel Sinclair uses the image of a "vortex" to contrast false and dangerous attempts at community with the liberating form provided by war, as she describes the historical events that signaled the beginning of organized feminism's fifty-year hiatus.

The novel, divided into three parts, focuses on Frances Harrison and her daughter Dorothy (or Dorothea), and it is Dorothy's story that demonstrates Sinclair's attitude toward feminism and the war. The two women are sharply contrasted, for while Frances lives in a comforting dream world that centers on her three sons,[5] Dorothy's sphere is very much the outside world of action. Dorothy is in many ways a feminist protagonist, for she refuses the conventional role as her parents' emotional support (at thirteen it is already clear that "Dorothy was not going to be her mother's companion, or her father's, either" [45]) and insists instead on a life of learning and political activity. Although readers might see her interest in political change as a function of her secondary status within the family, there is no suggestion that she makes this connection, but rather that she knows instinctively that certain rights—including the vote —must be fought for. Much of the novel chronicles Dorothy's participation in a militant suffrage organization, and she continues to be politically active even during the war; there is never any question about her commitment to social change, but the terms of that commitment and the definition of that change alter dramatically. Unlike the protagonists of other novels describing the suffrage movement, such as Elizabeth Robins's *The Convert*, Dorothy experiences no epiphany or sudden conversion to the feminist cause—

instead, her epiphany involves the *rejection* of organized feminism and the embracing of what she perceives as a larger cause, the war effort.

To understand Dorothy's movement from militant suffragist to war worker, and Sinclair's unusual analysis of the differences between war and other political activity, we need to look closely at the prevailing image of the "vortex."[6] For Sinclair and her characters, the vortex describes any group activity that involves mass emotion and threatens individuality, personal integrity, and self-control. The image names the long central section of the novel, which depicts Dorothy's involvement with feminism, but it appears in connection with any experience in which the characters fear a loss of self. In childhood, Dorothy's brother Michael gives the best description:

> "It's sort of—sort of forgetting things."
> "What things?"
> "I don't know, Mummy. I think—it's pieces of me that I want to remember. At a party I can't feel all of myself at once—like I do now." [18]

This image, though not always named, recurs in Michael's hatred of boarding school, where "you're expected to do everything when the other fellows are doing it, whether you want to or not, as if the very fact that they're doing it too didn't make you hate it" (87). When he becomes a poet he finds "the vortex of revolutionary Art" equally threatening (233), and as World War I begins he tries to resist the vortex of patriotism and violence and remain outside the conflict. These feelings—anxiety at the possibility of being swept up and disintegrated by mass emotion or collective behavior—are common to Dorothy, two of her brothers, and her mother, who typically fears the effects of the vortex on her sons. Frances's overriding fear is of their adulthood, their complete separation from her, and "she saw her children . . . swept every day a little farther from the firm, well-ordered sanctities, a little nearer to the unclean moral vortex that to her was the most redoubtable of all" (156). This "unclean moral vortex" is most threatening in the artistic circles favored by Michael and his brother Nicky: "These people lived in a moral vortex; they whirled round and round with each other; they were powerless to resist the swirl. Not one of them had any other care than to love and to make love after the manner of the Vortex. This was their honour, not to be left out of it, but to be carried away, to be sucked in, and whirl round and round with each other and the rest" (158).

For Dorothy, this same quality manifests itself in the feminist movement, for she sees it—particularly the militant organization she has joined—as demanding unquestioning allegiance and un- thinking emotion, but in contrast to her mother and brothers, the feminist vortex seems also to hold an almost perverse attraction for her. The word "vortex" is first used in connection with her friend Rosalind, who has, in Dorothy's view, fallen victim to the false sense of activity and control it generates: "She whirled in it now, and would go on whirling, under the impression that her move- ments made it move" (124). More important than Rosalind's vic- timization, however, is Dorothy's fascination, for she both fears the vortex and defines herself through her power to resist it: "She liked the feeling of her own power to resist, to keep her head, to beat up against the rush of the whirlwind, to wheel round and round out- side it, and swerve away before the thing got her" (124).

Despite these fears, however, Dorothy continues to take part in suffrage activities, refusing her fiancé's demand that she stop—an- other, more personal attempt to violate her autonomy—and finally being jailed for her role in a riot. In prison she welcomes solitary confinement as a relief from the intensity of the feminist vortex, and at a banquet honoring the release of Dorothy and other militant prisoners, she has her final confrontation with it:

> The singing had threatened her when it began; so that she felt again her old terror of the collective soul. Its massed emo- tion threatened her. She longed for her white-washed prison- cell, for its hardness, its nakedness, its quiet, its visionary peace. She tried to remember. Her soul, in its danger, tried to get back there. But the soul of the crowd in the hall below her swelled and heaved itself towards her, drawn by the Vortex. She felt the rushing of the whirlwind; it sucked at her breath; the Vortex was drawing her, too; the powerful, abominable thing almost got her. The sight of [her aunt] Emmeline saved her.
>
> She might have been singing and swaying too, carried away in the same awful ecstasy, if she had not seen Emmeline. By looking at Emmeline she saved her soul; it stood firm again; she was clear and hard and sane.   [225]

The contrast she sees between the "massed emotion" of the ban- quet and the "visionary peace" of her prison cell is crucial, for it is in prison that she has an epiphany which reveals to her the insignificance of the militant cause.[7] To Frank Drayton, her fiancé, she says: "The things that came to me were so much bigger than the things I went in for. I could see all along we weren't going to get it that way. And I knew we *were* going to get it some other way. I don't in the least know how, but it'll be some big, tremendous way that'll make all this fighting and fussing seem the rottenest game" (220). The prison banquet is the last we see of Dorothy's active involvement in militant feminism, for a year later the war has begun, the suffrage organizations have disbanded, and Dorothy has "settled down" to write reformist articles on marriage (232).

For 1917 readers of this novel it probably came as no surprise that the "bigger" thing Dorothy anticipated in her prison cell should turn out to be World War I, but for those interested in women's relation to war, it is a particularly revealing twist. First, Dorothy's perception of the suffrage struggle as "only . . . a small, ridiculous part" of a larger struggle for freedom (221) is an unusual position for an apparent feminist to take. This characterization goes beyond the common view of the time that other issues necessarily took a backseat to the crisis of war, for Dorothy's view of the suffrage movement as ultimately "ridiculous" and petty is reinforced by Sinclair's description of the final days of militant agitation:

> The Women's Franchise Union . . . ran riot up and down the country. It smashed windows; it hurled stone ginger-beer bottles into the motor cars of Cabinet Ministers; it poured treacle into pillar-boxes; it invaded the House of Commons by the water-way, in barges, from which women, armed with megaphones, demanded the vote from infamous legislators drinking tea on the Terrace; it went up in balloons and showered down propaganda on the City; now and then, just to show what violence it could accomplish if it liked, it burned down a house or two in a pure and consecrated ecstasy of Feminism.   [232–33]

Even more important is her identification of the collective emotion of the feminist movement as a hysteria threatening members with loss of self, a position that contrasts sharply with the views of other feminists, like Schreiner and Robins, who found such union spiritually fulfilling, creative, and enabling.[8] But most striking is the characterization of the war as totally unlike the mass annihilation of the group activities Dorothy and her family fear and abhor.

Given the prominence of the vortex image throughout this novel, we might expect to see the war as its ultimate expression, and indeed Michael does originally see it that way: "[I]n his worst dreams of what [the vortex] could do to him Michael had never imagined anything more appalling than the collective patriotism of the British and their Allies, this rushing together of the souls of four countries to make one monstrous soul" (327). But for Sinclair, and eventually for all of her characters, the war exemplifies just the opposite: in war is found the genuine community that the frenzied ecstasy of the various vortexes can only imitate. Paradoxically, the war is seen as far less threatening than the vortex of boarding school or art or feminism—even though every significant male character who enlists in the army is killed in action. Even Michael, whose initial reaction to the war is so intense, changes his mind and is moved to enlist when his brother Nicky is killed in battle.

While the term "vortex" is briefly applied to the war ("The little vortex of the Woman's Movement was swept without a sound into the immense vortex of the War" [299]), Sinclair's description of the experience of war makes it clear that this is a very different kind of whirlwind. The war is described as "reality itself," greater than the love Dorothy feels for Frank and "more than they" (313), and as Dorothy remembers after his death, Frank calls it "the biggest fight for freedom" (317). Even for civilians, war transforms long-held feelings, such as Frances's impatience over her husband's "invariable, irritating rightness," into pride and affection (322). Individuals become identified as parts or potential parts of the war effort: "[Frances] was proud of [Anthony], not because he was her husband and the father of her children, but because he was a man who could help England. They were both proud of Michael and Nicholas and John, not because they were their sons, but because they were men who could fight for England" (322). Internal family hostilities are resolved, and even Frances's three unmarried sisters "had ceased from mutual recriminations" and are "shocked into a curious gentleness to each other," despite a lifetime of antagonism (297). And Frances, whose entire adult life has been devoted to her children, now spends her days working "in a room behind [Anthony's] office, receiving, packing, and sending off great cases of food and clothing to the Belgian soldiers" (321).

But it is the experience of battle that points up the difference between the community of war and the "little vortex" of feminism. Nicky's letters home describe a powerful feeling that is "more than anything you could have imagined. . . . It grows more and more so, simply swinging you on to [the parapets], and that swing makes up for all the rotten times put together" (363–64). While he also describes the boredom and the shocking sights of corpses and destruction, the "horrible harmony" of war (366), it is the ecstasy of battle, the "gorgeous fight-feeling," that is foremost: "When you're up first out of the trench and stand alone on the parapet, it's absolute happiness. And the charge is—well, it's simply heaven. It's as if you've never really lived till then" (368).[9] Nicky disagrees with Michael's characterization of such feelings as "nothing but a form of sex-madness" (368), or a fellow soldier's idea that "it's simply submerged savagery bobbing up to the top—a hidden lust for killing, and the hidden memory of having killed" (369). For Nicky, the chance of being killed is far more significant than the act of killing: "You're bang up against reality—you're going clean into it—and the sense of it's exquisite" (369).

Michael's gradual realization that "the thing that threatened him had been, not the War but [the] collective war-spirit, clamouring for his private soul" (376) is crucial in distinguishing the various vortexes from the "exquisite" feelings Nicky describes. Despite his attempts to evade the war's obvious manifestations—drilling troops, departing soldiers—by retreating to the country, Michael has a slowly gathering epiphany which, like Dorothy's in her prison cell, shows him "that it was the greatest War of Independence that had ever been" (377), but it is only Nicky's death that prompts him to enlist: " 'Of course I shall go out now. I might have known that this would end it. *He* [Nicky] knew' " (380). Significantly, this decision lessens the pain of his brother's death: "[B]ecause he was going out, and because he would be killed, he was not feeling Nicky's death so acutely. . . . He had been let off that" (381).

Michael's conversion is far from painless, for he immediately experiences intense fear of the battles and destruction he will see, and he comes to believe that his long avoidance of the war has been only cowardice. Once he enters the fight, however, he too reports "exquisite" moments: "Nothing—not even poetry—can beat an infantry charge when you're leading it" (394). His newly found sense of community—"It feels as if you were drawing [all your men] up after you" (394)—contrasts sharply with his earlier anxiety about collective activity, and he describes an "ecstasy" that is connected to danger but "hasn't anything to do" with courage (395): "Doesn't it look as if danger were the point of contact with reality, and death the closest point? You're through. Actually you lay hold on eternal life, and you know it" (396). The feeling is like "the utter satisfaction when you see a beautiful thing" (397), and for Michael it transcends death, making the friends and family who have been killed somehow not dead, for their ecstatic souls live on.

It is important to note that, in contrast to many feminists, Sinclair was not a believer in women's equal contribution to the development of civilization. As she argued in her 1912 essay "A Defence of Men," "It is only by danger and hardship faced and endured by men that civilisation and comfort have been made possible for any of us,"[10] a clear reference to war and a belief that probably laid the foundation for the prowar stance of *The Tree of Heaven*. But there is far more going on here than simply the idea that men's participation in warfare makes civilization possible, for her depiction of the British war effort includes detailed descriptions of women's contributions to it, rolling bandages and knitting socks, driving ambulances, resettling refugees, working as nurses. (Sinclair herself spent seventeen days in Belgium as a member of an ambulance corps, an experience she describes in her 1915 *A Journal of Impressions in Belgium*.) The absence of any attention to the issues over which the war is fought (aside from vague references to freedom and ethnocentric remarks about the Germans) makes it impossible to read the novel as a justification of this war in particular.

This last aspect of the novel is important, because both feminism and World War I lose any specific political dimensions in Sinclair's presentation of them. The particular issues at stake—either in the women's movement or in the war—are apparently of no importance, for even questions of "bigger" or "lesser" struggles for freedom are only used as arguments for or against participation in a specific movement, and drop out of the picture as soon as this is resolved. Instead, both war and feminism become mere opportunities for either community or loss of self.

This may seem like an extreme statement. Perhaps the absence of concrete issues can be explained by the fact that readers were already familiar with them (did British citizens in 1917 really need to be told why they were at war?), or by the desire to engender even more passion for the war effort (don't general remarks about "the greatest War of Independence" ever fought seem more compelling than dry analyses of particular political issues?). But Sinclair's focus in this novel on questions of community suggests a more profound meaning to the ecstasy of battle than the simple glorification of World War I.

Resonating throughout *The Tree of Heaven* is an idea recently developed by Nancy Hartsock in *Money, Sex, and Power*, her study of power and notions of community. Hartsock points to the Homeric ideal of the warrior-hero, and subsequent Greek texts, as the basis for community structures founded on dominance, violence, and death, in contrast to the exchange model (favored by Marx and many others), which posits a community of interests. Her goal is to point toward a theory of power that will explain not only class conflict, as the exchange model does, but other relations of dominance and submission, particularly those centering on gender and race. To do so she examines the Homeric ideal in which, she argues, "[t]he political community *as community* exists only on the battlefield, where the collective good can be the primary concern of the hero."[11] Her defining example is Achilles, who must choose between honor through death in battle and long life at home, and who, being a hero, knows that the former is the only possible choice. In the agonal community typified by this choice, the preservation of life is secondary to the gaining of honor, and the existence of the political community—as opposed to the individual family household—depends on men's willingness to make this choice.

Hartsock's analysis is complex and sophisticated, entailing much more than this brief allusion can suggest, but it offers a compelling context for reading *The Tree of Heaven*, for we see in this novel a fictional embodiment of the very idea that, according to her, forms the foundation of contemporary male-dominated conceptions of community. While Hartsock claims that women who theorize about power come to radically different conclusions about the basis of community,[12] the vision we see here—created not only by a woman, but by a self-identified feminist—is almost identical to the male-centered one Hartsock describes. In *The Tree of Heaven*, almost all attempts at community (boarding schools, children's parties, artistic cliques) or collective political action (the militant suffrage movement) are doomed to failure because they require sublimation of the self into mass emotion and activity, yet produce no compensating vision or honor. Only in war can *individual* men find *individual* moments of ecstatic vision—moments that depend on immediate danger, risk, and expected loss of life. Paradoxically, it is the willingness to be destroyed, to die in battle, that permits the individual soul to prevail or, in Homeric terms, to achieve honor. The struggle that leads to such "exquisite" moments is simultaneously a collective and an entirely individual one, strangely divorced from whatever political issues might have led to the particular war or battle, and divorced, too, from personal concerns about family, home, art, and so on. Dorothy's vain attempts to remain an individual in the midst of collective feminist struggle underline the futility, in Sinclair's view, of seeking "exquisite" moments outside of war. Her experience in the suffrage riot is typical, for, while her arrest is the result of an individual act—trying to defend a woman attacked by police—she is swept up in the pantheon of feminist "heroes," as in the banquet celebrating her release from prison. From this perspective, as Hartsock suggests, war is the only legitimate public activity, and its values are necessarily opposed to those embodied in the home. In the novel, this opposition is reflected in Frances's mourning for her sons' *bodies*, while other characters recognize that it is their *souls*—now eternally ecstatic—that matter.

This recognition suggests that what is wrong with the vortex, in its various forms, is the vain attempt to impose the public value of self-denial (denial of selfhood) on lesser activities than war. While it is difficult to identify these activities as "private"—at least in the modern world, education, art, and political change are all part of the sphere conventionally defined as public[13]—it is clear that, for Sinclair, they fall short of the ideal of battle. One reason for this may be that, while they take place beyond the confines of the home, they do not involve the risk of life that transforms soldiers into heroes. (Most feminists today would see the suffrage activists as intensely "heroic" in their risk of reputation, position, family ties, and even health and physical safety, but Sinclair's highly critical portrait of the militant movement makes it obvious that she does not share this view.)

As Sandra Gilbert points out, Sinclair's description of wartime ecstasy "certainly . . . reflects a transference to men of the liberation she herself experienced when she worked in Belgium with the Munro [Ambulance] Corps."[14] Yet, in contrast to the other women writers Gilbert discusses, Sinclair seems a poor example—particularly in this novel—of the increased power and freedom women gained through the war. Among other things, Dorothy's explicit criticism of and withdrawal from collective activity with other women is quite different from the "union among women" Gilbert describes.[15] The emphasis throughout the novel on the dangers of the various vortexes, mere imitations and intimations of the war, underlines this contrast.

Through the character of Dorothy, Sinclair does hint at a feminist revision of the community of war: not surprisingly, she suggests women's participation in that community, not the redefinition of the community itself, and certainly neither the redefinition nor the abolition of war. Dorothy's original epiphany in prison is, as she herself points out, a smaller version of the ecstatic visions her brothers achieve, and both she and her cousin Veronica immediately understand the significance of these visions,[16] while Frances —above all a mother, and a representative of the private world of the home—cannot quite see their value. Dorothy is also courageous (as is Veronica), wishes she could take a larger part in the war— even be a soldier[17]—and is the first in her family to be able to articulate clearly the difference between war and the vortex's threat. Thus Sinclair hints that women are, or can be, capable of the heroism of warriors, and challenges the conventional assumption—including her own assessment of history—that war represents men's unique contribution to civilization.

But these are only hints, for Dorothy—like the other women in the novel and like the men, including her father, who are too old or otherwise unfit for military service—can only participate from the sidelines. Although women do go to the front as ambulance drivers and nurses, Dorothy stays home—working hard, yes, but never risking her life. And she stays home because Frank insists that women's presence at the front " 'won't make it easier for *us* to win the War. You can't expect us to fight so comfy, and to be killed so comfy, if we know our womenkind are being pounded to bits in the ground we've just cleared' " (313–14).[18] Thus the women are reduced to comforting symbols of home and England, inspiring their men to feats of valor through the need to protect these dependents, but never able to be heroes themselves. (It is easy to see what this equation means for the men who, because of age or physical disability, are unable to join the war: they, too, are denied the opportunity for the transcendence that can only be gained through battle, but being men, they can take little consolation from the "comfiness" they might inspire in those at the front.)

Because the vortex of the militant suffrage movement provides the major contrast to the genuine community of the war, the novel suggests that women are even less able to be heroic than Dorothy's courage and determination might imply. As Nancy Hartsock's analysis suggests, the site of heroic action and of meaningful community is the same, and that site is totally inaccessible to women. When women organize collectively to agitate for feminist change, their activities are ridiculous and even dangerous, their movement hysterical rather than ecstatic. When men organize collectively for war, they provide themselves with an avenue for transcendence of self. Militant women can create only a "little vortex"; military men can achieve "heaven."

Sinclair's attitude toward World War I was not unique to her, but not all prowar feminists went to such lengths to justify war in general, and her explicit contrast between feminism and war suggests the dangers of a feminist acceptance of certain cultural assumptions. In *The Tree of Heaven* we see a rejection, even a denial, of the satisfactions of collective action celebrated by many of her contemporaries and by feminists today. Even more important, Sinclair privileges traditional male-centered ideas of what sort of collective activity really counts by denying the importance of struggle in the private sphere. In Sinclair's view, as in the Homeric community Hartsock describes, the supposedly private values challenged by the feminist movement mean little beside the public world exemplified by warfare, and by maintaining the Homeric ideal of a heroic transcendence attainable only through battle, she also maintains the secondary position of women. At best, Sinclair hints that, by joining men in battle, women may hope to achieve an ecstasy similar to those her male characters experience. But by failing—in fact, refusing—to question the basic premise that war is the only real site of such ecstasy, she relegates the very movement she has championed, as well as the art she practices, to a position of triviality.

Notes

I am extremely grateful to Mary Lou Emery for her thoughtful reading of earlier versions of this essay; to the University of Wisconsin-Madison Women's Studies Program for support and community; and to Nancy St. Clair, who lent me the book.

1. This is the explanation that Olive Schreiner gives in her 1911 work of feminist theory, *Woman and Labor*, and reiterates in her posthumous novel, *From Man to Man*.

2. In the 1889 "Appeal against Female Suffrage," for example, Mrs. Humphry Ward and over a hundred other prominent women signed a letter that argued, among other things, that "women's direct participation [in Parliament, commerce, and the armed forces] is made impossible" by innate disability or "by strong formations of custom and habit resting ultimately upon physical difference. . . . Therefore it is not just to give to women di-

rect power of deciding questions . . . equal to that possessed by men" (260–61).

3. Schreiner, *Woman and Labor*, 174.

4. See for example Blanche Weisen Cook's collection *Crystal Eastman on Women and Revolution*, which includes essays on Eastman's antiwar and pacifist work, such as her participation in the Woman's Peace Party of New York City.

5. Exemplary of Frances's dreaming is her conflict with her husband Anthony over the tree of the novel's title:

> She had always dreamed of having a tree of Heaven in her garden; and he was destroying her dream. He replied that he didn't want to destroy her dream, but the tree really *was* an ash. You could tell by the bark, and by the leaves and by the number and the shape of the leaflets. And anyhow, this was the first he'd heard about her dream.
>
> "You don't know," said Frances, "what goes on inside me." [Sinclair, *The Tree of Heaven*, 11; subsequent references cited parenthetically in text]

Her habit of viewing the world entirely in terms of her children (actually, her sons) is typified by her interpretation of a game of tennis: "[I]t was not Vereker or Parsons or Norris that she loved or that she saw. It was Michael, Nicholas and John whose adolescence was foreshadowed in those athletic forms wearing white flannels; Michael, Nicky and John, in white flannels, playing fiercely" (38).

6. There is undoubtedly some connection between Sinclair's use of the term "vortex" and the Vorticism propounded by her friends Ezra Pound and Wyndham Lewis, but it is crucial that, for Sinclair, the concept is an entirely negative (though tempting) one.

7. For Elaine Showalter, Dorothy's prison experience is typical of the "turning inward" she finds in feminist writers of the period, a withdrawal from political activism and analysis to solitary meditation. See Showalter, *A Literature of Their Own*, 215, 239.

8. Both Schreiner in *Woman and Labor* and Elizabeth Robins in her collection of feminist essays, *Way Stations*, emphasize the spiritual gains women make through collective action with other women. Sinclair's characterization of the militant movement as hysterical is also strange, considering that her most extended published defense of feminism, a Women Writers' Suffrage League pamphlet called *Feminism*, is a critique of exactly such a characterization by rabid antifeminist Sir Almroth Wright.

9. The contrast between the genuine "heaven" Nicky describes and the pretended "tree of heaven" of the title is a telling one, suggesting as it does that men in battle achieve a happiness that women at home can only find by a fantastic reshaping of reality.

10. Sinclair, "A Defence of Men," 567.

11. Hartsock, *Money, Sex, and Power*, 188.

12. See especially 210–51, where Hartsock discusses Hannah Arendt's work and that of feminists theorizing about power.

13. I stress that these categorizations are modern ones, for in Homeric terms, as Hartsock emphasizes, the definitions of public and private are quite different. I am thankful to Mary Lou Emery for reminding me of this.

14. Gilbert, "Soldier's Heart," 440. Throughout *A Journal of Impressions in Belgium*, Sinclair describes feelings that she later ascribes to various characters in *The Tree of Heaven*. She recounts her initial fear before leaving for Belgium, her nervous anticipation of the horrors she will see, and the mounting excitement coupled with the tedium of waiting for something to do. There is even a hint of the threat and attraction of the vortex when she writes:

Odd how the War changes us. I, who abhor and resist authority, who hardly know how I am to bring myself to obey my friend the Commandant, am enamoured of this Power [of military authority] and am utterly submissive. I realize with something like a thrill that we are in a military hospital under military orders; and that my irrelevant former self, with all that it has desired or done, must henceforth cease (perhaps irrevocably) to exist. I contemplate its extinction with equanimity. [23–24]

The realization that she may actually be in danger prompts a feeling much like those Nicky and Michael describe: "It is as if my soul had never really belonged to me until now, as if it had been drugged or drunk and had never known what it was to be sober until now. The sensation is distinctly agreeable. And on the top of it all there is a peace which I distinctly recognize as the peace of God" (107). But the journal emphasizes most of all Sinclair's frustration over not being allowed to see (much less participate in) a real battle, and her envy of and feeling of being secondary to those exposed to immediate danger.

15. Gilbert, "Soldier's Heart," 428.

16. Veronica is a fascinating figure in this novel, particularly because of her sixth sense, which allows her to "see" those who love her at the moment of their deaths. Unlike Dorothy, she marches at the head of the suffrage parade and does not fear the collective vortex, but she is still removed from it: while everyone else sings the Women's Marseillaise, Veronica sings Heine and Schumann. Like Dorothy, she understands the "ecstasy" Michael and Nicky describe, but unlike Dorothy, she is able to feel happiness rather than pride or fear when confronting collective emotion; see for example 228–29, 230. She appears to function as a positive figure, perhaps even critiquing Dorothy's position, yet she is so clearly a secondary character that these differences do not significantly undermine Dorothy's view.

17.

[A]s Dorothea drove her car-loads of refugees day after day in perfect safety, she sickened with impatience and disgust. Safety was hard and bitter to her. Her hidden self was unsatisfied; it had a monstrous longing. It wanted to go where the guns sounded and the shells burst, and the villages flamed and smoked; to go along the straight, flat roads between the poplars where the refugees had gone, so that her nerves and flesh should know and feel their suffering and their danger. She was not feeling anything now except the shame of her immunity. [301]

18. In real life, Sinclair was irritated by this sort of male attitude, as is reflected in *A Journal of Impressions in Belgium* when she describes an ambulance driver who finds the idea of "women in a field ambulance" disgusting: "He is the mean and brutal male, the crass obstructionist who grudges women their laurels in the equal field" (99). The simile she uses for men's attitude toward women like herself, who want to be part of the war, is a telling one:

It is with the game of war as it was with the game of football I used to play with my big brothers in the garden. The women may play it if they're fit enough, up to a certain point, very much as I played football in the garden. The big brothers let their little sister kick off; they let her run away with the ball; they stood back and let her make goal after goal; but when it came to the scrimmage they took hold of her and gently but firmly moved her to one side. If she persisted she became an infernal nuisance.   [105–6]

From this perspective—and this is clearly reflected in Dorothy's "shame" over her "immunity" (see n. 17)—what is wrong with war, and with women's position in relation to it, is that it is confined to men. War seems to represent, in these passages, a male-only club that women like Sinclair and Dorothy desperately wish to join.

Works Cited

"An Appeal against Female Suffrage." *Nineteenth Century* 148 (1889): 781–88. Reprinted in *Free and Ennobled: Source Readings in the Development of Victorian Feminism*, edited by Carol Bauer and Lawrence Ritt, 260–62. Oxford: Pergamon Press, 1979.

Cook, Blanche Weisen, ed. *Crystal Eastman on Women and Revolution.* Oxford: Oxford University Press, 1978.

Gilbert, Sandra M. "Soldier's Heart: Literary Men, Literary Women, and the Great War." *Signs* 8, no. 3 (Spring 1983): 422–50.

Hartsock, Nancy C. M. *Money, Sex, and Power: Toward a Feminist His-*

torical Materialism. Boston: Northeastern University Press, 1985.

Robins, Elizabeth. *The Convert.* 1907. Reprint. Old Westbury, N.Y.: Feminist Press, 1980.

_____. *Way Stations.* New York: Dodd, Mead, 1913.

Schreiner, Olive. *From Man to Man (or Perhaps only . . .).* 1927. Reprint. Chicago: Academy Press, 1977.

_____. *Woman and Labor.* 4th ed. New York: Frederick A. Stokes, 1911.

Showalter, Elaine. *A Literature of Their Own: British Women Novelists from Brontë to Lessing.* Princeton, N.J.: Princeton University Press, 1977.

Sinclair, May. "A Defence of Men." *English Review* 11 (1912): 556–66.

_____. *Feminism.* London: Women Writers' Suffrage League, 1912.

_____. *A Journal of Impressions in Belgium.* New York: Macmillan Co., 1915.

_____. *The Tree of Heaven.* New York: Macmillan Co., 1918.

Sharon
O'Brien Combat Envy and Survivor Guilt:

Willa Cather's "Manly Battle Yarn"

Writing in the Lincoln *Courier* in 1895, Willa Cather announced her profound disgust with women writers who could not transcend such limited feminine subjects as romantic love to attempt such universal masculine subjects as war. "I have not much faith in women in fiction," she wrote. "Women are so horribly subjective and they have such scorn for the healthy commonplace. When a woman writes a story of adventure, a stout sea tale, a manly battle yarn, then I will begin to hope for something great from them, not before."[1] Although by 1895 Cather had discarded the masculine dress she first began to wear during her Red Cloud adolescence, she identified with males no less than she had at fourteen when she transformed herself into William Cather, jr. Associating maleness with the power and autonomy she wanted for herself, Cather saw in war and combat (what historian Jackson Lears calls the late nineteenth century's "martial ideal"[2]) the apotheosis of masculinity, a temporary refuge from social definitions of feminine identity, linked in her mind with passivity and victimization.

The young journalist's belligerent advice to the aspiring woman writer reveals the hearty endorsement of masculine aesthetics, plots, and values that we can see elsewhere in Cather's writings of the 1890s. In an 1893 commentary on football, for example, she praised the sport as a rousing, bone-crushing cure for foppishness, "chappieism," and Eastern effeminacy. After conceding impatiently that football was "brutal," she went on to say: "So is Homer brutal, and Tolstoi; that is, they alike appeal to the crude savage instincts of men. We have not outgrown all our old animal instincts yet, heaven grant we never shall! The moment that, as a nation, we lose brute force, or an admiration for brute force, from that moment poetry and art are forever dead among us" (*KA*, 212).

Admiring and associating "brute force" with sport, warfare, and creative power, during the 1890s Cather applied the decade's cult of virility to her literary opinions. Her ideal artist was a heroic warrior, forceful, chivalric, potent; someone like Robert Louis Stevenson, who had "died with his spurs on," as she noted approvingly (*KA*, 556), or his successor Rudyard Kipling, who "had conquered an empire before he was out of his 'teens."[3] She celebrated Kipling for creating "manly" men and urged him to tell more war stories, praised Bliss Carman and Richard Hovey's poetry as "thoroughly manly and abundantly virile," and recommended Stevenson, Kipling, and Anthony Hope to her readers because they allowed their heroes to "love and work and fight and die like men" (*KA*, 317, 354, 232).

In addition to viewing the writer and the literary profession through the masculine and military ideology dominating the period, at times Cather described the writer's relationship to both reader and subject as a power struggle like that enacted on the gridiron or battlefield.[4] If the artist were a conqueror or warrior, then the reader would be his colonized subject: art was like the "Roman army," she thought, for in overwhelming readers, viewers, or listeners, art "subdues a world, a world that is proud to be conquered when it is by Rome" (*KA*, 54).

Although Cather was influenced by the cult of manhood and strenuous living many Americans endorsed during the 1890s, her fascination with the virile soldier or warrior had a familial as well as a cultural source. When the adolescent girl was seeking alternatives to the feminine role, she began to identify with the family's military hero, her maternal uncle William Boak, who died fighting for his Virginia regiment in the Civil War. Later she wrote a poem (1903) and a story (1907) inspired by this imagined bond, both entitled "The Namesake." In the poem (dedicated to "W. S. B., of the thirty-third Virginia") Cather celebrated the inheritance of power she had received from her soldier uncle: "Proud it is I am to know / In my veins there still must flow, / There to burn and bite alway, / That proud blood you threw away."[5] In later years Cather maintained this myth of origins and descent by informing even close friends that she had been named for her uncle William Boak, whereas family letters reveal that she was the namesake of an aunt Wilella who had died, unheroically, of diphtheria.

When Cather began to write her own "manly battle yarn" in 1919, she was inspired by the loss of another male relative who died in combat—another version of the family drama that had been central to her construction of an autonomous and creative self. *One of*

Ours (1922) originated in her profound emotional response to the death of her nephew G. P. Cather, killed in 1918 at Cantigny. After reading his letters to his mother Cather felt compelled to tell his story; as she wrote friend and fellow novelist Dorothy Canfield, she sensed a kind of blood-identity with her nephew, and compared the link she felt with him after his death to the bond between Siegmund and Sieglinde, the reunited brother and sister in Wagner's *Die Walküre.* Cather spent the next four years enjoying what she later termed a perfect companionship with the novel's protagonist Claude Wheeler—an imaginative rendering both of her nephew and of a male figure whom she came to view as her other self.[6]

In doing so, she produced a novel that portrays World War I as the arena for Claude's liberation, maturation, self-discovery, and heroism. Because Cather seemed to be endorsing a sentimental, naive view of war as the realm of heroic, noble sacrifice—an ideology widely held during the war but stiffly repudiated by intellectuals and writers during the 1920s—*One of Ours* has been dismissed since its appearance (except by the Pulitzer Prize Committee) as a woman writer's romanticized, inauthentic view of modern combat. Although reviewers and critics generally praised the first half of the novel, set in Nebraska, most agree with H. L. Mencken that in the second half, in which Cather takes her hero to the French battlefields, the narrative suffers an abrupt decline in power and realism. As Mencken phrased it, in the war scenes Cather becomes a "lady novelist."[7] Mencken's labeling of Cather as a "lady" to explain why the second half is inferior reveals two challenges to her literary authority: as a woman writer, she lacked the experience of war and so lacked the authority to invade the male genre of the war novel; as a woman (and a civilian) writer, Cather perpetuated the romantic stereotypes defining war as an elevated, noble enterprise.

We can see both charges—inauthenticity and romanticism—in Hemingway's famous comment on the novel in a letter to Edmund Wilson: "You were in the war weren't you? Wasn't that last scene in the lines wonderful? Do you know where it came from? The battle scene in *Birth of a Nation.* I identified episode after episode, Catherized. Poor woman she has to get her war experience somewhere."[8] Mencken's and Hemingway's judgments—which assume that Cather, by virtue of her gender, was incapable of writing a convincing, antiromantic war novel—have been echoed by later critics who have failed to distinguish Claude Wheeler's point of view from Cather's.[9] In his study of the World War I novel in America, although acknowledging the realism in Cather's portrayal of Nebraska life, Stanley Cooperman found *One of Ours* "often typical of wartime writing," by "lady authors" such as Temple Bailey and Mary Raymond Shipman Andrews, in which God-fearing, virtuous American soldiers waged a holy war against a bestial foe.[10]

If we were to judge solely from the evidence of the young Cather's male-identification and the reviewers' assessments, we would be forced to view *One of Ours* as an unusual novel indeed—a war story written by a male-identified "lady novelist." But we should not identify the young writer's praise of manly battle yarns with her writing of *One of Ours* or conflate the adolescent's identification with her uncle with the adult writer's identification with her nephew. By 1918, the year she began the novel, Cather had questioned and redefined the social constructions of gender that she had accepted in the 1890s. Her reconciliation of artistic vocation and female identity is evident in *O Pioneers!* (1913) and *The Song of the Lark* (1915), in which artistic inheritance is portrayed as matrilineal. Moreover, her rejection of the aggressive masculinity she had once identified with war, sport, and violence can be seen in several of the stories she wrote in the early 1900s, including "Paul's Case" and "The Professor's Commencement," as well as in her first novel—*Alexander's Bridge* (1912)—where her virile engineer hero plunges into the St. Lawrence River along with the outmoded masculinity Cather by then found self-destructive, ineffectual, and a bit silly.[11]

Thus Cather turned to *One of Ours* not in the midst of her preoccupation with male values, but after having demonstrated her discovery of a creative power linked with femininity and receptivity (rather than with masculinity and violence). So she did not begin the novel in order to celebrate the "brute force" she had admired in the 1890s; in fact, as she later confided to Dorothy Canfield, she had never intended to attempt a war novel and waited six months before beginning to write, finally doing so because the story would not leave her alone. She had also not consciously intended to write a story with a male protagonist, she told Canfield, but felt that she was implicated in G. P. Cather's story by an accident of birth. Some of her was buried with him in France, she wrote, and some of him was living in her.[12] Given her sense that she had become psychic twins with her fallen nephew, Cather evidently felt that she possessed the authority, as well as the inspiration, to invade male literary territory and write a war novel. As her letters to Canfield show, she felt that this was a problematic genre for a woman writer; but she had been claimed by her subject, and this was the story that demanded narration.

The novel that resulted from Cather's response to her nephew's death is neither the chest-thumping, Kiplingesque celebration of militarism and patriarchy that a William Cather might have written nor the sentimental, stereotypic hymn to the American fighting man that her reviewers attributed to the "lady" author's feminine limitations. It is a complex text filled with seemingly contradictory and anomalous elements; like many novels by women writers, it contains an encoded narrative that is far more interesting and potentially subversive than the surface plot. There is the overt story of the hero's maturation and self-discovery (structured by Cather as a quest plot, with parallels to the Grail legend); this was the product of what I am calling Willa Cather's combat envy. This narrative is admittedly a stirring account of military glory and heroism, although not as formulaic and romantic as the reviewers imagined since Cather was detached from, as well as identified with, her hero. But below the surface *One of Ours* tells a contradictory story associating war not with male heroism but with mutilation, infantilization, and emasculation in which women gain the power men relinquish. This submerged narrative at once reveals Cather's antiromantic vision of the realities of war and betrays the woman writer's survivor guilt and anxiety of authorship.

By concentrating on the issues of gender, sexuality, and power portrayed in the text, we can examine the relationships between the overt and covert narratives and explore the ways in which the same issues structured Cather's experiences in writing and publishing *One of Ours*. In this way we can perhaps discover why the novel's process of composition, like the text itself, was marked by tensions and contradictions; why Cather found the writing of *One of Ours* at once joyful and anxiety-ridden.

Despite her love for France, Willa Cather was not at first overly distressed by the war. She was involved in her own developing literary career, riding the surge of creativity that resulted in *The Song of the Lark* in 1915 and *My Ántonia* in 1918. Even after the American entry into the war in 1917, when her friend Elizabeth Sergeant left for France as a correspondent for *The New Republic*, Cather's own work came first. "Willa clearly realized that I had to go," Sergeant remembers. "She was herself, however, in no wise drawn to do anything but get on with her new story."[13] After her nephew's death, however, Cather's view of the war—in particular of the men who fought in the war—changed. Rather than being distressed by loss, suffering, and death, Cather became fascinated by the transformation in identity soldiers experienced in battle. Her nephew, who had been a sullen, discontented country boy, seemed to her to have found dignity and purpose, symbolized by his death at Cantigny. It was testimony to the transforming power of war, she suggested to Canfield, that someone so disinherited of hope should have something so glorious happen to him.[14] David Hochstein, a young violinist whom she knew slightly, likewise seemed to have been mysteriously ennobled by his experience in battle. After reading Hochstein's letters to his mother, published after the war, Cather observed that "something very revolutionary had happened in Hochstein's mind; I would give a good deal to know what it was!"[15]

One of Ours was in part inspired by Cather's desire to "know what it was" that happened to her nephew and soldiers like Hochstein. To find out the secrets of battle, she first read Hochstein's and G. P. Cather's letters to their mothers; she then had many conversations with returned soldiers, some of whom she interviewed in the hospital, some of whom she invited to her Bank Street apartment; and, one summer in her Jaffrey, New Hampshire, retreat she came across a military doctor's journal that became the source of Book 4, "The Voyage of the *Anchises*."

Although as a woman and a civilian Cather was far removed from the experience of war, her letters to Dorothy Canfield show how strongly she identified with G. P. Cather and, by extension, with the American doughboy. In addition to describing her sense of "blood-identity" with her nephew (we were very much alike, she told Canfield), Cather stresses their shared dislike of Nebraska's constricted life and desire for escape. Hence she could invest Claude Wheeler with her own desire to flee bourgeois oppression, her distaste for materialism, and her quest for authentic, creative selfhood without feeling that she was falsifying the experience of her cousin or other American farm boys who believed they would play more exciting parts in the theater of war. Her correspondence with Canfield further reveals that Cather found it natural to compare her own experiences to those of the war's participants and victims. Referring to the years of storm and struggle she and Dorothy had weathered, she suggested that someday they might get together and compare their scars, like doughboys. In Cather's view, her own

experience of life's struggles and scars gave her the emotional authority to write the last half of *One of Ours*; getting the material
for the last part was not easy, she told Canfield—a great deal of
living went into it.[16]

Difference as well as similarity sparked Cather's imaginative response to her nephew and the American soldier. As she confided to
Canfield, G. P. Cather was her opposite as well as her double,
Siegmund to her Sieglinde. The cultural and psychological difference marked by his gender was intensified by his experience of
combat and soldier's death; Cather's male "double" had been transformed by experiences that were forbidden to women. No matter
how strong her identification with her uncle and nephew who died
in battle, she could not "know" what they knew; but by inventing
Claude Wheeler, she could symbolically possess their experience
and share their secrets. So her creative process was generated by
both identification and difference, and the novel was itself a bridge
between seemingly separate realms: male and female, soldier and
writer, dead and living. Cather's letters to Canfield are filled with
imagery of blurred boundaries and interpenetration, as if the emotional bond she shared with Claude, who was simultaneously self
and other, legitimated the woman writer's foray into male literary
and social territory. She spoke of resting herself in Claude's younger, stronger body; of being drained by Claude; of having him in
her blood; and of the creative process as an experience of complete
possession, in which she was simultaneously possessing, and possessed by, her protagonist.[17]

The novel that resulted from Cather's conviction that soldiers
like G. P. Cather and David Hochstein had enjoyed a glorious transformation can be seen in the dominant plot of *One of Ours*, the
narrative that aroused Mencken's disappointment and Hemingway's contempt. In a Nebraska characterized by smug materialism
and narrow religiosity, Claude finds no social role in which to express his idealism and vitality, but in France Cather grants him the
death of his old self and the birth of a new. She connects his sense
of "ever-widening freedom" with a return to childhood idealism.
The war is like "something he imagined long ago" before the re-
strictions and self-divisions of adolescence, and the revitalized
Claude feels that he is "having his youth in France" and "beginning
over again."[18]

Cather attributes Claude's fulfillment to the discovery of a rich,
traditional culture in France, to his exhilarating discovery of male

comradeship, and to the self-realization he attains in devoting himself to the war's noble cause. She also portrays Claude's move from peacetime to war as a rite of passage into manhood. In Nebraska he is weakened and emasculated by women—the wife who denies him sex and the mother who denies him separation—but in France, strengthened by his love for David Gerhard and the men in his unit, he attains the virility that seems possible only in an all-male world.[19] He dies without disillusionment in a literally heightened moment as he leaves the trench for a parapet where he inspires his men and attracts enemy fire. He dies with his newly acquired mastery, vitality, and potency intact: "The blood dripped down his coat, but he felt no weakness. He felt only one thing; that he commanded wonderful men. When David came up with the supports he might find them dead, but he would find them all there. They were there to stay until they were carried out to be buried. They were mortal, but they were unconquerable" (386).

Paradoxically, it is the presence of passages like this—displaying the ideology of masculinity popularly associated with the rigors of war—that marked *One of Ours* as the work of a "lady author." By the 1920s, such rhetoric had been associated by writers like Hemingway and Dos Passos with the empty abstractions of a bankrupt Western culture: real men did not use inflated language, even if they continued to associate war with masculine power and identity.

Most of Cather's reviewers failed to note that in the concluding pages she mutes the novel's romanticism and clearly detaches her perspective from Claude's by suggesting that he dies before an inevitable disillusionment, "believing his own country better than it is, and France better than any country can ever be. And those were beautiful beliefs to die with. Perhaps it was as well to see that vision, and then to see no more" (390). Drawing on this conclusion as well as a pattern of authorial irony, Jean Schwind has countered the Mencken and Hemingway views of the novel by arguing that Cather consistently undercuts Claude's romanticism.[20]

But in my view Cather's detachment from Claude's perspective is unstable and shifting. At times she maintains ironic distance from his thrilled discovery of self in combat, but at other times she identifies with it. Although occasionally providing an antiromantic authorial perspective, the novel still offers plentiful support for the view that Claude Wheeler creates a new, and in Cather's opinion an enriched, self in World War I. An article Cather wrote for *Red Cross Magazine* in 1919—"Roll Call on the Prairies"—reveals the glorification of the soldier's heroism that can also be found in *One of Ours*, which she was working on at the same time. Speaking of the casualty lists that she had read every morning in her New York papers, Cather commented that the names of obscure Midwestern towns "came out one after another with the name of some boy who brought his home town into the light once and gloriously." This roll call of sacrifice and death was "terrible," but it was also "wonderful."[21]

The romantic story of Claude Wheeler's death and transfiguration arose from what I have termed Cather's combat envy: her belief that something "wonderful" had happened to men in battle, her sense of exclusion from that arena of experience, and her desire to represent and to possess that experience vicariously through the act of writing. And yet *One of Ours* also tells a much less optimistic story of war's transforming power, a story that has been obscured by the surface plot. To find this antiromantic vision we should look not to the last two pages or to occasional authorial irony but to a subtext that subtly undermines the dominant plot. If we turn our attention from Claude to minor and peripheral characters—soldiers on the plot's sidelines—we see a novel much closer to those produced by the male writers whose unsentimental exposés of World War I's brutalities gained the critical praise that *One of Ours* never enjoyed. In the margins of the text we find a tale of infantilization rather than of manhood, of mutilation rather than wholeness, of emasculation rather than of virility.

We see this contrasting pattern as soon as Claude ships out for France on the troopship *Anchises*, embarking on his rite of passage. An influenza epidemic rages and the healthy Claude—who has left illness behind in Nebraska—is soon surrounded by weakened, diseased, and dying men. While Claude seems to be growing up, moving into the adult male's power and authority, he is surrounded by men who return to infancy either through fear, like the soldier Claude discovers "snivelling and crying like a baby" (251), or through illness, like the "giant baby" Corporal Tannhauser who reverts to the "language of his early childhood" in delirium and dies whispering " 'Mein' arme Mutter!' " (257, 254, 256).

Once in France, Claude encounters men dismembered rather than made whole by the war: he watches a girl cradling a one-armed soldier in her lap, "stroking his head so softly that she might have been putting him to sleep"; the next morning he sees a wounded soldier who has lost "everything that belonged to health" and learns that " '[i]n the beginning that one only had a finger blown off; would you believe it?' " (284, 285). Surrounding Claude with amputees and disfigured men, near the end of the novel Cather introduces the most grotesque image of dismemberment—the hand of a German corpse that keeps reaching out of the earth, refusing to stay buried (380). Such images suggest that—even as she was honoring Claude's heroism—Cather was not glossing over the cruelties of war. Portraying mutilation and dismemberment, she in fact was confronting what Elaine Scarry reminds us is the "main purpose" of war—injuring.[22] In connecting war's power to injure with dismemberment, Cather may also have been influenced by the war's atrocity stories, according to which "the Germans—and the Allies as well—were cutting off the heads, noses, genitals, or legs of enemy soldiers."[23]

One of the most interesting minor characters Cather introduces is the physically and psychically dismembered soldier who has lost both an arm and half his memory—that concerned with women. "He can remember his father, but not his mother," a doctor tells Claude; the "women are clear wiped out, even the girl he was going to marry" (287–88). "Maybe he's fortunate in that," Claude responds. A dutiful son who carries his mother always in his memory, Claude is attracted to this form of obliteration; evidently he too wants to "wipe out" the women.

This interchange calls attention to the consequences (and perhaps the causes) of male powerlessness and victimization in the novel: Cather's war is a mother-son story in which women gain the power men relinquish. Consequently the prevailing imagery of infantilization and emasculation is connected not only with Cather's desire to portray the real injuries of war, but also with her realization that war might weaken rather than strengthen male dominance. Commenting on the sex-role reversals caused by World War I, Sandra Gilbert observes that "women seemed to become . . . ever more powerful." Taking over men's jobs, taking over men's health, women could be seen as embodying the once-nurturing but now demanding "home front" for which men were dying, becoming the inheritors of the culture the soldiers sacrificed themselves to protect.[24]

In her article on the home front, "Roll Call on the Prairies," Cather portrays the same role reversal in describing the increased power domestic women enjoyed in wartime, as "diet and cookery, the foundation of life," became transformed under women's surveillance. Men who were not at war became increasingly subject to women's authority: "When my father absent-mindedly took a second piece of sugar at breakfast, he felt the stony eyes of his womenfolk and put it back with a sigh." Citing women's contributions to the war effort—through conservation of supplies and volunteer work—Cather concluded, "The women were 'in the war' even more than the men. Not only in their thoughts, because they had sons and brothers in France, but in almost every detail of their daily lives."[25]

Cather does not address the subject of women's increased power directly in One of Ours, just as she places the images of male mutilation at the margins of her narrative. But several seemingly anomalous events and images suggest that the war—supposedly the realm of masculine power—causes power to flow from men to women, and specifically from sons to mothers. In a small French church Claude sees a mutilated statue of the Virgin and Child: the Virgin is untouched, but a "little foot sticking to her robe showed where the infant Jesus had been shot away." Claude's French guide tells him consolingly, " 'Le bébé est cassé, mais il a protégé sa mère,' " but given the context it seems that sons—in the act of protecting mothers—are being sacrificed for (or to) them (324).

Other brief, almost nightmarish images suggest that men's weakness somehow underlies women's strength: in a tableau recalling the Pietà, a woman cradles a one-armed soldier in her lap; a soldier calls out his mother's name (in his mother tongue) when he is dying; and David Gerhardt wonders to Claude if when the "sons of the gods were born, the mothers always died in agony? Maybe it's only Semele I'm thinking of." But now, he speculates, it may be the sons' turn to die: "I've sometimes wondered whether the young men of our time had to die to bring a new idea into the world" (348). The equation Cather makes between childbirth and war in this comment recalls men's original dependence on the female body as well as suggests that men's destructive power in war may somehow be causally linked to women's reproductive power. If, as Nancy Huston contends, "men make war because women have children" (emphasis in original) in order to rival and escape this realm of female power, then Cather further suggests through the Semele reference that men make war to appropriate the mother's role in creation.[26] But this is a futile quest, as One of Ours demonstrates, since in war—in contrast to the Semele myth—it is men who die and women who live.[27]

Claude at first seems to have escaped the emasculation Cather associates with men's subjection to mothers and maternal women. Entering the war, he leaves behind Enid Royce, the woman who nursed him during a debilitating illness and then, after marriage, refused him sex, leaving him "unmanned" (169). He also leaves behind his mother—beloved, caring, yet connected with a repressive piety as well as a lover's desire to possess him. Their farewell scene suggests that Claude needs to go to war to escape her desire for him, as well as his for her:

> She rose, reaching toward him as he came up to her and caught her in his arms. She was smiling her little, curious intimate smile, with half-closed eyes.
>
> "Well, is it goodby?" she murmured. She passed her hands over his shoulders, down his strong back and the close-fitting sides of his coat, as if she were taking the mould and measure of his mortal frame. Her chin came just to his breast pocket, and she rubbed it against the heavy cloth. Claude stood looking down at her without speaking a word. Suddenly his arms tightened and he almost crushed her.
>
> "Mother!" he whispered as he kissed her. He ran downstairs and out of the house without looking back.   [225]

While Claude may have eluded Enid and Mrs. Wheeler, he soon reconstitutes the family as he becomes son to Madame Joubert and luxuriates in her maternal presence. Cather thus provides even in the sequences in France an ironic counterpoint to the story of Claude's maturation into manhood: "It was good to lie again in a house that was cared for by women. He must have felt that even in his sleep, for when he opened his eyes he was thinking about Mahailey and breakfast and summer mornings on the farm. The early stillness was sweet, and the feeling of dry, clean linen against his body. There was a smell of lavender about his warm pillow" (297–98). Returning to the Joubert's welcoming home after a few days at the front, Claude savors once more the child's pleasures: "Perfect bliss, Claude reflected, as the chill of the sheets grew warm around his body, and he sniffed in the pillow the old smell of lavender. To be so warm, so dry, so clean, so beloved!" (343).

Cather also counterpoints the manhood-through-violence story with suggestions that war—precisely because it is an all-male environment—offers men erotic and emotional possibilities that male roles do not allow in civilian life. Men in war are allowed, momentarily, to enter the female realm of love and sentiment in their friendships with their comrades and to take on roles associated with domesticity, as Claude does when he helps to nurse dying men on the *Anchises* and begins housekeeping with David Gerhardt in their "comfortable little hole" of a dugout (311).

There seems to be a fine line between the regression Claude momentarily experiences as he nestles in the "perfect bliss" of his lavender-scented bed and the child's return to and absorption by a powerful mother, linked here, as elsewhere in Cather's fiction, with the loss of self in death. Claude seems to find manhood through violence as he jumps to the parapet to direct his faltering men (who, having turned "soft" through fear, "become like rock" through his leadership [385]), but Claude's escape from maternal power is somewhat ambiguous. Although he dies a hero's death, once he is dead his continued vitality depends upon women's memory. "By the banks of Lovely Creek, where it began, Claude Wheeler's story still goes on," the narrator tells us (389). Claude's story continues because he is preserved by—and in a sense contained and absorbed by—his two mothers, Mrs. Wheeler and the servant Mahailey. The novel ends with Mrs. Wheeler reading Claude's letters; she, not Claude's father, is his link with the future. And we learn that Mahailey sometimes addresses Mrs. Wheeler as "Mudder" when she is "thinking of Claude" and "speaking for Claude" (390). Silenced in death, Claude has lost the power of language to the women who survive him.

The novel's muted conclusion, in which a mother reads her son's letters and takes over the power of narration, leads us back to the relationship between the woman writer and her subject. Willa Cather was one of the women who survived Claude's death, just as she survived the deaths of William Boak and G. P. Cather. If her combat envy contributed to the heroic story of Claude's rebirth and death, then the woman writer's survivor guilt underlay the imagery of mutilation, infantilization, and impotence that undercuts the surface plot. In part, these disturbing patterns reflect Cather's awareness that World War I might have maimed its participants psychologically as well as physically rather than offering them the heightened self-realization she granted her hero. Yet these patterns also reflect Cather's experience of the creative process, which she found disturbing as well as joyful. To put it bluntly, Cather's muse was a dead man. Inspired by G. P. Cather's letters, she was taking over his power of speech, removing the pen from his hand in order to tell his story.[28] This transferal of power was exhilarating, as her letters to Dorothy Canfield suggest. But it evidently also aroused the guilt and anxiety surrounding the act of writing that she had seemingly quelled several years before when she reconciled gender with artistic vocation.

Since the novel had its source in dead, dying, or wounded men's stories—the letters of G. P. Cather and David Hochstein to their mothers, the conversations Cather had with returned soldiers, the doctor's diary—as their literary inheritor Cather was taking on the maternal role that is portrayed so ambiguously in the novel. Like Mrs. Wheeler and Mahailey, she was the mother who lived to tell the son's story. However altruistic her motives, in a sense she was profiting at the soldiers' expense, deriving a release of creative energy from their suffering and death.

Cather characteristically experienced the creative process as a replay of the psychological dynamics of the mother-child bond in which she could simultaneously play the roles of daughter and mother. If, as psychoanalyst Anthony Storr contends, creative desire is one example of the human impulse to recapture the lost connection with the mother, then writing can be thought of as a symbolic reunion with the mother's life-sustaining body—an equation Cather once suggested when she declared that the writer must know her subject as intimately as "the babe knows its own mother's breast."[29] In essays and interviews in the 1920s and 1930s she frequently portrayed the imitative or unsuccessful writer as "starving" and the writer who had found her subject as "fed" by her creativity; she once told an interviewer that inspiration drove her to write "exactly as food makes a hungry person want to eat."[30] While she was working on a novel Cather generally developed profound attachments to her characters, at times resembling the child relying upon a maternal presence. She had so "depended on Thea" (the heroine of *The Song of the Lark*) that when the book was finished and the "close inner tie was severed, she felt the pang and emptiness of one deserted," as if the book were the mother leaving the child.[31]

Cather's metaphor of the severed "inner tie" also portrays the writer as mother and the book as the child being born. If for men the metaphoric equivalence of childbirth is war, for Willa Cather, the childless woman writer, it was writing. "She once explained to a friend how a story started. First she felt it in the front of her head, where it enlarged as a baby grows in its mother's womb. And finally, it reached the back of the head where it lay heavy and painful awaiting delivery. Then she would be obsessed by the fear that something would prevent her bringing it to life."[32] As a novelist who so strongly associated her books with their protagonists that in letters she refers to a novel as "him" or "her," Cather was also the mother who nourished her characters until they were independent enough to leave home.

Although Cather could be both child and mother in the creative process, in writing *One of Ours* she seems to have experienced herself more frequently in the maternal role. In her first letters to Canfield, G. P. Cather/Claude Wheeler played the roles of lover, brother, and other self, but as her work on the novel progressed she more and more implied that her protagonist was her child. In one letter Cather recalled that she had once taken care of her nephew when he was a child, and in writing the novel she replayed that maternal role; she always knew, she told Canfield, that she would be able to feed Claude during a day's work.

But if she was a mother who gave life to her son, she also derived life from him; an intense morning of work, she told Canfield, always gave her the wonderful feeling of resting herself in his stronger, younger body. And finally, of course, she had to kill off the child she had brought to life—once when she wrote the death scene, again when she completed the book. When she finished proofreading, she wrote Canfield, she felt as if she were putting away a dead lad's things.[33] Cather always referred to the manuscript as "Claude," the title emphasizing the extent to which she identified the text with her protagonist. She only agreed to Alfred Knopf's strong recommendation that the novel be retitled *One of Ours* with reluctance, doubtless because the first-name title symbolized the personal bond she felt with her book/child.

The maternal bond Cather experienced with her book and her protagonist characterized more than the creative process: it also marked her dealings with her publishers, contributing to (and perhaps legitimating) her decision to leave Houghton Mifflin for Knopf. While she was writing *One of Ours* Cather was considering this move. Dissatisfied with Houghton Mifflin's attention to book design, advertising, and publicity, and skeptical of their commitment to her and her books, she was attracted by the aesthetic and commercial possibilities she saw in Knopf's new firm. In writing her Houghton Mifflin editor Ferris Greenslet, Cather adopted a maternal role both to threaten and to dismiss him, first informing Greenslet that Claude was getting big enough to care for himself, and that she would not give him to anyone who would not do a great deal for him. Later she told Greenslet of her decision to move to Knopf by explaining that she was leaving the firm for Claude's health.[34] Even after she had finished the novel and had signed a contract with Knopf, Cather continued to regard Claude as her child. Anticipating the possibility of hostile reviews, she imagined rescuing her protagonist from the text. Even if the book fell down, she told Dorothy Canfield, she would want to save Claude, to have him jump from the book as from a burning building, and she would catch him in a blanket.[35]

Thus power was flowing from sons to mother in the creative process as well as in the narrative. As the novel's creator, like Mrs. Wheeler and Mahailey, Cather was preserving the soldier's memory, ensuring that both the character and his real-life source would have an enduring life in fiction. This sense of the artist's maternal life-giving power underlay the joy and exhilaration she felt in writing *One of Ours.* But she was also absorbing, containing, and replacing her nephew, just as she was required to write Claude's death scene and "put away a dead lad's things," and the guilt surrounding this survival and substitution may have lay behind her comment to an interviewer that it was "presumptuous" of her to have written this novel.[36] Quite likely, too, her fear of public criticism for telling a soldier's story contributed to the pervasive imagery of mutilation and dismemberment, which reflects her literary anxieties as well as her desire to portray male psychic and physical injury. As her letters to Canfield show, Cather was quite aware that she was a woman writer venturing into hostile territory.

Throughout her life Cather associated creative power with the hand and frequently suffered from pain and paralysis in her right hand, which at times prevented her from writing. Images of mutilation and castration in her fiction and real-life problems with her right hand and arm frequently occurred at times of professional and personal stress when she was attempting to "rise" as a writer. We see this pattern when she first began to write fiction ("The Clemency of the Court"), when she took Henry James most directly as her mentor ("The Namesake" and "The Profile"), when she moved from the short story to the novel ("Behind the Singer Tower"), and when she wrote her first and only war novel. Cather seems to have invested the peripheral characters in *One of Ours* with the punishment she may have felt she deserved for attempting this masculine genre—the inability to write any more. The one-armed men Claude pities cannot write, and the partial amnesiac has lost the source of Willa Cather's major fiction—her memories of beloved and powerful women.

If the woman writer's survival power and guilt are responsible for the darker elements in this novel, Cather's sense that she was fulfilling an ambiguous maternal role may be responsible for her somewhat perplexing decision to dedicate the novel to her mother. This is a strange novel, we might think, to be dedicated to a proper Southern lady. But upon reflection the dedication makes psychological and emotional sense. Virginia Cather had also been a survivor who preserved her fallen brother's memory, keeping his flag and sword and telling his story to her daughter. In a sense she gave Cather her adolescent identification with William Boak, which may have been the earliest source of *One of Ours*. Like the novel itself, the dedication suggests that mothers (and the daughters of mothers) may both appropriate and pass on the power to tell men's stories.

But this is not the novel's final story. After writing the dedication, Cather had to send her war novel out to the reviewers who would judge it. She feared entering this literary battlefield; as her letters to Canfield and to Greenslet show, she was aware that she was taking a risk in writing a war novel, but she kept insisting that she had been compelled to do so because of her attachment to Claude. Cather's supplicating letter to H. L. Mencken, written before he reviewed *One of Ours*, reveals that gender was the source of her anxieties. Evidently she became more aware of the seeming contradiction between gender and genre as the novel reached the reviewers' hands. Could he let her know as soon as possible what he thought of the novel, she asked; she might be hit by a taxicab before he got round to reading it in the regular course of things. Mencken would be a good man to smell out falsity, she assured him, since he would be prejudiced against the subject matter, and against the sentiment on which the latter part of the novel was. built. She might be guilty of special pleading, but she wanted to give this boy every chance. And if she had done a sickly, sentimental, old-maid job on him, Mencken should tell her so loudly, like a man, rub it in, pound it down; she would deserve it and need it for her soul's salvation. She knew that her knowledge and desire were at the mercy of the feeble hand, the hand made unsteady by the fullness of truth.[37]

As if responding to Cather's fear, in his review Mencken did give her the pounding she half thought she deserved when he said that she had fallen into the company of lady writers. The first half of the book (where Cather stuck to her Nebraska material) Mencken liked, but the last half (where she crossed into male territory) degenerated, he charged, to the "level of a serial in the *Ladies' Home Journal*."[38]

Cather was distressed by the novel's reviews, the openly announced failure of her feeble hand. *One of Ours* was the novel with which she had felt most emotionally engaged, and she found it hard to remain detached from the public criticism. Given her maternal feelings for Claude, she may have been disturbed by this confrontation with the limits of a mother's power. Even though she had safely brought her novel to life, battling her own anxieties and leaving her first publisher in the process, she could not protect the novel from the reviewers. But her close bond with her literary child persisted, and eventually Claude's injury was balanced by her own. In the summer of 1923 Cather went to France, hoping to work on a new novel, but she suffered a painful attack of neuritis in her right arm and found herself unable to write.

Notes

1. Cather, *The Kingdom of Art*, 409. Hereafter cited in the text as *KA*.

2. Lears, *No Place of Grace*, 117–24.

3. Cather, *The World and the Parish*, 1:556.

4. For an analysis of how Cather later dismantled and subverted that ideology in her first novel, see Ammons, "The Engineer as Cultural Hero."

5. Cather, *April Twilights*, 26.

6. Willa Cather to Dorothy Canfield [Fisher], April 7, 1922.

7. Mencken, "Four Reviews," 12. For other reviews, see Schroeter, *Willa Cather and Her Critics*, 25–34, and Murphy, *Critical Essays on Willa Cather*, 165–68.

8. Wilson, *The Shores of Light*, 118.

9. For an analysis of this issue, and an argument that Cather consistently views Claude's romanticism with detachment and irony, see Schwind, "The 'Beautiful' War."

10. Cooperman, *World War I*, 30, 21.

11. See Ammons, "The Engineer as Cultural Hero," and O'Brien, "Willa Cather: The Emerging Voice," 381–93.

12. Cather to Canfield, March 8, 1922, Dorothy Canfield Fisher Papers.

13. Sergeant, *Willa Cather: A Memoir*, 146.

14. Cather to Canfield Fisher, March 8, 1922, Dorothy Canfield Fisher Papers.

15. Sergeant, *Willa Cather: A Memoir*, 179.

16. Cather to Canfield, n.d. [1922], Dorothy Canfield Fisher Papers.

17. Cather to Canfield, April 7, 1922; March 8, 1922, ibid.

18. Cather, *One of Ours*, 259, 349. Future references included in the text.

19. Cooperman, *World War I*, has an interesting analysis of Claude as a "war lover" who finds erotic fulfillment in violence. Although he does not give Cather credit for intentionally creating this psychologically and socially rich perspective, he does see a contradiction between surface and subtext: "Indeed, her book, beneath its sentimentality and intrusive rhetoric, can be seen as a case history of a man for whom the idea of death is the only possible aphrodisiac" (129).

20. Schwind, "The 'Beautiful' War," 55.

21. Cather, "Roll Call on the Prairies," 27–30.

22. Scarry, "Injury and the Structure of War," 1.

23. Cooperman, *World War I*, 13.

24. As Gilbert, "Soldier's Heart," suggests, the war had overturned "the rule of patrilineal succession, the founding law of patriarch society itself" (432).

25. Cather, "Roll Call on the Prairies," 27.

26. Huston, "The Matrix of War," 119-36. For a psychoanalytic analysis that links men's need to dominate—and to wage war—with the early dependence on the mother, see Dinnerstein, *The Mermaid and the Minotaur*.

27. According to the myth, when Zeus appeared in his full majesty to Semele, she was burned to ashes; he then took her unborn child, Dionysus, and sewed him into his thigh until the time of delivery—thus becoming at once mother and father.

28. Gilbert observes that several women writers felt that "their art had been subtly strengthened, or at least strangely inspired, by the deaths and defeats of male contemporaries." Vera Brittain, Edith Wharton, Katherine Mansfield, and H.D., among others, felt themselves empowered to write by the loss, death, or weakening of brothers, lovers, and husbands ("Soldier's Heart," 446–47).

29. Storr, *The Dynamics of Creation*, 181; Sergeant, *Willa Cather: A Memoir*, 137.

30. For references to starving and feeding, see the "Preface" and "Katherine Mansfield"; also Merrill, "A Short Story Course."

31. Sergeant, *Willa Cather: A Memoir*, 137.

32. Bennett, *The World of Willa Cather*, 212. For an analysis of the ways in which male and female writers have used the childbirth metaphor differently, see Friedman, "Creativity and the Childbirth Metaphor."

33. Cather to Canfield, March 8, 1922; April 7, 1922; May 8, 1933, Dorothy Canfield Fisher Papers.

34. Willa Cather to Ferris Greenslet, May 30 [1919]; Willa Cather to Ferris Greenslet, January 12, 1921, Willa Cather Papers.

35. Cather to Canfield, [March 13, 1922], Dorothy Canfield Fisher Papers.

36. Sergeant, *Willa Cather: A Memoir*, 172.

37. Cather to Mencken, February 6, 1922, H. L. Mencken Papers.

38. Schroeter, *Willa Cather and Her Critics*, 10.

Works Cited

Ammons, Elizabeth. "The Engineer as Cultural Hero and Willa Cather's First Novel, *Alexander's Bridge*." *American Quarterly* 38, no. 5 (Winter 1986): 746–60.

Bennett, Mildred. *The World of Willa Cather*. Lincoln: University of Nebraska Press, 1961.

Cather, Willa. *April Twilights (1903)*. Edited by Bernice Slote. Bison edition. Lincoln: University of Nebraska Press, 1968.

———. "Katherine Mansfield." *Not Under Forty*. New York: Alfred A. Knopf, 1936.

———. *The Kingdom of Art. Willa Cather's First Principles and Critical Statements, 1893–1896*. Edited by Bernice Slote. Lincoln: University of Nebraska Press, 1966.

———. *One of Ours*. New York: Alfred A. Knopf, 1922.

———. Papers. Houghton Library, Harvard University, Cambridge, Massachusetts.

———. "Preface." *Alexander's Bridge*. Boston: Houghton Mifflin, 1922.

———. "Roll Call on the Prairies." *Red Cross Magazine*, July 1919.

———. *The World and the Parish: Willa Cather's Articles and Reviews, 1893–1903*. 2 vols. Edited by William Curtin. Lincoln: University of Nebraska Press, 1970.

Cooperman, Stanley. *World War I and the American Novel*. Baltimore: Johns Hopkins University Press, 1967.

Dinnerstein, Dorothy. *The Mermaid and the Minotaur: Sexual Arrangements and Human Malaise*. New York: Harper & Row, 1976.

Fisher, Dorothy Canfield. Papers. Bailey/Howe Library, University of Vermont, Burlington, Vermont.

Friedman, Susan Stanford. "Creativity and the Childbirth Metaphor: Gender Difference in Literary Discourse." *Feminist Studies* 13, no. 1 (Spring 1987): 49–82.

Gilbert, Sandra. "Soldier's Heart: Literary Men, Literary Women, and the Great War." *Signs* 8, no. 3 (Spring 1983): 422–50.

Huston, Nancy. "The Matrix of War: Mothers and Heroes." In *The Female Body in Western Culture: Contemporary Perspectives*, edited by Susan Rubin Suleiman, 120–36. Cambridge, Mass.: Harvard University Press, 1986.

Lears, T. J. Jackson. *No Place of Grace: Antimodernism and the Transformation of American Culture, 1880–1920*. New York: Pantheon, 1981.

Mencken, H. L. "Four Reviews." In *Willa Cather and Her Critics*, edited by James Schroeter. Ithaca, N.Y.: Cornell University Press, 1967.

———. Papers. Enoch Pratt Free Library, Baltimore, Maryland.

Merrill, Flora. "A Short Story Course Can Only Delay, It Cannot Kill an Artist, Says Willa Cather." *New York World*, April 19, 1925.

Murphy, John J., ed. *Critical Essays on Willa Cather*. Boston: G. K. Hall, 1984.

O'Brien, Sharon. *Willa Cather: The Emerging Voice*. New York: Oxford University Press, 1987.

Scarry, Elaine. "Injury and the Structure of War." *Representations* 10 (Spring 1985): 1–41.

Schroeter, James, ed. *Willa Cather and Her Critics*. Ithaca, N.Y.: Cornell University Press, 1967.

Schwind, Jean. "The 'Beautiful' War in *One of Ours*." *Modern Fiction Studies* 30, no. 1 (Spring 1984).

Sergeant, Elizabeth. *Willa Cather: A Memoir*. Lincoln: University of Nebraska Press, 1963.

Storr, Anthony. *The Dynamics of Creation*. New York: Atheneum, 1972.

Wilson, Edmund. *The Shores of Light: A Literary Chronicle of the Twenties and Thirties*. New York: Farrar, Straus & Young, 1952.

Sara   "Seeds for the Sowing":
Friedrichsmeyer
              The Diary of Käthe Kollwitz

I n the decades since Käthe Kollwitz (1867–1945) began exhib-
iting her graphic works and sculptures, critical response to her
art has varied greatly, usually depending on the favor accorded
the socially committed work of a woman artist.[1] One constant
in many of the discussions, however, has been the perception of
Kollwitz as a "revolutionary" artist. Even contemporary critics who
deal with her oeuvre frequently describe her as "revolutionary," referring not only to the implicit call throughout her work for radical
social change, but linking her to a revolutionary political credo as
well.[2] The largely unpublished diary that Kollwitz kept for almost
thirty-five years is the most important source for assessing her political position.[3] Begun in 1908, continuing through the years of the
First World War and the Weimar Republic, and ending only in 1943
shortly before she was evacuated from Berlin, her diary not only
puts into clear perspective the revolutionary fervor that did indeed
inspire her well-known early works, but also demonstrates what
should be seen as her evolution from political revolutionary to
pacifist. Although it documents her revolutionary vision for a more
just society, it challenges any final assessment of Kollwitz as an
artist doing her part to achieve that goal through an art calling for
the forceful overthrow of existing political and social systems.

Because the diary's themes are all interwoven and, in fact, interdependent, separating them for discussion runs the risk of placing
undue emphasis on a particular thematic concern. Nevertheless,
the following discussion concentrates on Kollwitz's development to
a pacifist position, with the proviso that it is only one of several
major themes in her writing and intricately related to every other.

Although the artist's early graphic works dealt with revolutionary
themes, they were inspired not by contemporary but by historical
events. *The Weavers' Rebellion*, for example, exhibited in 1898 and
the series with which the public continued for years to associate
her name, depicted the 1844 revolt of the Silesian weavers. *The*

Peasant War, for which she was awarded a year's stay in Italy in 1907, was based on another unsuccessful uprising, this time the sixteenth-century peasants' war.[4] By the time she began her diary, however, Kollwitz had been living for many years in a working-class neighborhood in Berlin where her husband, a physician for the poor, had his practice. The numerous anecdotes in the journal about the workers with whom she came into contact offer convincing proof that her interest in events of the past was gradually being replaced by a concern for the everyday life around her. After August 1, 1914—a date noted in her journal with the one word "War" stretched across the page in large letters—Kollwitz's interests were never again with the past, but instead with the world in which she lived and worked.

Her writings from the first days in August present a dramatic account of the German war effort. To be sure, there are entries that point to the apprehension and unrest mobilization brought to a mother with two sons, but the majority reflect the romanticized, heroic version of war so typical throughout Germany in 1914. That perception of war was tested when her younger son Peter decided to volunteer for service; as the diary entry of August 10, 1914, reveals, it was Kollwitz herself who helped persuade her husband to support his decision. In retrospect she realized her anxiety had been overcome by the even more powerful desire to do her duty and by the rhetoric of sacrifice. And sacrifice she did, for her son died in the first months of the war. The reader feels her anguish as she writes of his death and her efforts to accept it, a process made more difficult by her own increasing skepticism toward the cause for which he had given his life.

Between 1914 and 1918 Kollwitz made almost daily entries, adapting her journal to her changing needs. What had begun August 1 as a war diary recording daily events soon became a means for expressing and controlling grief,[5] and then later a forum for exploring her growing opposition to the war and to violence.[6] Not at all a linear development, this reassessment of the fighting and the intense self-examination accompanying it were marked by much ambivalence and frequent contradictions as she sifted through her altering feelings and beliefs to find a position she could uphold.

The entry for October 30, 1914, which records the event that forced her reassessment of the war, is a single sentence poised in the middle of one page: " 'Your son has fallen.' " Eleven days after this news, which she follows with a blank page marking a sure break with a part of her past, Kollwitz begins to write of her son, but initially only as others remember him. The entries written two days later to express her own feelings, addressed to her son as "you," reflect her prostration and overwhelming need to reestablish their intimacy. Occasionally entire passages are written to him, but more typical are the sudden outpourings of emotion that interrupt the diary narrative, even in entries dated years later. On August 28, 1915, for example, with a cry intensified by its lack of punctuation, she breaks into her narrative with "Oh my son a year ago at this time I could still see you."

Although she does not allow herself many expressions of grief in the journal, the message of almost uncontrollable pain is also carried by the handwriting: for months after her son's death, words look as if they were forced onto the paper. Her emotional state during that period can also be read from the confusion in her journal, from the frequent crossouts and dates that do not match the entries. Even her use of tenses carries the message of sorrow. The happy experiences of the past she relives by recalling them in the present tense.

It was Kollwitz's custom each New Year's Eve to summarize in her journal the past year, weighing its joys against the suffering it had brought. In her review for 1914 she is able to speak of her son in the past tense. The first line reads: "1896–1914. Then your life was ended." Though written to her son, the message is of a life that is over. But even as she begins to assign his death to the past, she comes to perceive of the distance she has gained as a threat to their bond, and she reacts in the diary by vowing to "keep faith" with her dead son. As the ensuing discussion makes clear, she understands that avowal to include loving her country as he did. Although she begins even within the next months to have doubts about the fighting, as numerous entries demonstrate, this promise ties her to a spirit of sacrifice and support for her country that interferes with her ability to assess the war impartially.

Throughout the months of 1915 Kollwitz's diary continues to provide her with a way to deal with her loss. But although emotional calls to Peter as "you" still occur, she is increasingly able to talk about him without hurt, and by July 1915 can record periods when she is almost free of pain. About this time, not coincidentally, the focus of her writing changes. Instead of seeking only to control her grief, she now begins to concentrate on the long process of working out her own position to the war, a process characterized by an almost paralyzing bewilderment as she tries to balance loyalty to her son's memory with the horrible reality of the fighting.

The majority of the entries for 1915 document Kollwitz's ambivalence toward the war. She records, for example, in November 1915 the horrifying statistic that five hundred thousand German soldiers have already died, but in the same months quotes and supports—if weakly—a poem urging those who have suffered losses to prove themselves "worthy heirs" of the dead by dedicating themselves to the war effort. She is aware of the inconsistency in her views, and in October 1915 expresses her conflict well: She *sees* only the "criminal insanity" of the war, but thoughts of Peter lead her to *feel* "the other." By the end of the year, however, what she "sees" has begun to prevail. In her New Year's Eve entry for 1915, slipping into a voice addressing her dead son as "you," she acknowledges without anguish her failure in making "your attitude toward the war . . . mine" and admits without apology to questioning the German cause.

Although the themes of family and work gain increased importance again during 1916, the war continues to dominate Kollwitz's thinking. Her growing skepticism is implicit in the material she chooses to discuss and quote in the early months of the year. On January 19, for example, she lists the reasons for which the English excuse their soldiers from fighting, singling out one for emphasis by quotation marks: " 'because going to war is against their conscience.' " The following day she summarizes a newspaper article stressing the unfortunate German equation of duty with loyalty to country. On April 22 she copies portions of a letter naming "simply death" as the greatest experience of war. Although she has not progressed far enough to present such opinions as her own, it is clear from the number of such entries and the absence of contending views that they reflect—and indeed are used to reinforce—her own thinking. Alongside such passages are also accounts detailing the harsh reality of war and its effects on human lives. On June 14, for example, she records hearing the following conversation as an aged mailman entered a restaurant where she and her husband were eating. "They greet him in a friendly manner, he is sad. Then someone says: 'Yours has fallen?' 'Yes —mine has fallen.' 'My sympathy.' Handshake. Silence. The old man goes again." The episode also demonstrates her ability to convey emotion with few words. It is, just as numerous others she records, a story of grief reduced to its essentials.

As was the case the previous year, the first entry for August 1916 marks with large letters another year of war. And by this time, after two years of fighting, Kollwitz has begun, if hesitantly, to find her own words to express her antipathy to the fighting. On August 27, after writing of the general situation—by now over 5 million young men have been killed and again as many lives have been destroyed —she asks: "Is there anything that justifies that?" Again it is an article that motivated this assessment, but here and in other passages over the following months she goes beyond merely quoting antiwar sentiments to register her growing opposition in her own words. Although her reaction in this entry is in the form of a question, it is obviously rhetorical. The subsequent discussion indicates that her main interest is in the writer's resistance to ideals, to sacrifice, and to dying for a "lifeless" ideal, that is, for love of country. Tentatively acknowledging that, at least according to the author of this article, her son died for just such a reason, she uses the journal to explore her own ideals, primarily what she recognizes as her dedication to "duty."

Although she claims in this long, searching entry to be "worn out" and incapable of understanding the varying perspectives with which she is confronted, it is apparent to the reader that the problem is not a lack of comprehension. Her conflict remains unresolved because she still cannot integrate what she sees and knows to be true with the ideals she has always referred to in judging issues and events, especially her unswerving loyalty to country. One phrase she quotes from the article—"For a pair of happy eyes the collected doctrines of the world's wisdom"—says what she is as yet unable to articulate. The urgency of this entry is underscored by its visual impression. While in the middle of the sentence linking her son to a death for a lifeless ideal, she comes to the end of the last page of her third journal; rather than interrupting her thoughts by looking for a new book or a loose piece of paper, she continues this important entry on the back cover of the volume, not her usual custom.

But her struggles are not yet over. Only a few weeks later, on September 9, 1916, a discussion reveals the depths of her emotional loyalty to the German cause, which she is still trying to overcome. The entry revolves around someone close to her sister's family who has been called to the fighting. Kollwitz seeks to understand the discomfiture with which she herself has heard the news and with unrelenting honesty—though certainly straining the reader's credibility—wonders if perhaps her reaction has been motivated by envy because her older son Hans has still not served on the front. Up until now, she suggests to herself, perhaps she has felt "privileged" because in contrast to her sister, she has already sacrificed one son. This, the most extreme statement of emotional patriotism in the journal, is a tentative conclusion, phrased in questions. And the questions seem to have served a purpose, for after having expressed her patriotism so negatively, she is soon able to leave behind her idealization of sacrifice.

Although she is still hesitant to speak with authority and is more comfortable expressing her views in someone else's words or by using them as the basis for her own reaction, she begins in the last months of 1916 to refer to her own experience to substantiate her resistance toward the fighting. Her observations of October 11 show she is still struggling, but more successfully now, with the concept of ideals. Juxtaposed against her admission that she frequently sees only the absurdity of war is, to be sure, her assertion that "life must be placed in the service of an idea." But while claiming in this entry her inability to understand "all this," she nevertheless works out an important distinction between "lifeless" ideals, specifically love for one's country, and other ideals, as yet undefined, that are worthy of lifelong devotion. From her statement that her son and the soldiers of all warring nations have died for love of country, she now is able to draw the logical but difficult conclusion that all were betrayed by dedication to a lifeless ideal. Had her son known what she now knows, she implies, he would not have volunteered.

This is an important juncture in her analysis, for having come to such a realization, she can now separate herself from the promise to her son that has bound her to his perception of the war, and allow herself to view the fighting more critically. Her response to a story she relates in the same entry indicates she is doing just that. The story, told by a pastor to her son and other volunteers in 1914, involved a Roman youth's sacrifice for a collective; his leap into an abyss somehow threatening it had caused the abyss to close. Even as she copied the account into her diary on October 4, 1914, Kollwitz indicated some reservations. Her analysis on October 11, 1916, clearly a reflection of her increasing aversion to war, is blunt and uncompromising: Sacrifices have been made, and yet "the abyss has not closed. It has devoured millions and is still wide open. And Europe, all of Europe is still offering like Rome its most beautiful and most precious." The thematic concerns of the following days confirm the impression that with this 1916 entry, Kollwitz has come to terms with the issue of her son's sacrifice. It has taken her more than two years, but after October the reader detects a new emphasis as she becomes more confident about articulating her now unequivocal hatred for war and begins, if haltingly at first, to speak and write of peace.

To call for peace in 1917 meant risking a confrontation with the Wilhelmine bureaucracy. Although Kollwitz did not join a peace group, she does write of her participation in peace demonstrations and her willingness to contribute various works to peace organizations. Subsequent entries, such as those showing a new interest in acquaintances who support a peace initiative, also document her growing abhorrence of war. Her yearly review for 1917 indicates that her hopes for an immediate peace, however, are very slight. Perhaps the most "positive" event of the year, she writes, was the Russian Revolution, for her a "new hope." Although her attitude toward events in Russia was conditioned by hope rather than reality and at times demonstrated what can only be called political naiveté, her description of what she thought was taking place there outlines the kind of political system which she could support and which she elsewhere defines as Socialism: "ethical motives" and "justice," she writes, were the determining features of the new Russian system, not "power."

An antiwar book by Henri Barbusse that she read early in 1918 reinforced her commitment to nonviolence. She alludes to the book on several different days, and by March 3 when she finally discusses it, she does so in her own voice, with confidence in her own thinking. The book should be published in millions of copies, she writes, for "[i]f the war is as he describes it—and it is indeed so—how is it then possible that humanity—*knowing about this suffering*, would ever repeat it?" Her antagonism toward war continues to be a dominant theme of the journal throughout 1918. On September 29 she even inserts into its pages a poem clipped from a newspaper, the first two stanzas of which depict the worsening situation for the German empire. The third stanza calls on all Germans to "give the ultimate" to save their country, a plea with which the Kollwitz of 1914 would have been in sympathy. But in 1918 she dates the poem, underlines its call to sacrifice, and writes beside those lines in large, underlined letters a simple, unequivocal "no."

As the war drew to a close, Kollwitz's convictions only deepened.

When in October 1918 the poet Richard Dehmel issued a call for volunteers to support a final war effort, she responded with an open letter. Published in two newspapers, it demonstrated publicly and without ambivalence the dramatic shift in her thinking. Dehmel had based his call for volunteers on the need to defend Germany's honor. Her refutation, which she copied into her diary on October 30, counters with the emotional plea: "Enough have died! No more should die!" Passionate, well-reasoned, and unyielding in its demand, her letter argues that the Germans should have learned during the previous four years a lesson that would invalidate such a response to the ever more certain German defeat. Addressed to the Germans through Dehmel, the letter speaks eloquently of the emptiness of the traditional concept of honor, redefining that virtue as a spirit of commitment to rebuilding the country. Just as the letter reflects Kollwitz's attitude toward war, it also summarizes by implication her development to that position. When she writes that the four years of war have caused the population to seriously reassess its earlier views, she is speaking from her own experience.

The change in Kollwitz's political thinking is difficult to imagine without her experience as diarist. That her diary offered an outlet she required and depended on between 1914 and 1918 is clear: its importance to her emotionally as a method of controlling grief and intellectually as a forum for working out her attitude to war can be discerned not only from the content, but also from the length and frequency of the entries through the war years. Of the ten books she wrote between 1908 and 1943, one entire volume is devoted to the first eight months of 1916. But there was more to the diary's appeal. Kollwitz had a Protestant sense of life as a gift to be used or, negatively expressed, of life as an obligation. She communicates to the reader a lingering fear of not living up to her potential, of not performing her duty. The journal, one can assume, offered her a chance to validate her life and affirm herself in her various roles—including those of woman, mother, wife, daughter, sister, friend, and artist. Although her diary documents this desire throughout most of her life, it was especially acute during the war years.[7]

Her writing was also important to her development for other reasons. She was, according to her older son Hans, a very private person, reserved in talking about or showing love and disinclined to "speak about feelings . . . or about any personal matters." To others she gave the impression of being "impregnable"; "only in her diaries," he wrote in the introduction to the selection of her writings published in 1955, "can you see how she struggled."[8] The greatest struggle of her life, according to the evidence of the diary, took place between 1914 and 1918. During that time when she was trying so desperately to work out her attitude to the war, the relatively private, unrestricted genre allowed her the freedom to deal with problems from many different perspectives and as often as she desired; over a period of years it allowed her through stylistic experiments and thematic digressions to relive the past and spiral into the future as often as necessary. With its emphasis on process instead of goal, the diary also assured the continuity and sense of involvement she required. It provided her a private space to outline her ideas slowly, to question preconceived notions, to formulate her ideas and reactions without fear of criticism, to seek her own "truth" in her own way. Above all, as she pushed to understand her own feelings and integrate them with what she knew intellectually to be true, her writing helped her develop confidence in her own thinking.

Kollwitz's refutation of Dehmel's call for volunteers in 1918 is surely a testimony to the diary's importance in her life. She may have arrived at the same conclusion without her years as a diarist, although the process would most assuredly have been even slower and more painful, but it is doubtful that she would have developed the self-assurance to make that refutation publicly and through the medium of language if she had not learned through the years of journal writing to trust her own voice and the experiences that had created it.

When Kollwitz finally did reject war and all violence, it was for a number of complicated, interrelated reasons; to see one of them as the supposedly "natural" link between women and pacifism as some critics would want to do would be a mistake. Although hers is a woman-centered art,[9] and although her diary documents the centrality of her own experience of motherhood, Kollwitz was no more naturally or biologically "determined" to be against war than other women and mothers. Even though she frequently expressed regret that her years of mothering were behind her (cf. January 17, 1916) and wrote of mothering as the most intense and happy experience of her life (June 17, 1920), she did not condemn the war when it began. As her diary testifies, she had to *learn* to reject violent confrontation. Through a long and painful intellectual struggle she had to *learn* to see the emptiness of her emotional loyalty to the German cause and to assess the war without the interference of an idealized frame.

Kollwitz's rejection of war and all violence cannot be linked to biology. Instead it came about largely through an increased awareness of self and a growing trust in her own experiences as a woman and mother. As a socialist, Kollwitz believed that the resolution of the class conflict would restore the natural equality between the sexes. She had no vocabulary for feminism and certainly no theory. Lacking both, her diary was of immense value because it granted her the freedom to explore privately a variety of women's issues. This exploratory writing helped reinforce the view of women and mothering which she had acquired from her own experience, and which in turn continued to be of paramount importance for her art and life. Although her journal does not articulate an alternative to her loss of faith in "lifeless" ideals, it does demonstrate beyond a doubt that her response was a clearer grounding in physical reality, in her own existence as woman and mother, and in the artistic rendering of that experience.

Critics agree that Kollwitz's graphic works and sculptures demonstrate a lifelong compassion for suffering humanity, and her diary can only substantiate that claim. But one can refine the focus to point out that in both her visual art and writings, the "humanity" for which she showed so much compassion is most often represented by mothers and their children. This was the case even before the war; after 1918 they became the major focus in both forms of expression. Her cultural reality, reinforced during the war and detailed in the diary, was the conviction that the victims of social injustice and war are always women and children. Appropriately, her first graphic series after the war combined her focus on women's experience with what she had learned was its logical, not "natural" consequence. In six of the seven plates of the series called simply "War," loving and grieving mothers and widows provide the dominant perspective and speak forcefully of the need for peace.

Her experiences as a woman and a mother, which contributed so directly to her rejection of war, were for Kollwitz not linked to archetypal or instinctual responses, and her concept of mothering had very little in common with the idealized, sentimental view of that role so prevalent in Germany at the time.[10] Bound up instead with the flow of daily life and with activities that affirmed it, her experiences and her understanding of the mother-child relationship were thus almost prescriptive for an embrace of the pacifist cause.

Catherine Krahmer, who has written the best biography on Kollwitz to date, has stated that Kollwitz "experienced the war as a woman and opposed it in her art with the instinct of a mother."[11] One could more accurately conclude that Kollwitz, with the *intelligence* of a woman who realized after a painful intellectual struggle that the values she espoused as a woman and mother could in no way be interpreted to support war, *learned* to oppose all violence.

In an article titled "Preservative Love and Military Destruction: Some Reflections on Mothering and Peace," Sara Ruddick has provided a philosophical framework for understanding the connection between mothering and pacifism which, I believe, helps to explain Kollwitz's rejection of war and all violent resolutions to conflicts. It must be stressed that for Ruddick, mothering is a social, not a biological category; it is not even gender-specific. Further, her discussion of maternal practice distinctly rejects any attempt to idealize motherhood. Instead she bases the link between the activities of mothering and a rejection of violence on a belief that what mothers or other people in mothering roles do influences the way they think. As she phrased it in an earlier article, "out of maternal practices [arise] distinctive ways of conceptualizing, ordering, and valuing."[12] The basis for female pacifism, Ruddick emphasizes, comes not from "ovarian adventures," but from the "complicated social activity of preservative love," the special kind of life-affirming love that mothering people engage in and which is "incompatible with military destruction."[13]

In both her visual art and her journal, Kollwitz's underlying theme was always human life and how it could and should be maintained and improved. But she did not become conscious of this concrete, life-affirming orientation or accept the consequences of such a value system until she had learned the limitations and potential hazards of loyalty to abstract ideals.[14] Ironically, the death of her son with its link to the emotional patriotism of 1914 delayed her from heeding the prerogatives her maternal practice endorsed. Only after she began to analyze her years as a mother and to grapple intellectually with the values imparted by that experience could she see that, when measured by the horrible reality of the previous four years, the heroic ideals of "country" and "honor" had proven themselves not only meaningless, but dangerous as well. Only then could the woman who in 1914 had sent her younger son to war with flowers and a copy of *Faust* emerge as an antagonist of all war. Although she did not articulate the social or political ramifications of her maternal practice and its preservative love, her visual art and written expression provide a different kind of testimony to the love which preserves not just the life of the individuals being mothered, but which extends itself to preserving life for its own sake. Her work is testimony to a kind of caring that leads ultimately to a belief in the inviolacy of all life.

Throughout the years of the Weimar Republic, Kollwitz remained a loyal diarist, although her struggles were never again so emotionally wrenching as those of the war years. One of the articulated themes of the Weimar period was her attempt to locate herself on the postwar political spectrum, which she explored in terms of revolutionary versus evolutionary change. This was an especially difficult task because she did not consider herself very perceptive about political affairs; the volumes of the diary in fact depict a woman who was more interested in ideas than in politics, who supported the causes she believed in without concern for their ideological linkages. Thus, it was with irony that she noted in November 1916 that people were beginning to think of her as politically wise, a development she rejected with the admission that she usually just repeated what her husband said. And, to be sure, one of the authorities she often quoted during the war was her husband. After the war, however, her diary discussions in general depend much less on argument by authority, except for that of Goethe, whom she continued to read, cite, and "live with" for the rest of her life.[15] After 1918 she writes with more self-confidence and her writing requires fewer corrections.

When Philip Scheidemann declared the Weimar Republic into existence, Kollwitz was a part of the enthusiastic crowd in front of the Reichstag building. But any optimism was of short duration, and just two days later she began her reportage of the conflicts between the various parties seeking to control the government. The struggle that interested her in the early days of the Republic was, as she saw it, between the Majority Socialists, who were willing to let socialism develop gradually, to "evolve," and the Independent Socialists—by this time associated with the Spartacist League and the German Communist party—who condoned the use of force to ensure an imminent socialist government on Prussian soil.

Although her early political sympathies had always been with the parties calling for radical social change, Kollwitz emerged from the war an opponent not just of war but of all violence; politically that meant support for the Majority Socialists, for she equated the Spartacists with revolution, and revolution quite simply with war. With a feeling of "terrible pressure," she records on December 8, 1918 her decision to vote for the Majority Socialist candidate rather than for the "revolutionaries." But even as she knows she would not vote for the Spartacists, she is most aware of the debt owed them for their role in forcing the Kaiser to abdicate. And it is also clear that emotionally she is still on their side. Without their constant pressure, she writes, there would have been no overthrowing of "all the militarism." They were the ones who had been and still were willing to "push forward . . . even," she adds, "if Germany is destroyed in the process." With that offhanded comment she defines her postwar conflict, a struggle between the revolutionary causes which she still emotionally supports, and the destruction to which she believes they almost inevitably lead.[16]

In many entries over the next two years, Kollwitz ponders and agonizes over her political beliefs. Only in an entry dated October 1920, while acknowledging her shame in belonging to no political party and suggesting as a reason her own cowardice, does she finally identify the reason for her continuing turmoil. She is, she finally realizes, "not a revolutionary, but an evolutionary." Because of their link with war and violence, revolutionary politics no longer attract her. But that recognition brings with it the awareness of another problem, one that has in fact contributed much to her difficulty in defining her own beliefs. Since the public, remembering her from her early graphic series, continues to see her and praise her as the "artist of the proletariat and of the revolution," she has, she writes, been forced "more firmly into that role," until she now finds herself reluctant to continue playing it. "I *was* revolutionary," she insists, and if she were younger, she believes, she probably would join the Communist party, but not in 1920. Having been through the war and having seen the hatred and death that accompanied it, she adds, her longing now is only for peace; and she does not see peace as the legacy of a political party dedicated to revolution.

Throughout the following year she continues to articulate and struggle with her rejection of revolutionary politics, striving despite that break with her past to find continuity in her life. Seeing Gerhart Hauptmann's drama *The Weavers* once again in the summer of 1921 leads her to a long assessment of her political development. As a young artist trying to perfect her technique and prove wrong her father's admonition that becoming a wife and mother precluded any accomplishments as an artist, she had been so impassioned by the première of the drama in 1893 that, as she recorded in a brief memoir written for her son Hans in 1941, she began at once her own graphic interpretation of the weavers' 1844 uprising.[17] Her fame as well as the epithet she was trying to escape dated from that series.

On June 28, 1921, she records the same feeling of "an eye for an eye, a tooth for a tooth" that she had had on first seeing the play, but with a difference: her desire for the justice that confrontation might bring is now outweighed by her resistance to all violence. Since first seeing the play, she writes, she has been through a revolution and learned from it that she is no revolutionary. Her childhood dreams of fighting on the barricade, she continues with a hint of sadness, will never be fulfilled because now that she has seen a barricade, she would never approach one. Only when an artist like Hauptmann transfers revolution into art, she writes, does she feel again like a revolutionary, in danger of falling "into the same old illusions."

In 1919 the family of Karl Liebknecht asked Kollwitz to create a memorial to the murdered Spartacist leader. She accepted the commission, knowing it would not be easy to find the right form for a memorial to the man whose death she had written about in her diary with genuine horror and repulsion but whose political position she had not shared. Over the next two years her efforts to find an appropriate means of expression paralleled her gradual acceptance of her repudiation of revolution as a means of achieving social justice. The inner struggle over the memorial was climaxed by the same October 1920 entry in which she recognized that her revolutionary sympathies were in the past. Claiming once again her inability to see clearly "these insanely complicated relationships," she asserted there her right as an artist to do the memorial as she chose. This assertion was then followed by a question—"Or not?!" —which she apparently answered in the affirmative, for she went on to create a memorial that is less a tribute to Liebknecht than to the group of workers filing past his bier. The solidarity with the workers remains, but without the anticipated call to revolution.

After the 1920s, Kollwitz's diary no longer played such an important role in her life. She was over sixty years old and, as the entries of the remaining years demonstrate, her major struggles were behind her. When she did write, it was mainly to explore issues concerning her family and work. As the Nazi years approached, however, she proved herself again a clear-eyed observer of contemporary events. In December 1930, for example, she noted that the film based on Erich Remarque's antiwar novel *All Quiet on the Western Front* could no longer be shown. "A difficult time is coming," she wrote and then added, "or *this is* a difficult time." And for her the Hitler years were difficult indeed. Because she signed a manifesto shortly before the election of 1933 calling for the parties of the left to unite against the Nazis, she, the first woman elected to the Prussian Academy of Arts, was forced to resign soon after the election put Hitler in power. She lost her teaching position and atelier and after 1936 was forbidden to exhibit her works.[18] After being questioned by the Gestapo, who threatened her with removal to a concentration camp, she recorded in July 1936 her pact with her husband to commit suicide should they return.[19] She did not use the diary after 1933 to weigh political events, but noted them only with terse, sometimes caustic comments that left no doubt as to her perspective.

When the war came, she remained in Germany, and there are those who might criticize her for having done so. She did, however, continue for the last few years of her life to work in the ways still left to her for her vision of a socially just and nonviolent world. Although she had written and demonstrated in many ways her opposition to war, she did not define herself as a pacifist until near the end of her life, perhaps because of her skepticism toward all movements and ideologies, but also because—to read between the lines of several entries—the term to her implied a passivity she found unacceptable. Only in 1944, after she had been moved from Berlin, did she apply the term to herself, and then only after a personal revision of its meaning. The kind of pacifism she wanted to be associated with, she declared in a letter to her daughter-in-law on February 21, was "not passive waiting" but "work, hard work." As she insisted to her granddaughter shortly before her death, the word pacifism meant not just an absence of war, but was connected as well with the spirit of universal friendship and equality.[20]

In the same letter of February 21, 1944, she summarized her antiwar position one final time, emphasizing her concern for a world beyond her own family and country. The worst thing about war, she wrote, was that "*every war carries within it another war as its answer. Every single war is answered by a new one*" until "everything, everything has been destroyed."[21] She was not referring merely to buildings or countries. As she had so cogently argued in her diary on March 21, 1922, violence of all kinds must be avoided precisely because the memory of its deeds can never be erased from the minds of the perpetrators or their victims. Every act of violence thus "contributes to the destruction of humanity. . . . and what use are the gains of war to human beings already destroyed from within?"

After having had to give up her studio space in the academy, she no longer worked with any regularity, but some of her last accomplishments combine the dominant themes of her life in ways that demonstrate what she had learned from her experience. More than ever before, the mother-child bond emerges in these last works as the exemplary human relationship. Although there had been a time, especially after World War I, when she had tended to depict her mother figures as passive victims, she avoids in these last works any such link. Kollwitz had learned to assert consciously her own values in her art and life. That strength speaks out from her last works, two of which underscore the roots of the artist's pacifism: they are paradigmatic for her unyielding, mother-centered demand for a nonviolent world. In 1938, when she was seventy-one years old, she finished a small bronze sculpture called "Tower of Mothers" depicting strong, defiant mothers banded together in a solid circle to protect their children. Her last lithograph, completed in 1942 after the bombing of Berlin had begun and after the death of her grandson, another Peter, in the fighting, also combines her faith in protesting mothers with her opposition to war.

When she titled this final lithograph *Seeds for the Sowing Must Not Be Ground*, she was consciously testifying to a continuity in her life despite the shifts it had entailed in her thinking, for the title that she now used as a summation of her beliefs was a phrase she had borrowed from Goethe several times before. On February 6, 1915 she had used the phrase in her diary, placing it dramatically on the page with spaces above and below, to comment on the meaninglessness of her son's death. It was a purely private grief that evoked this first response to the line. Then later that month in an entry dated merely February 1915, after a long discussion concentrated on her own life, she found in the lines a reason to go on living: With her younger son dead, she saw herself as responsible for achieving through her art what he, with a similar talent, might have accomplished. Later, after having worked out her rejection of war, she used Goethe's line and his authority as the irrefutable conclusion to her own letter opposing Dehmel's call for volunteers. In 1941, at a time when she knew she did not have long to live, she discussed the line with her older son Hans and, as the diary records in December of that year, claimed it as her testament.

To illustrate this theme, which she had referred to at critical junctures of her life, she now for her last lithograph turned to motifs she had also used so often in the past and drew once again an angry, yet proud, physically powerful mother enclosing and protecting her children in her arms. If a context for the work is needed, she provided it in her journal, where in December 1941 she stressed that the lithograph was meant not only to encourage an end to all war, but to "demand" it.

Seeds for the Sowing in many ways provides a fitting summation for Kollwitz's life and beliefs. In contrast to the artist of the early graphic series, the artist of this final lithograph is the woman who had learned to place a higher value on life than on abstract and "lifeless" ideals; it is the work of a woman who had finally come to recognize that the social changes she longed for and worked for in her art could take place only in a nonviolent world. The "demand" of this work for an end to all war is also directly linked to the artist's long years as a diarist, for it was her writing which afforded her the opportunity to explore her changing beliefs and which then helped her find the courage and self-confidence to accept the consequences of those changes. When future biographies of Kollwitz are written, it is the artist of *Seeds for the Sowing* who should be remembered, the woman whose private intellectual struggles on the pages of her diary led her to active, even assertive, participation in the cause of a socially just, nonviolent world.

Notes

I would like to thank the Kollwitz family and Dr. Walter Huder, Director of the Kollwitz Archive in the Akademie der Künste in West Berlin, for permission to read the artist's largely unpublished, handwritten diary. I would also like to thank the German Academic Exchange Service (DAAD) for funding to carry out the research. The translations from the diary and from other German sources are my own.

1. Kaiser Wilhelm rejected her depictions of workers as "art of the gutter," but during the years of the Weimar Republic those works and others she created in that period were well known and highly regarded. Officially

denounced in the 1930s as "degenerate" and dismissed during the 1950s as "sentimental" and "propagandistic," the same works by the 1970s were hailed as examples of socially responsible art. For a summary of the critical reception to Kollwitz's works up to the 1970s, see Lippard's introduction in *Käthe Kollwitz: Graphics, Posters, Drawings.* Today many art historians all but ignore Kollwitz's work, a neglect attributable to her gender and medium; she is known primarily as a graphic artist, and the graphic arts have long been considered an inferior means of artistic expression. Only in 1986 were galleries opened in West Germany to exhibit the spectrum of her work. Their status as private galleries reflects the disinterest of the national museums and their curators in collecting and showing her art. See Kipphoff's comments to the opening of the West Berlin gallery in "Die Gesten der Frau."

2. In Harris and Nochlin's recent book *Women Artists,* for example, Nochlin calls Kollwitz a "political activist" whose work was intended as an incitement to "radical social change" (65); this judgment accompanies a discussion of Kollwitz's early works, which did advocate political revolution, but leaves the impression that it applies to her entire oeuvre. Lippard, who along with Nochlin and others has done much to bring Kollwitz to the attention of the art world, links her to Rosa Luxemburg and calls her an artist "who understood politics" (*Voices of Women,* 4). In *Eva und die Zukunft,* the 1986 catalog edited by Werner Hofman for the Hamburg Kunsthalle's exhibit of women in art since the French Revolution, Kollwitz is well represented, but almost entirely with works supporting this view.

3. The ten volumes of the diary are housed in the Kollwitz Archive of West Berlin's Akademie der Künste. Throughout this paper I will cite from the handwritten manuscript. Since Kollwitz did not date all her entries, they will be identified in the text by the last-mentioned date; frequently that will be only month and year. Her letters are cited according to her *Tagebuchblätter und Briefe,* edited by Hans Kollwitz.

4. In both series, the artist placed herself unequivocally on the side of the oppressed victims of history.

5. Kollwitz was not alone in using a diary for this purpose. See Rosenblatt's *Bitter, Bitter Tears.*

6. Although the way in which certain passages are heavily inked out—along with the very fact that she saved the ten volumes—indicates that Kollwitz considered the possibilty that others might read her writing, she wrote primarily for herself, and not for any real or imagined audience.

7. Such a need for self-affirmation has recently been identified as a primary concern in much of women's autobiographical writing. See, for example, Jelinek's Introduction to *Women's Autobiography,* Goodman's *Dis/-Closures,* and Smith's *Poetics of Women's Autobiography.*

8. Hans Kollwitz, Introduction to *Diary and Letters,* 2.

9. This view of her art is beginning to find its way into the critical litera-

ture; see, for example, Lippard's Introduction to *Voices of Women* and Nochlin's contribution on Kollwitz in Harris and Nochlin's *Women Artists*.

10. See Koonz, *Mothers in the Fatherland*, and the anthology *When Biology Became Destiny*, edited by Bridenthal, Grossmann, and Kaplan, for discussions on the ideology of mothering in Germany during the early twentieth century.

11. Krahmer, *Käthe Kollwitz*, 85.

12. Ruddick, "Maternal Thinking," 224.

13. Ruddick, "Preservative Love," 235–36, 240.

14. See the discussion in Ruddick's "Preservative Love" on the connection between warfare and abstract thinking and between mothering and a more concrete orientation (249–52). See Gilligan, *In a Different Voice*, for further elaboration on these linkages.

15. Jutta Kollwitz, "Aus der letzten Zeit," 192.

16. The entry also documents the difficulty Kollwitz had in dismissing patriotism as a "lifeless" ideal. There was a certain variant of German Idealism operative in her thinking that enabled her to continue a sentimental attachment to country even after she came to espouse internationalism.

17. Käthe Kollwitz, *Tagebuchblätter und Briefe*, 41–42.

18. Compare her February 1933 letter to a friend in her *Tagebuchblätter und Briefe* (150) with her diary entry of February 15, 1933. The manifesto is reprinted in her *Bekenntnisse*, edited by Volker Frank (71–72).

19. Heinrich Mann, who also signed the manifesto and who was therefore also forced to resign from the Prussian Academy of Arts, left Germany six days after this expulsion. The "inner emigration" of those who, like Kollwitz, chose to remain, was not without compromise. In the same entry Kollwitz records that the Gestapo's threats did induce her to retract some measure of her previously published support for the Soviet Union. See Krahmer's *Käthe Kollwitz* (113) for documentation that she did not, however, reveal the name they were seeking of another Soviet supporter.

20. Jutta Kollwitz, "Aus der letzten Zeit," 191.

21. Käthe Kollwitz, *Tagebuchblätter und Briefe*, 161–62.

Works Cited

Bridenthal, Renate, Atina Grossmann, and Marion Kaplan, eds. *When Biology Became Destiny: Women in Weimar and Nazi Germany.* New York: Monthly Review, 1984.

Gilligan, Carol. *In a Different Voice: Psychological Theory and Women's Development.* Cambridge, Mass.: Harvard University Press, 1982.

Goodman, Katherine. *Dis/Closures: Women's Autobiography in Germany*

Between 1790 and 1914. New York University Offendorfer Series. New York, Berne, Frankfurt: Peter Lang, 1986.

Harris, Ann Sutherland, and Linda Nochlin. *Women Artists: 1550–1950.* New York: Alfred A. Knopf, 1977.

Hofman, Werner, ed. *Eva und die Zukunft: Das Bild der Frau seit der Französischen Revolution.* Munich: Prestel, 1986.

Jelinek, Estelle C. Introduction to *Women's Autobiography: Essays in Criticism,* edited by Estelle C. Jelinek. Bloomington: Indiana University Press, 1980.

Kipphoff, Petra. "Die Gesten der Frau." *Die Zeit,* June 20, 1986, 16.

Kollwitz, Hans. Introduction to *The Diary and Letters of Kaethe Kollwitz,* edited by Hans Kollwitz, and translated by Richard and Clara Winston. Chicago: Henry Regnery, 1955.

Kollwitz, Jutta. "Aus der letzten Zeit." In *Käthe Kollwitz: Tagebuchblätter und Briefe,* edited by Hans Kollwitz, 190–92. Berlin: Mann, 1948.

Kollwitz, Käthe. Diary. Unpublished handwritten manuscript. Akademie der Künste, West Berlin.

———. *Käthe Kollwitz: Bekenntnisse.* Edited by Volker Frank. 2d ed. Leipzig: Philipp Reclam, 1984.

———. *Käthe Kollwitz: Tagebuchblätter und Briefe.* Edited by Hans Kollwitz. Berlin: Mann, 1948.

Koonz, Claudia. *Mothers in the Fatherland: Women, the Family, and Nazi Politics.* New York: St. Martin's Press, 1987.

Krahmer, Catherine. *Käthe Kollwitz.* Reinbek bei Hamburg: Rowohlt, 1981.

Lippard, Lucy. Introduction to *Käthe Kollwitz: Graphics, Posters, Drawings,* edited by Renate Hinz. New York: Pantheon, 1981.

———. Introduction to *Voices of Women,* edited by Cynthia Navaretta. New York: Midmarch, 1980.

Rosenblatt, Paul. *Bitter, Bitter Tears: Nineteenth-Century Diarists and Twentieth-Century Grief Theories.* Minneapolis: Minnesota University Press, 1983.

Ruddick, Sara. "Maternal Thinking." In *Mothering: Essays in Feminist Theory,* edited by Joyce Trebilcot, 213–30. Totowa, N.J.: Rowman & Allanheld, 1984.

———. "Preservative Love and Military Destruction: Some Reflections on Mothering and Peace." In *Mothering: Essays in Feminist Theory,* edited by Joyce Trebilcot, 231–62. Totowa, N.J.: Rowman & Allanheld, 1984.

Smith, Sidonie. *A Poetics of Women's Autobiography: Marginality and the Fictions of Self-Representation.* Bloomington and Indianapolis: Indiana University Press, 1987.

Susan
Schweik A Needle with Mama's Voice:

Mitsuye Yamada's *Camp Notes* and

the American Canon of War Poetry

A recent, useful bibliography of American war literature by
David Lundberg acknowledges one of its significant gaps
in a note: "There have also been no studies of Japanese-
American war literature, even though a number of memoirs and novels about the relocation experience have appeared in
recent years."[1] At least one widely available scholarly study of the
literature of relocation, a section of Elaine Kim's ground-breaking
Asian-American Literature, was in print at the time of the bibliography's compilation, but this fact does not exactly invalidate Lundberg's statement; Kim's project nowhere defines itself as an examination of texts about "war."[2] Americans tend to reserve that term
for narratives characterized by the description of armed combat,
victors and vanquished, a space for masculine action called the battlefield. In accounts of the American canon of war literature, the
enforced exile, imprisonment, economic losses, and dehumanizing
treatment that Japanese-American civilians endured and recorded
are, at best, relegated to footnotes.

Experiences and responses specific to Japanese-American *women*
disappear entirely. Lundberg's one reference to women's writing
about war, a short discussion of Great War novels by Wharton and
Cather, concludes that these authors "continued to believe in the
war because as women they never experienced combat at firsthand"
(380). Many American women who have sought to write about
World War II have faced the problem of their distance from the
zones of actual military occupation and confrontation. But Japanese-American women—either denied citizenship or stripped of
their rights as citizens, forcibly exiled from their homes, exposed to
humiliation and violence, imprisoned in desert camps in the interior of an ostensibly sheltered and sheltering nation—experienced
the war very much "at firsthand." The texts they produced in response to internment challenge assumptions about both gender and

warfare that have informed the aesthetics of the prevailing canon of war poetry.

This essay focuses on one group of poems written by one Japanese-American woman, a body of work that reflects the shaping forces of the camp and relocation experience: Mitsuye Yamada's *Camp Notes*. The poems that make up the central section of *Camp Notes* were written in part during or not long after the war. They were kept from publication, however, until 1976, when the early poems appeared in conjunction with the publication of more recent poems by Yamada that gloss and expand on the wartime "notes" themselves. "My affectionate thanks," says a note by the author on the first page of the 1976 edition, "[go] to Alta and Angel who have coaxed *Camp Notes* out of mothballs."[3] These are the first things Yamada's text teaches us: that its central section has been both hidden and preserved, closeted and mothballed, by its owner (the "mothball" metaphor suggests a domestic, protective silence both docile and subversively secretive, not unlike the material aura of Emily Dickinson's neatly sewn fascicles); that these poems have been recovered not by a solitary act of will, but at the loving urge of two friends; and most important, that they have been shut up for a long time, and that this long silence is both a fact about the poems and a major issue within them. "It took forever," Yamada wrote in 1981 of Asian-American women's emergence as a vocal force in American society.[4] "Forever" here is an unabashed hyperbole, a sign of the emotional eternities of silence undergone by the women of whom Yamada speaks. "Perhaps it is important to ask ourselves," she goes on, "why it took so long." My question here is a condensed version of that larger inquiry: Why did *Camp Notes* take so long, and what do the poems themselves tell us about their long arrival?

The postponement of *Camp Notes* should be understood first of all in the context of the general factors that impeded Japanese-American writing and excluded it from view during the war. Toshio Mori's collection of short stories, *Yokahama, California*, for example, was scheduled for publication, with an admiring introduction written by William Saroyan, in 1941; nine years later it finally came out, with a small postscript by Saroyan barely and uneasily noting the delay.[5] Mori's book was literally suppressed by its publishers. Other texts written by Japanese-American authors were suppressed or repressed at earlier stages, harder to trace. From 1941 until well after 1945, any narrative or for that matter any act of public speech by a Japanese-American posed an unacceptable threat to the national fictions embodied and organized in established U.S. literary institutions.[6] Dominant constructions of national identity, permissible representations of the "American people" as they faced their Enemies, depended, first of all, on an almost complete elision of the existence of a Japanese-American population. Annette Kuhn's work on the British wartime documentary "Desert Victory" describes its representation of national identity in words that could easily be applied to constructions of "Americanness" in the majority of American texts that represented the war: "The People is constructed by the collective mode of address as a group politically united by ties of nationhood, undivided by class—or for that matter gender or race—and having the same interests as the institutions responsible for the conduct of war, and indeed of representations of the war."[7] The American myth of a united people—undivided by racial tensions, standing up together against racist enemies—provided new publishing opportunities for "loyal" Asian-American writers, Filipino-American or Chinese-American authors, for instance.[8] But the disturbing fact of the concentration camps, and the realities of the Japanese-American population the camps contained, threatened dominant representations of a nation "all in it together." Books like Mori's, which explored Japanese-American culture in detail, constituted double threats, both in their subject matter and in their very existence.

Yokahama, California was already written and accepted for mainstream publication well before Pearl Harbor and before the Executive Order that enforced the evacuation and internment procedures. If Mori's book could not escape censorship, texts written from the camps that treated the matter of imprisonment and relocation and their effects on Japanese-American people were even less likely to come to light beyond the camps or to be written at all.

I have traced elsewhere the obstacles to writing that the various generations of Japanese-American *women* in particular encountered during the Second World War.[9] In recent essays Yamada has written eloquently about those obstacles. Her most extended analysis of the forces that suppressed, strained, and shaped her early work can be found in "Invisibility Is an Unnatural Disaster: Reflections of an Asian American Woman," an essay published in 1981:

> Like the hero in Ralph Ellison's novel *The Invisible Man* [sic], I had become invisible to white Americans, and it clung to me like a bad habit. . . . I first recognized how invisible I was in my

first confrontation with my parents a few years after the outbreak of World War II. . . . By this time I had met and was much
influenced by a pacifist. . . . When my parents learned about
my "boy friend" they were appalled and frightened. . . . I was
devastated to learn that they were not so much concerned
about my having become a pacifist . . . [as] about the possibility
of my marrying one. . . . my father reassured me that it was "all
right" for me to be a pacifist because as a Japanese national and
a "girl" it *didn't make any difference to anyone.* . . . Those
who feel powerless over their own lives know what [that] is
like. . . . The poor know it only too well, and we women have
known it since we were little girls.   [36–37, 38–39]

The situation described here presents the Japanese-American
woman with a paradoxical impasse. As one who can be seen to be of
Japanese ancestry, she is perceived within the dominant culture as
a political threat, and thereby subject to continual constraints and
even assaults. As a woman and a daughter, however, she is denied
any capacity for independent political behavior, either as patriot or
traitor (even by or especially by her own family). Forced by U.S.
authorities to define and maintain a clear and acceptable political
identity, she finds herself at the same time identified only in powerless relation to men. Marked by her visible difference, she still
"makes no difference to anyone."

Not surprisingly, Yamada's *Camp Notes* reveals an imagination
skirting between two perils: the danger of invisibility and the danger of visibility. At the book's center, the "archival" materials that
comprise the original "Camp Notes" recount in detail Yamada's
imprisonment from arrest to release. The last three poems in these
"Notes," which form an independent shorter narrative, provide a
useful focus for a closer study of the differences making no difference makes. "Notes" culminates in the second-to-last poem, "Cincinnati," framed by one "before" poem entitled "The Night before
Goodbye," and one "after" poem, the last one in the "Notes," called
"Thirty Years Under." "Night before Goodbye" begins the story in
the present tense:

Mama is mending
my underwear
while my brothers sleep.
Her husband taken away by the FBI
one son lured away by the Army

now another son and daughter
lusting for the free world outside.
She must let go.
The war goes on.
She will take one still small son
and join Papa in internment
to make a family.
Still sewing
squinting in the dim light
in room C barrack 4 block 4
she whispers
Remember
keep your underwear
in good repair
in case of accident
don't bring shame
on us.

[28]

The speaker's "Mama" at the start of the poem is mending, a familiar, intimate, domestic practice; but when the household in which she operates is "room C barrack 4 block 4," her homemaking sphere is threatened and subverted. Her power to mend works in minimal opposition to the power to shred that the war works against her best caretaking efforts. The poem moves from terse description of the mending to broken explanations of the adversaries to mending, the strong and violent forces that rend the family apart. Those threats are outward and alien first of all—the structures of internment that police the Japanese-American family, the pressure on the younger generation to relocate, the political conflict of the war itself. But outside threats to the fabric of the family coexist with, and motivate, forces from inside the family as well; "lure" and "lust" will send the daughter who speaks here and her brothers away from this scene, toward the ironically designated "free world" (which in this "before" poem still retains the illusions of freedom). "Night before Goodbye" arrests the mother sewing in the dark at the moment before it abandons her. What the poem chooses as significant to remember is a gift of mending, and it poses the puzzle of what that gift is worth, what its inheritance means for the daughter who is singled out after dark to receive it.

Like many literary and actual gifts passed down from mother to daughter, this one is accompanied by a strong (and in this poem so familiar and embarrassing as to be almost parodic) admonition, the poem's conclusion: "Remember / keep your underwear / in good repair / in case of accident / don't bring shame / on us." In another context, this collapse into maternal cliché would be ludicrous, though still ominous. Spoken to any daughter by any mother, the statement evidences a disturbing obsession with the daughter's decorum at the expense of concern for her actual well-being: "If you get hurt or die," it seems to suggest, "I will be more worried about the spotless and holeless state of your panties than about your body itself. Better dead than despoiled." The mama in this poem anxiously socializes her daughter on Papa's behalf, in order to ensure the daughter's survival within several partially opposing cultures. As a result, she becomes an implicated participant in the process of policing the daughter's body that internment imposes. She expects her daughter to internalize that policing more deeply than a learned "lust" for freedom; the daughter must now do for herself what her mother has done for her. To be a good daughter, she must render herself doubly invisible, as impervious to notice or comment as possible, even at the moments of greatest vulnerability and display of her body. The mother presumes, of course, that all such moments of real display will be genuine "accidents," results intended neither by her daughter nor by the world around her.

The blank rest of the page that follows seems to represent all of the unknowable freedoms of a world beyond the camps and beyond the reach of Mama's oppressive needle. At the same time, however, though the adolescent daughter as character resists merely obeying, merely listening to, her mother, the adult daughter as poet insists on listening, empathetically and emphatically. And the poem has been published in a larger text, which begins with the words, "What your mother tells you now / in time / you will come to know" (1), suggesting that even the half-comic prescription which concludes "Night before Goodbye" cannot be ignored and must, in fact, be learned once more by the daughter for herself. The next poem both proves the point and disproves it; for what happens next, in "Cincinnati," is a hard lesson that is no accident.

"Freedom at last / ," the daughter speaker begins, ". . . My first day / in a real city / where / no one knew me."

No one except one
hissing voice that said

dirty jap
warm spittle on my right cheek.
I turned and faced the shop window
and my spittled face
spilled onto a hill
of books.
Words on display.   [29]

The violence and violation that occur here confirm the mother's fears even as they render her injunctions meaningless. The most perfectly mended underwear, the most docile demeanor in the world provide no defense against this hissing voice. But the consciousness at stake here is the younger, not the older, woman's. It is the daughter who must turn to look at herself with spit on her face, and it is she who must make sense out of this event, must turn it into harsh irony, in the writing of the poem.

The medium through which she comes to see herself is, significantly, not a mirror but a store window, and not just any window but one full of books, "words on display." The books here represent the full weight of "national fictions"; they embody the dominant popular culture to whose angers, desires, and fears the identity of the Japanese-American woman is subjected and by whose words she is defined. In opposition to the hill of books stands the single image of the speaker's "spittled face." That face, spat-upon and, as the poem will reveal, crying, signifies both the brutalities "words on display" evade and the subjectivity of a woman for whom "words on display" do not speak. The intensity of the outward and inward violence experienced by the speaker is suggested by the submerged battlefield imagery in these lines: the injured face "spills" or spatters onto the landscape.

Two quotations from recent feminist analyses of the representation of women in popular culture provide helpful glosses on the image of the face superimposed over and against a wartime book display. "An image of a woman's face in tears," writes Judith Williamson,

will be used by a paper or magazine to show by impression the tragedy of a war, or the intensity of, say, a wedding. From the face we are supposed to read the emotion of the event. But conversely, it is the event that gives the emotion to the face; we have to know whether it is a war or a wedding to interpret

correctly its well of meaning. Similarly in films . . . close-ups
. . . function as an imprint of the action, like a thermometer
constantly held up to the narrative. And no matter what the
nature or content of the imprint, it is this imprintedness itself
which seems to constitute femininity.[10]

And in her "Tales of War and Tears of Women," Nancy Huston remarks on the regularity in war narratives of the appearance of a
crying woman: "[She] has two possible pretexts for weeping: either
the infringement of her physical integrity—paradigmatically, she
can be raped by the Enemy—or else bereavement, in the event that
the Hero is killed in battle.[11]

How do we interpret Yamada's tears? Accurate as these two passages are about dominant modes of representation of war, neither
one fairly or completely accounts for Yamada's text. The speaker
cries here, certainly, in response to a brief but violent "infringement of her physical integrity," represented with nightmarish detail
by the "warm spittle" on her face. Her relation to the Enemy, however, is far more complicated than that of women in the standard
war narrative Huston defines. In her own country, the Japanese-
American woman is herself perceived as the Enemy; there is no
hope of release from the fear of assault imagined in the context of
this poem, no possible protection or victory. Turning to see her own
reflection, the speaker must realize that fact and then begin to interpret for herself the image of her face covered not only with tears
but also with spit, which means interpreting her own imprintedness. If that image conveys, as Judith Williamson puts it, the
"tragedy of war," it does so very differently from, say, a photograph
of a grieving war widow on the front page of a newspaper; the
mourning widow is not spat upon. The "nature or content" of this
imprint involves a primary realization of the impossibility of freedom in a racist society. What is at issue here, however, is also the
way in which being marked by race works to constitute the daughter's femininity. "Cincinnati," which centers on a moment of im-
printing, is as much about femininity as it is about the inescapa-
bility of being targeted by racial hatred.

The rest of the poem offers a portrait of temporary paralysis, focusing with agonized slow motion, as the crowds in "Government
Square" rush past the speaker, on the lifting of her hand to wipe her
face. At this point the revisionary relation of this poem to "Night
before Goodbye" becomes particularly apparent, for "Cincinnati"

moves into a close-up of another mother-made, protective domestic object linked in thematic implication to the mended underwear of the previous poem, a "bleached laced / mother-ironed hankie":

My hankie brushed
the forked
tears and spittle
together.
I edged toward the curb
loosened by fisthold
and the bleached laced
mother-ironed hankie blossomed in
the gutter atop teeth marked
gum wads and heeled candy wrappers.

Everyone knew me.   [29]

The loss of innocence represented by the defiled handkerchief entails a specific crisis of femininity: the loss of a sense that the practice of daughterly duty, a certain kind of modest womanhood taught by the mother, could make the world safe for the speaker. Being squeaky-clean, bleached, and lacy does not protect her from the taunt "dirty jap"; and being womanly, simply being a woman, increases the ways in which she is vulnerable to the barely deflected violence represented by "teeth-marks" and "heels." The threat of rape for the young woman relocated by herself, muted but real, haunts the end of this poem.

The next poem, the final one in the "Camp Notes" series, emphasizes the general experience of racial oppression shared by all nonwhite women *and* men in the United States:

I had packed up
my wounds in a cast
iron box
sealed it
labeled it
do not open . . .
ever . . .
and travelled blind

for thirty years
until one day I heard
a black man with huge bulbous eyes

say
there is nothing more
humiliating
more than beatings
more than curses
than being spat on

like a dog.   [30]

As its title suggests, "Thirty Years Under" accounts retrospectively for the long repression of the "Camp Notes" poems and of
the memories to which they bear witness. It begins with a heavy-
handed allegory, replacing the striking image of the soiled handkerchief from the poem before with a clumsier and more abstract image of repression as a cast-iron box. The poem achieves greater
power as it abandons its initial visual conceit and ends, as "Night
before Goodbye" ended, with the transcription of a single voice.

Yamada's poetic method is characterized throughout *Camp Notes*
by a reliance on the "transcription" of voices. Voice has been a
primary threat in the short narrative sequence of the three final
poems that I have been examining closely; in "Cincinnati," the
"hissing voice" represents and carries racist violence. At the same
time, however, *Camp Notes* privileges powers of voice over all
other human powers; its own authority derives from its claim to
vocal veracity and authenticity, its representation of itself as a particular woman's voice speaking up, telling her own story, a true
story. The volume resembles several political feminist documentary films that offer narrative histories or biographies through interviews and reminiscence; it is worth noting that many readers of
Yamada have discovered her work through the documentary *Mitsuye and Nellie: Two Asian-American Woman Poets*.[12] Documen-
tary-like itself, the text offers in turn a series of anecdotal vignettes
in which various people's stories are told. The majority of poems
in the volume offer themselves as simple and incontrovertible accounts of actual events, many of which happened to the speaker,
others of which are tales of relatives—the mother's story, or the
grandmother's, or the father's.

It is appropriate, then, that the speaker of "Camp Notes" is represented as learning the ability to remember her ordeal, to validate
her outrage, and to possess the necessary authorial control over her
story through someone else's testimony, the voice of the blind
black man in "Thirty Years Under." This concluding poem of the

"Notes" is, in essence, about what voice can transmit. The encounter between the poem's speaker and the one who presents the moral, between the Japanese-American woman and the black man she sets up as her counterpart, may be taken as a model for the reader's ideal relation to Yamada's project. If the testimony of *Camp Notes* works, we should be brought to revelation, to recovery, to an "unlocking" of our own woundings and dealings in a racist society.

"Thirty Years Under" has an explicit moral, articulated by the black male speaker: a refusal to dismiss the particular suffering of one who is spat upon; an insistence on the intensity of the violence of a "hissing voice"; an argument for a certain kind of interchangeability of oppression in the United States shared by blacks and Japanese-Americans alike. But the text is also about the process by which its author has discovered refusal, insistence, and argument as rhetorical and moral possibilities. The outrage expressed in another's voice here will be claimed directly in the speaker's own voice in later poems (see, especially, "To the Lady"), and the text often seems to suggest through its own implicit fictions of transmission that out of overheard stories, stories of the listener's own will naturally issue, that militance and self-respect are catching.[13]

At other moments, however, *Camp Notes* offers a less easy or confident view of the uses of anecdote and the possibilities of transmission. The reader moves toward the archival "camp" material at the center of the book through a series of poems that narrate family stories—poems presumably meant to teach us how to read Yamada and her culture. The two that concern the Nisei speaker's attempts to understand Japanese culture through dialogue with her father, "Enryo" and "A Bedtime Story," are both narratives of failed translations, characterized by impasses between the storytelling father and the listening child. These failures stand in marked contrast to the poems in which the mother narrates the stories, achieving an almost seamless identification of mother and daughter. The daughter disappears, except to the degree that we feel her behind the scene or between the lines as an empathetic listener; the mother's voice speaks without interruption, without mediation—even when the story it recounts is one of painful separation between mother and daughter, as in "Homecoming, from Tillie Olsen." The workings of these early poems conform to a general pattern: in the "mother" poems, narrative works, stories are recovered and found to be worth the telling; in the "father" poems, narrative warps, stories fall on deaf ears, fall short.

What appears to be, by my description, a narrative gender gap in *Camp Notes* may be perceived by some of my readers as an unfair stacking of the cards against the male voice; and to the extent that Yamada's text, and other feminist projects like it, imply a painless transmission of history from mothers to daughters or an inevitable progression toward a universal liberation of women achieved by the telling of anecdotes, there may be good reason to regard them with distrust. Noel King has provided a model of such distrust in his useful questions about the implications of unproblematic use of witness testimony in political documentaries (films with which, I have already suggested, Yamada's work has much in common). Calling for a reading which, "[g]iven that it is the function of a classical narrative system to suppress and suture . . . potentially discontinuous or contradictory features, . . . [would] notice precisely how that suturing occurs," King argues that the documentaries he examines work to suppress analysis of social forces or institutions outside the individual, presenting instead a world in which individual testimony against injustice is enough in itself to bring about social change. He goes on to cite Michel Foucault's warning about "the desire to make historical analysis the discourse of continuity and the desire to make human consciousness the originating subject of all learning and all practice. This system conceives of time in terms of totalization."[14]

Does Yamada's text, with its seemingly effortless and complete transmissions of the mother's history, establish a false "discourse of continuity"? I would argue no, and I would also maintain that there is a valid reason for the differences between "mother" and "father" poems in the opening section of *Camp Notes*, one that might be deduced from the one exception to the rule I have set up about their divergences. The exception is the poem called "P.O.W." in "Camp Notes," which consists entirely of translations from the Japanese of two *senryu* poems written by "Jakki," the pen name of Yamada's father. Here, although the daughter identifies herself as translator and thereby separates herself from her father in a way that does not take place when she retells her mother's stories, she has still, clearly, undertaken a task of transmission for her father's sake, without protest or misunderstanding.

Why should these short, bitterly but quietly ironic poems be translatable while the father's other narratives are rejected and called into question? The answer, I would argue, lies in the father's *senryu*'s marginal relation to dominant histories. In "Bedtime

Story" or "Enryo," we hear him playing the role of acculturator, using his stories in an attempt to shape and dominate his daughter's behavior; in the "P.O.W." poems he speaks only for himself, from a place of exclusion. Like the mother's narratives in "Marriage Was a Foreign Country" and "Homecoming," each of which relates a story that has clearly for years gone unspoken, "P.O.W." represents itself as a written history that came very close to being unwritten, one that may be written off once again.

The father's "Bedtime Story" can be read as an example of an attempt to construct what Foucault calls "total" and "totalizing" history, the kind of official history that draws "all phenomena around a single centre—the principle, meaning, spirit, worldview, overall form of a society or civilization," in this case traditional Japanese civilization. The Americanized daughter to whom the story is told greets it with great skepticism: "That's the *end?*" she shouts at its conclusion, debunking its totality for better or worse (the story is appealing), refusing to be drawn into its circle. No one shouts "That's the end?" at the end of "P.O.W." It's not necessary; the two sad, short poems question themselves from inside. Their quality of self-questioning, the sense they give of severe, radical discontinuity and of contradictions between and within cultures, is precisely what allows the "P.O.W." poems to be translated by the daughter. The histories Yamada's text admits intact are those that exhibit the qualities Foucault has attributed to "general" histories, which provide alternative modes of approach to the past. General histories, unlike "total" histories, as Foucault defines them, narrate and incorporate "segmentation, limits, difference of level, time-lags, anachronistic survivals, possible types of relation."[15] *Camp Notes* constructs Yamada's history itself as a part of "general history": a story not of center but of circumference; a retelling of the story that never allows either teller or listener to forget its limits, its lags, the differences that threaten to circumscribe or silence it; a transcription of the story that never pretends to be the *whole* story. Permanently marginal, perpetually in opposition to dominant versions of its events, energized by its interruptions, *Camp Notes* reaches toward the construction of a discourse of discontinuity.

Reaches only, for the text's insistence on what is discontinuous, what is made peripheral and fragmented, is matched and countered by its celebration of complex but enduring personal and cultural identities. Like the act of mending performed by the mother in "Night before Goodbye," Yamada's poetic project both takes note of threats to the integrity and unity of the self's fabric and demonstrates how, in response to those threats, suturing may still occur. "Night before Goodbye" itself enacts, simultaneously, both separation from and connection to the mother and the Japanese-American Issei culture she represents, both continuities and discontinuities.

Narratives of discontinuity are not, of course, the special property of women writers or Japanese-American writers; and canonical war literature, perhaps even more than most types of contemporary literature, tends to exhibit strategies that heighten incoherences and incompletions. Dominant antiwar literature, from Owen and Sassoon through Jarrell and Pynchon to Vietnam-era poetry, has presented itself as replacing an imperious, totalizing narrative with a much truer and far more disjointed "real story." Of the many examples of texts by white male writers that I might cite here, perhaps the most striking is Louis Simpson's postponed poetic rediscovery of his own war, both nightmare and reportage, which he describes in his autobiographical *Air with Armed Men*:

> I enlisted in the U.S. Army in 1942. . . . I got through the war all right, but afterwards, when I was back in the States, I had a "nervous breakdown," and was hospitalized. I had amnesia; the war was blacked out of my mind. . . . In 1948, when I was living in Paris, one night I dreamed that I was lying on the bank of a canal, under machine gun and mortar fire. The next morning I wrote it out, in the poem "Carentan O Carentan" and as I wrote I realized it wasn't a dream, but the memory of my first time under fire.[16]

Simpson's amnesia reminds us that being at what Clausewitz called the "true center of gravity in war,"[17] the battle, may rob a soldier of discourse—of identity and life itself—instead of granting him any personal center of gravity from which to speak. In Simpson's war poem "Carentan O Carentan," there is no center, only scattered, disconnected, barely coherent violence.

But if Simpson's repressed dispatches from the nightmare battlefront prove that dispossessions and discontinuities are not a feminine problem alone, their power derives from their refusal like many feminist texts, to construct a history of war along the lines of the coherent national histories of conquest and military strategy that *have* been written, by and large, by and for men. Nancy Huston, in the discussion of women and weeping to which I referred earlier, asks, "If a war gave rise to no narrative, would it have taken place? The question," she goes on, represents neither paradox nor provocation; it is rooted in a problematic with which everyone is familiar: the strong connection between narrativity and the idea of conflict. . . .

> . . . going off to war, men have always sought to demonstrate their ability not only to "make" history, but also to *write* it. . . . When listeners marveled at the precision with which Bernal Diaz evoked battle scenes of fifty years before (he had been a soldier under Cortes in the Conquest of Mexico), he explained that the Spaniards used to gather together every evening to recount the day's combats. . . . This virtually simultaneous translation [allowed] the conquistadors . . . to be able to *read History for themselves*, im-mediately, in order to grasp its meaning and to foresee its probable evolutions. [272]

The internment of Mitsuye Yamada and her family in Minedoka, Idaho, and of her father in prison in New Mexico; her terror as a young woman released from the camps in an atmosphere of intense racial hatred; the modes of survival she and her family devised: these things took place, though for a long time they gave rise to no published or shared narrative. Still, as a young writer at work on the early poems in *Camp Notes*, Yamada did, covertly, read her history for herself. We need a different way of speaking about war narratives, as Nancy Huston herself insists, to encompass those like Yamada's that come slowly and haltingly, not simultaneously.

But what distinguishes Yamada's war story from others more likely to be included in bibliographies of war literature is not simply the fact of its postponed publication. After all, the amnesiac gap between Louis Simpson's war experience and his war poems seems to contradict, as directly as *Camp Notes*, the model of masculine war narrative Huston sets up. "Carentan O Carentan," by Simpson's account, is a war story neither immediate nor "virtually simultaneous"; neither is *A Farewell to Arms*, published ten years after the events it describes, nor *Catch-22*, a World War II novel published two decades later. If Yamada had access to popular anthologies of war literature published during the forties, she might even have been instructed in postponement as a canonical criterion of excellence. Ernest Hemingway's introduction to *Men at War* (1942), for instance, describes a canon of war literature composed almost exclusively of stories originally withheld under the force of censorship and trauma: in general, only "after the war," Hemingway writes, do "the good and true books finally start . . . to come out."[18]

Camp Notes seems to fit without disruption, then, into a conventional paradigm of postponement such as Hemingway employs. But the subtitle of *Men at War* reminds us of how sharply Yamada's situation and purpose differ from Ernest Hemingway's. *Men at War: The Best War Stories of All Time* has been edited, Hemingway states in his preface, so that his three sons "can have the book that will contain the truth about war as near as we can come by it," one that will show "what all the other men that we are a part of had gone through" (xxvii, xi). "*The* book," "the best of all time," "all other men we are a part of": Hemingway's terms suggest an active consciousness both universal and elite. He envisions an endlessly repeated, totalizing war story, brutal and noble both at once, easily surviving and transcending petty censorship and relatively short periods of silence.

Yamada, reading this anthology in 1942, could have identified herself nowhere—neither with the "little monkeys" who are Hemingway's Japanese nor with the white sons to whom the book is dedicated. "During a war," Hemingway writes confidently, "censorship can conceal. . . . But after the war, all of these acts have to be paid for . . . the people know what has really happened . . . the men who fought the war come home" (xxi). Writing her own poems in the war years, knowing that the forces that silenced her would not disappear on V-J Day, Yamada produced a book that resists incorporation into any scheme of "best war stories of all time," or even "best internment stories of all time." She wrote it for her time, in and of a camp in Idaho, and then put it away.

The model for *Camp Notes*'s narrative of postponement is not, then, the immediate tale told by a soldier to his comrades around a campfire, nor the true war story passed on haltingly from father to son, but, perhaps, something closer to the story Jeanne Wakatsuki Houston tells of her return to the internment camp where she grew up, in her *Farewell to Manzanar*:

This visit, this pilgrimage, made comprehensible, finally, the traces that remained and would always remain, like a needle. That hollow ache I carried during the early months of internment had shrunk, over the years, to a tiny sliver of suspicion about the very person I was. . . . I heard Mama's soft, weary voice from 1945 say, "It's all starting over." . . . Manzanar would always live in my nervous system, a needle with Mama's voice.[19]

"A needle with Mama's voice": this is a striking, resonant, and paradoxical phrase. If it represents the self-suspicion and the gnawing sense of fear that present the major psychological obstacle to writing for a female survivor of internment, it also represents a source of wisdom passed on from the mother, the useful survival skill of memory. It is a *speaking* needle, the constant reminder of a narrative which resists the forces that would silence it, but which must also acknowledge its own incompleteness, its own suppressions and suturings, its own internal silences. The needle jabs, but it can also be turned to mending and to creating. For Yamada, writing, rediscovering, adding to, and publishing "Camp Notes" meant acknowledging the "needle with Mama's voice" in all its contradictions.

Notes

1. Lundberg, "The American Literature of War," 386. Subsequent references to this work are included parenthetically in the text.

2. I am indebted to Kim's important work throughout this essay. Another widely disseminated analysis of camp writing in print at the time of Lundberg's formulation appears in Chin et al., *Aiiieeeee!*, xxxiv–xxxvii. See also Yamamoto, "I Still Carry It Around."

3. Yamada, *Camp Notes*, 1. Subsequent references to this work are included parenthetically in the text. Yamada's book is named after its central section; I refer to that section as "Camp Notes" and to the volume as a whole as *Camp Notes*.

4. Yamada, "Invisibility," 36. Subsequent references to this work are included parenthetically in the text.

5. See the discussion of Mori in Kim, *Asian American Literature*, 163–72.

6. I take this phrase from Gerachty's report, "National Fictions," on the 1983 British Film Institute Summer School, whose subject was "Struggles over the Meaning of World War Two."

7. Kuhn, " 'Desert Victory,' " 58.

8. See Kim, *Asian American Literature*, 18–22, 59–60, 73–74.

9. One chapter in my forthcoming book *A Gulf So Deeply Cut* traces in detail the conditions that shaped, hindered, and permitted women's writing in the camps and offers an expanded and reconsidered analysis of Yamada's camp poems along with the work of other Japanese-American women poets of the period.

10. Williamson, "Images of 'Woman,'" 103–4.

11. Huston, "Tales of War," 275. All subsequent references to this work are included parenthetically in the text.

12. Light and Saraf, *Mitsuye and Nellie*.

13. I am indebted here to King's discussion of the representation of militance in political documentaries as "univeral, timeless, always waiting below the surface," in his "Recent 'Political' Documentary," 15.

14. Ibid., citing Foucault, *Archeology of Knowledge*.

15. This summary enters my text third-hand—from Kaplan's introduction to *Women and Film*, 3, which condenses terms from Lentricchia, *After the New Criticism*. Lentricchia in turn is summarizing Foucault's *Archeology of Knowledge*. I am indebted to Kaplan's application of Foucault's distinctions to feminist constructions of history.

16. Simpson, *Air with Armed Men*, 109.

17. Clausewitz, *On War*, 248.

18. Hemingway, *Men at War*, xv. All subsequent references to this work are included parenthetically in the text.

19. Houston and Houston, *Farewell to Manzanar*, 170.

Works Cited

Chin, Frank, Jeffery Chan, Lawson Fusao Inada, and Shawn Hsu Wong, eds. *Aiiieeeee!: An Anthology of Asian-American Writers*. Washington, D.C.: Howard University Press, 1974.

Clausewitz, Carl von. *On War*. Edited by Michael Howard and Peter Paret. Princeton, N.J.: Princeton University Press, 1976.

Foucault, Michel. *Archeology of Knowledge*. Translated by Alkan Sheridan. New York: Pantheon, 1972.

Gerachty, Christine. "National Fictions." *Screen* 24 (1983): 94–96.

Hemingway, Ernest, ed. *Men at War: The Best War Stories of All Time*. New York: Crown, 1942.

Houston, Jeanne Wakatsuki, and James D. Houston. *Farewell to Manzanar*. Boston: Houghton Mifflin, 1973.

Huston, Nancy. "Tales of War and Tears of Women." *Women's Studies International Forum* 5, no. 3/4 (1982): 271–86.

Kaplan, E. Ann. *Women and Film: Both Sides of the Camera*. New York: Methuen, 1983.

Kim, Elaine. *Asian American Literature: An Introduction to the Writings and Their Social Context*. Philadelphia: Temple University Press, 1982.

King, Noel. "Recent 'Political' Documentary: Notes on *Union Maids* and *Harlan County, U.S.A.*" *Screen* 22 (1982): 7–20.

Kuhn, Annette. "'Desert Victory' and the People's War." *Screen* 22 (1982): 45–68.

Lentricchia, Frank. *After the New Criticism.* Chicago: University of Chicago Press, 1980.

Light, Allie, and Irving Saraf, producers. *Mitsuye and Nellie: Two Asian-American Woman Poets.* San Francisco: Light-Saraf Films, 1981.

Lundberg, David. "The American Literature of War: The Civil War, World War I, and World War II." *American Quarterly* 36 (1984): 381–92.

Schweik, Susan. *A Gulf So Deeply Cut: American Women Poets and the Second World War.* Madison: University of Wisconsin Press, forthcoming.

Simpson, Louis. *Air with Armed Men.* London: London Magazine, 1972.

Williamson, Judith. "Images of 'Woman.'" *Screen* 24 (1983): 103–5.

Yamada, Mitsuye. *Camp Notes and Other Poems.* San Lorenzo, Calif.: Shameless Hussy Press, 1976.

———. "Invisibility Is an Unnatural Disaster: Reflections of an Asian American Woman." In *This Bridge Called My Back: Writings by Radical Women of Color.* Watertown, Mass.: Persephone Press, 1981.

Yamamoto, Hisaye. "I Still Carry It Around." *Rikka* 3/4 (1976): 11–19.

Carol J.
Adams Feminism, the Great War,

and Modern Vegetarianism

What is civilization? What is culture? Is it possible for a healthy
race to be fathered by violence—in war or in the slaughter-house—
and mothered by slaves, ignorant or parasitic? Where is the historian who traces the rise and fall of nations to the standing of
their women?—Agnes Ryan, "Civilization? Culture?"

Twentieth-century British and American women writers
have struggled with one of the literary consequences of
the Great War: experience at the front has customarily
been understood as entitling one to write about war
while being at the home front has been thought to foreclose this
right. In response to this literary standard silencing most women
because they were not at the front, some writers strategically expand the terrain of war. The front, they suggest, exists not only in
traditionally viewed warfare, but also in what they view as the war
against nonhuman animals, typified by hunting and meat eating.[1]
Women, too, their argument goes, are located at this front, and are
thus entitled to speak about war. From this expanded front, these
writers correlate male acts of violence against people and animals;
vegetarianism becomes, along with pacifism, a challenge to war. In
the wake of the Great War, many modern women writers trace the
causes of both war and meat eating to male dominance.

Drawing together the numerous references to vegetarianism in
works by twentieth-century women writers, this essay identifies a
tradition of literary texts that expands the front and in so doing
establishes the links between vegetarianism and pacifism. Because
the Great War catalyzed the assimilation of vegetarianism into the
antiwar vision of women writers, it is the context against which we
should read this tradition. For the purposes of this essay I am identifying vegetarianism as a theme in a novel only when the author
has clearly articulated it. Vegetarians are figured in literature either

when the characters so declare themselves or when there is specific reference to the elimination of meat in their diets. Through the textual strategy of "interruption," modern women writers introduce vegetarian incidents into their novels. Four themes aligned with the notion of the expanded front arise when a vegetarian "interruption" occurs. These themes include rejection of male acts of violence, identification with animals, repudiation of men's control of women, and the positing of an ideal world composed of vegetarianism, pacifism, and feminism as opposed to a fallen world composed in part of women's oppression, war, and meat eating. A consideration of the narrative strategies and thematic concerns of several illustrative works will suggest the depths of the linkage between vegetarianism and pacifism in women's writings of the twentieth century. Further, it will reveal some of the costs of our failure to discern this conjunction.

II

When times are normal people and governments are inclined to pursue lines of least resistance; that is, to continue practices and customs not because they are best but because of habit, but it is during abnormal periods that we do our best thinking. . . . I have long had in mind a book on "Wheatless and Meatless Menus," but the time to bring it out was not ripe until now.—Eugene Christian, *Meatless and Wheatless Menus*, 1917

As an individual choice, pre–Great War vegetarianism can be traced back to writers such as Porphyry and forward to George Bernard Shaw.[2] As a movement its heyday was from 1790 to 1850. In England it was called the Pythagorean diet, in the United States, Grahamism; it became the adopted diet of many of the utopian communities that sprang up in these countries. Yet, by the time the word "vegetarian" was coined in 1847, much of the movement had been diffused, although individuals such as WCTU president Frances Willard and English theosophist and feminist Annie Besant carried it forward to the turn of the century.

As an attribute of fictional characters, few literary examples of vegetarianism antedate the Great War. The modernization of vegetarianism occurred when it began to figure, as a theme or incidental element, in novels. The Great War quickened vegetarianism, propelling it as a movement into the twentieth century and as a subject into the novels of women writers. Events of the Great War yoked the heretofore sporadically linked notions of pacifism and vegetarianism. Philosopher Mary Midgley views the Great War as a turning point in attitudes toward animals, suggesting that after the war there was an upsurge of interest in and scientific proof of the continuities between animals and human beings. After citing examples of good-hearted tolerance of egregious acts of hunting, she writes, "For most of us, however, the light seems somehow to have changed—indeed, it probably did so during the First World War."[3]

During the war, soldiers' imaginations became alerted to what Shaw and other vegetarians had claimed for decades: corpses are corpses. How could the soldier avoid thinking of his commonality with animals as he sat in the trenches watching large black rats consume soldier and horse? The horrors of this war were also found in the slaughterhouse. The editor's introduction to L. F. Easterbrook's article on "Alcohol and Meat" explains, "In 1918 the spectacle of a herd of scared and suffering cattle hustled together in a van, and being conveyed to a slaughter yard, struck the writer of this note as being at least as abominable, and as degrading to our civilisation, as anything he had recently witnessed on several hard fighting fronts in France and Italy."[4]

Individual women took these insights to heart. For instance Mary Alden Hopkins remarked: "I reacted violently at that time against all established institutions, like marriage, spanking, meat diet, prisons, war, public schools, and our form of government."[5] Agnes Ryan and her husband Henry Bailey Stevens, both editors of *The Woman's Journal* and pacifists, became vegetarians during the Great War. In 1917, Maud Freshel, author of the definitive vegetarian cookbook for that time, *The Golden Rule Cookbook*, resigned from the Christian Science church when it supported the entry of the United States into World War I. Ryan describes Freshel's address on war and meat eating to a 1915 Fabian Society meeting: "Here was a new type of woman; here was a new spiritual force at work in the universe. . . . [S]he clearly stressed the idea that wars will never be overcome until the belief that it is justifiable to take life, to kill—*when expedient*—is eradicated from human consciousness."[6] During the Great War, feminist, pacifist, and vegetarian Charlotte Despard would not allow the soup kitchen operated on her property in a poor area of England to serve meat. At least four American vegetarian feminists traveled on the Ford Peace Ship in 1915.

The rationing of food during the Great War provided a positive, though transitory, vegetarian environment for civilians, especially women, who could turn to books such as Christian's *Meatless and Wheatless Menus* or *The Golden Rule Cookbook*. This rationing provided one researcher the largest survey population attainable, the entire nation of Denmark. Dr. Mikkel Hindhede describes it as "a low protein experiment on a large scale, about 3,000,000 subjects being available."[7] After directing the rationing program necessitated by the war—"a milk and vegetable diet"—Hindhede found that it had improved the Danish people's mortality rates.

During the Great War some feminists argued that male domination and the absence of female power caused war.[8] In the wake of the war, this position intersected with the view that meat-eating cultures were war cultures (even though not all meat-eating cultures were then at war). As feminists and vegetarians acknowledged their shared critical positions, they discovered that the destructive values of patriarchal culture were not limited to the battlefront.

III

Scarcely a human being in the course of history has fallen to a woman's rifle; the vast majority of birds and beasts have been killed by you, not by us. . . . —Virginia Woolf, *Three Guineas*

"I expect after you have many times seen a deer or woodchuck blown to bits, the thought of a human being blown to bits is that much less impossible to conceive."—Medieval scholar Grace Knole in *The James Joyce Murders*

Does a man revisit the Great War by recalling his days as a fox hunter? Yes, according to Siegfried Sassoon, whose *The Memoirs of George Sherston*, which culminates in 1918, begins with *Memoirs of a Fox-Hunting Man*.[9] How else should Robert Graves begin his farcical, satirical, humorous memoir—his book that turned the war and everything else on its end—but by introducing us to a vegetarian?[10] Can there be a *Case for the Vegetarian Conscientious Objector*, as Max Davis and Scott Nearing believed in 1945? Where else should a novel anticipating the Great War begin but with a male-only shooting party? All of these works suggest a connection between eating meat (and/or hunting) and war. This sense of connection was both verified and intensified once examined through a feminist lens, revealing that it was *Man* the Hunter and *Man* the Soldier—the phrases are Charlotte Perkins Gilman's from a poem that opens her penultimate book, *His Religion and Hers*, written after, and influenced by, World War I.[11]

Man the hunter, man the soldier: this refrain not only links disparate acts of violence—the killing of people and the killing of animals—but also focuses on the sex of the killer. The tradition of vegetarian feminist novels by women writers that I explore in this essay recalls Gilman's approach. This tradition originates with the recognition of an expanded front that exists wherever animals are killed. A constellation of feminist insights, which I have isolated into four distinct themes, seems to follow this recognition. (1) The theme of rejection of male acts of violence: While their complicity in meat eating locates women *at* the front, a heightened sensitivity to the consumption of animal flesh also generates a comprehensive antiwar critique *from* the front. (2) The theme of identification with animals: Women are allied with animals because they too are objects of use and possession. Women's oppression is expressed through the trope of meat eating. (3) The theme of vegetarianism as rejection of male control and violence: Through the adoption of vegetarianism women simultaneously reject a warring world and dependence on men. This dependence not only manifests itself in the need to be protected by men, but also the need to project on men tasks that women prefer not to think of themselves as doing, such as functioning as killers. (4) The theme of linked oppressions and linked ideal states: Male dominance is seen to cause women's oppression, war, and meat eating; conversely, in discussions of that perfect world before the fall, vegetarianism and pacifism become linked with women's equality. While the works in this tradition are unified by their inclusion of animals within a pacifist vision, none of them attempts to include all four themes in any one text, nor is there any chronological order to the development of these themes. In essence, while the texts are united by a recognition of an enlarged war front, they vary according to the distinct themes evolving from the particular configuration they choose to explore.

Isabel Colegate's Great War novel *The Shooting Party* (1980) anchors the texts securely within the antiwar tradition.[12] By exploring the connection between hunting and war from a woman's perspective, Colegate demonstrates, like Sassoon, that hunting is the perfect prelude and pattern for judging a warring world. Colegate provides a female twist, however, by including women in the expanded front. If hunting is the appropriate mirror against which to judge war, then women can gain a voice in judging what they do not share—the battlefront—by judging what they do share as spectators—the experience of the hunt.

Colegate's tightly constructed novel depicts the evening of the second day and the third day of a traditional shooting party. It is a stunning evocation of prewar innocence and a dark foreshadowing of a bloody war. But the shooting party—with its army of uniformed beaters (68) following campaign plans (151), moving from the bivouac of lunch to the front line of the shooting, with loaders scurrying in a no-man's-land retrieving the thickly strewn corpses—is not a mere intimation of things to come, but a depiction of a war itself. "War might be like this," thinks Olivia, "casual, friendly and frightening" (131). Indeed, male competition, culminating in the accidental death of a beater—who propelled the frightened pheasants forth to their slaughter at the guns of the upper-class shooters—represents the eternal cause of war. A hunter eager for the most animals "bagged" mistakenly shoots the beater.

Colegate places more spectators at the "front" than shooters. We find there the beaters, the upper-class women, an activist vegetarian, a young child worried about his pet duck, a maid. Their thoughts about the shooting act as counterpoints to the escalating competition of the male shooters. Olivia, appalled by her husband's concern for social niceties and pursued by an earnest poet willing to fight the coming war for her sake, represents the female spectator. By positioning her women at the shooting party, Colegate establishes their right to voice criticisms such as Olivia's: "And I am often aware at shooting parties how differently I feel from a man and how, more than that, I really would like to rebel against the world men have made, if I knew how to" (20–21). Olivia articulates Colegate's theme of rejection of male violence. In Colegate's novel, women's presence in, but opposition to, the violent world men have made is constantly reiterated.

Through the analogy of the shooting party as war, Colegate expands the front to where women are, empowering their articulations. When the war is referred to as "a bigger shooting party [which] had begun, in Flanders," (188) empowerment to speak of *this* front implicitly exists. Thus, *The Shooting Party* becomes one answer to the recurring twentieth-century question posed to women writers: how does a woman condemn war if she cannot be a soldier?[13] This issue is dissolved if she criticizes war by criticizing its equivalent, of which she *is* a part, as witness as well as subsequent consumer: the shooting party.

During the Great War the chasm between the soldier at war and the woman spectator was intentionally widened by soldier-writers who condescendingly dismissed—for lack of experience at the front —any writings by noncombatants. This legacy of condescension and dismissal carried into the Second World War as well. By showing that women, prior to the Great War, had a right to voice their perspective on war through the corollary experience of participating in, and responding to, a shooting party, Colegate brilliantly restores a right of articulation. The suggestion her novel leaves, therefore, is not that one must be at the war front to have the right to speak, but that one may speak by linking one's own experience *to* war, through making the connection between hunting and/or meat eating and war. So, one can claim one's voice. Wilfred Owen and other Great War writers erred not by restricting authentic experiences to the front alone, but by their too-limited definition of where the front can be found.

At the expanded front, the theme of identification with animals arises: with whom do the women located there align themselves, the hunter or the hunted? Identification with animals is a pivotal moment for two novels in this tradition of women writers. For Margaret Atwood's and Marge Piercy's heroines, meat eating becomes a trope of their own oppression. Women come to see themselves as being consumed by marital oppression at the domestic front; they grapple with the recognition that their bodies are battlegrounds and view animals with the new awareness of a common experience. The third theme, related to their identification with animals, expresses their sense of shared violation. Linking sexual oppression to meat eating, Atwood's and Piercy's heroines forego the traditional romantic ending by giving up marriage and associating male dominance in personal relationships with meat eating. Thus, they give up meat as well.[14]

The character who most successfully rejects both meat and marriage is Beth, in Marge Piercy's *Small Changes* (1972). Newly married, she finds herself one night eating meat loaf at the kitchen table. Though shaken by a vehement argument during which her husband, angered by her apparent independence, had flushed her birth control pills down the toilet, she sits and contemplates her situation. As she chews the meat loaf she realizes her status as simultaneously victim and victimizer: "A trapped animal eating a dead animal" (41). She imprints this realization on her memory: "Remember the cold meat loaf. From the refrigerator she got the ketchup and doused it liberally. Then it was less obnoxious. Meat, a dead animal that had been alive. She felt as if her life were something slippery she was trying to grab in running water." (42) Grasping her life, she flees her domestic front, becoming a conscientious objector to the war against women and animals.[15] Beth undergoes numerous "small changes" on which Marge Piercy centers her novel. Beth's first and abiding change is her rejection of meat: "The revulsion toward eating flesh from the night of the meat loaf remained. It was part superstition and part morality: she had escaped to her freedom and did not want to steal the life of other warm-blooded creatures" (48). Her insights of an expanded front catalyze her education into feminism, her evolution into lesbianism, and, finally, her important enactment of antiwar activism through a Traveling Women's Theater. Inevitably she denounces all war fronts.

Though Margaret Atwood's *The Edible Woman* takes place far from war it is in the midst of a war zone. There are no civilians there, only hunter or hunted, consumer or consumed. Atwood's heroine, Marian, is the target of a hunt by her fiancé, a hunter with an arsenal of weapons. Her man has already taken up metaphoric arms against her by dominating her, and she now realizes that not only is she *at* the front, she is *the* front. Marian's job is to assess the impact of a Moose beer ad that features hunting: "That was so the average beer-drinker, the slope-shouldered pot-bellied kind, would be able to feel a mystical identity with the plaid-jacketed sportsman shown in the pictures with his foot on a deer or scooping a trout into his net" (25). But Marian identifies wih the victim and cries after hearing her fiancé describe his experience at the "front" as a hunter: " 'So I whipped out my knife, good knife, German steel, and slit the belly and took her by the hind legs and gave her one hell of a crack, like a whip you see, and the next thing you know there was blood and guts all over the place. All over me, what a mess, rabbit guts dangling from the trees' " (70). An emotional argument over dinner propels Marian to understand her own relation to that "front": She watches her fiancé skillfully cut his meat and remembers the Moose beer ads, the hunter poised with a deer, which reminds her of the morning newspaper's report of a young boy who killed nine people after going berserk. She imagines that he was someone who could not hit anyone, but that the rifle he had used allowed him a distancing from violence. Again she ponders her fiancé carving his steak and remembers her cookbook's diagram of a "cow with lines on it and labels to show you from which part of the cow all the different cuts were taken. What they were eating now was from some part of the back, she thought: cut on the dotted line." Then she casts her eyes at her own food. "She looked down at her own half-eaten steak and suddenly saw it as a hunk of muscle. Blood red. Part of a real cow that once moved and ate and was killed, knocked on the head as it stood in a queue like someone waiting for a streetcar. Of course, everyone knew that. But most of the time you never thought about it" (155).

After this, Marian's unconscious attitude toward food changes: her body rejects certain foods and she realizes to her horror that she is becoming a vegetarian, that her body has taken an ethical stand: "[I]t simply refused to eat anything that had once been, or (like oysters on the half-shell) might still be living" (183). Both meat eating and first-person narration are suspended once Marian intuits her link to other animals, suggesting that a challenge to meat eating is linked to an attack on the sovereign individual subject. The fluid, merged subjectivity of the middle part of the book finds mystical identity with things, especially animals, that are consumed. Only when she can deal with her own sexual subjugation is Marian released from her body's refusal to eat. She confronts her fiancé with a truly edible woman, a cake she has made, and accuses: " 'You've been trying to destroy me, haven't you. . . . You've been trying to assimilate me' " (279). Domestic dynamics, a sexual war, lead to the interpenetration of vegetarian and pacifist sensibilities. But so profound a challenge to the status quo seems too much to sustain: after breaking her engagement and freeing herself from subjugation to her fiancé, Marian both reclaims first-person narration and regains control over her body's selection of foods. Freed from domestic oppression, she has difficulty sustaining insights in opposition to the dominant worldview, and the pleasure of her own autonomy renders her less sensitive to others' oppression. Her consciousness of being (at) the front subsides. She begins to eat meat again.

If male dominance catalyzes the feminist insight of an expanded front and subsequent vegetarianism, feminist vegetarianism offers men a way to reject war by rejecting meat eating. As opposed to Piercy's and Atwood's controlling, masculine men, whose relationships with women catalyze the ineluctable insight that meat eating and sexual oppression are linked, Agnes Ryan's unpublished feminist, vegetarian, pacifist novel "Who Can Fear Too Many Stars?" figures a romance of vegetarian conversion for a liberated man. Writing in the 1930s, Ryan introduced an unusual motivation for vegetarianism: love of a New Woman. Vegetarianism is the standard against which the new man is measured. As Ryan described her work in a letter to the author of *The Golden Rule Cookbook*: "I would like to make it a ripping love story, hinging on meat-eating."[16] Ruth, an independent, professional woman, is opposed to marriage yet finds herself in love with John Heather. Fearing that it will make their love "go asunder," Ruth withholds from John one vital piece of information. She will not "take anybody into [her] inner circle who can think and know—and still eat flesh." Unfortunately, John is a meat eater. He struggles to become a vegetarian for the woman he loves, but, at Christmas, all romance collapses when he sends Ruth fox furs. Horrified by the gift and the lack of comprehension it reveals—John has not really understood her complete repugnance at exploiting animals—Ruth sends the furs back and flees. Deeply in love, John resolves to learn as much as possible about vegetarianism by reading, among others, Anna Kingsford (a nineteenth-century vegetarian) and Shaw. The journal he keeps during this time reveals to Ruth that he is now fully a vegetarian, and as a result they can be married.

Vegetarianism and feminism act as antiphonal voices in this novel, not as a unified vision, except to demonstrate Ryan's theme "that there are many modern thinking women who mean to stiffen the case for men—or not marry."[17] While John reads vegetarian writings, Ruth receives a tract against marriage that warns "To be a bride is to become a slave, body and soul" (131). Ryan introduces vegetarian and feminist arguments into the novel through references to books, diaries, pamphlets; for her, texts mediate the conversion to vegetarianism and feminism. Whatever John and Ruth read, we must read as well as readers of Ryan's novel; thus we encounter both the literal and literary arguments for vegetarianism and feminism. But there is an imbalance there: while John reads his way into vegetarianism, Ruth avoids confronting the implication of romantic love. His fate as a male in love with a "modern thinking woman" is redemption. Ruth's fate as a modern thinking *married* woman will be to live in oppression. Ryan thus acknowledges there are some things that vegetarianism cannot redeem and that reading cannot accomplish. The text fails at this point: for what can be the fate of a woman in a ripping love story hinging on meat eating? As a vegetarianism redeemed through romantic love is written into the text, *she* is written out of it. The novel collapses into itself and becomes a tract such as the ones that John and Ruth encounter.

Ryan's novel presents a variant formulation of vegetarianism as rejection of male control and violence: rather than portraying a woman who simultaneously rejects violence and dependence on a man, like Piercy's and Atwood's heroines, it figures a man who, through his love for a woman, discovers the ability to reject a warring world. John represents Ryan's husband, Henry Bailey Stevens, who held that humanity was initially vegetarian, goddess worshipping, and pacifist. These characteristics embody the fourth theme available for exploration in works by twentieth-century women writers, such as Charlotte Perkins Gilman's *Herland* and June Brindel's *Ariadne*.

In *The Recovery of Culture*, Henry Bailey Stevens proposes that a plant culture—which he considers anthropologically and horticulturally verified—was replaced with a "blood culture." In a section entitled "The Rape of the Matriarchate" he writes: "The truth is that animal husbandry and war are institutions in which man has shown himself most proficient. He has been the butcher and the soldier; and when the Blood Culture took control of religion, the priestesses were shoved aside" (105). Novelists and short-story writers joined Stevens in locating the cause of meat eating and war in male dominance; some twentieth-century women writers imagine a world before the fall that was feminist, pacifist, and vegetarian. In the short story "An Anecdote of the Golden Age [Homage to *Back to Methuselah*]" Brigid Brophy suggests that male behavioral change is at the root of war, women's oppression, and the killing of animals. Brophy's Golden Age is one in which immortals consume bounteous food from the garden. Naked women menstruate openly and their blood is admired by everyone for its rare beauty. However, men discover that they too bleed when two men engage in a bloodletting fist fight, and paradise is lost. Menstruation is tabooed and fruit—moments ago cherished food—is now disdained by one of the men, Strephon. He bombs another man's pagoda and offers this justification: " 'Corydon was a murderer,' Strephon said sulkily. 'He was fair game. Which reminds me: I shall kill the animals next' " (35). Strephon confines his menstruating female to the house, "and preferably the kitchen, in which unglamorous setting she would be least attractive to other men." Brophy concludes her cautionary tale: "Strephon, the only one of the group to be truly immortal, is in power to this day" (36).

Though obviously having a romp in this piece, Brophy suggests that as long as men are in power, patriarchal violence and its attendant oppressions of women and animals will continue. This theme of the male overthrow of a prepatriarchal vegetarian era also appears in June Brindel's *Ariadne: A Novel of Ancient Crete*. Blood sacrifice here is associated with male control. Ariadne—called by her author "the last Matriarch of Crete"—attempts to introduce the ancient rituals of worship featuring milk and honey but no blood. Brindel's feminist-vegetarian-pacifist mythopoesis figures a vegetarian time of powerful priestesses worshipping goddesses. The triumph of patriarchal control simultaneously introduces the slaughter of animals and the worship of male gods: "Daedulus would ask a question about the ritual, cautiously. 'The invocation to Zeus, when was that introduced into the ceremony? I do not find it in the oldest texts.' Or, 'The earliest records of offerings to the Goddess list only grains and fruit. When was the slaughter of animals added?' " (76). As women's power is displaced, Ariadne escapes to the mountains and pronounces that the labyrinth of Theseus is patriarchal thought that has killed the center, the Mother Goddess. Brindel, like Brophy, evokes a female-centered Golden Age where there are no fronts and no wars.

Through diets for a peaceful vegetarian life, feminist utopias enact the critiques of the expanded front, imagining a world without violence. This aspect of the fourth theme is initially depicted in the first feminist, vegetarian, pacifist utopia written by a woman, Charlotte Perkins Gilman's *Herland*, published during the Great War.[18] In *Herland*, we find menus recalling *The Golden Rule Cookbook*: "The breakfast was not profuse, but . . . this repast with its new but delicious fruit, its dish of large rich-flavored nuts, and its highly satisfactory little cakes was most agreeable" (27). Gilman's narrator, the American intellectual male of 1915, at once notices the absence of meat in *Herland* and queries: " 'Have you no cattle—sheep—horses?' " (47). In a novel that demonstrates the need for a feminine loving kindness, what Gilman called Maternal Pantheism, we might expect that their vegetarianism is one expression of mother love and the corollary belief that meat eating causes aggressive behavior such as male dominance and war. But it is not. Instead, it is a politically astute and ecologically sound conclusion:

wars can be avoided if meat eating is eliminated. They did not have any cattle, sheep, horses because they did " 'not want them anymore. They took up too much room—we need all our land to feed our people. It is such a little country, you know' " (47). What wartime had required of Denmark, the prevention of war required of *Herland*.

Gilman's *Herland* is a feminist gloss on the ecological position enunciated in Plato's *Republic*.[19] Gilman's subtext about land use resulting in war is in opposition to the overt text, which suggests that motivations arising from Mother Love determine Herland's policies. Through her use of the classical ecological argument of preventing wars through controlling diet, Gilman acknowledges that women living on their own would still have a potential for violence against each other *if* they left their diet uncontrolled. Thus women are not exempted from future wars, as Maternal Pantheism would imply. By extension, the Great War could not be the war that ends all wars if meat eating continued. The issue of vegetarianism is an inevitable part of *Herland* because Gilman, while emphasizing women's strengths and abilities, deconstructs the essentials of patriarchal culture at its many fronts.

While *Herland* is the initial text in which a modern woman writer posits the configuration of feminism, vegetarianism, and pacifism, Dorothy Bryant's more recent *The Kin of Ata are Waiting for You* extends Gilman's treatment by situating animals within the moral order. *The Kin of Ata* depicts an egalitarian utopian society in which men and women share child care, gardening, and cleaning. Dried fruits and nuts, grains and legumes, root vegetables and herbs provide great variety to the diet. And the reason for the diet is Bryant's 1970's equivalent to Maternal Pantheism: "I knew better than to suggest that we eat birds or animals, or even fish. They would have reacted the same way as if I'd told them we should eat the children.... [N]o one would have thought of killing any of them" (159).

Rachel Blau DuPlessis comments that the "erasure of the dualism of public and private spheres is one part of the critique of ideology in women's writings."[20] Together the four themes arising from the insight of the expanded front exemplify this erasure. The meaning of the public front invades the private sphere, prompting a redefinition of the location of the front. Additionally, taken together these themes challenge the dualism separating the consequences of violence for animals and human beings. These works argue that domestic oppression and meat eating, usually considered private occurrences, are vitally connected to waging war, while vegetarianism, an apparently private act, constitutes the public rejection of war as a method of conflict resolution. At the front, the connections between male dominance, the killing of animals, and the killing of human beings become clear. In feminist novels, vegetarianism destabilizes the male culture of war.

IV

The symbolism of meat eating is never neutral. To himself, the meat-eater seems to be eating life. To the vegetarian, he seems to be eating death. There is a kind of gestalt-shift between the two positions which makes it hard to change, and hard to raise questions on the matter at all without becoming embattled.
—Mary Midgley, *Animals and Why They Matter*

We have examined novels in which feminist insights catalyze connections between vegetarianism and political violence. Each of these novels appears to employ the same literary technique for summoning these connections—a technique I call interruption. Interruption provides the gestalt-shift by which vegetarianism can be heard. Technically, it occurs when the movement of the novel is suddenly arrested, and attention is given to the issue of vegetarianism in an enclosed section of the novel. The author provides signs that an interruption has occurred. Dots or dashes; the use of the word "interruption"; stammering, pauses, inarticulateness, or confusion in those who are usually in control; the deflection of the story to a focus on food and eating habits; or the reference to significant earlier figures or events from vegetarian history: all become the means for establishing an interruption, a gap in the narrative in which vegetarianism can be entertained. Although the interruption is set apart, the meaning it contains speaks to central themes of the novel, unifying the interruption and the interrupted text through acute critical comments about the social order and meat eating.

In the works of modern women writers the intrusion into the text of a vegetarian incident announces a subversion of the dominant world order, enacted through the subversion of the text itself by the textual strategy of interruption. What was once silenced breaks into the text, deflecting attention from the forces that generally silence it, both thematically and textually. Interruption of others is the method by which silencing is overcome. Interruption provides an opportunity for refocusing the trajectory of the text, as well as providing a protected space within the novel for expanding the front. Interruption does battle with the novel for meaning, wresting meaning from the dominant culture as represented in the text itself.[21] In essence, expanding the front requires extending the scope of the novel, taking it to new topical territory, and this is the function of interruption.

Isadora Duncan's meditation on the connection between war and meat eating, in her autobiography *My Life*, exemplifies the interruption of narrative. She interrupts a discussion about her life during the Great War to assert: "Bernard Shaw says that as long as men torture and slay animals and eat their flesh, we shall have war. I think all sane, thinking people must be of his opinion." From her wartime experience she concludes:

> Who loves this horrible thing called War? Probably the meat eaters, having killed, feel the need to kill—kill birds, animals— the tender stricken deer—hunt foxes.
> The butcher with his bloody apron incites bloodshed, murder. Why not? From cutting the throat of a young calf to cutting the throats of our brothers and sisters is but a step. While we are ourselves the living graves of murdered animals, how can we expect any ideal condition on the earth?   [309]

Duncan's interruption is clearly announced to readers by her beginning reference to Shaw and her ending with a literal invocation of what she believed to be his words. However, she provides a distinctly feminist interpretation to Shaw's insights. By positioning the masculine pronoun between the butcher and the bloody apron, she implicitly indicts male behavior.

The most notable interruption in a text occurs during a Thanksgiving dinner in France, described in Mary McCarthy's *Birds of America*. The novel moves forward without much regard to any specific ethics of consumption. Suddenly, a vegetarian speaks: attention becomes riveted to what the vegetarian is saying and not eating. The interruptions occur on many levels. Roberta Scott, a young American, refuses both dark and light meat from her host, a NATO general. Shocked, he must set down his carving knife before he can say, " 'No turkey?' " With the carving knife he has arrogated power, and each slice of speared meat reinforces his military presence. Her refusal challenges his use of these symbolic implements and thus his power. His implements remain unused as he learns of her vegetarianism, and he must resort to playing "impatiently" with them as he solemnly informs his guest, " 'This is Thanksgiving!' " (166) Later, his wife asks, " 'What made you decide to take up vegetarianism? I don't mean to be intrusive, but tell us, do you really think it's cruel to kill animals?' " Again, the general's actions are arrested by the presence of vegetarianism: "[T]he general, who was carving seconds, paused with his knife in mid-air to await the verdict" (171). In the midst of this interruption we find Miss Scott's precise echoing of the vegetarian position on warfare, artfully introduced into the text prior to a heated argument about the war in Vietnam: " 'Why, some people actually claim that it's a flesh diet that's turned man into a killer of his own kind! He has the tiger's instincts without the tiger's taboos. Of course that's only a hypothesis. One way of testing it would be for humanity to practice vegetarianism for several generations. Maybe we'd find that war and murder would disappear' " (172).

McCarthy's chapter uses domestic events to figure the claim that meat eating causes war, as it traces the slowly escalating rage of the general, for whom carving recalls his military might. He announces that he is "in command here," and discounts Miss Scott's refusal by giving her turkey anyway. But she will not eat it, nor any of the gravy-polluted foods he proffers (168). Her refusal implies that if meat eating and war are related, as *some* people claim, then the dining room table is a part of the extended front; her vegetarianism functions as a condemnation of war. The table soon becomes a site of simulated warfare, as an enlistee makes the sounds of an automatic machine gun. Meanwhile, the general perceives the subtle condemnation and escalates the verbal battle as he argues for the bombing of Hanoi. Pinpointing the cause of his bellicosity his wife confides: " 'Between you and me, it kind of got under his skin to see that girl refusing to touch her food, I saw that right away' " (183). McCarthy's novel pursues the question of how far moral obligations should extend; this interruption suggests that they extend to the quintessential bird of America.

The interruptions of *The Shooting Party* are caused by the appearance of Cornelius Cardew, earnest vegetarian activist who actually interrupts the hunting by picketing at the front. He shoulders his "Thou Shalt Not Kill" banner and marches "straight down the line in front of the guns" (92). Some of the shooters refuse to cease their firing, especially the most competitive one: "The interruption had not caused him to lose a single shot," but for the others, "their concentration had been broken by the interruption" (93). By Cardew's interruption, the historical alliance between feminism and vegetarianism is suggestively summoned; he hands out his own pamphlet, "The Rights of Animals, a Vindication of the Doctrine of Universal Kinship." Colegate here evokes past writers of vindications: Mary Wollstonecraft and her *A Vindication of the Rights of Women*, and Percy Shelley, who in 1812 ingeniously entitled his first essay on vegetarianism *A Vindication of Natural Diet*. She also summons a third vindication through her use of Henry Salt as the historical figure upon whom Cardew is based.[22] Salt knew of both of these vindications; he edited Shelley's *Vindication* and used one response to Wollstonecraft's work to demonstrate in *Animal Rights* "how the mockery of one generation may become the reality of the next" (5). Here he was referring to the first published attack on Wollstonecraft, a parody by Thomas Taylor that was entitled *A Vindication of the Rights of Brutes*. The sense that efforts for women's rights can be undercut by implying that consideration of animals will be next—the message of *Rights of Brutes*—is cleverly evoked in Colegate's novel: "Sir Reuben Hergesheimer was describing to Minnie how a lunatic had appeared waving a placard and how he had taken for granted that it must be a suffragette and been astonished to find out that the agitation was on behalf of animals. 'Votes for pheasants, I suppose.' " (111).

As all three examples demonstrate, the interruptions contain their own legitimating mechanism by summoning historical figures who endorsed what the interruptions convey—the message of the expanded front. For instance, Henry Salt's *The Creed of Kinship*, which Cardew's "Vindication of the Doctrine of Universal Kinship" recalls, contains a section entitled "Two Similar Pastimes: Sport and War." Essentially, vegetarian tradition provides the authority for interrupting the text with vegetarianism. Shaw is summoned by Duncan and Brophy, Salt by Colegate, the Doukhobors (Russian pacifist-vegetarians who migrated to Canada) by McCarthy and Atwood,[23] and Kingsford by Ryan. In addition, this historical invocation of past vegetarians imprints a distinctly feminist hermeneutic: Duncan's view of male butchers as inuring the world to bloodshed; McCarthy's female challenge to male bellicosity through dietary choice; Colegate's allusions to Wollstonecraft and Shelley as well as

Salt. Situating historical reference within the interruption suggests that the notion of an expanded front is one that recurs in history. And through the feminist hermeneutic brought to vegetarian history, a causal link with male dominance and war is effected. Interruption destabilizes the text and the culture it represents.

V

[T]here is not always encouragement and acceptance for those who try to introduce meanings for which there is no conceptual space in the social order. . . . —Dale Spender, *Man-Made Language*

[T]here is a kind of seductiveness about a movement which is revolutionary, but not revolutionary enough.—Mary Daly, *Beyond God the Father*

The convergence of vegetarianism, pacifism, and feminism in modern women writers' works constitutes a tradition that has been ignored. How can we explain this heightened sensitivity by twentieth-century women writers to violence against animals and the failure among literary critics to remark on this sensitivity? The answer lies in the concept of dominance and mutedness that has been well explored in other areas of feminist literary criticism. The difficulty of introducing meanings for which there is no conceptual space has been theorized by anthropologist Edwin Ardener as a problem of dominance and mutedness. As Elaine Showalter describes it, explaining the appropriation of his insights to feminist literary criticism: "[W]omen constitute a *muted group*, the boundaries of whose culture and reality overlap, but are not wholly contained by, the *dominant (male) group*." The term "muted" connotes issues of language and power; "muted groups must mediate their beliefs through the allowable forms of dominant structures."[24] Mutedness is a form of interruption that silences speech: how appropriate to undo mutedness through interruption, the tactic that causes mutedness in the first place. Vegetarianism, like women's words, has been a muted argument in the dominant meat-eating ethos of our times. And through a conscious redefinition of the front, vegetarianism is in muted discourse with a continuously warring world.

Vegetarians face the problem of making their meanings understood within a dominant culture that accepts the legitimacy of meat eating. The gestalt-shift Midgley perceives between the meat eaters' perspective and the vegetarians' is that between the majority who have assimilated a prevailing dominant belief and a minority who have not. This gestalt-shift is suggested by the feminist detective in Lynn Meyer's *Paperback Thriller* who opines early in the novel, "I could tell you now that I'm a vegetarian, but let's just leave it at that. I won't go into the reasons. If you don't understand them, there's not much I can say; and if you do there's no need for me to say anything" (45).

When female marginality is "in dialogue with dominance" it invokes the position of animals, who are also on the margins.[25] Part of the otherness with which women writers identify is the otherness of the other animals.[26] The "assertive repossession of voice"[27] includes the expression of voice through identification with those who have none. Through specific female-identifications catalyzed by male oppression, the character reflects on the question "How would you like it if this were done to you?" When Margaret Atwood's Marian cannot think of herself as "I," when her first-person singular identity is interrupted, her body becomes alert to the oppression of the other animals. What evolves is a poetics of engagement between women and animals, and a belief that violence against other animals carries the same seriousness as violence against people: where meat eating is, there is the front. Vegetarianism becomes, then, a necessary accompaniment to pacifism. Challenging the dominant ethos that animals exist for human consumption by extension challenges a world at war.

The theory of dominance-muteness not only explains why women expand the front but also why their focus on this issue has not been apprehended in feminist literary criticism. Generally women as well as men hold to the powerful, dominant ethos regarding animals, just as Marian returns to eating meat once she is able to think again in the first-person singular. This causes the muting of a tradition that does not hold to the dominant ethos. The tradition in which modern women writers confront the meaning of meat eating within the context of war is one of a dialectic between silencing and risking speech. It is a tradition that speaks through specificity (i.e., naming what is eaten), interrupting a meal, interrupting a man's control, interrupting the male tradition with female voices. When women writers raise the issue of vegetarianism, they touch upon their dilemma of being silenced in a patriarchal world. Vegetarianism becomes a complex female meditation on being dominated and dominator.

While modern vegetarianism interrupts modern women's writing and hence disrupts it as a way of finding space and power to speak, on a deeper level it confirms women's work. By redefining the front and locating it wherever meat eating is, modern women writers make a powerful statement on the rights of women and women writers to have a voice during wartime.

Notes

1. The term nonhuman animals has been adopted by animal rights scholars to emphasize that we, too, are animals; see, for instance, Singer, *Animal Liberation*, ix. For the purposes of this essay, whenever I refer to animals I mean animals excluding human beings.

2. Women are notably absent from most historical catalogues of vegetarianism because of the male-centered bias of the chroniclers. My larger work in progress, "Against the Texts of Meat," seeks both to explain and redress this exclusion.

3. Midgley, *Animals and Why They Matter*, 15.

4. Editor's note to Easterbrook, "Alcohol and Meat," 306.

5. Hopkins, "Why I Earn My Own Living," 44.

6. Ryan, "The Heart to Sing," 314–15.

7. Hindhede, "Food Restriction during War," 381.

8. Wiltsher, *Most Dangerous Women*, 67.

9. Fussell, *The Great War*, 91.

10. In Graves's *Good-bye to All That*, the first paragraph of the first chapter ends: "or Mr Eustace Miles the English real-tennis champion and vegetarian with his samples of exotic nuts, I knew all about them in my way" (9). See also Fussell, *The Great War*, 203–20.

11. In his introduction to *The Home*, O'Neill maintains that Gilman "published very little after the war," and attributes this to the fact that "World War I, and the changes that accompanied it, destroyed the moral foundation of her career" (x). In contrast, I would argue that the war confirmed her claim of the need to involve women and women's values in decision making, and that *Herland* and *His Religion and Hers* suggest in opposite ways, first positively and then negatively, the conclusion that violence was a result of male dominance.

12. Page references for the novels and other primary works discussed in the remainder of this essay are given parenthetically in the text.

13. This issue is discussed in Schweik's "A Word" and her essay in this volume.

14. I am indebted here to DuPlessis's analysis, in *Writing beyond the Ending*, of women writers' strategy for challenging traditional romance.

15. These metaphors are mine and not Piercy's. I use them to suggest that from her epiphanic moment in her kitchen, Beth adopts a systematic, ongoing rejection of a male, meat-eating culture that can be best represented by using metaphors from the antiwar movement.

16. Ryan, letter to Maud Freshel, October 14, 1936, Box 6.

17. Ryan, letter, March 23, 1937, Box 4.

18. It could be argued that Shelley's *Queen Mab* is the first feminist, vegetarian, pacifist utopia.

19. Socrates tells Glaucon that meat production necessitates large amounts of pasture. Resultingly, it will require cutting "off a slice of our neighbours' territory; and if they too are not content with necessaries, but give themselves up to getting unlimited wealth, they will want a slice of ours." Thus Socrates pronounces, "So the next thing will be, Glaucon, that we shall be at war" (2.371). See Lappé, *Diet for a Small Planet*, 67–74.

20. DuPlessis, *Writing beyond the Ending*, 113.

21. War images in this sentence remind us that the patterns of war have been adopted in the style and content of discourse.

22. Cornelius Cardew is based on Salt's life in many pertinent ways. Cardew became a vegetarian while at public school. Salt tells us in his memoirs: "Thus gradually the conviction had been forced on me that we Eton masters, however irreproachable our surroundings, were but cannibals in cap and gown—almost literally cannibals, as devouring the flesh and blood of the higher non-human animals so closely akin to us" (*Seventy Years among Savages*, 64). Salt and his wife set up housekeeping in a cottage near Tilford after leaving Eton; Cardew lives with his wife in a cottage in the Surrey hills. Salt was close friends with Shaw; Cardew imagines what he shall put in a letter to Shaw. Salt founded the Humanitarian League, a reform-oriented group that like Cardew concerned itself with animals' rights, the extension of the franchise, land reform and socialism, among other issues.

23. It is striking that two different texts linking vegetarianism and pacifism insert the name of the Doukhobors, who maintained their vegetarianism and pacifism in rigorous circumstances—persecution and banishment in Russia as well as migration as a group (estimated as high as 7,500 individuals) to Canada. The Doukhobors become grounding figures. This tradition of providing additional authority through historical references is a version of what any embattled group does, that is, evoking touchstone figures who in feminist terms we might consider "role models."

24. Showalter, "Feminist Criticism," 261, 262.

25. DuPlessis, *Writing beyond the Ending*, 115.

26. This does not preclude sensitive male writers such as Shelley, Shaw, Salt, and Stevens from also exploring the issues of animals' and women's

otherness. Indeed, the conclusion to be drawn from their writings and their lives is that men as well as women can enact lifestyles sensitive to issues of feminism, pacifism, and vegetarianism.

27. DuPlessis, *Writing beyond the Ending*, 107.

Works Cited

Atwood, Margaret. *The Edible Woman*. New York: Warner Books, 1969.

Brindel, June Rachuy. *Ariadne: A Novel of Ancient Crete*. New York: St. Martin's Press, 1980.

Brophy, Brigid. "An Anecdote of the Golden Age [Homage to *Back to Methuselah*]." In *The Adventures of God in His Search for the Black Girl*. Boston: Little, Brown & Co., 1968.

Bryant, Dorothy, *The Kin of Ata Are Waiting for You*. Originally titled *The Comforter*. Berkeley: Moon Books, 1976.

Christian, Eugene. *Meatless and Wheatless Menus*. New York: Alfred A. Knopf, 1917.

Colegate, Isabel. *The Shooting Party*. New York: Avon Books, 1980.

Cross, Amanda. *The James Joyce Murders*. New York: Macmillan Co., 1967.

Daly, Mary. *Beyond God the Father*. Boston: Beacon Press, 1973.

Davis, Max. *The Case for the Vegetarian Conscientious Objector*, with a Foreword by Scott Nearing. Brooklyn: Tolstoy Peace Group, 1944.

Duncan, Isadora. *My Life*. New York: Liveright, 1927, 1955.

DuPlessis, Rachel Blau. *Writing beyond the Ending: Narrative Strategies of Twentieth-Century Women Writers*. Bloomington: Indiana University Press, 1985.

Easterbrook, L. F. "Alcohol and Meat." *Nineteenth Century and After* 95 (February 1924): 306–14.

Freshel, Maud. See Sharpe, M. R. L.

Fussell, Paul. *The Great War and Modern Memory*. London, Oxford, New York: Oxford University Press, 1975.

Gilman, Charlotte Perkins. *Herland*. New York: Pantheon, 1979. First serialized in *Forerunner* 6 (1915).

———. *His Religion and Hers: A Study of the Faith of Our Fathers and the Work of Our Mothers*. London: T. Fisher Unwin, 1924.

Graves, Robert. *Good-bye to All That*. Hammondsmith, Eng.: Penguin Books, 1957.

Hindhede, Mikkel. "The Effect of Food Restriction during War on Mortality in Copenhagen." *Journal of the American Medical Society* 74, no. 6 (February 7, 1920): 381–82.

Hopkins, Mary Alden. "Why I Earn My Own Living." In *These Modern Women: Autobiographical Essays from the Twenties*, edited by Elaine

Showalter. Originally published 1926–1927 in *The Nation.* Old Westbury, N.Y.: Feminist Press, 1978.

Lappé, Frances Moore. *Diet for a Small Planet: Tenth Anniversary Edition.* New York: Ballantine Books, 1982.

McCarthy, Mary. *Birds of America.* New York: New American Library, 1972.

Meyer, Lynn. *Paperback Thriller.* New York: Random House, 1975.

Midgley, Mary. *Animals and Why They Matter.* Athens: University of Georgia Press, 1983.

O'Neill, William. Introduction to *The Home,* by Charlotte Perkins Gilman. Urbana: University of Illinois Press, 1972.

Piercy, Marge. *Small Changes.* Greenwich, Conn.: A Fawcett Crest Book, 1972.

Plato. *The Republic of Plato.* Edited by Francis MacDonald Cornford. New York and London: Oxford University Press, 1966.

Ryan, Agnes. "Civilization? Culture?' " Notes for *Vegetarian Pocket Monthly.* Box 2, file no. 33, "Vegetarian Writings, circa 1952–53." Agnes Ryan Collection. Arthur and Elizabeth Schlesinger Library on the History of Women, Radcliffe College, Cambridge, Mass. Permission to publish material provided by the Schlesinger Library and the late Henry Bailey Stevens.

———. "The Heart to Sing." Agnes Ryan Collection. Arthur and Elizabeth Schlesinger Library on the History of Women, Radcliffe College, Cambridge, Mass.

———. "Who Can Fear Too Many Stars?" Agnes Ryan Collection. Arthur and Elizabeth Schlesinger Library on the History of Women, Radcliffe College, Cambridge, Mass.

Salt, Henry. *Animals' Rights Considered in Relation to Social Progress.* Clarks Summit, Penn.: Society for Animal Rights, 1980. Reprint of 1892 edition.

———. *Seventy Years among Savages.* London: George Allen & Unwin, 1921.

———. *Two Similar Pastimes: Sport and War.* (Reprinted from *The Creed of Kinship.* 1935.) London: National Society for the Abolition of Cruel Sports, 1947.

Schweik, Susan. "A Word No Man Can Say for Us: American Women Writers and the Second World War." Ph.D. dissertation, Yale University, 1984.

Sharpe, M. R. L. *The Golden Rule Cookbook: Six Hundred Recipes for Meatless Dishes.* Cambridge, Mass.: The University Press, 1908.

Shelley, Percy Bysshe. *A Vindication of Natural Diet 1812. The Complete Works of Percy Bysshe Shelley,* vol. 6. Edited by Roger Ingpen and Walter E. Peck. New York: Gordian Press, 1965.

Showalter, Elaine. "Feminist Criticism in the Wilderness." In *The New*

Feminist Criticism: Essays on Women, Literature and Theory, edited by Elaine Showalter, 243–70. New York: Pantheon, 1985.

Singer, Peter. *Animal Liberation: A New Ethics for Our Treatment of Animals*. New York: New York Review, 1975.

Spender, Dale. *Man-Made Language*. London: Routledge & Kegan Paul, 1980.

Stevens, Henry Bailey. *The Recovery of Culture*. New York: Harper & Row, 1949.

Taylor, Thomas. *A Vindication of the Rights of Brutes*. London, 1792.

Wiltsher, Anne. *Most Dangerous Women: Feminist Peace Campaigners of the Great War*. London, Boston: Pandora Press, 1985.

Wollstonecraft, Mary. *A Vindication of the Rights of Woman*. 1791. Reprint. New York: W. W. Norton & Co., 1967.

Woolf, Virginia. *Three Guineas*. 1938. Reprint. London: Hogarth Press, 1968.

Esther Fuchs   Images of Love and War

in Contemporary Israeli Fiction:

A Feminist Re-vision

*I*n an essay on the new Israeli story, Baruch Kurzweil argues
that since the early 1960s, Israeli fiction has demonstrated an
increasing obsession with the subject of Eros. He refers to
Eros not in its Freudian sense of the life instinct but in the
sense of "the temptations of woman," and as such he uses it as a
term of opprobrium: "But this special conspicuousness of Eros,
which is so characteristic of so many Israeli stories, testifies to the
lack of a real goal in life. This mania for Eros in the Hebrew story is
not a sign of effervescent vitality, but of something sick. It signifies
an escape from the emptiness of life."[1] Kurzweil goes on to interpret the proliferation of the stories about the sexual "temptations
of woman" not only as a manifestation of existential nausea, but
also as an expression of self-hatred, an attempt to flee from Jewish
identity, a suicidal pursuit of false Western idols. Although he calls
attention to an important development in what came to be known
as the literature of the New Wave (which emerged in the late 1950s
and early 1960s in reaction to the confined realism and socialist
Zionist ideology of their predecessors), Kurzweil ignores the fact
that Eros (in his sense) is often linked to Thanatos, the human
desire to die. By failing to note the punitive element in the association in the literature of the 1960s and 1970s of "the temptations of
woman" with the motif of death, Kurzweil implicitly endorses the
androcentric vision which couples woman's sexuality with destruction. It is this tendency in the new Israeli story, to couple woman
with destruction, that I would like to examine here.

The thematic relationship between heterosexual love and national war has pervaded Israeli fiction since its inception in the late
1940s. Yet the presentation of this relationship has undergone radical structural transformations from its bipolar appearance in the
works of S. Yizhar and Moshe Shamir to its interdependent presentation in the works of Yitzhak Ben Ner, Ya'akov Buchan, and David

Schütz. Whereas in the Palmah fiction romantic love and national war appear as dichotomously opposed indices of happiness and anguish, hope and despair, peace and violence, life and death, in the fiction of the generation of the state, the boundaries between the thematic poles seem to have dissolved: love and war are not only inextricably intertwined, but, in terms of their ideational function, virtually reversed. Heterosexual love is exposed as a power struggle, a relentless war leading to atrophy, to psychical and even physical death; whereas military confrontation emerges as a kind of refuge. The female character, previously symbolic of peace and love, turns into a pernicious victimizer. Romantic love—previously idealized as the loftiest human drive—is translated into lifeless, exploitative, and mechanical sex, degrading and debilitating for both man and woman. Perhaps the most dramatic expression of the thematic complementarity of love and war in Israeli narrative fiction can be found in war-related stories, in which the horror of war is both highlighted and counterbalanced by a subplot revolving around romantic love. In addition, most stories about romantic heterosexual love contain war-related subplots and/or war-related thematic kernels. Another common feature in this context is the identification of national war with male characters, and the complementary identification of love and sex with female characters—a tendency which, in view of the active involvement of women in Israel's military history, should not be taken for granted. The agenda of this study is then threefold: first, to illustrate the dialectical relationship of love and war in stories by the most prominent writers of the 1960s and 1970s; secondly, to analyze the implications of the results within the context of sexual politics; and thirdly, to suggest some general explanations for the most common configurations observed in our examples.

The transformation of woman from an icon of peace and romantic love (e.g., in Yizhar's *Yemei Tsiklag* [The days of Ziklag, 1959]) into one of death is illustrated in Yoram Kanyuk's *Himo melekh yerushalayim* (Himo king of Jerusalem, 1966). The novel revolves around the peculiar love of Hamutal Hurvitz, a young and beautiful nurse, for Himo, a casualty of the 1948 War of Independence. The only unmutilated remainder of what used to be a dashing young officer is Himo's lips, which convulsively and incessantly mumble, "Shoot me! Shoot me." The rest of his body, including, most significantly, his genitals, have been irreparably damaged. Undeterred by Himo's ghastly physique, Hamutal showers all her love and devotion upon him, to the astonishment and envy of the other wounded soldiers in the hospital. Finally, however, Hamutal gives up and decides to poison Himo in order to put an end to his agony. Ironically, Himo undergoes a strange transformation just as Hamutal is preparing the fatal injection. He is shown suddenly to recover his long-extinct desire to live: "He is pleading for his life. His mutilated body is writhing now, he tried to stretch out his hands imploringly; he pleaded like a starving dog, but he could no more say a word."[2] The juxtaposition of the upright stature of the beautiful nurse, gripping boldly the poisonous injector, determined and all but immune to the dramatic reversal of events, and the victimized man writhing helplessly at her feet, dramatizes the reversal in traditional power relations between male and female that are often occasioned by war.[3] I would like to suggest that the transformation of Hamutal from an icon of love to an angel of death reveals a male fear of the radical transition that wars in patriarchal societies tend to bring about in the status of women, changing them overnight from passive dependents to active participants in the economy and in leadership roles on both the civilian and military fronts. While wars are likely to empower the "weak" sex, they also tend to emasculate the "strong" sex. War casualties find themselves at the mercy of female nurses, and even male survivors discover their dependency on female services and nurturance. Himo, who used to be the epitome of virility, is not only sexually emasculated and physically incapacitated, but also emotionally dependent on Hamutal.

By ending with a calm and collected Hamutal stopping at a coffee shop several years later, only to remember the tragic incident in passing, Kanyuk's novel subverts the romantic image of woman in the Palmah literature as protective mother/lover, as well as that of the perennial mourner.[4] It is true that Hamutal's love for Himo supplies the motivation for the larger part of the novel, but the ironic denouement challenges the impression heretofore created. Hamutal's decision to kill Himo turns out to be just as irrational and unpredictable as her unyielding love for him: neither one serves the desires and needs of the male victim. Woman's proverbial selflessness and concern for the male war victim are here exposed as irrational and transient.[5] Even her deepest identification with the male victim, even the most passionate love, is shown to have its limits. At best, woman is an outsider in war. At worst, she is a dangerous enemy under the guise of a caring, nurturing female role model.[6]

In Amos Oz's novel, *Michael sheli* (My Michael), the symbolic representation of woman as Thanatos in the guise of Eros becomes even more explicit. Although this novel also presents the man, Michael, as victim, and the woman, Hana, as victimizer, the novel celebrates the male victim's quiet victory over his destructive enemy. Despite Hana's refusal to cooperate with Michael either as wife or as mother, and despite her exploitative and humiliating treatment of him, it is she who finally degenerates through successive stages of boredom, passivity, and physical sickness into psychosis, while Michael succeeds in launching a brilliant academic career, moving progressively toward greater professional accomplishment and economic stability. Hana's perverse attitude toward her husband is most eloquently dramatized in her sexual exploitation of him: "I would wake up my husband, crawl under his blanket, cling to his body with all my might. . . . Nevertheless, I ignored him; I made contact only with his body: muscles, arms, hair. In my heart I knew that I betrayed him over and over again with his body."[7] Hana's sexual abuse of her husband is a perversion and prevarication of Eros. Using Michael as a sex object (the traditional literary role of the female), she turns what constitutes the ultimate symbolic expression of love into a ritualistic enactment of war.[8] Having failed to vitiate her husband's virility by other means, she attempts to castrate him by exhausting him sexually. Sexual relations in *Michael sheli* become a metaphor for the power relations between man and woman, and it is a woman who is blatantly responsible for this perverse reversal. Hana is incapable of and uninterested in love; what she seeks is sadomasochistic titillation, a luxury her dedicated husband does not afford her. She therefore resorts to erotic fantasies in which she is both the commander and the victim of Halil and Aziz, her Palestinian childhood playmates, who she imagines have become terrorists. It is significant that Hana first starts to fantasize about Halil and Aziz when Michael is drafted during the war of 1956. The analogy between the husband, who is fighting the Egyptians in the Sinai Peninsula, and the wife, who indulges in erotic fantasies about the Arab twins, dramatizes not only Hana's infidelity, but also her national disloyalty.[9] This becomes even more pronounced at the end of the novel as Hana imagines herself sending her Palestinian lovers/servants on an anti-Israeli terrorist mission: "I will set them on. . . . A box of explosives, detonators, fuses, ammunition, hand grenades, glittering knives."[10]

The presentation of woman as conjugal and national enemy reveals, among other things, a deep-seated suspicion of woman's allegedly passive role in wartime. The notion that married women stay home, secure and relatively invulnerable, while men sacrifice their lives to defend them has powerful implications for relations between the sexes in a country constantly threatened by war. It must be remembered that despite the compulsory draft in Israel, only 50 percent of draftable women actually join the armed forces. Religious, illiterate, married, and pregnant women are exempted from the draft. Furthermore, the law bars women from combat duties; consequently, the majority of women serve in auxiliary jobs (e.g., as secretaries, clerks, teachers, drivers, wireless operators, parachute folders).[11] These circumstances create the impression that women are not really involved in the war effort, that their suffering and sacrifices are negligible compared to the price paid by male fighters. This impression is shared by both men and women in Israel. Two factors are all too often forgotten in this context: first, that women were not consulted when, in 1948, as the War of Independence was underway, it was decided to pull them out of the front and confine them to noncombat duties;[12] and secondly, that war takes a heavy psychological toll on Israeli mothers and wives, especially *because* of their inability to contribute to the war effort more substantially. This imposed impotence results in anxiety, guilt, alienation from the national scene, and a loss of self-esteem.[13] While in reality war ends up damaging the status of women both inside and outside the army, mythical thinking, which often serves as grist for literary creativity, tends to envision women as protected and secure, and perceive men as vulnerable and victimized by war.[14] Mythical thinking, to which Amos Oz, like other New Wave writers, is especially susceptible, ignores social, economic, and legal constraints, and tends to perceive the human world *sub speciae aeternitatis*.[15] A literature inspired by mythical thinking will construe a social situation not as the outcome of external constraints, but as the product of human nature. From this perspective, woman stays home because she is inherently passive, confined, indifferent to war. In the volatile political context of Israel, a country continually on the brink of military conflagration, willful passivity entails treachery or, worse, a perverse subconscious love for the enemy: Eros bound with Thanatos, Thanatos in the guise of Eros. Fostered on the one hand by the archetypal association of treachery with female sexuality, and on the other by the

Freudian theory concerning woman's alleged masochism, this vision spawns an image very much like that of Hana Gonen, a woman who indulges in orgiastic fantasies of rape by Palestinian terrorists while her husband fights for the common weal.[16]

If the implicitly incriminating portrait of Hana Gonen derives from the subconscious mistrust of the homebound passive woman, Ben Ner's "Nicole" (1976) is inspired by the apparently opposite distrust of the active army woman. While Hana's passivity and unsociability are essentially excoriated by the standards of socialist Zionism, Nicole's participation in the army is criticized by the traditional Judeo-Christian endorsement of woman's place in the home. Like Hamutal and Hana, Nicole is beautiful and sexy; like Hana, Nicole wields her sexuality as a weapon in her eternal contest with men she wants to subdue. Unlike Hana, however, Nicole is not content with fantasies of self-destruction. In order to satisfy her sadomasochistic proclivities, she joins the army and ends up destroying others. What attracts Nicole to a career in the army is not patriotism or even a professional interest, but the vulnerability of the sex-starved soldiers, the perfect potential victims for her narcissism and nymphomania. The story focuses on Nicole's sexual campaigns and conquests, especially after her affair with Lt. Col. Baruch Adar, or Barko, whom she seduces away from his lawful wife, as she has done with all her previous lovers. On the eve of the fateful Yom Kippur of 1973, she convinces Barko to spend the night with her in a hotel whose location remains undisclosed to their brigade. When the war breaks out, the soldiers are unable to contact Lieutenant Colonel Barko, which results in confusion, disorientation, and ultimately defeat. Although Barko blames himself for the tragic blow to his brigade, the story implies that the military defeat is the product of Nicole's wiles. The aetiological linkage of one of the most traumatic wars in Israel's military history with woman's role in the army reveals a deep-seated distrust of women soldiers, especially those endowed with authoritative status and power. When allowed to affect the public scene, woman evolves from a personal to a national enemy; her vampiric bite affects not only the individual man, but the entire army.

In addition to the distrust of women in power—who endanger the traditional power-structured status quo between the sexes—the story reveals a deeper discontent with woman's encroachment into what appears to be an exclusively male domain. The next monologue, in which Amiram castigates Nicole for her neglect and irresponsibility, reveals not only contempt for women in power, but also a vision of woman as an outsider who is incapable of comprehending even the most basic facts about the army: "Look madame, this is the army. This is an army at war for life or death. In such a war, things must be decided like that, sharply, this or that way. You have been among us long enough to understand this, haven't you?"[17] Amiram implies that despite Nicole's status and experience, she remains a woman, a "you," an outsider, against "us," the male insiders. The hostility toward military women corresponds to a masculinist insecurity rooted in the identification of virility with military prowess. In a patriarchal and militarized culture, successful military women may compromise the self-image of men as fighters and defenders of the civilian population, namely helpless women and children.[18] Furthermore, a military woman constitutes a threat to male bonding, of which the army is one of the remaining socially sanctioned mainstays.[19] Finally, symbolically identified with sex, gentleness, pleasure, and sensuality, woman embodies all the values that threaten the military ethos, which thrives on coarseness, vulgarity, toughness, and the suppression of Eros.[20] In a military context, woman is reduced to a sex object, and sex to a mechanical activity, intended to relieve physiological tensions rather than gratify emotional needs. Because it is necessary not to give in to normal human needs for love and intimacy, women and sex become the subjects of vulgar jokes, and objects whose importance must be defied in order to sustain the psychic balance necessary for military efficiency.[21]

Like Hamutal Hurvitz and Hana Gonen, Nicole is an epitome of the castrating bitch who, under the guise of love, emasculates her male victims: "She is so glad to know that he [Barko] is afraid. At last. He should be afraid. She wants him to be afraid."[22] Like Hana Gonen, Nicole sadistically tortures her man in an attempt to vanquish his male pride and subject him to her will. Realizing how guilty Barko feels about his brigade's defeat, she calls him up, pretending to be a widow of one of his dead soldiers. But in this battle between the sexes, Nicole, like Hana, cannot win. With resentment and exasperation, Nicole admits her defeat: "But, damn it, he does not crawl, break down, quiver, cry, scream, writhe helplessly; he keeps rising from his downfalls."[23] Once again, man is victimized not by national but by sexual war—the real enemy is not the Arab across the border, but the Israeli woman inside the hospital, the home, the camp. The most fatal blows come not from firearms, but from the "loving" arms of woman. Death lurks not in violence, but in sexuality; love is not the opposite, but the motivating principle of war.

Although the interdependence of Eros and Thanatos is conspicuous in Israeli literature, it pervades other literature as well. The motif of man's fatal entrapment by a sexually irresistible woman has deep roots in the Western literary tradition; from Samson and Delilah, to Holofernes and Judith and to John the Baptist and Salomé, from the Sirens and the Sphinx to the Lorelei, woman serves as the composite symbol of Eros and Thanatos. Karen Horney suggests that this ubiquitous phenomenon derives from man's castration anxiety, which is related to his realization of the difference between his genitalia and that of the female, and from man's dread of physical flaccidity/weakness/death after coitus.[24] To conceal his anxiety and dread, man either glorifies woman, putting her on an unreachable pedestal, or objectifies her as evil and dreadful, thus rationalizing and justifying his dread. " 'It is not,' he says 'that I dread her; it is that she herself is malignant, capable of any crime, a beast of prey, a vampire, a witch, insatiable in her desires. She is the very personification of what is sinister.' "[25] This psychoanalytic explanation has a political dimension that Horney does not go into. Since men have been the primary producers of canonic religion, art, literature, and culture until fairly recently, their representations of women have become a hegemonic perspective through which both men and women perceive themselves. The representation of woman as the embodiment of Eros and Thanatos then serves as an important weapon in the hands of patriarchal hegemony; by wielding this image, the patriarchal system succeeds in both fostering man's distrust of woman as well as in keeping woman in her proper place.[26] One can conclude, then, that war and love appear together so frequently because love, as perceived in Western culture, is a kind of war.[27] Romantic love in Western society perpetuates the power imbalance between the sexes; rather than drawing them together, as it often purports to do, it intensifies the enmity between them.[28]

To return to our specific case study, it is clear that contemporary Israeli literature has not invented the thematic and compositional interdependence of Eros and Thanatos; as an essentially Western literature, it has inherited this vocabulary of images and concepts. Nevertheless it is unique in its quantitative and qualitative use of this vocabulary. Here Eros and Thanatos are usually polarized and then welded together as, respectively, sex and war. Eros is usually represented not as a love or life instinct, but rather as a sexual drive; Thanatos is normally associated with violent death—usually war. In this context, man is the victim of woman, who is out to destroy both his virility and his life.

Israel's protracted war with its surrounding neighbors, a war whose inevitability and complexity began to emerge in Israel's national consciousness after the war of 1956, has created what Marcuse calls "a repressive society," a society in which death is either feared as constant threat, glorified as supreme sacrifice, or accepted as inescapable fate.[29] In a repressive culture, Eros is feared as a distracting, energy-consuming principle. Instead of allowing human sexuality to sublimate itself into Eros—a life-giving social order—a repressive system suppresses it by trivializing it, reducing it to a biological need and presenting it as potentially dangerous. Under repressive circumstances, especially in the context of war, which sanctions and often sanctifies the destruction of life, sex, symbolically represented as woman, is depicted as life-threatening. The cultural acceptance of Thanatos brings about a reversal where woman, the giver of life and the principle of Eros, is depicted as a deathly victimizer, while man, who does the killing, is perceived as the victim. On a less abstract level, Israel's protracted war and the sexual division of labor within the army produce a suspicion of women who seem not to do quite their share, despite their traditional nurturant and protective roles as wives and mothers outside the army, or nurses and auxiliary soldiers within it. On the other hand, the constant threat of war and continuous political instability create a strong need for security within the private sphere, a need that is often translated into a nostalgic and regressive move back to traditional—namely patriarchal—patterns of intersexual and marital relations. In this context, women who seem to defy traditional power relations inspire anxiety and distrust.

Contemporary Israeli literature reflects not only the effects of war and siege; to a large extent, it is also what Yosef Oren calls a literature of disillusionment.[30] The disenchantment with both Israel's political and military constraints and with the gradual transformation of what used to be a pioneer society—dedicated to utopian and idealistic visions—into an organized, bureaucratized state that often sacrifices ideals for pragmatic considerations, is sharply registered in Israel's canonic literature. The internecine relations between husband and wife and the degeneration of love into mutually destructive sexual relations serve as metaphors for what Israeli writers perceive as Israel's ideological disorientation and social disintegration. As Oren points out, "The writers of the new generation dramatize an extreme scene that has not yet been established in Israeli reality, and [they] ask us to accept it as an authentic testimony to the reality of our lives."[31] Identified with the family (the fundamental unit of society), woman came to signify the stultifying and corrupt society from which the Israeli male hero constantly flees, often right into the arms of war. Thus the romanticized nurturant mother/lover of the Palmah generation—often the symbol of civilian life—became the vampiric bitch in the literature of the 1960s and 1970s, just as the idealistic, victorious, and admirable male fighter turned into a pathetic victim.[32] In so far as private relations serve as allegorical constructs signifying a national reality, the vampiric woman reflects not only the exasperated society, but also the devouring country with its insatiable demand for sacrifices, with its endless hunger for male corpses. The land of Israel is often symbolically portrayed as a female principle, a conception with deep biblical roots.[33] Just as in Hebrew-Palestinian utopian literature, this country is often depicted as a loving mother/wife waiting for her son/lover to return to her; in contemporary Israeli literature, it appears as a deathly woman exacting endless sacrifices from her male lover.

Baruch Kurzweil was right in observing the increasing prevalence of what he calls Eros in Israeli literature, but his interpretation of this development can only be accepted if we consider its full range. It is not merely the increasing preponderance of women (especially in the capacity of sexual agents) that conveys a sense of disorientation and existential nausea. It is rather the presentation of women as symbolic of death that may perhaps signal an expression of despair, disorientation, and demoralization in Israeli fiction. It is the pervasive combination of Eros with Thanatos that may convey what Kurzweil sees as the flight from affirming values to self-hatred and self-destruction.

Notes

I would like to thank the editors of this volume and John Bormanis for their editorial assistance in the preparation of this article, which also appeared (in a modified version) in *Modern Judaism* 6 (1986): 189–96. See also Fuchs, *Israeli Mythogynies*.

1. Kurzweil, *Hipus hasifrut hayisraelit*, 67. This and all the following quotations from Hebrew sources are based upon my own translations.

2. Kanyuk, *Himo melekh yerushalayim*, 170–71.

3. In her article on British literature during and after World War I, Sandra M. Gilbert notes that "the unmanning terrors of combat lead not just to a generalized sexual anxiety but also to a sexual anger directed specifically against the female, as if the Great War itself were primarily a climactic episode in some battle of the sexes that had already been raging for years" (Gilbert, "Soldier's Heart," 424).

4. Yigal Mossinsohn appears to be the exception in the overall tendency of the writers of the late 1940s and 1950s to portray woman as a symbol of peace and normal civilian life. His portrayal of women as adulterous traitors suggests that it is man's failure to assert himself, rather than woman's innate power, that is the true cause of his defeat.

5. Although this is not one of the major themes of the novel, Hanoch Bartov's *Pitsei bagrut* (Acne, 1965) offers an analogous example of woman's transient commitment to the male warrior. Likewise, Benjamin Galai, in "Al haholkhim" (On the travelers who will not return), writes, "For not forever will your girl cry, and not forever cast down her eyes" (313–15).

6. Woman also appears as outsider in Yitzhak Orpaz's *Masa daniel* (The voyage of Daniel, 1969).

7. Oz, *Michael sheli*, 178.

8. Yitzhak Orpaz's *Nemalim* (Ants) offers an analogous description of internecine relations between husband and wife.

9. An allegory of the political situation of Israel as a state in siege, Orpaz's *Nemalim* also presents woman as a potential national threat.

10. Oz, *Michael sheli*, 197.

11. On the status of women in Zahal, the Israeli Defence Force, see Yuval-Davis, "The Israeli Example," 73–78; Hazelton, *Israeli Women*, 112–61; Rein, *Daughters of Rachel*, 44–54; Lahav, "The Status of Women," 107–29; and Padan–Eisenstark, "Are Israeli Women Really Equal?" 538–45.

12. Women protested indignantly against the decision to exclude them from combat duties. See Rein, *Daughters of Rachel*, 46–7; Yehuda, *1948—Bein hasefirot*, 277–81.

13. Only recently have Israeli women begun to give expression to their frustrations in wartime. See Sharron, "Women and War," 8.

14. In Amos Oz's "Minzar hashatkanim" (The Trappist monastery, 1965), the male protagonist sets out on a reprisal mission against an Arab village while his girlfriend stays at the army base. A. B. Yehoshua also casts his male heroes as victims and his female characters as passive outsiders who are, in the final analysis, the enemies of their male counterparts. See his "Besis tilim 612" (Missile base 612, 1975) and Shamai Golan's *Moto shel uri peled* (The death of Uri Peled, 1971), where woman appears not only as

passive, indifferent, and treacherous, but also as the perpetrator of her husband's death.

15. The New Wave emphasized the universal and unchanging patterns of human behavior, rather than the peculiarities of the Israeli situation, and hence its frequent use of allegory, archetype, and myth. See Shaked, *Gal hadash basiporet haivrit*.

16. The association of woman, and especially female sexuality, with treachery has a long tradition in Western culture and literature; see Hays, *The Dangerous Sex*; Rogers, *The Troublesome Helpmate*. For a critique of Freud's theories on female masochism, see Horney, *Feminine Psychology*, 214–33. For a more general revision of Freudian theories on female sexuality and psychology, see Chodorow, *The Reproduction of Mothering*, 141–58.

17. Ner, "Nicole," 170.

18. Natalie Rein, *Daughters of Rachel*, 47, suggests that the reluctance to credit women for their contribution to the underground groups of Etsel and Lehi, as well as to the Palmah, manifests the unwillingness of male Jews, who have come from generations of emasculated manhood, to share with women the experience of asserting their newfound virility. The reluctance to acknowledge women's military contribution is a rather common phenomenon. Despite their participation in Europe's modern armies, mostly in service jobs, women are barely mentioned in most military histories; see Hacker, "Women and Military Institutions," 643–71.

19. According to Lionel Tiger, for example, women are by nature incapable of bonding, and as such threaten male bonding, which he sees as one of the major forces of social cohesiveness (see Tiger, *Men in Groups*). On the hostile responses to integrating women into regular combat forces in modern armies, see Rogan, *Mixed Company*.

20. Amos Elon notes that the continuous and repeated periods of war and military tensions in Israel have produced a cult of toughness. On the effect of this cult on intersexual relations, he points out, "The letters written by young Israelis to their sweethearts are notoriously dry, unimaginative, and frequently, oddly impersonal. They are often so skimpy in exclamations of love, devotion, or longing—indeed of any feeling whatsoever—that a reader may suspect a near total lack of sensitivity and refinement. Or else he may suspect that the young writers, if they have feelings, are so frightened by them—or so ashamed and embarrassed—that they have apparently resolved to keep them permanently concealed. One does not talk of feelings, one rarely admits that they exist" (Elon, *The Israelis*, 238).

21. See Fetterley (*The Resisting Reader*, 51) on the analogous attitude toward women and sexuality in Hemingway's *A Farewell to Arms*.

22. Ner, "Nicole," 179.

23. Ibid., 180.

24. Horney, *Feminine Psychology,* 107–18; 131–46.

25. Ibid., 135. Horney also points out that Freud himself objectifies the male dread of woman when ascribing this fear to woman's actual hostility toward the male, a hostility that is allegedly generated by the pain and discomfort of defloration. See Freud, "The Taboo of Virginity," 70–86.

26. On the political dimension of male-authored literature describing women and intersexual relations, see Millett, *Sexual Politics,* 3–31; 331–505.

27. See Rougemont, *Love in the Western World.*

28. For a political analysis of romantic love in Western culture, see Firestone, *The Dialectic of Sex,* esp. 126–45.

29. Marcuse, *Eros and Civilization,* 222–36.

30. See Oren, *Hahitpakhut.*

31. Oren, *Hahitpakhut,* 24.

32. This is only one aspect of the parodic treatment of the Palmah literature by the New Wave. For further analysis, see Gertz, "Haparodia," 272–77.

33. The words referring to the concept or object of the land of Israel are all of the feminine gender in Hebrew. For example, "erets" (country), "adama" (earth), "moledet" (homeland), "medina" (state). Biblical literature, notably prophetic writings, and later Jewish traditional literature often identify the land of Zion as an abandoned wife or a widow. The symbolic presentation of the land as female has had an enormous impact on modern Hebrew literature, as well as on contemporary Israeli writers. In a recent treatise on Zionism, A. B. Yehoshua identifies the land of Israel as the long-neglected symbolic mother of the Jewish people. See Yehoshua, *Bizkhut hanormaliut,* 55–62.

Works Cited

Ben-Yehuda, Netiva. *1948—Bein hasefirot* (1948—Between the calendars). Jerusalem: Keter, 1981.

Chodorow, Nancy. *The Reproduction of Mothering.* Berkeley: University of California Press, 1978.

Elon, Amos. *The Israelis.* New York: Rinehart & Winston, 1971.

Fetterley, Judith. *The Resisting Reader: A Feminist Approach to American Fiction.* Bloomington: Indiana University Press, 1971.

Firestone, Shulamith. *The Dialectic of Sex.* 2d ed. New York: Bantam Books, 1979.

Freud, Sigmund. "The Taboo of Virginity." In *Sexuality and the Psychology of Love,* 70–86. 2d ed. New York: Macmillan Co., 1974.

Fuchs, Esther. *Israeli Mythogynies: Women in Contemporary Hebrew Fiction.* Albany: State University of New York Press, 1987.

Galai, Benjamin. "Al haholkhim shelo yashuvu" (On the travelers who will not return). In *Modern Hebrew Poetry*, edited and translated by Ruth Fein-Mintz, 313–15. Berkeley: University of California Press, 1966.

Gertz, Nurith. "Haparodia behilufei hadorot basifrut ha'ivrit" (Parody in generational transitions in Hebrew literature). *Siman keriah* 12–13 (1981): 272–77.

Gilbert, Sandra M. "Soldier's Heart: Literary Men, Literary Women, and the Great War." *Signs* 8, no. 3 (Spring 1983): 422–50.

Hacker, Barton C. "Women and Military Institutions in Early Modern Europe: A Reconnaissance." *Signs* 6 (1981): 643–71.

Hays, H. R. *The Dangerous Sex: The Myth of Feminine Evil.* New York: G. P. Putnam's Sons, 1964.

Hazelton, Lesley. *Israeli Women: The Reality behind the Myth.* New York: Simon & Schuster, 1977.

Horney, Karen. *Feminine Psychology.* New York: Norton, 1967.

Kanyuk, Yoram. *Himo melekh yerushalayim* (Himo king of Jerusalem). Tel Aviv: Am Oved, 1966.

Kurzweil, Baruch. *Hipus hasifrut hayisraelit* (In search of Israeli literature). Ramat Gan: Bar Ilan University, 1982.

Lahav, Pnina. "The Status of Women in Israel: Myth and Reality," *The American Journal of Comparative Law* 22 (1974): 107–29.

Marcuse, Herbert. *Eros and Civilization.* Boston: Beacon Press, 1966.

Millett, Kate. *Sexual Politics.* New York: Ballantine Books, 1970.

Ner, Yitzhak Ben. "Nicole." In *Shkiah kafrit* (Rustic sunset). Tel Aviv: Am Oved, 1976.

Oren, Yosef. *Hahitpakhut basiporet hayisraelit* (The disillusionment in Israeli narrative fiction). Tel Aviv: Yachad, 1983.

Orpaz, Yitzhak. *Masa daniel* (Daniel's Voyage). Tel Aviv: Am Oved, 1969.
———. *Nemalim* (Ants). Tel Aviv: Am Oved, 1968.

Oz, Amos. *Michael sheli* (My Michael). Tel Aviv: Am Oved, 1968.
———. "Minzar hashatkanim" (The Trappist Monastery). In *Artsot hatan* (Lands of the Jackal). Tel Aviv, 1965.

Padan-Eisenstark, Dorit D. "Are Israeli Women Really Equal? Trends and Patterns of Israeli Women's Labor Force Participation: A Comparative Analysis." *Journal of Marriage and the Family* 35 (1973): 538–45.

Rein, Natalie. *Daughters of Rachel: Women in Israel.* New York: Penguin Books, 1979.

Rogan, Helen. *Mixed Company: Women in the Modern Army.* New York: G. P. Putnam's Sons, 1981.

Rogers, Katherine M. *The Troublesome Helpmate: A History of Misogyny in Literature.* Seattle: University of Washington Press, 1966.

Rougemont, Denis de. *Love in the Western World.* Translated by M. Belgion. 2d ed. Princeton, N.J.: Princeton University Press, 1983.

Shaked, Gershon. *Gal hadash basiporet haivrit* (A new wave in Israeli fiction). 2d ed. Tel Aviv: Poalim, 1974.

Sharron, Nomi. "Women and War." *The Jerusalem Post: International Edition*, November 7–13, 1982, 18.

Tiger, Lionel. *Men in Groups*. New York: Random House, 1969.

Yehoshua, A. B. "Besis tilim 612" (Missile Base 612). In *Ad Horef* (Till Winter). Tel Aviv: Hakibbutz Hameuchad, 1975.

_____. *Bizkhut hanormaliut* (The right of normalcy). Tel Aviv: Schocken Books, 1980.

Yuval-Davis, Nira. "The Israeli Example." In *Loaded Questions: Women in the Military*, edited by W. Chapkis, 73–78. Amsterdam: Transnational Institute, 1981.

Gillian   Nuclear Domesticity:
Brown
           Sequence and Survival

D uring the past few years a chain letter, which originated
in Japan, has circulated through the academic profession urging a worldwide movement for nuclear disarmament. The same week this letter reached me there arrived in my mail a chain letter of the usual type promising me
wealth and success if I passed the letter on to my friends and associates, and threatening financial reverses or even death if I broke the
chain. The arrival of the second letter brought into relief the informing structure of the nuclear chain letter: a systematic coercion
to maintain sequence. It is the role of sequence in thinking about
nuclear danger that I wish to consider here—how sequence, as the
ordering principle and rhetorical figure of domesticity, our cultural
institution of continuity, governs the language and gestures generated by both nuclear protest and postnuclear planning movements.

Typical chain letters, much like protection rackets, seek to scare
us into subscription. This terrorization is what makes them such
unwelcome mail. For chain letters mobilize fear against fear itself,
disseminating threats in order to insure a proliferation of responses
against those threats. The chain letter might therefore appear an
odd or inappropriate form of address for nuclear protest to employ
(unless, perhaps, it is understood as a tactic thematizing the force of
the nuclear threat). I want to suggest, however, that there is an
aspect of chain letter logic that resonates with the preservationist
values of nuclear disarmament.

As chain letters work by implementing a continuous sequence
of multiplication and circulation against the threat of loss or annihilation, antinuclear rhetoric pits (versions of) the nuclear family
against nuclear war. While chain letters characteristically operate
as commercial schemes, and the annals of the nuclear protest letter
(the lists of addressees become addressors) likewise chronicle a professional self-perpetuation, the nuclear chain letter would draft us
into a more urgent and essential enterprise of self-advancement, a
commitment to perpetuation per se. Asking us to continue the

chain as an expression of support for a worldwide movement for nuclear disarmament, the nuclear protest chain letter becomes itself a model of continuity, community, and reproduction, the familiar features of domesticity.

This characterization of the chain letter as a representation of domestic life and human ties seems at first much less compelling than the impression of a shakedown that chain letters generally make. Yet it is from this domestic aspect of the imperative to maintain sequence that the chain letter's exhortation gathers force; for the chain letter form works on a principle of safety in numbers, the lure of a simultaneous particularity and commonality for the individual, which recalls the domestic milieu's production of individuality whereby the individual inheres in its relations. Put another way, networks make persons—persons *are* networks—and persons persist through the activities of their connections. Not only does the chain letter mime domestic reproduction of individuality, but it also condenses a domestic moment. Whatever fears chain letters marshall, they mainly build upon hope and desire, wagering futures and fortunes, and in this gambling gesture, they intensify and make immediate the bourgeois domestic narrative of human comfort and continuity. In gambling and get-rich-quick schemes, the usual time and labor of accumulation are bypassed for an instantaneous return. It is upon this characteristically capitalist escalation of economic process that the nuclear protest letter constructs an engine of perpetuity; gambling for domesticity speeds up and subsumes the generation of the individual to a phenomenon of self-generation. Another key aspect of the chain letter gamble is of course the desire that one succeed in this self-generating process, that one benefit from a fortune not available to everyone. Foregrounding the domestic appeal in the chain letter's invitation to maintain sequence, the nuclear protest interestingly recharges capitalist culture's faith in self-projection: the ideal of generating from ourselves more of ourselves. The domestic motifs invoked by the chain letter and highlighted by the nuclear disarmament chain letter harness our capacity to fabricate futurity to the fate of self-generation. We can thus trace in our present association of survival with seriality, often expressed as an alliance between femininity and futurity, the operations of the domestic machinery through which this self-generating individuality ensues.[1]

To explore the function of domesticity in nuclear rhetoric is not in any way to discredit the admirable and courageous efforts of the

antinuclear movement; nor can all antinuclear activities be characterized as domestic narratives. Interventionist gestures such as
placing one's body in the path of a train carrying supplies to a nuclear power plant belong to a different tradition. Rather, this exploration is advanced in order to help clarify why the pressure of nuclear anxiety and protest that has inhabited and shaped political
realities for decades now has so little wrinkled the surface of everyday life.

I

The self-projective pattern of the chain letter format, which the
nuclear protest recapitulates and refines, recurs throughout contemporary antinuclear statements and literature; the 1985 Ribbon
in memory of the fortieth anniversary of the bombings of Hiroshima and Nagasaki literalized the imagery of human bonding in a
fabric frieze sewn from yard-long panels, each representing what
the maker could not bear to think of as lost forever in a nuclear
war, the whole forming a giant ribbon that demonstrators then attempted to wrap around the Pentagon.[2] Perhaps the most striking
example of the commitment to affiliation and continuity in the
literature of nuclear protest is Jonathan Schell's jeremiad in *The
Fate of the Earth* on our responsibility to preserve the possibility of
life for the unborn. "If our species does destroy itself, it will be a
death in the cradle," Schell writes, "a case of infant mortality." It is
thus to parental bonds that witnesses of the nuclear predicament
appeal; domesticity is repeatedly invoked as the stay against extinction. As in the history of domestic ideals since the eighteenth century, this current revivification of faith in the domestic constitutes
a domesticity transcendent to worldly problems. In committing
ourselves to the survival of the species, Schell continues, "we do
not yet ask for justice, or for freedom, or for happiness, or for any of
the other things we may want in life. We do not even ask for our
personal survival; we ask only that we *be survived*."[3] As in the
history of the family thus far, future history depends upon denials
and inequities; we are urged to accept a deterring, self-denying, preserving role, the traditional domestic position of the mother. Freeman Dyson makes the link between the domestic and the antinuclear even more explicit in his book *Weapons and Hope* when he
characterizes debates about the nuclear as debates between the war-

riors and victims, between warrior men and victimized women and
children; many feminists share this view, aligning men with the
technology of the bomb and women, who appear "smothered by
masculine invention," with the natural order, reproduction, and
peace.[4]

Without in any way denying the urgency of the nuclear predicament, I want to explore here some implications of this resurgence
of domestic values and divisions in nuclear rhetoric. Not only does
the threat of nuclear war engender domestic angels of peace but it
also resurrects the domestic manual in the form of the Shelter
Management Handbooks produced by the Federal Emergency Management Agency (FEMA). A reading of this literature reveals how
domesticity may be congruent and compatible with the technology
that threatens it. The first act of civil defense directors in a nuclear
emergency, the FEMA guide instructs, should be "to duplicate in
large numbers and distribute" the handbook itself.[5] Apart from the
absurdity of looking for copy machines in the wake of a nuclear
explosion, this recommendation is remarkable and almost poignant
for its avowal of the survival of reproductive operations. Like the
nuclear chain letter's linkage of futurity to the multiplication of
the letter, this faith rests in the durability of reproductive machinery. It is as if the sentiment usually accorded to pregnant women
were transposed to machines. Our recent technologies of human
generation, test tube babies, artificial insemination, and surrogate
motherhood, in which invention or ingenuity approximate creation, culminate a long-term personification of and identification
with our technologies. An increasing acceptance and practice of
these alternative modes of reproduction reflects the extent to
which technology inhabits, and replaces, the traditionally feminine
domain of reproduction. In the context of such transformations,
nuclear survivalism may represent less a reponse to fears of perdition than a strong regard for the scope of human invention: a
guarded hope that technology will indeed preserve us now that it
both augments and creates human life. At any rate, the FEMA scenario of beginning the world anew with the distribution of its
words suggests an account of nuclear power as infinitely productive. Far from destroying signs of life, a nuclear explosion would
appear in this account to generate a hum of productivity.

Indeed, the FEMA handbook might be read as a blueprint for a
surrogate domesticity, a new procedure for reproducing and sustaining personal life in a postnuclear age. This management of the fu-

ture would be nonsexist. Newer editions of the FEMA guides assure us that gender distinctions will not persist: "In the following pages, the manager and staff are referred to as 'he,' which term is intended only as a space-saving convenience, with no implication whatever of any sexual discrimination. In the event of nuclear disaster, women will be playing major roles as Managers and other key staff in helping our nation to survive and recover."[6] Nuclear survivalism will maintain affirmative action. A member of the Campaign for Nuclear Disarmament (a London-based group that runs a bookstore devoted to antinuclear literature and publishes the journal *Sanity*) has pointed out that "[g]ender divisions between men and women's occupational roles would be wiped out" in a nuclear war because "*[e]verybody* would become powerless"—everybody would become simultaneously a combatant and a noncombatant in the sense of being a possible target and playing no role in military decisions or actions. Men and women alike "would be placed alongside objects, buildings, machinery, all recipients of undiscriminating missiles."[7]

Oblivious to the leveling effects of a nuclear explosion, the progressive survivalist program stresses its (albeit futile) liberalism in order to accentuate the presence of women in the postnuclear world. In the very irrelevancy of its nonsexist rhetoric, survivalism continues to identify women's work with futurity, even as the procreativity of the female body is severely constrained, or possibly extinguished. What I am suggesting is that the seemingly empty survivalist gesture of fair play to women strategically reiterates a traditional domestic usage of the feminine, the symbolic value of women to the reproduction of culture. What gets affirmed in the effort to cope with nuclear disaster is not gender equality but the domestic sentiments still attached to women. The association of femininity with futurity registers and allays anxiety about the displacement of human functions by human inventions. Invoking the feminine to naturalize and domesticate nuclear generativity, nuclear emergency reinvigorates domesticity at the moment of its deformation or decimation.

The FEMA guide provides instructions for living in shelters after a nuclear attack; in addition to operational advice about decontamination of water, sanitary disposal of the dead, radiation exposure measurements, organization, communication, and record keeping, the guide recommends educational, religious, and recreational activities. Another FEMA guide, *How to Manage Congregate Lodging Facilities and Fallout Shelters*, specifies that such activities should include religious services, group singing, arts and crafts, and board games. "Improvising checkerboards and pieces, cards, etc., is an important part of your recreational program," the guide says, "and is a team effort that will bring people together." But not too much together. Even the most private matters are monitored in this surrealistic reconstruction of community: "High social standards, particularly for sexual behavior, should be maintained."[8]

What begins to emerge here is a better-policed version of domestic life; more remarkable than the inscription of a New Right agenda into these designs for living after the bomb is the imagination of the fallout shelter as the promise of the future. "The best lesson that your population can learn in the fallout shelter is to know they can survive and to believe in a future in which our society can be rebuilt."[9] Domesticity survives to continue its reproductive function and reassurances of continuity, as in the final image of Jason Robards returned to the rubble of his home in the TV film *The Day After*. Elaine Scarry touches on the simultaneous devastation and hope encoded in this image when she notes that "the unmaking of the world requires a return to, and mutilation of the domestic, the ground of all making." Writing on the destructive and creative uses of human artifacts in her profound and compelling study *The Body in Pain: The Making and Unmaking of the World*, she locates in "the protective, narrowing act of the domestic" "the human being's most expansive potential." Yet however much the domestic surely "expresses the most benign potential of human life,"[10] it also bears witness to dislocations and disappearances caused by the human progress it both signifies and sponsors.

Historically, domesticity has performed the role of easing the absorption and assimilation of unsettling transformations wrought by the development of market capitalism. When textile manufacture replaced household production in the mid-nineteenth century, the memory of household production was retained by the new mass-produced fabric—called "domestic"—and by the ideology of domesticity that clothed the individual with a sense of enduring value in private life.[11] Forwarding and fostering the succession of one reality by another, the domestic thematizes as it sanctions a progressive replaceability. The tautological turn by which the domestic encapsulates nostalgia for itself works as the mainspring of a fable of continuity.

The world as it was known in the nineteenth century was unmade and remade in the name of domesticity; the FEMA guide's

promise of the same sequential pattern for coping with the ultimate transformation (if the virtual extinction of the species can
still be considered within temporal terms) espouses a continued
faith in progress, whatever may vanish in its wake. Imaged as the
return to a devastated home, the imagined situation of survival,
however attenuated, still operates under the sign of the domestic,
even if a mutilated domestic. For the mutability registered by the
domestic's preservative project is precisely the guarantee of the wager for self-preservation. Survivalism banks on evanescence; houses
mutate into fallout shelters and life goes on.

The incongruity of the FEMA guides' fantastic vision of life as
normal during the nuclear catastrophe is compounded by the fact
that no adequate shelter facilities other than a few privately built
shelters exist in the United States. According to Freeman Dyson,
Americans cannot accept and plan shelters because (unlike, for example, the Swiss, who have an elaborate, well-built system of shelters and a history of coping with war) they cannot accept the notion
of open housing and shared resources.[12] Our present problems
housing the increasing numbers of the homeless would seem to
confirm this. Resistance to shelters, in this line of thought, signifies resistance to an underground utopian domesticity at odds with
our traditions of privacy and individual homes. Visions of a collective domesticity, in fact, recur throughout our domestic ideology;
against the mainstream of domesticity float such proposals as the
great Christian neighborhood envisaged by Catharine Beecher and
Harriet Beecher Stowe in 1869.

The Beecher sisters devoted the penultimate chapter of their
best-selling housekeeping manual *The American Woman's Home*
to domestic solutions for "the homeless, the helpless, and the vicious." For an alternative to crowded city tenements and street living, they proposed communal apartment houses run by philan-
thropic women, an arrangement decades later put into effect by
Jane Addams. The Beecher sisters believed domestic economy
should be applied to the entire society, in order "to save the world"
from "the great struggle of humanity in all ages . . . to rise higher."
Against the privilege and exclusivity of the wealthier classes, they
urged "a revival of the true, self-denying spirit of Christ." Their
communitarian Christian interpretation of domestic ideology rejects the value of human goods and the material logic of futurity
structured upon the survival of such goods. "Nothing goes into the
future world as a good secured but training our own and other im-

mortal minds." "We are to spend all to save the world," for "no-where [in the New Testament] do we find any direction or approval of laying up money for self or children."[13]

Nuclear survivalism would seem to censure this utopian narra-tive of domesticity and affirm the values of exclusivity and priva-cy promulgated and sold in the architect Andrew Jackson Down-ing's popular house designs. Instead of an expansive, public-spirited domesticity, Downing stressed the removal and individuality of home, "the solitude and freedom of the family home in the coun-try." Downing's accentuation of privacy in his secluded country homes has held sway in the domestic ideal since the nineteenth century. The domestic ideology upon which the present imagina-tion of survival is founded develops a misanthropic and miserly strain in the domestic, the preference for an exclusionary peace apart from what Downing called "the battle of life, carried on in cities." Those tumultuous cities hold the homeless, helpless, and vicious Beecher and Stowe sought to house. Though the cities ex-hibit the evidence of problems of space availability and uneven dis-tribution of wealth, Downing celebrates "the ease of obtaining a house and land, and the ability of almost every citizen to build his own house" in America.[14] So Downing's ideal domesticity is founded on the distinction of ownership as well as the distinction between the country and the city. Or, more succinctly, ownership distinguishes the secure freedom of the country home from prob-lematic and uncertain urban living in a capitalist culture. The drive to privacy in Downing's domesticity reflects and privileges an indi-viduality soldered to private property.

Owning property effectively guarantees one's difference from those who remain subject to the operations of property owners; ownership, the enjoyment of exclusive rights to a given property, thus signifies one's particularity, one's individuality. To assure this individuality amidst maintenance costs and shifting property val-ues, Downing counsels buying a house according to this standard inquiry: "Can the proprietor afford to leave it to one of his chil-dren?—or, at the most, is it an expenditure that will not prove a serious loss, should they be compelled to part with it?"[15] Since property is transferable, the value of the individual home rests in the stability of ownership. The individualistic domesticity defined by Downing and instituted in nineteenth-century America elabo-rates, like Downing's Gothic Revival designs, upon an older tradi-tion of individualism, the seventeenth-century concepts of what

C. B. MacPherson has termed possessive individualism. According to this formulation of the individual "as an owner of himself" and "the proprietor of his own person or capacities," ownership determines freedom and self-realization. "The human essence is freedom from dependence on the wills of others, and freedom is a function of possession."[16] Nineteenth-century domestic ideology identified individualism and freedom with the possession of home; in the domesticity of nuclear survivalism, individual existence continues by virtue of its exclusive proprietorship—of a bomb shelter.

Nuclear domesticity then amplifies and reiterates the economic problems built into the possessive individualism perpetuated through the domestic; the getting of shelter replays anxieties about self-proprietorship, about self-perseverence through the preservation of the property that reflects and registers presence in the world. Nuclear shelter exemplifies the imbrication of sequence with accumulation, the identification of continuity with the accretion and consolidation of things. This is an association at the heart of domestic experience, first learned at home in nursery rhymes, which offer children a way to place themselves and other objects in the world. These rhymes not only teach by repetition, but teach repetition, committing to the child's memory a pattern of succession, resonance, and continuity. In this pedagogical practice, children learn the world by reconstructing it from one man—call him Jack—and reproducing the productions of man by recounting all the things that go in the house that Jack built. The domestic storage and incorporation of the world chanted here links the individual to things as an owner; all the animals on Old MacDonald's farm echo the pleasures of an expanding proprietorship. Consequent concerns of government, relation, and order in this world-populating enterprise become apparent in "The Farmer in the Dell," where a specific chain of being extends from the proprietorial farmer down to the inanimate, nonaggressive cheese who stands alone. As these narratives recount a descending order in a chain of proprietorship (for example, from farmer to cheese), they also exemplify how the extension of the domestic circle depends upon substitutions in the sequence (wife for farmer, dog for wife, and so on, ending in cheese for mouse). In the accrual of property and construction of the world, the self disappears to reappear in sequences that identify the proprietor with the property—the individual reverberates through the things of his taking and making.

"The function of belongings within the economy of the bourgeois subject is one of supplementarity," Susan Stewart observes in her fascinating study of narrative and metaphors of subjectivity, "a supplementarity that in consumer culture replaces its generating subject as the interior milieu substitutes for, and takes the place of, an interior self." Stewart is describing here the formation of subjectivity within industrial capitalism, the imprint and internalization of a particular political economy. While I would quarrel with Stewart's assumption of a self anterior to cultural relations and reflections (that is, her distinction between an interior milieu and an interior self), I think her description particularly apt for its illumination of proprietorship as supplementarity and its focus on the seriality of that proprietorship. According to the logic of possessive individualism (which, as MacPherson emphasizes, is an account of individualism that has persisted with market relations), the supplement of property extends rather than replaces the individual through what might be called a serial of self. The construction of subject and world enacted in the nursery rhymes' miniaturization of society relies upon the generative power of the series to reflect and augment the individual. In this spiral of self-reproduction, the items of the series are the subject's property and representation (that is, they belong to and stand for the subject), and it is in their common frame of reference, or in Stewart's words, "in the interdependence of the elements of the series that their regenerative power resides."[17] As in the epistolary exercise of the chain letter, which of course also belongs to this narrative tradition of serial self-projection, the greater the number of elements in one's series or within one's purview, the more assured one's self-possession.

Sequence thus operates as survival by stockpiling—not only in the case of nuclear survivalism but in the very concept of self circulated through domestic traditions. The gesture to the future that domesticity and sequence signify depends upon our constantly taking inventory of the things by which we project ourselves from day to day. This is the principle built into the threatening logic and insistent sequentiality of chain letters: the circulation and reproduction of the self in its markers, whether family, furniture, land, livestock, pets, or letters. The method to nuclear-survivalist madness lies in this catalogue tradition of self-perpetuation; antinuclear thematics of affiliation and associationism share with pronuclear survivalism this desire for sequence and the narrative of possessive individualism it reprises. Thinking about the nuclear, then, is itself a sequence in the history of liberal humanism, a sequence that foregrounds the dynamic of disappearance and reappearance in the logic of self-proprietorship. It is not entirely facetious here to recall the cheese standing alone, marking the limit of the farmer's purview by closing the circle of consumption. The farmer and his sequence end in the solitary cheese, unitary because inanimate. But the cheese's moment of stationary solitude returns, like all the possessive movements, to the fact of the farmer in the dell.

What replacements of sequence effect is a continual reconstruction of the individual, whose property, however immobile, perpetuates its owner. This, I think, explains why domestic property and props figure so prominently and powerfully in programs for survival, regardless of political and temporal vantages. The structure of self-extensive individuality informing the survivalist imagination of shelter life also underlies antinuclear contemplations of futurity. Thus the powerful argument against nuclear arms advanced by Schell and other proponents of disarmament stresses the nuclear potential to destroy the material and social bases of our individuality. Because "our transmission of ourselves, the substance and continuity of our existence, is not confined to what we inherit genetically, but exists outside ourselves," Kate Soper of the Campaign for Nuclear Disarmament writes, "we cannot identify survival simply with the salvaging of the physical body." And because we "acquire our individuality through what might be called a continuous 'extension' of ourselves in an objective realm—for example, in our children, friends, lovers, work, hobbies, pets, and so on," nuclear war, in annihilating these self-extensions, would mean the "failure of *human* survival."[18] It is through human paraphernalia that humanity will perdure.

II

I have argued so far that survivalists and antinuclear activists alike employ the identification of survival with domesticity and sequentiality, and thus the individualistic conception of self as materially embodied and memorialized. This thesis is not meant to deny the very real differences between the politics of survivalism and the politics of disarmament, but to delineate and delimit the horizon of individualism in which both the prospect of postnuclear domesticity and the preservation of humanity are articulated. However compelling and intuitively correct we may find antinuclear emphasis on the human dimension of survival, its focus on the particular-

ity of human existence and history merits an inquiry into the construction of that particularity. While such a maneuver may seem to
defer nuclear danger to more domestic matters, to submerge the
imminence of nuclear holocaust in the history of individualism, it
reflects rather than deflects the gravity of nuclear peril. For it is
precisely because the nuclear threat has become an occasion for the
reassertion of individualism that we should attend to the domestic
contexts of nuclear discourse; after all, the intensity of nuclear concerns is identical to the immediacy and intimacy of our self-
interest.

The domestication of the nuclear and mobilization of the domestic I have traced in the imagery and rhetoric about the nuclear peril
manifest a common interest in a mode of self-perpetuation that
continually accelerates us into the future and new forms of ourselves. When the antinuclear chain letter enjoins us to take a stake
in futurity, or when the nursery rhyme reconstructs our self-extension in the world, they epitomize our familiarity with and reliance
on a notion of projection in which we ourselves *are* our (possible)
futures. If this structure of risk, deferral, and faith defines and organizes individuality, the fact that we have invented the ultimate risk
in nuclear weaponry seems perfectly continuous with our practices
of self-perpetuation. The work of survival, then, may require calls
not only for nuclear disarmament but also for a disarmament of the
ideology of sequential self-extension.

The endurance and embellishments of the concept of possessive
individualism evident in the domestic rhetoric of the nuclear debate also account for the enormity of the task feminism faces in
critiquing and changing domestic institutions. Over the last fifteen
years, feminism has persistently challenged the narrative of domesticity I have traced here. And one result of this challenge has been
the recovery of alternate domestic models such as the Beecher-
Stowe collective domesticity. But the ease with which the feminist
project is appropriated by nuclear domesticity suggests that it
would be useful to consider how feminism itself remains under the
aegis of the individualistic domestic.

Since narrative and its sequential mechanisms shape and sustain
the association of self-perpetuation and domesticity, much recent
feminist criticism has devoted itself to analyzing and revising the
domestic narratives of the eighteenth- and nineteenth-century
novel. Central to this project is the mode of reading instituted by
Sandra Gilbert and Susan Gubar's highly influential *The Mad-*

woman in the Attic, which traces in nineteenth-century women writers "a common female impulse to struggle free from social and literary confinement."[19] Such feminist rereadings of the novel highlight the heroines who escape domesticity through adultery, disease, or death. In the heroine's end begin feminist visions of alternative plots; exits such as the anorectic deaths of Clarissa and Catherine Earnshaw, the drowning of Maggie Tulliver and the death by fire of Bertha Mason, the suicides of Emma Bovary and Edna Pontellier, the ascensions to heaven by Little Eva, Beth March, and other female (usually tubercular) invalids all variously signify a refusal of conventional femininity and its narratives. Leaving the narrative, these characters indicate the unsatisfactory nature of novelistic closure, the identity of the customary novelistic happy ending with conventional prescriptions for women: marriage and family. Breaking this sequence and circumventing its expected conclusion, the feminist heroine appears to signal disruption of traditional self-definitions.

The feminine has long been considered a threat to aesthetic order because of its identity on the one hand with the triviality of the everyday and on the other with the violence of the repressed.[20] Feminine exits from the novel are now characterized as necessary protests of that order and the political economy it articulates. While such a characterization uncovers a very important tradition of feminist protest, it also tends to overlook the place of this tradition within the history of the novel as a document of individualism. When the novel under consideration is one of the great representations of romantic individualism, such as Emily Brontë's *Wuthering Heights,* the complications in the relation between feminism and domesticity emerge with particular clarity.

Wuthering Heights has provided feminists with a powerful example of the disappearing rebellious heroine in Catherine Earnshaw, who, according to Gilbert and Gubar, "longs equally for the extinction of parlor fires and the rekindling of unimaginably different energies." Yet what makes this novel so compelling a document for feminists, I submit, is not the "quenchless will" of a protesting "female nature,"[21] but its overwhelming individualism: the individualism epitomized in the novel's double allegiance and movement to perdition (the deaths of the first two generations) and rehabilitation (the succession of the next generation). What makes Catherine so memorable a figure for feminism is her claim to sovereignty in both the existent and future order of things; what makes her so haunting a figure in *Wuthering Heights* is her sheer staying power in the narrative of individualism kindled by parlor fires. Far from proposing the extinction of domesticity, *Wuthering Heights* detects unimaginably different energies in the domestic.

If Catherine's death detaches her from a domestic destiny, her exploitation of the productive powers of disappearance reaffirms the self-perpetuating logic of the domestic. *Wuthering Heights* is saturated with Catherine's presence despite the fact she so early exits the narrative. As all readers of the novel recall, Catherine dominates the narrative; the (first) film version emphasizes and sexualizes this powerful presence as the romantic passion of Merle Oberon and Laurence Olivier. Yet in the novel itself, there is less the sense of the eternity of great characters than the impression of the principle of perpetuity through which the individuals Catherine and Heathcliff perdure. It is in the ways the principals continue to loom in others' consciousness, in the power of persons as effects, that Catherine and Heathcliff achieve indelibility.

The haunting perpetuity chronicled in *Wuthering Heights* is announced and condensed in the famous opening dream sequence detailing the events and logic of Catherine's survival. Catherine enters the book, chronologically reenters and returns, through the childhood effects discovered by the narrator Lockwood—her signature, her books, and her diary penned in the margins of those books. After reading Catherine's account of the corporal punishment and separation from Heathcliff she suffered for not attending to the religious observances dictated by the family servant Joseph, Lockwood dreams that he is beaten by a congregation with their pilgrim's staves for refusing to submit to a sermon by the Reverend Jabes Branderham (one of the writers whose text's margins served as Catherine's journal space). Waking from this nightmare, Lockwood realizes that the sound of the wooden staves he heard in his sleep is in fact emitting from a tree branch beating against the window. He then dreams again: that he opens the window in order to detach the rapping fir bough and in stretching out his arm grasps the icy hand of a ghost-child, who identifies herself as Catherine Linton, the married name of Catherine Earnshaw twenty years previously at the time of her death. To break her "tenacious grip," and prevent her from entering, Lockwood violently pulls her "wrist on to the broken pane," and rubs "it to and fro till the blood ran down and soaked the bed-clothes."[22] Making the ghost bleed, he restores Catherine to human form, and to her childhood. These metamorphoses of signature into story into staff into tree limb into hand again reincarnate Catherine through a series initiated by her autographical etchings in the windowsill.[23] The serial return and revivification of Catherine staged in Lockwood's dreams mark the child's imprint on her world, and thus multiply and affirm the signs of her presence, testifying to her impact on the world.

The world of Wuthering Heights, where resemblances between relations, between persons and beasts (Isabella Linton wonders if Heathcliff is a man or devil), and between live and dead animals (Lockwood mistakes a pile of dead rabbits for a sleeping cat family) are so emphatic, seems particularly receptive to human imprints; it remains suffused with the effects of its inhabitants. These effects are not limited to the conventional human reproduction of successive generations. Though the names, appearances, and even characters of one generation reappear in the next, perpetuity also derives from a seemingly supernatural mode of reproduction. The ghost of Catherine, and finally the ghost couple of Catherine and Heathcliff, haunting the moors between Wuthering Heights and Thrushcross Grange in 1802, signifies and mythifies the other productive powers and possibilities of individualism emerging in the nineteenth century. *Wuthering Heights* magnifies the childhood rehearsal of individualism into a drama of lasting proprietorship: the futurity of proprietorship in a redoubled individualism charted in the novel's story of the fate of family property.

In the story of Catherine and Heathcliff, *Wuthering Heights* describes the consolidation of an individualism tied to landed gentry like the Lintons and Earnshaws with the bourgeois individualism of Heathcliff, the orphan who mysteriously and swiftly rises to the status of gentleman and proprietor. Heathcliff's era of control over both family estates only strengthens family identity since the estates eventually revert to Catherine's nephew Hareton Earnshaw, descendant and namesake of the Hareton Earnshaw whose name was inscribed in 1500 on the original threshold of Wuthering Heights. Moreover, Heathcliff's ownership never really takes Wuthering Heights from the Earnshaws for, as Catherine says, Heathcliff is "more myself than I," and furthermore, "I *am* Heathcliff." It is Catherine who persists through Heathcliff's proprietorship, haunting him and accruing and lasting in him. He bears out her belief in "an existence of yours beyond you." "If all else perished and *he* remained, I should still continue to be," she asserts. And (s)he does remain; despite Lockwood's wonder that "anyone could ever imagine unquiet slumbers for the sleepers in that quiet earth," the little shepherd boy at the end of the novel reports seeing "Heathcliff and a woman."[24]

III

The legacy *Wuthering Heights* leaves for feminism, I think, consists in Emily Brontë's extraordinary prescience in recognizing the simultaneously reassuring and horrific possibilities for the self in an amended individualism. The fact that the idea of miraculous generative energies extends the horizon of individualism and furthers the prospect of nuclear domesticity might remind us that the category of the unimaginable has historically denoted transformations already accomplished or within reach. It is an exaggeration in the process of entering the scale of the normal. Whereas Gilbert and Gubar attribute to *Wuthering Heights* the imagination of unimaginably different energies in place of parlor fires, the novel itself calls attention to the unimaginable issuing from those fires. *Wuthering Heights* demonstrates how the domestic houses new conventions of individualism, including those that generate liberal feminism. The domestic ideology feminism would undo sustains its enabling principle, the widening franchise for female proprietorship.

The trope of the feminine as the tear in the social and literary fabric, the impediment to uniformity—and therefore, the site of revisionary intervention—has figured in the novel since its inception. Clarissa's tragedy haunts Pamela's success; the precariousness of the marital (or any) destiny is built into the novel as an operating premise of replaceability, the anticipation of changes in sequence. As in the epistolary model upon which the novel embroiders, such removals of the subject clear the way for the substitutions by which forms of seriality like the novel reproduce and preserve the individual. If breaking narrative order and the social chains it represents is an eventuality anticipated and built into the novel, then it might be said that the novel in its humanistic mission of representing interiority has invented forms of the feminine and feminism as mechanisms for its own reproduction and transformation.[25] The effectiveness of this transformative device is currently reflected in the achievement of feminist criticism in revitalizing literary interests and debates.

The domestic heritage of feminism shows the historical role of the feminine in nurturing the imagination of the new or the otherwise. In the convergence of feminism, individualism, and survivalism I have traced in the domestic imagery and rhetoric of the nuclear peril, we can see that it is both the strength and limitation of feminism to bear this reproductive role. While feminism might engender and implement different forms of the self, these, too, become conventions of the individualistic narrative. It may be the particular plight—and potential—of feminism in our time to disenfranchise the individual from the traditions of self-perpetuity.

The arsenals of self-erasure and self-projection by which the self persists protect the logic of sequence, which is the logic both sides of the nuclear debate—all of us in the nuclear predicament—share. The durability of this procedure of self-ratification should alert us to the unreassuring familiarity bred so far by deployments of disappearance and deferral. As long as our concerns about nuclear holocaust maintain the logic of sequence, they retain this scenario of the wagered self. Thinking about the nuclear poses (as it exposes) a crucial difficulty for feminism: how to disjoin women from the domestic narrative and yet prevent a reprise of their disappearance from general view. The difficulty in which feminism is placed, the predicament which we all face, implies that perhaps we should be less concerned with what the nuclear annihilates than with what nuclear rhetoric reproduces. What makes the rehearsals of sequence in chain letters so threatening, finally, is not the dangers of breaking the chain but the spectre of rampant self-proliferation.

Notes

Portions of this essay appeared in the *Yale Journal of Criticism* (Fall 1988).

1. My thinking on nuclear catastrophe and individualism is much indebted to the invaluable essay by Ferguson, "The Nuclear Sublime." I have also benefited from discussions with Miriam Hansen, Howard Horwitz, George Levine, and, especially, Barbara Freeman, with whom this work began when we cochaired an MLA special session on feminist nuclear criticism in 1986.

2. Syracuse Cultural Workers Project, "The Ribbon—August 1985."

3. Schell, *The Fate of the Earth*, 182–84.

4. Dyson, *Weapons and Hope*. I take the phrase "smothered by invention" from the title of the feminist anthology of essays *Smothered by Invention: Technology in Women's Life*, edited by Wendy Faulkner and Eric Arnold.

5. Federal Emergency Management Agency, "Shelter Management Handbook."

6. Quoted in Zuckerman, *The Day after World War III*, 120.

7. Assiter, "Womanpower and Nuclear Politics," 200–201.

8. Quoted in Zuckerman, *The Day after World War III*, 97–124.

9. Quoted in ibid., 124.

10. Scarry, *The Body in Pain*, 38–45.

11. On the rise of domesticity and transformations in textile production, see Cott, *The Bonds of Womanhood*, 63–100; Dublin, *Women at Work*; Strasser, *Never Done*, 125–44.

12. Dyson, *Weapons and Hope*, 110–17. In Dyson's intriguing exploration of the paradoxes in the American "antipathy toward shelters," he points out that the very privileges of private property shelters exemplify have become an ethical reason to reject shelters as reasonable survival strategies. But though Americans are not building shelters in the 1980s, FEMA is producing its shelter plans.

13. Beecher and Stowe, *The American Woman's Home*, 433–52. On the evolution of this disjunction of domestic economy from the existent political economy, which I take to be the contribution of Stowe to her older sister's domestic philosophy, see my "Getting in the Kitchen with Dinah," 503–23.

14. Downing, *The Architecture of Country Houses*, xix, 3.

15. Ibid., 269.

16. MacPherson, *The Political Theory of Possessive Individualism*, 3. See also MacPherson's introduction to *Property: Mainstream and Critical Positions*, 1–13.

17. Stewart, *On Longing*, xi. Stewart's acute analysis of the miniature as a narrative of interiority has helped to shape my account of the individualistic narrative of nursery rhymes.

18. Soper, "Contemplating a Nuclear Future," 176–79.

19. Gilbert and Gubar, *The Madwoman in the Attic*, xii.

20. Schor, *Reading in Detail*, 1–22.

21. Gilbert and Gubar, *The Madwoman in the Attic*.

22. Brontë, *Wuthering Heights*, 30.

23. I am here developing a different account of the process of metamorphosis in *Wuthering Heights* so eloquently described by Bersani in *A Future for Astyanax*, 189–229. Following Bersani, I am stressing the novel's presentation of the "self as a potentiality for metamorphoses"; but where Bersani takes this self to have renounced both "the closed circle of family repetitions" and "the limiting definitions of individuality," I maintain that the metamorphosing self is indicative of a fantasy of limitlessness within domesticity and individuality.

24. Brontë, *Wuthering Heights*, 72–74; 265–66. In an interesting sequel to the logic of perpetuity presented in *Wuthering Heights*, Clarke's chil-

dren's book *The Return of the Twelves* tells the story of the discovery and reanimation of the Brontë children's toy soldiers.

25. On the crucial role of women (as readers, writers, and subjects) in the evolution of the novel, see, among others, Miller, *The Heroine's Text;* Moers, *Literary Women;* and Watt, *The Rise of the Novel.*

Works Cited

Assiter, Alison. "Womanpower and Nuclear Politics: Women and the Peace Movement." In *Over Our Dead Bodies: Women against the Bomb,* edited by Dorothy Thompson, 200–201. London: Virago, 1983.

Beecher, Catherine, and Harriet Beecher Stowe. *The American Woman's Home.* New York: J. B. Ford & Co., 1869.

Bersani, Leo. *A Future for Astyanax.* Boston: Little, Brown & Co., 1969.

Brontë, Emily. *Wuthering Heights.* New York: Norton Critical Edition, 1972.

Brown, Gillian. "Getting in the Kitchen with Dinah: Domestic Politics in *Uncle Tom's Cabin.*" *American Quarterly* 36, no. 4 (Fall 1984): 503–23.

Clarke, Pauline. *The Return of the Twelves.* New York: Coward, McCann, 1963.

Cott, Nancy. *The Bonds of Womanhood.* New Haven: Yale University Press, 1977.

Downing, Andrew Jackson. *The Architecture of Country Houses.* New York: Dover, 1969.

Dublin, Thomas. *Women at Work: The Transformation of Work and Community in Lowell, Massachusetts 1826–1860.* New York: Oxford University Press, 1979.

Dyson, Freeman. *Weapons and Hope.* New York: Harper & Row, 1984.

Faulkner, Wendy, and Eric Arnold. *Smothered by Invention: Technology in Woman's Life.* London: Pluto Press, 1985.

Federal Emergency Management Agency. *Shelter Management Handbook.* Washington, D.C.: U.S. Government Printing Office, May 1984.

Ferguson, Frances. "The Nuclear Sublime." *Diacritics* 14, no. 2 (Special Issue on Nuclear Criticism, Summer 1984): 4–10.

Gilbert, Sandra, and Susan Gubar. *The Madwoman in the Attic: The Woman Writer and the Nineteenth-Century Literary Imagination.* New Haven: Yale University Press, 1979.

MacPherson, C. B. *The Political Theory of Possessive Individualism.* New York: Oxford University Press, 1962.

_____. *Property: Mainstream and Critical Positions.* Toronto: University of Toronto Press, 1978.

Miller, Nancy. *The Heroine's Text.* New York: Columbia, 1980.

Moers, Ellen. *Literary Women.* New York: Doubleday, 1977.

Scarry, Elaine. *The Body in Pain: The Making and Unmaking of the World*. New York, Oxford: Oxford University Press, 1985.

Schell, Jonathan. *The Fate of the Earth*. New York: Alfred A. Knopf, 1982.

Schor, Naomi. *Reading in Detail: Aesthetics and the Feminine*. New York: Methuen, 1987.

Soper, Kate. "Contemplating a Nuclear Future: Nuclear War, Politics and the Individual." In *Over Our Dead Bodies: Women against the Bomb*, edited by Dorothy Thompson, 176–79. London: Virago, 1983.

Stewart, Susan. *On Longing: Narratives of the Miniature, the Gigantic, the Souvenir, the Collection*. Baltimore: Johns Hopkins University Press, 1984.

Strasser, Susan. *Never Done: A History of American Housework*. New York: Pantheon, 1982.

Syracuse Cultural Workers Project, "The Ribbon—August 1985." Syracuse, N.Y., 1985.

Watt, Ian. *The Rise of the Novel*. Berkeley: University of California Press, 1957.

Zuckerman, Edward. *The Day after World War III*. New York: Viking, 1984.

Barbara
Freeman "Epitaphs and Epigraphs:

'The End(s) of Man' "

A s my reader may have already noted, the quotation marks in my title are somewhat perplexing. But they are there for a reason, and since their story is bound up with this essay's inception, I would like to begin by recounting it. A version of this paper was presented at a special session that Gillian Brown and I organized, under the title of "Ends and Beginnings: Feminist-Nuclear Criticism," at the 1986 MLA convention. The title of my paper bears the traces of its institutional origin. I did not know that the MLA Program Committee reviews and may disallow the title of each paper, and was shocked when "Epigraphs and Epitaphs: The End(s) of Man" (originally with no added quotation marks) was returned with "Man" circled and the following comment: "Organizer—We must change to avoid sexist language. Alternatives might be *life*, or *human life*. Please let us know which you prefer or provide another word." I was not willing to change it. The word "man" had been chosen not only to illustrate my paper's subject, but the issues at stake in the entire session; indeed, the MLA's objection itself presented an example of the kind of question I wanted to explore: in the context of nuclear catastrophe, is "man" really equivalent to "human life"? I wrote in response that the title referred to Derrida's essay "The Ends of Man,"[1] and suggested that putting single quotation marks around it might solve the problem. Fortunately the committee accepted the compromise and let the amended title stand. But I have retained the punctuation thereby necessitated because the story of how it comes to be there raises an important issue regarding sexual difference, sexism, and deterrence.

Why, for example, was my (or Derrida's) use of the word "man" considered an instance of sexist language? Perhaps because it employs the name of one sex to refer to both men and women, thereby denying sexual difference by implying that femininity is identical to or the same thing as masculinity. But although the title might appear sexist in that it gives to all of human life the name of only one gender, it was formulated to engage the following questions:

When we speak of nuclear technology and discourse, are the ends of men, women, or both at stake? Is the possibility of nuclear destruction the symptom of a specifically masculine imagination? When Derrida, for example, writes that "the stakes of the nuclear question are those of humanity, of the humanities,"[2] ought we to read the "man" in "humanity" and "the humanities" as gender-specific? If there is such a thing as nuclear desire, does it have a gender? Let me pose this question in another way.

Ought the Constitution of UNESCO, which starts with the words, "Since wars begin in the minds of men, it is in the minds of men that the defenses of peace must be constructed,"[3] be taken as an example of sexist language? The very naturalness of linking the words "war" and "men" would problematize the claim that man and human life are equivalent, or at least interchangeable. According to a certain view, men are implicated in war and the production of nuclear weapons in a way that women are not. Now it is precisely this assumption I wish to interrogate: the extent to which the ends of women, and perhaps of a certain feminism, are implicated and complicit in man's potential end as represented by the possibility of nuclear war; that is, the ways in which, in relation to nuclear war and discourse about it, the term "human life" cannot be employed as a substitute for the word "man."

I propose, then, that we look for the logistics of war where we might, consciously or not, presume its exclusion, and one place to start is by thinking about couples—the way they work, the ideologies they support, and particularly the logic according to which two of the most influential couples ever constructed, man/woman and war/peace, have come to be coupled, that is, defined in terms of one another.

By investigating the junction of two kinds of couples I would like to point out first that Western representations of sexual difference are dependent upon and determined by the structure of the couple, and second that the couple is the precondition for war in the sense that a war cannot take place without at least two sides. In this regard it is useful to juxtapose Hélène Cixous's insight into the relationship between couples and sexual difference with Elaine Scarry's arguments concerning the nature of war.

According to Cixous, not only does the couple provide the most basic organizational pattern of Western thought, but every opposition is also sexed; it has a gender. As she puts it:

Thought has always worked through . . . dual, hierarchical oppositions . . . [e]verywhere (where) ordering intervenes, where a
law organizes what is thinkable by oppositions. . . . And all
these pairs of oppositions are *couples*. Does that mean something? Is the fact that Logocentrism subjects thought—all concepts, codes, and values—to a binary system, related to "the"
couple, man/woman?[4]

If Cixous is correct, such couples as active/passive, mind/body,
speech/writing, and war/peace are not only, as Alice Jardine points
out, "intrinsic to the ensemble of symbolic systems in the West,"
but would also "appear to be modeled on *the couple*: Man/Woman,
Masculine/Feminine."[5] In other words, every couple—each term in
every pair of opposites—conceals a gender, and with it, an ethic. For
a couple is in fact a disguised hierarchical arrangement, or contest,
which leads to privileging and provides the grounds for debasing
one half of the couple at the expense of the other—like war itself.

Scarry's discussion of the structure of war in *The Body in Pain*
and her definition of it as a contest shows that the couple is one of
war's most necessary components, without which war as such
could not exist. Coupling, in other words, is at the very heart of all
conflict. According to Scarry:

War is a contest where the participants arrange themselves into
two sides and engage in an activity that will eventually make it
possible to designate one side the winner and one side the
loser. . . . [I]n consenting to enter into war, the participants enter into a structure that is a self-cancelling duality[,] . . . a formal duality, that, by the very force of its relentless insistence
on doubleness, provides the means for eliminating and replacing itself by the condition of singularity. A first major attribute
here is the transition, at the moment of entry into war, from
the condition of multiplicity to the condition of the binary; a
second attribute is the transition, at the moment of ending the
war, from the condition of the binary to the condition of the
unitary.[6]

If, as Scarry's work so eloquently demonstrates, war depends upon
the structure of the couple, which is from the outset bound up with
certain unconscious attitudes toward and representations of sexual
difference, it is interesting to note that in many current feminist

antiwar critiques the masculine/feminine couple is not only un-examined but positively valorized and reendorsed: man is equated with war and destruction, woman with peace and creativity. Examining some typical feminist critiques of nuclear war and the arms race enables us to investigate the ideology at work in this particular couple and allows us to ask if a certain humanistic feminism is not, however well-intentioned, supportive of the very values and behavior patterns it wishes to resist.

Dr. Helen Caldicott, who is perhaps the champion of a physiological and psychological feminist-essentialism in which "man" is synonymous with violence and war and "woman" is equated with peace and life, provides an almost too-perfect example of such a couple. In her best-selling *Missile Envy: The Arms Race and Nuclear War*, she holds that men are totally responsible for war, which is a product of the masculine as opposed to the feminine mind. Indeed, "bombs are not the cause of the problem, but only the symptoms of the deranged thought processes of man's mind,"[7] and when Caldicott says "man" she indeed means male and not female people. Her description of the "typical woman" is a parody of conventional, cliché-ridden assumptions about an inborn womanhood: "A typical woman . . . is very much in touch with her feelings, cries when necessary, has a very strong and reliable intuition, which serves her in good stead. . . . [W]omen are nurturers. They are generally born with strong feelings for nurturing the life process" (316). Men, on the other hand, are not only "more psychologically aggressive than women"; Caldicott even suggests that "something about men's most primitive feelings makes them enjoy killing" (318). She concludes, therefore, that the "hideous weapons of killing and mass genocide may be a symptom of several male emotions: inadequate sexuality and a need to continually prove their virility plus a primitive fascination with killing" (321). If "the children of the country and the world" are to be saved from "man's war and destruction," the only hope is that women "rapidly become elected to the highest offices in the country and change America's national policies from those of death to life." Thus may the "positive feminine principle" become "the guiding moral principle in world politics" (322). It's ironic that Caldicott's prototypically feminist use of the word "man" to refer to men instead of women may be interpreted as sexist in that it reaffirms patriarchial stereotypes about the sexes (women are idealized as not only different from but inherently better than men) at the same time that it conforms to the MLA's injunction that gender terms be used "genderically" and not generically, guidelines adopted precisely so as to avoid sexism. The question, however, is not who is making the politically correct, feminist gesture—Caldicott, who says that war in general and nuclear war in particular is a uniquely male phenomenon, a symptom of man's peculiar ends, or the MLA's belief that it is sexist to use the word "man" to refer to male and female persons—but whose interests such an understanding of sexual difference serves.

Caldicott's views are not, unfortunately, simply an extreme or eccentric example of feminist positions regarding nuclear war, but rather typify the concept of sexual difference put forward by the Women's Peace Movement, namely, that women are innately peace-loving and therefore have an inherent and special relation to the preservation of life. The extremely popular British Women's Peace Movement publication, *A Handbook for Women on the Nuclear Mentality*, for example, reemphasizes Caldicott's belief that human reality is basically of two kinds: male and destructive versus female and creative. One of the very premises of the book is as follows:

> The world is presently caught in an imbalance of male and female energy. We believe, in fact, that the destructive path exemplified by the nuclear industry has resulted from a heavy overload of male-defined power in our society. While we do not want to insinuate that the masculine is necessarily all bad, we do believe that the dominating force within all of us which we label animus or male has taken over and created a destructive imbalance on our planet. We feel strongly that the value of anima or female energy has been largely lost to each individual, man and woman, and certainly to the Earth as a whole. It is our intention, therefore, to illustrate this imbalance, and to suggest ways for restoring the female principle.[8]

And another British Women's Peace Group, "Nottingham WONT," further underscores the view that war is a primarily male phenomenon, its technology the product of a uniquely masculine desire:

> The so-called masculine, manly qualities of toughness, dominance, not showing emotions or admitting dependence, can be seen as the driving force behind war. . . . Nuclear technology is built on the arrogance and confidence of mastery (over nature as over women) which this has fed.[9]

Whereas historically woman has been viewed as the originator of sin and evil and the cause of war, as in Eve's role in man's fall from the Garden of Eden or Helen's part in starting the Trojan War, according to regnant feminist ideologies that burden has now shifted to men: femininity is held to be the better half of a Manichean couple in which men give rise to war and death while women are peaceful and life-affirming. But although the roles have been reversed, the fundamental concept of sexual difference as an opposition in which one sex is innately good and the other innately evil has not changed. Such a polarization does not deter war, but rather provides the means by which the unitary term, in this case masculinity and all that is attributed to it, can triumph over femininity, the secondary term that copulates with and enables it. Here the war between the sexes mimes or is mimed by that between nations, for the very tactic that is supposed to resist war—attempting to isolate the problem by shifting responsibility for it to men and trying to change their behavior—participates in the framework that allows, indeed is indispensable to, the conflict in the first place.

What is crucial for an effective resistance to war is not a reversal of the same themes, but a displacement of the very structure that produces it. Paul Virilio observes, "[T]he original war machine is a man and a woman. The couple is not only good for making babies. Marriage is in reality a war machine, not a machine for production."[10] If he is right, one begins to suspect that the feminist tactic of coupling man with war and woman with peace reenacts what Richard Klein has called the "dialectic of mimetic rivalry,"[11] which, far from deterring war, threatens to replicate the conflict it ostensibly resists and helps to reproduce the condition it supposedly critiques. But then the unavoidable question becomes, if the traditional feminist position does not act as a deterrent, is there another, perhaps alternative kind of feminist criticism that could? Or might?

In order to defer this question, if only momentarily, I would like to suggest that the man/war, woman/peace equation be read as a couple whose sustained encounter threatens to "take place on the grounds of a catastrophe,"[12] and that the specific contours of this catastrophe are inseparable from a certain logic of apocalypse—indeed, already written in the Book of Revelation two thousand years ago. A discussion of this text allows us to explore two possibilities: first, that the nuclear bomb is part of the inheritance the Book of Revelation proposes, its heir or legacy; and second, that the very notion of apocalypse (the prophetic revelation of imminent catastrophe, from the Greek *apokalypto*, translated from the Hebrew *gala*) is a consequence of writing in general, and fiction in particular—with the act of imagining and describing an event that has never occurred. I will also suggest that the Book prefigures, maybe even authors, the bomb, and that the bomb externalizes the Book, threatening to enact precisely what the Book of Revelation describes. My wager is that the bomb's invention has been built into the Book, as if the desire at work in the last chapter of the New Testament were indeed the end of human life. I am also supposing, perhaps mistakenly, that the Book of Revelation was written by people and not by God, and is a sociohistorical, literary artifact.[13]

If revelation is understood as the disclosure of knowledge to humans by a supernatural agency, in the Book of Revelation it occurs only through an intermediary. The last book of the Bible begins by setting up a kind of postal service between Jesus, the Angel who transmits God's message, and John, who receives the message and redelivers it to the Seven Churches. John reports hearing behind him "a great voice, as of a trumpet" (1:10), which belongs to Jesus' appointed messenger. The Angel tells John that he will have a vision, and instructs him: "What thou seest, write in a Book, and send it unto the seven churches. . . . Write the things which thou hast seen, and the things which are, and the things which shall be hereafter" (1:11–19). John, God's faithful servant, is also his first official mailman, the bearer of the original apocogram.[14]

It is perhaps no accident that apocalypse finds its most appropriate symbol in the Book. Faced with the task of self-representation, apocalypse is led with a certain necessity to this particular image: not only is John told to write down what he sees, but the apocalyptic message per se is contained within and triggered by a virulent, exploding book, for the world's destruction is brought about by the opening of its seals. Everything happens as if the New Testament could end only by inventing a book-within-a-Book that portrays the end of the world, and its details bear such a remarkable similarity to descriptions of nuclear destruction they may be read as if they were in fact predicting it.[15]

In successive chapters, seven angels sound trumpets that mime a bomb's explosion in that each blast sets off a particular catastrophe: fires, earthquakes, falling stars, a blackout, blinding flashes of light, intense heat, scorched bodies:

The first angel sounded, and there followed hail and fire min-
gled with blood, and they were cast upon the earth, and the
third part of trees was burnt up, and all green grass was burnt
up.   [8:7]

And the second angel sounded, and as it were a great mountain
burning with fire was cast into the sea, and the third part of the
sea became blood.   [8:8]

And the third angel sounded, and there fell a great star from
heaven, burning as it were a lamp, and it fell upon the third
part of the rivers, and upon the fountains of water.   [8:10]

And the fourth angel poured out his vial upon the sun; and
power was given unto him to scorch men with fire. And men
were scorched with great heat, and blasphemed the name of
God. . . .   [16:8, 9]

It is precisely such an "apocalyptic reading" of the Book of Revelation, in which the Book's thematic resemblance to a nuclear explosion may be interpreted as predictive of it and a relay system is
set up whereby the Book's truth is reconfirmed, that I would like to
critique. Read in such a light, the Book of Revelation is indeed
apocalypse's vehicle, for it has the power actually to bring about the
catastrophe it seems merely to announce. What I would like to
emphasize, however, is the Book's double nature. On the one hand
it presents itself as the epitome of what a humanist might like to
believe a book can be and do: not only is its act of destruction the
instrument of salvation, a means of ushering in "a new heaven and
a new earth" (21:1); in addition it is the medium through which
God assures us of His presence and goodwill, the very source of
Truth itself. But the book-within-the-Book also has the destructive
power of nuclear weaponry, for to open it is equivalent to detona-
tion. Here a text functions exactly like a nuclear bomb: it blows up
the world. What a nonapocalyptic reading reveals is the Book's capacity to destroy as well as redeem—for the book itself is a bomb.

The notion of apocalyptic mail suggests that the logic at work in
the Book of Revelation is similar to that which produced the bomb,
as if John the mailman had perhaps not yet delivered his message,
and the Book kept in transit a missile that might explode at any
time. For nuclear weaponry, which brings with it the possibility of a
specific kind of catastrophe and death, both threatens to enact the

Christian text and gives rise to books about it, as if the Book and the bomb were co-conspirators in a mutual process of reproduction.

Scenarios of nuclear winter, which describe the probable aftermath of a nuclear war, are particularly striking in light of these parallels. This theory, which may be read as a contemporary version of the Book of Revelation, originated in 1982 when the editors of *Ambio*, the environmental journal of the Royal Swedish Academy of Sciences, commissioned Dutch scientist Paul Crutzen and his American colleague John Birks to investigate the effects of nuclear war on the atmosphere.[16] Rather than focusing on the increased amounts of ultraviolet radiation, as had previous studies, it occurred to them that heavy clouds of smoke and soot rising from fireballs ignited by nuclear weapons could block out sunlight from half the earth's surface for weeks on end; in short, that summer could be turned into winter in a week or two. The original study has given birth to a proliferation of texts that attempt to render scenarios of nuclear winter ever more precise.[17] Computer models, for example, indicate widespread crop destruction from the torrents of smoke that would be sent skyward by burning cities and forests, causing a chilling of the earth's climate, and speculate that damage to interdependent plant and animal populations might cause mass extinction.

If, before Crutzen and Birks, no one had convincingly calculated the effect of smoke, which is now believed to be the major determinant of the postnuclear climate, describing its consequences is an essential feature of nuclear winter narratives:

> After the explosions, and as the fires burned, the clouds of smoke would drift downwind, spreading outwards as they went. At first, near the fires, they would be so dense that the sunlight would be reduced to darkness, except for the light of the fires. They would drift hundreds of miles in hours and thousands of miles around the world in a week or two. After a few days the sunlight might begin to penetrate through, but only enough to raise the level of illumination to that of moonlight or twilight. Within a week or two, one could expect a continuous band of smoke and dust around the world, mostly between the latitudes 30 and 70 degrees North, where most of the World's population lives and where most of our crops are grown. By then it might be like twilight or a heavily overcast day, even at noon.[18]

Given the context, it is perhaps not surprising that the smoky darkness covering the earth after the opening of the Book's last seal is resonant with descriptions of nuclear winter: "And the fifth angel sounded, and I saw a star fall from heaven unto the earth: and to him was given the key of the bottomless pit. And he opened the bottomless pit; and there arose a smoke out of the pit, as the smoke of a great furnace; and the sun and the air were darkened by reason of the smoke of the pit" (9:1–2). Details such as these suggest that nuclear winter narratives may function as the Book's twin. For although there are important differences between Christian and nuclear apocalypse (one is divinely ordained and constructed, not made by human beings; one leads to a better world, the other to no world at all), both share a faith in the capacity of the word to bring about salvation; both assume that the truth does not partake of, and therefore can save us from, disaster, and that we can rely on knowledge—either in the form of a divinely inspired vision, or a computer-generated model—to protect us from catastrophe.

Nuclear winter is apocalyptic not only in that it provides a narrative that describes the end of the world; its theorists also believe the scenarios will act as a preventive measure. Robert J. Lifton, a psychiatrist who has studied nuclear winter imagery, emphasizes that the hypothesis helps justify the prediction that full-scale use of nuclear weapons might mean the end of civilization, and he is confident that describing the aftermath of a nuclear war will keep it from happening: "Nuclear winter tells us, loud and clear, precisely where hope lies: not in shelters, evacuation plans, and rebuilding from the ruins, but *only* in prevention."[19] And according to Carl Sagan, one of the nuclear winter theory's most influential American proponents, the policy implications of the new findings are "inescapable": "They point to . . . the necessity of moving as rapidly as possible to reduce the global nuclear arsenals below levels that could conceivably cause the kind of climactic catastrophe and cascading biological devastation predicted by the new studies."[20]

In spite of man's destructive history and continuing aggressivity, Sagan, like other proponents of the nuclear winter theory, is convinced that the word has an entirely prophylactic function, and that the more specific and detailed the scenario, the more likely it will be to function as a deterrent. Perhaps for this reason what is most at stake in nuclear winter narratives is the attempt to depict the aftermath of a nuclear war as meticulously as possible. Theorists of nuclear winter aim for maximum specificity regarding its effects, such as the size and extent of the fires that nuclear explosions would generate; and they construct graphs, formulae, charts, boxes, and diagrams so as to make increasingly precise calculations regarding the various details of the outcome of a nuclear war. Painstaking attention is given to calculating possible variations in, for example, the height of "smoke plumes of city fires ignited by thermonuclear weapons" and the approximate heights of mushroom clouds. It is as if the authors believe that the accuracy with which they are able to describe what has not yet occurred can influence whether or not the event will in fact take place, as if there were an inverse relationship between the text's capacity for deterrence and the precision of its details.[21]

Proponents of the nuclear winter theory do not question that describing the bomb's aftermath plays an important part in preventing its use. What they fail to consider is that the very mechanisms that produce and give birth to the one are also at work in the other. For if, as the Book of Revelation has shown, the Book and the bomb are two faces of the same coin, then the Book can kill as well as cure, and there is always the chance that it may bring about our destruction rather than save us from it. The Book cannot be trusted to deter the bomb because it is part of the very logic that produces it. And any theory—be it of representation or deterrence—that does not proceed from an awareness of the Book's double nature runs the risk of being complicit in and perpetuating what it seeks to prevent.

That the desire at work in the Book may not be radically different from that which produced the bomb: this is in part what humanism in its various guises—traditional feminist critiques and proponents of nuclear winter theory among them—cannot consider. Perhaps for this reason, they fail to examine two vital issues: the extent to which language in and of itself may be relied upon to function as a deterrent to the production and potential use of nuclear weapons, and the possibility that there is an atom in writing and its attendant technology that turns on and provokes an inadmissible desire: a desire for a nuclear end. A certain relationship between teleology and termination, in the sense of a proclivity for disaster, is built into what nuclear missiles bear with them and transport. For the possibility of nuclear extinction reintroduces the question of desire no longer on the scale of the individual or of a chosen race, but of the species. If every fear encases a desire, the site of an unthinkable

wish, then "nuclear desire" might be defined as that for a monstrous engulfment of individual entities and identities.[22] Its very
language—phrases such as "blows me away, cracks me up, awe-
some, wasted, what a blast"—incorporates this catastrophic desire
or desire for catastrophe, such that nuclear war would be its perverse, or sublime, fulfillment.

One of the tasks of a posthumanistic feminist criticism, then,
may be to investigate what more traditional criticisms preclude:
the notion of a desire, shared by both sexes, for annihilation or
apocalypse, and the possibility that a version of nuclear desire
might actually be at work within language itself. In this regard it is
important to examine *Hiroshima Mon Amour*, for Marguerite Duras's scenario confronts the very issues that the humanistic texts
we have encountered ignore.

Its very title announces the possibility of a seemingly impossible
conjunction: that between Hiroshima, the site of nuclear devastation, and "mon amour," the object of a woman's passionate love. In
so doing, it displaces the proper name's relationship to its referent,
for if "Hiroshima" can name one's lover and the city in which mass
destruction occurred, the same word has contradictory meanings—
it can signify collective violence and passionate love. *Hiroshima
Mon Amour* invites us to consider the relationship between po-
litico-historical and personal trauma, between "Hiroshima" and
"my love affair," death and eros. Its title thus encapsulates the very
issues at stake in the film, for the relationship between the name
and its referent—signifying the merger of public and private, political and erotic, universal and personal—is emblematic of this central question: who or what is named by "Hiroshima"?[23]

Hiroshima Mon Amour suggests a powerful critique of nuclear
war, and does so precisely in terms of its representation of gender. If
humanistic feminism reverses and reifies one term of a couple, and
in so doing unwittingly supports the binaristic thinking that is one
of patriarchy's principal strategies of self-maintenance, *Hiroshima
Mon Amour* lays waste to it. Rather than strengthening the line
that divides war from peace, sexuality from speech, or man from
woman, it blurs the difference between the two. In their place we
find Duras's meticulous exploration of her heroine's desire, the
agency by virtue of which these oppositions are dismantled. It is
probably no accident that Duras chooses a feminine protagonist,
calling her simply the anonymous "elle," to exemplify a desire that
humanism in its various guises refuses to acknowledge or allow. In

this context the name "Hiroshima" becomes synonymous with what the heroine desires—and fears, for what might occur when "Hiroshima" becomes identical to "my love"?

The kind of eroticism depicted is itself a violent merger in which individual identities are absorbed in a moment of blackout that is also equivalent to amorous union. The text suggests that erotic passion and destructive violence may be intimately bound up with one another, that "Hiroshima" and "mon amour" may have more in common than we might like to think. The very first image—an atomic mushroom cloud slowly disintegrates and reveals two figures embracing—makes it impossible for the viewer to decide, merely on the basis of what is seen, the difference between lovemaking and death. As Duras puts it, "In the beginning of the film we don't see this chance couple. Neither her nor him. Instead we see mutilated bodies—the head, the hips—moving—in the throes of love or death—and covered successively with the ashes, the dew, of atomic death—and the sweat of love fulfilled."[24] Duras implies that "atomic death" and "the sweat of love fulfilled" have something profoundly in common, such that one image can substitute for, or be confused with, the other. She invites speculation as to whether eroticism signifies love, death, or both at once, not in order to imply that there is no difference between the two, but rather to underscore the points at which they overlap. I suggest that sustaining rather than denying their points of intersection may offer a strategy of deterrence, in that it raises a question most critiques of nuclear weaponry do not: can Hiroshima be represented and, if so, how?

"Elle," a French actress whose name is never given, has come to Hiroshima to make "an enlightening" (edifiant, 64) film on Peace. ("It's not necessarily a ridiculous film," explains Duras, "merely an enlightening one" [39].) She meets and has a brief love affair with a Japanese architect, himself identified with death in that he is one of Hiroshima's "survivors," and they make love aware that whatever is thereby created will also be illuminated by the memory of total destruction. The opening dialogue, which takes place during their embrace, both emphasizes the interchangeability of love and death and interrogates the capacity of vision to convey the full significance of Hiroshima. His first words, "You saw nothing in Hiroshima. Nothing" (15), deny that *seeing* Hiroshima bears any necessary relationship to knowledge of it. "Elle" nonetheless insists: "I saw *everything. Everything*" (15), and enumerates it: the hospital, Peace Square, and various documentations of the catastrophe: the

Museum ("the people walk around, lost in thought, among the photographs, the reconstructions, for want of something else, among
the photographs, the photographs, the reconstructions, for photographs, the photographs, the reconstructions, for want of something
else, the explanations, for want of something else" [17]); newsreel
shots of Hiroshima taken after August 6, 1945; and photographs
showing Hiroshima's mutilated survivors. "Listen," she says finally, "I know. I know *everything*. It went on." "*Nothing*," he repeats, "You know *nothing*" (21). The film thus begins by interrogating the presumed equivalence of vision and knowledge. In so doing
it problematizes the authority of its own medium, questioning the
extent to which narrative forms based on reproducing what is
seen—museum exhibits, photographs, even documentaries—can
indeed convey the meaning of what they depict. For Duras the
name "Hiroshima" thus raises a complex epistemological question:
through what means, or medium, can nuclear war and its effects be
known?[25]

Duras's solution is to portray the perplexing intersection of nuclear and erotic desire. "Elle's" sexuality becomes the pivot around
which the possibility of symbolizing Hiroshima turns; and her capacity to articulate it coincides with the possibility of ever representing or mourning Hiroshima. As her first monologue reveals,
what she desires is an erotic effacement that may substitute for
nuclear catastrophe;[26] erotic pleasure becomes identical to absolute
erasure, simulating the total extinction that took place at Hiroshima:

> . . . I meet you.
> I remember you.
> Who are you?
> You destroy me.
> You're so good for me.
> How could I have known that this city was made
>   to the size of love?
> How could I have known that you were made to
>   the size of my body?
> You're great. How wonderful. You're great. . .
> How slow all of a sudden.
> And how sweet.
> More than you can know.
> You destroy me.

You're so good for me.
Plenty of time.
Please.
Take me.
Deform me, make me ugly.
Why not you?
Why not you in this city and in this night so
    like the others you can't tell the difference?
Please . . .   [24–25]

"I meet you, I remember you," says the heroine. The night at
Hiroshima is a repetition, but a repetition of what?[27] Not only of
her own history, whose most decisive event was a doomed first love
affair with a German soldier in her birthplace of Nevers during
World War II; it is also unquestionably a repetition of atomic catastrophe. It is as if the loss that took place there might be repaired
only by a semiotic-erotic explosion in which body and word con-
verge and leave nothing in their wake, save for the reiteration of an
impossible demand: "[Y]ou destroy me (tu me tues, 35), you're so
good for me." This phrase, whose repetition haunts the scenario
like a phantom or a caress, portrays Hiroshima's legacy as the
merger of nuclear devastation and desire, in which being deformed
or destroyed, and healed or made love to, are irreparably linked.[28]

Duras implies that identifying with Hiroshima's victims may be
a point of access to knowledge of it. The sentences "Please. Take
me. Deform me, make me ugly," are repeated near the end of the
script with a significant difference: "Take me. Deform me to your
likeness so that no one, after you, can understand the reason for so
much desire" (77). The wish in both instances is that her lover do
to her what the bomb did to Hiroshima's victims, to make her
body a simulacrum of its survivors, to deform her body as theirs
were deformed. But the latter phrase further suggests that the wish
for deformation produces rather than diminishes desire, and that
embracing such a desire is the condition for its transformation.
Eroticism is revealed to have an epistemological function, for it
displaces the assumption that sight is the privileged source of
knowledge and replaces it with touch as a means of representing
Hiroshima.

Words may take the place of a caress, but serve the same function. It is essential that the Japanese enable her to experience the
erotic intensities nuclear desire instills. Making love with him al-

lows her to identify with and then articulate the possibility of her own nonexistence; it renders transparent the ways in which erotic passion is also marked by death. The bond, or disfigurement, established erotically allows her to tell the Japanese the story she's never told. Shortly before leaving Japan, ("all we can do now is kill the time left before your departure; still 16 hours before your plane leaves" [52]), she describes her love for the German, who was killed by her countrymen the day Nevers was liberated, and its aftermath: she goes mad, and is locked in the cellar by her parents as punishment (she scrapes the skin of her hands and licks them as if to taste her lover's blood). When she regains sanity, she can no longer remember him. She survives, but as one deformed, a war victim with invisible wounds.

Language can also become a kind of fallout, resulting from amorous fusion. The condition for being able to tell her story is that the Japanese substitute for the German. The phrase "I meet you, I remember you," means that meeting the one reminds her of the other; desire brings the dead back to life, and allows a certain "resurrection" to take place: "When we see them now they are almost happy. They don't notice the time passing. A miracle has occurred. What miracle? The resurrection of Nevers" (53). Duras employs traditional religious terminology in a way that parodies and displaces Christian thought. What is at stake is the articulation of a "miracle" that neither participates in nor reinscribes the logic of apocalypse and revelation. In this text there is no possibility of averting death; no hope for an eternal life in the world to come (their love, for example, leads toward rather than away from a final separation); no assurance that we can prevent the reoccurrence of a nuclear catastrophe. This miracle offers neither salvation nor insurance against trauma; on the contrary, confronting and reexperiencing what has been lost is its necessary precondition. The revelation is rather that the dead may return to life only in symbolic form. Representation provides the sole nonapocalyptic afterlife; and burial precedes the dead's preservation. But in the posthumanistic logic of *Hiroshima Mon Amour*, neither eros nor the Word can protect us from loss—or nuclear disaster; and if they function as deterrents they do so only when we proceed from the awareness that both are complicit in and partake of what they are employed to critique. The question that remains, finally, is not whether we can open the Book or keep it closed, but instead ask how to read, and reenact, it.

Notes

I would like to thank Helen Cooper, Adrienne Munich, and Susan Squier for their many helpful critical responses to earlier versions of this paper; Frances Ferguson, whose essay "The Nuclear Sublime," provided its inspiration; and Gillian Brown, for her friendship.

1. This essay, a meditation on the politics (and "ends") of humanism, particularly in relation to Heidegger's concept of Dasein ("human reality"), has no ostensible relation to the topic of nuclear war. Nonetheless its emphasis on "the human" makes it an interesting precursor to Derrida's "No Apocalypse, Not Now," cited below.

2. Derrida, "No Apocalypse, Not Now," 22.

3. Osmanczyk, "UNESCO Constitution," 827.

4. Cixous, "Sorties," 63–64.

5. Jardine, "Death Sentences," 120.

6. Scarry, *The Body in Pain*, 87–88.

7. Caldicott, *Missile Envy*, 316. All subsequent references are to this edition and are given parenthetically within the text.

8. Koen and Swaim, *Aint No Where We Can Run*, 1.

9. Nottingham WONT, "Working as a Group," 23.

10. Virilio and Lotringer, *Pure War*, 110.

11. Klein, "*Diacritics* Colloquium on Nuclear Criticism," 2.

12. The phrase is Ronell's. See *Dictations: On Haunted Writing*, xv.

13. I am responding in part to Derrida's suggestion that the epoch of the book and that of theology and divinity are intimately bound up with one another. In *Of Grammatology*, for example, he argues that "the sign and divinity have the same place and time of birth. The age of the sign is essentially theological. Perhaps it will never *end*. Its historical *closure* is, however, outlined." See Derrida, *Of Grammatology*, 14. The interested reader might also see Derrida's persuasive remarks on the relationship between fiction, rhetoric, and nuclear weaponry in "No Apocalypse, Not Now," cited earlier.

14. For Derrida's reading of the "apocalyptic tone" put forward by the Book of Revelation, especially as pertaining to the metaphysics of postal systems, see "Of an Apocalyptic Tone," 3–37.

15. David Dowling's *Fictions of Nuclear Disaster*, a comprehensive study of fictional treatments of the bomb, also remarks upon the similarities between the Book of Revelation and a nuclear explosion. His discussion, however, focuses only on their shared thematics, emphasizing common patterns of imagery: Dowling does not investigate the possibility of a structural affinity. Perhaps for this reason he does not notice that a book serves the function of a bomb in the Book of Revelation, and he takes it for granted that fiction acts as a deterrent to the bomb's use: "Fictions of nuclear disaster . . . call on the power of the word to de-fuse the power of the

fused atom" (218). See in particular "Apocalypse and Revelations" in *Fictions of Nuclear Disaster*, 115–44.

16. Crutzen and Birks, "The Atmosphere after a Nuclear War," 114–25.

17. For a description of current nuclear winter literature, see Greene, Percival, and Ridge, *Nuclear Winter*, 71–76.

18. Ibid., 59.

19. Lifton, "Imagining the Real," 93.

20. Sagan, "Nuclear War and Climatic Castastrophe," 11.

21. Unfortunately nuclear winter scenarios have not functioned to deter the production of U.S. nuclear missiles. According to the *Statistical Abstract of the United States*, the estimated number of U.S. strategic nuclear forces has changed very little since 1978. Between 1978 and 1984 the estimate was for 2,100 long-range intercontinental missiles, with a total of 9,854 warheads. The 1985 edition revised the estimate for 1983 to 1,884 missiles and 9,439 warheads. And the 1986 edition, valid for 1985, shows a total of 1,963 missiles with 10,398 warheads. There are evidently slightly fewer missiles, but 544 more warheads in circulation today than there were when the nuclear winter theory originated. See the *Statistical Abstract of the United States: 1986*, 339.

22. These speculations regarding a possible "nuclear desire" owe a great deal to Freud's controversial theory of the "death drive" developed in *Beyond the Pleasure Principle*. Here Freud argues that the fundamental tendency of every living being is to return to the inorganic state. Although lengthy analysis is impossible in this context, "nuclear desire" might be distinguished from the Freudian death drive in that it would not wish for the reduction of tension to zero-point (although a nuclear bomb certainly would accomplish precisely that), but rather for a fusion or a merger of organic and inorganic that could not definitively be separated from, or opposed to, eros in the way that Freud often appears to wish.

23. For an especially interesting essay on the relationship between historical and personal narratives in *Hiroshima Mon Amour*, see Glassman, "The Feminine Subject."

24. Duras, *Hiroshima Mon Amour*, 8 (9–10 in French edition). All subsequent references are from the English edition and will be given in parentheses within the text. Whenever the resonance of the original is pertinent, I have preserved the French in parentheses followed by the page number of the French edition.

25. My reading is particularly indebted to Sharon Willis's insightful and original study of the work of Marguerite Duras. For her illuminating treatment of *Hiroshima Mon Amour*, especially as pertaining to issues of femininity, hysteria, and writing, see "*Hiroshima Mon Amour*: Screen Memories," in Willis, *Marguerite Duras: Writing on the Body*, 33–62.

26. For a discussion of erasure and eroticism in *Hiroshima Mon Amour*, see Ames, "Writing, Violence and Memory."

27. See Sanford S. Ames's study of repetition and forgetfulness in the films of Marguerite Duras, "The Skin of Film, the Edge of Talk," 27–31. I am greatly indebted to this essay as well as Ames's "Writing, Violence and Memory."

28. See Julia Kristeva's discussion of *Hiroshima Mon Amour* as pertaining to notions of postmodern love in "The Pain of Sorrow."

Works Cited

Ames, Sanford S. "The Skin of Film, the Edge of Talk: Marguerite Duras." *Cream City Review* 6, no. 1 (Fall 1980): 27–31.

———. "Writing, Violence and Memory: Marguerite Duras." *Cincinnati Romance Review* 2 (1983): 60–69.

Caldicott, Helen. *Missile Envy: The Arms Race and Nuclear War.* New York: Bantam Books, 1985.

Cixous, Hélène. "Sorties." In *The Newly Born Woman*, translated by Betsy Wing, 63–132. Minneapolis: Minnesota University Press, 1986.

Crutzen, P. J., and J. W. Birks. "The Atmosphere after a Nuclear War: Twilight at Noon." *Ambio* 11 (1982): 114–25.

Derrida, Jacques. "The Ends of Man." Translated by Edouard Morot-Sir, Wesley L. Piersol, Hubert L. Dreyfus, and Barbara Reid. *Philosophical and Phenomenological Research* 30 (1970): 31–57.

———. "No Apocalypse, Not Now: Full Speed Ahead, Seven Missiles, Seven Missives." Translated by Catherine Porter and Philip Lewis. *Diacritics* 14, no. 12 (1984): 20–31.

———. "Of an Apocalyptic Tone Recently Adopted in Philosophy." Translated by John P. Leavey, Jr. *The Oxford Literary Review* 6, no. 2 (1984): 3–37.

———. *Of Grammatology.* Translated by Gayatri Chakravorty Spivak. Baltimore and London: Johns Hopkins University Press, 1976.

Dowling, David. "Apocalypse and Revelations." In *Fictions of Nuclear Disaster*, 115–44. Iowa City: University of Iowa Press, 1987.

Duras, Marguerite. *Hiroshima Mon Amour.* Translated by Richard Seaver. New York: Grove Press, 1961.

———. *Hiroshima, mon amour.* Paris: Gallimard, 1960.

Freud, Sigmund. *Beyond the Pleasure Principle.* Translated and edited by James Strachey. New York: W. W. Norton & Co., 1961.

Glassman, Debbie. "The Feminine Subject as History Writer in *Hiroshima Mon Amour*." *Enclitic* 5, no. 1 (Spring 1981): 45–53.

Greene, Owen, Ian Percival, and Irene Ridge. *Nuclear Winter: The Evidence and the Risks.* Cambridge, Mass.: Polity Press, 1985.

Jardine, Alice. "Death Sentences: Writing Couples and Ideology." *Poetics Today* 6, nos. 1–2 (1985): 119–31.

Klein, Richard. "Proposal for a *Diacritics* Colloquium on Nuclear Criticism." *Diacritics* 14, no. 2 (Summer 1984): 2.

Koen, Susan and Nina Swaim. *Aint No Where We Can Run: Handbook for Women on the Nuclear Mentality*. Norwich, Conn.: WAND, 1980.

Kristeva, Julia. "The Pain of Sorrow in the Modern World: The Works of Marguerite Duras." *PMLA* 102, no. 2 (March 1987): 138–52.

Lifton, Robert J. "Imagining the Real." In *The Long Darkness*, edited by Lester Grinspoon, 90–114. New Haven: Yale University Press, 1986.

Nottingham WONT. "Working as a Group: Nottingham Women Oppose the Nuclear Threat." In *Keeping the Peace*, edited by Lynn Jones, 18–29. London: Women's Press, 1983.

Osmanczyk, Edmund Jan. "UNESCO Constitution." *Encyclopedia of the United Nations and International Agreements*. Philadelphia and London: Taylor & Francis, 1985.

Ronell, Avital. *Dictations: On Haunted Writing*. Bloomington: Indiana University Press, 1986.

Sagan, Carl. "Nuclear War and Climatic Catastrophe." In *The Long Darkness*, edited by Lester Grinspoon, 8–21. New Haven: Yale University Press, 1986.

Scarry, Elaine. *The Body in Pain: The Making and Unmaking of the World*. New York, Oxford: Oxford University Press, 1985.

U.S. Bureau of the Census. *Statistical Abstract of the United States, 1986*. 106th ed. Washington, D.C.: U.S. Government Printing Office, 1985.

Virilio, Paul, and Sylvere Lotringer. *Pure War*. Translated by Mark Polizotti. New York: Semiotext(e), 1983.

Willis, Sharon. *Marguerite Duras: Writing on the Body*. Urbana and Chicago: University of Illinois Press, 1987.

Jennifer A Bibliography of
Clarke
Secondary Sources

Adam-Smith, Patsy. *Australian Women at War*. Melbourne, Victoria: Nelson, 1984.

Anderson, Karen. *Wartime Women: Sex Roles, Family Relations, and the Status of Women during World War II*. Westport, Conn.: Greenwood Press, 1981.

Andrews, Matthew Page, comp. *The Women of the South in War Times*. Baltimore: Norman, Remington Co., 1920, 1924.

Arendt, Hannah. *The Human Condition*. Chicago: University of Chicago Press, 1958.

———. *On Revolution*. New York: Penguin Books, 1977.

Barash, Carol L. "From Feminism to Literature: *Freewoman's* Debate with the Suffragettes." Forthcoming in *Literary Studies*.

Batsleer, Janet, Tony Davies, Rebecca O'Rourke, Chris Weedon, eds. *Rewriting English: Cultural Politics of Gender and Class*. London: Methuen, 1985.

Beard, Mary Ritter. *Woman as Force in History: A Study in Traditions and Realities*. 1946. Reprint. New York: Farrar, Straus & Giroux, 1981.

Berkin, Carol R., and Clara M. Lovett, eds. *Women, War, and Revolution*. New York: Holmes & Meier, 1980.

Binkin, Martin, and Shirley J. Bach. *Women and the Military*. Washington, D.C.: Brookings Institution, 1977.

Bradbury, Malcolm. "The Denuded Place: War and Form in *Parade's End* and *U.S.A.*" In *The First World War in Fiction*, edited by Holger Klein. London: Macmillan & Co., 1976.

Braybon, Gail. *Women Workers in the First World War: The British Experience*. London: Croom Helm; Totowa, N.J.: Barnes & Noble, 1981.

———, and Penny Summerfield. *Out of the Cage: Women's Experiences in Two World Wars*. New York: Methuen (Pandora Press), 1987.

Bridenthal, Renate, and Claudia Koonz. *Becoming Visible: Women in European History*. Boston: Houghton Mifflin, 1977.

Bruce, Jean. *Back the Attack!: Canadian Women during the Second World War—at Home and Abroad.* Toronto: Macmillan of Canada, 1985.

Buck, Pearl S. *Of Men and Women.* New York: John Day, 1941.

Byles, Joan Montgomery. "Women's Experience of World War I: Suffragists, Pacifists, and Poets." In *Women's Studies International Forum* 8, no. 5 (1985): 473–87.

Byrd, Barthy. *Home Front: Women and Vietnam.* Berkeley, Calif.: Shameless Hussy Press, 1986.

Cadogan, Mary, and Patricia Craig. *Women and Children First.* London: Gollancz, 1978.

Calder, Angus. *The People's War: Britain, 1939–45.* New York: Pantheon Books, 1969.

Caldicott, Helen. *Missile Envy: The Arms Race and Nuclear War.* New York: Morrow, 1984.

Cambridge Women's Peace Collective, eds. *My Country Is the Whole World: An Anthology of Women's Work on Peace and War.* Boston: Routledge & Kegan Paul, 1984.

Campbell, D'Ann. *Women at War with America: Private Lives, Patriotic Era.* Cambridge, Mass.: Harvard University Press, 1985.

Carr, Jean. *Another Story: Women and the Falklands War.* London: H. Hamilton, 1984.

Chafe, William. *The American Woman: Her Changing Social, Economic, and Political Roles, 1920–1970.* New York: Oxford University Press, 1972.

Chapkis, Wendy, ed. *Loaded Questions: Women in the Military.* Amsterdam and Washington: Transnational Institute, 1981.

Clausewitz, Carl von. *On War.* Edited and translated by Michael Howard and Peter Paret. Princeton, N.J.: Princeton University Press, 1984.

Cohn, Carol. "Sex and Death in the Rational World of Defense Intellectuals." *Signs* 12, no. 4 (1987): 687–718.

Cooke, Miriam. *War's Other Voices: Women Writers in the Lebanese Civil War.* Cambridge, Mass.: Cambridge University Press, 1988.

Cottam, K. J., ed. and trans. *The Golden-Tressed Soldier.* Manhattan, Kans.: MA/AH Publishing, 1983.

———. *Soviet Airwomen in Combat in World War II.* Manhattan, Kans.: MA/AH Publishing, 1983.

Davis, Natalie Zemon. "Men, Women, and Violence: Some Reflections on Equality." *Smith Alumnae Quarterly* 69 (April 1977): 12–15.

Dullea, Georgia. "Women Who Served in Vietnam Emerge as Victims of War Strain." *New York Times*, March 23, 1981, pp. 1, B-12.

Duras, Marguerite. *War*. New York: Pantheon Books, 1986.

Eastman, Crystal. "How I Dare Do It." In *Crystal Eastman on Women and Revolution*, edited by Blanche Cook. New York: Oxford University Press, 1978.

Ellet, Elizabeth F. *The Women of the American Revolution*. 3 vols. New York: Haskell House, 1850. Reprint 1969.

Elshtain, Jean Bethke. *Public Man, Private Woman: Women in Social and Political Thought*. Princeton, N.J.: Princeton University Press, 1981.

––––––. *Women and War*. New York: Basic Books, 1987.

––––––. "Women as Mirror and Other: Toward a Theory of Women, War, and Feminism." *Humanities in Society* 5, no. 2 (Winter–Spring 1982): 32.

––––––, and Sheila Tobias. *Women, Militarism, and War*. Totowa, N.J.: Rowman & Littlefield, forthcoming.

Enloe, Cynthia. *Does Khaki Become You? The Militarization of Women's Lives*. Boston: South End Press, 1983.

Foley, Helene P., ed. *Reflections of Women in Antiquity*. New York: Gordon & Breach Science Publishers, 1981.

Foulkes, A. P. *Literature and Propaganda*. London, New York: Methuen, 1983.

Fourcade, Marie-Madeleine. *Noah's Ark*. New York: E. P. Dutton, 1974. Originally published as *L'Arche de Noe*. Paris: Fayard, 1968.

Fourtouni, Eleni, trans. and comp. *Greek Women in Resistance: Journals, Oral Histories*. New Haven: Thelphini Press; Chicago: Lake View Press, 1986.

Fussell, Paul. *The Great War and Modern Memory*. London, Oxford, New York: Oxford University Press, 1975.

Garner, Shirley Nelson, Claire Kahane, Madelon Spregnether, eds. *The (M)Other Tongue: Essays in Feminist Psychoanalytic Interpretation*. Ithaca, N.Y.: Cornell University Press, 1985.

Giffen, Frederick C., ed. *Woman as Revolutionary*. New York and Scarborough, Ontario: New American Library, 1973.

Gilbert, Sandra M. "Soldier's Heart: Literary Men, Literary

Women, and the Great War." *Signs* 8, no. 3 (Spring 1983): 422–50.

Gluck, Sherna Berger. *Rosie the Riveter Revisited: Women, the War, and Social Change.* Boston: G. K. Hall, 1987.

Goldman, Nancy L. *Female Soldiers: Combatants or Noncombatants? Historical and Contemporary Perspectives.* Westport, Conn.: Greenwood Press, 1982.

Goldsmith, Margaret. *Women at War.* London: L. Drummond, 1943.

Gordon, Sarah. *Hitler, Germans, and the "Jewish Question."* Princeton, N.J.: Princeton University Press, 1984.

Gray, J. Glenn. *The Warriors: Reflections on Men in Battle.* New York: Harper Colophon, 1970.

Greenwald, Maurine. *Women, War, and Work: The Impact of World War I on Women Workers in the United States.* Westport, Conn.: Greenwood Press, 1980.

Gribble, Francis Henry. *Women in War.* New York: Dutton, 1917.

Halloran, Richard. "Women, Blacks, Spouses Transforming the Military." *New York Times*, August 25, 1986, 1.

Hartmann, Susan M. *The Home Front and Beyond: American Women in the 1940's.* Boston: Twayne, 1982.

———. "Prescriptions for Penelope: Literature on Women's Obligations to Returning World War II Veterans." *Women's Studies* 5 (1978): 223–39.

———. "Women's Organizations during World War II: The Interaction of Class, Race, and Feminism." In *Woman's Being, Woman's Place: Female Identity and Vocation in American History,* edited by Mary Kelley. Boston: G. K. Hall, 1980.

Hartsock, Nancy C. *Money, Sex, and Power: Toward a Feminist Historical Materialism.* Boston: Northeastern University Press, 1985.

———. "Prologue to a Feminist Critique of War and Politics." In *Women's View of the Political World of Men,* edited by Judith H. Stiehm. Dobbs Ferry, N.Y.: TransNational Publishers, 1984.

Hewison, Robert. *Under Siege: Literary Life in London. 1939–45.* London: Weidenfeld & Nicholson, 1977.

Hibbert, Joyce, ed. *The War Brides.* Toronto: Peter Martin Associates, 1978.

Higonnet, Margaret Randolph, Jane Jenson, Sonya Michel, and Margaret Collins Weitz, eds. *Behind the Lines: Gender and the Two World Wars.* New Haven: Yale University Press, 1987.

Honey, Maureen. *Creating Rosie the Riveter: Class, Gender, Propaganda during World War II.* Amherst: University of Massachusetts Press, 1984.

Howard, Michael. *The Causes of War.* Cambridge, Mass.: Harvard University Press, 1984.

Humphreys, Sally. *The Family, Woman, and Death.* Boston: Routledge & Kegan Paul, 1983.

Huston, Nancy. "The Matrix of War: Mothers and Heroes." In *The Female Body in Western Culture: Contemporary Perspectives,* edited by Susan Rubin Suleiman, 120–36. Cambridge, Mass.: Harvard University Press, 1986.

———. "Tales of War and Tears of Women." *Women's Studies International Forum* 5, no. 3/4 (1982): 271–82.

Katz, Esther, and Joan Miriam Ringelheim, eds. Proceedings of the Conference on Women Surviving the Holocaust. New York: Institute for Research in History, 1983.

Kennedy, David M. *Over Here: The First World War and American Society.* New York: Oxford University Press, 1980.

King, Olive. *One Woman at War: Letters of Olive King, 1915–1920.* Edited and with an introduction by Hazel King. Melbourne: Melbourne University Press, 1986.

Kristeva, Julia. *Powers of Horror.* Translated by Leon S. Roudiez. New York: Columbia University Press, 1982.

Laska, Vera. *Women in the Resistance and the Holocaust: The Voices of Eyewitnesses.* Westport, Conn.: Greenwood Press, 1983.

Leed, Eric. *No Man's Land: Combat and Identity in World War One.* New York: Cambridge University Press, 1979.

McArthur, Judith N. "From Rosie the Riveter to the Feminine Mystique: An Historiographical Survey of American Women and World War II." *Bulletin of Bibliography* 44 (March 1987): 10–18.

Macdonald, Sharon, Pat Holden, and Shirley Ardener, eds. *Images of Women in Peace and War: Cross-cultural and Historical Perspectives.* Houndmills, Basingstoke, Hampshire, and London: The Macmillan Press Ltd., 1987; Madison: University of Wisconsin Press, 1988.

McGuigan, Dorothy G., ed. *The Role of Women in Conflict and Peace.* Ann Arbor: University of Michigan Press, 1977.

McLaren, Barbara. *Women of the War.* New York: George H. Doan Co., 1918.

McMillan, James F. *Housewife or Harlot: The Place of Women in*

French Society, 1870–1940. New York: St. Martin's Press, 1981.

Milkman, Ruth. *Gender at Work: The Dynamics of Job Segregation by Sex during World War II.* Champaign: University of Illinois Press, 1987.

Minns, Raynes. *Bombers and Mash: The Domestic Front, 1939–1945.* London: Virago Press, 1980.

Mitchell, David. *Monstrous Regiment: The Story of the Women of the First World War.* New York: Macmillan Co., 1965.

———. *Women on the Warpath: The Story of the Women of the First World War.* London: Jonathan Cape, 1966.

Moore, Frank. *Women of the War: Their Heroism and Self-Sacrifice.* Hartford, Conn.: S. S. Scranton, 1867.

Pierson, Ruth Roach. *They're Still Women after All: The Second World War and Canadian Womanhood.* Toronto, Ontario: McClelland & Stewart, 1986.

Playne, Caroline E. *Society at War, 1914–1916.* Boston: Houghton Mifflin, 1931.

Polenberg, Richard. *War and Society: The United States, 1941–1945.* Philadelphia: Lippincott, 1972.

Reardon, Betty. *Sexism and the War System.* New York: Teachers College Press, 1985.

Reilly, Catherine W., ed. *Chaos of the Night: Women's Poetry and Verse of the Second World War.* London: Virago Press, 1984.

———. *Scars Upon My Heart: Women's Poetry and Verse of the First World War.* London: Virago Press, 1981.

Ridd, Rosemary, and Helen Callaway, eds. *Caught Up in Conflict: Women's Responses to Political Strife.* Houndmills, Basingstoke, Hampshire: Macmillan Education in association with Oxford University Women's Studies Committee, 1986.

Riley, Denise. *War in the Nursery: Theories of the Child and the Mother.* London: Virago Press, 1983.

Rogan, Helen. *Mixed Company: Women in the Modern Army.* New York: G. P. Putnam's Sons, 1981.

Rossiter, Margaret L. *Women in the Resistance.* New York: Praeger, 1986.

Ruddick, Sara. "Maternal Thinking." In *Mothering: Essays in Feminist Theory,* edited by Joyce Trebilcot. Totowa, N.J.: Rowman & Allanheld, 1984.

———. "Pacifying the Forces: Drafting Women in the Interests of Peace." *Signs* 8, no. 3 (Spring 1983): 471–89.

———. "Preservative Love and Military Destruction: Some Reflections on Mothers and Peace." In *Mothering: Essays in Feminist Theory*, edited by Joyce Trebilcot. Totowa, N.J.: Rowman & Allanheld, 1984.

Rupp, Leila J. *Mobilizing Women for War: German and American Propaganda, 1939–1945*. Princeton, N.J.: Princeton University Press, 1978.

Saxonhouse, Arlene. "Men, Women, War, and Politics: Family and Polis in Aristophanes and Euripedes." *Political Theory* 8 (February 1980): 65–81.

Saywell, Shelley. *Women in War*. Ontario: Viking; New York: Viking Penguin, 1985.

Scarry, Elaine. *The Body in Pain: The Making and Unmaking of the World*. New York, Oxford: Oxford University Press, 1985.

Scharr, Adela Riek. *Sisters in the Sky*. Gerald, Mo.: Patrice Press, 1986.

Schreiner, Olive. "Woman and War." *Women and Labor*. London: T. F. Unwin, 1911. Reprint. London: Virago Press, 1978.

Schweik, Susan M. "A Word No Man Can Say For Us: American Women Writers and the Second World War." Ph.D. dissertation, Yale University, 1984.

Shorer, Michele. "Roles and Images of Women in World War I Propaganda." *Politics and Society* 5 (1975): 469–86.

Stiehm, Judith Hicks. *Bring Me Men and Women: Mandated Change at the U.S. Air Force Academy*. Berkeley: University of California Press, 1981.

———, ed. *Women and Men's Wars*. Special issue of *Women's Studies International Forum* 5, no. 3/4, (1982).

Steinson, Barbara J. *American Women's Activism in World War I*. New York: Garland Publishing, 1982.

Summerfield, Penny. *Women Workers in the Second World War: Production and Patriarchy in Conflict*. London: Croom Helm, 1984.

Summers, Anne. *Angels and Citizens: British Women as Military Nurses, 1854–1914*. London, New York: Routledge & Kegan Paul, 1988.

Thebaud, Françoise. *La femme au temps de la guerre de 14*. Paris: Stock, 1986.

Theweleit, Klaus. *Male Fantasies*. Translated by Stephan Conway in collaboration with Erica Carter and Chris Turner. Minneapolis: University of Minnesota Press, 1987.

Thomas, Mary Martha. *Riveting and Rationing in Dixie: Alabama*

Women and the Second World War. Tuscaloosa: University of Alabama Press, 1987.

Thomson, Dorothy, ed. *Over Our Dead Bodies: Women Against the Bomb.* London: Virago Press, 1983.

Walzer, Michael. *Just and Unjust Wars: A Moral Argument with Historical Illustrations.* New York: Basic Books, 1977.

Warner, Lavinia, and John Sandilands. *Women Beyond the Wire: A Story of Prisoners of the Japanese, 1942–1945.* London: M. Joseph, 1982.

Warner, Marina. *Joan of Arc: The Image of Female Heroism.* New York: Vintage Books, 1982.

Whalen, Robert Weldon. *Bitter Wounds: German Victims of the Great War, 1914–1939.* Ithaca, N.Y.: Cornell University Press, 1984.

Willenz, June A. *Women Veterans: America's Forgotten Heroines.* New York: Continuum, 1983.

Wiltsher, Anne. *Most Dangerous Women: Feminist Peace Campaigners of the Great War.* London: Pandora, 1985.

Winther, Sophus K. *The Realistic War Novel.* Folcroft, Pa.: Folcroft Press, 1969.

Women's Division of Soka Gokkai. *Women Against War.* Translated by Richard L. Gage, with an introduction by Richard H. Minnear. Tokyo: Kondansha International, 1986.

Woodward, C. Vann, and Elisabeth Muhlenfeld, eds. *The Private Mary Chesnut: The Unpublished Civil War Diaries.* New York: Oxford University Press, 1984.

Yedlin, Tova, ed. *Women in Eastern Europe and the Soviet Union.* New York: Praeger, 1980.

Young, Agnes Brooks. *The Women and the Crisis: Women of the North in the Civil War.* New York: McDowell, Obolensky, 1959.

Zanotti, Barbara. "Patriarchy: A State of War." In *Reweaving the Web of Life,* edited by Pam McAllister. Philadelphia: New Society Publishers, 1982.

The Contributors

Carol J. Adams is a feminist writer and activist who has been involved over the past ten years with the issues of domestic and sexual violence, vegetarianism and animal rights, and low-income housing and white racism. Her activities have included founding a Hotline for Battered Women and chairing the Housing Committee for Governor Cuomo's Commission on Domestic Violence. She has a Master of Divinity from Yale University. With a grant from the Culture and Animals Foundation she is finishing a book—"Against the Texts of Meat"—which explores how a patriarchal culture authorizes meat eating. Previous articles on this subject include "The Rape of Animals, the Butchering of Women," (in *Critical Matrix*, 1988) and "The Sexual Politics of Meat" (in *Heresies*, no. 21). Her article "The Male Gaze and Animal Experimentation" will appear in an anthology on the relationship between women and animals forthcoming from Cleis Press.

Gillian Brown has published essays on domestic politics in *Uncle Tom's Cabin* and on representations of motherhood and agoraphobia. She teaches in the English Department at Rutgers University.

Patricia Francis Cholakian teaches French at Hamilton College. Her publications include coauthorship of *The Early French Novella*, a critical introduction to Marie de Gournay's *Le Proumenoir de M. de Montaigne*, and articles in *Romance Notes*, *The French Review*, *Theatre Journal*, *Prose Studies*, and *Seeking the Woman in Late Medieval and Renaissance Writings*. At present, she is studying "feminine writing" in the *Heptameron*.

Jennifer Clarke is Assistant to the President at the State University of New York at Stony Brook, where she received her doctorate in the Department of English. Her study is entitled, " 'Know This Is Your War': British Women Writers of the Two World Wars." Her review of *Behind the Lines: Gender and the Two World Wars*, edited by Margaret R. Higonnet et al., is in *the minnesota review*, Fall 1987.

Helen M. Cooper teaches Victorian literature and feminist theory at the State University of New York at Stony Brook. She is author of *Elizabeth Barrett Browning, Woman and Artist* (University of North Carolina Press, 1988). She is coeditor of *the minnesota review: a journal of committed writing.*

Barbara Freeman teaches Western Culture and Feminist Studies at Stanford University. Her work has appeared in *Cahiers du GRIF, Oxford Literary Review, Paragraph,* and *Sub-Stance.*

Sara Friedrichsmeyer is Associate Professor of German at the University of Cincinnati, Raymond Walters College, where she teaches courses in both German and Women's Studies. She has published in the areas of German Romanticism and feminist literary theory, and is currently working on a monograph on German women's autobiographical writing.

Esther Fuchs is an Associate Professor of Hebrew Literature at the Department of Oriental Studies, the University of Arizona, Tucson. She is the author of numerous essays on women (both authors and characters) in modern and biblical Hebrew literature. She is the author of *Israeli Mythogynies: Women in Contemporary Hebrew Fiction* (SUNY Press, 1987). Her forthcoming book, from Indiana University Press, is *Sexual Politics in the Biblical Narrative: Toward a Feminist Hermeneutics of the Hebrew Bible.*

Lorraine Helms, Assistant Professor of English at Simmons College, teaches dramatic literature and theater history. She has written on both classical and Renaissance drama and is currently completing *The Saint in the Brothel: Or, Eloquence Rewarded,* a study of the rhetoric of gender and violence in English Renaissance drama.

Margaret R. Higonnet, Professor of English at the University of Connecticut, has written essays on romantic and modern literary theory; she has coedited *The Representation of Women in Fiction* (Johns Hopkins University Press), *Behind the Lines: Gender and the Two World Wars* (Yale University Press), and several volumes of the journal *Children's Literature.* Her current projects include a book on eighteenth-century French suicide and a study of the feminist contribution to comparative criticism.

June Jordan is Professor of English and Director of the Poetry Center and the Creative Writing Program at the State University of

New York at Stony Brook. Her most recent book of poetry is *Living Room, New Poems, 1980–1984* (Thunder's Mouth Press, 1985); *On Call, New Political Essays, 1981–1985* was published by South End Press in 1985.

James Longenbach is Associate Professor of English at the University of Rochester. He is author of *Modernist Poetics of History: Pound, Eliot, and the Sense of the Past* (Princeton University Press, 1987) and *Stone Cottage: Pound, Yeats, and Modernism* (Oxford University Press, 1988).

Jane Marcus, Professor of English, CUNY Graduate Center and the City College of New York, is the author of *Art and Anger: Reading Like a Woman* (Ohio State University Press, 1988), and *Virginia Woolf and the Language of Patriarchy* (Indiana University Press, 1987), and editor of three collections of essays on Woolf. Her most recent collection is *Suffrage and the Pankhursts* (Routledge & Kegan Paul, 1987).

Laura Stempel Mumford is a feminist writer and scholar living in Madison, Wisconsin. She has written about Olive Schreiner, feminist writing, popular culture, and the pain of academic displacement.

Adrienne Auslander Munich teaches Victorian Literature and feminist theory at the State University of New York at Stony Brook. She is author of *Andromeda's Chains: Victorian Interpretation and Gender* (Columbia University Press, 1989) and editor of *Browning Institute Studies: An Annual of Victorian Literary and Cultural History*. Her published articles are on feminist theory, Queen Victoria, and "Tootsie," among other subjects.

Sharon O'Brien is Professor of English and American Studies at Dickinson College. She is the author of *Willa Cather: The Emerging Voice* (Oxford University Press, 1987), and the editor of *The Library of America Willa Cather, Volumes I and II* (Literary Classics of the United States). Her current projects include a study of Irish women writers and of the culture of tourism.

Jane E. Schultz, Assistant Professor of English at Indiana University-Indianapolis (IUPUI), is at work on a manuscript about American women at the Civil War battlefront.

Susan Schweik is an Assistant Professor of English at the University of California at Berkeley and author of the forthcoming *A Gulf*

So Deeply Cut: American Women Poets and the Second World War, to be published by the University of Wisconsin Press.

Susan Merrill Squier teaches Modern British literature and feminist theory and criticism at the State University of New York at Stony Brook. She is editor of *Women Writers and the City: Essays in Feminist Literary Criticism* (University of Tennessee Press, 1984), and author of *Virginia Woolf and London: The Sexual Politics of the City* (University of North Carolina Press, 1985). She is a co-editor of *the minnesota review: a journal of committed writing*.

Index

DATE DUE

APR 05 '91			
38-297			